P9-CKG-212

PRAISE FOR OTHER BOOKS BY JUDY ALLEN

EVENT PLANNING

The Ultimate Guide to Successful Meetings, Corporate Events, Fund-Raising Galas, Conferences, Conventions, Incentives and Other Events

(ISBN: 978-0-470-15574-5)

"Allen is a good teacher. Wise planners will add *Event Planning* to their personal reference library as a useful working guide."
—*Meeting Professional Magazine*

"A blueprint for executing events for 50 or 2,000, with budgets of a few thousand dollars to hundreds of thousands."
—*Success Magazine*

"*Event Planning* will save beginning event planners from plenty of heartbreak and headaches."
—*Lisa Hurley, Editor, Special Events Magazine*

"*Event Planning* gives readers a blueprint for planning and executing special events with flair. Consider the book as preventative maintenance."
—*Sales Promotion Magazine*

"A guide to well planned events. *Event Planning* is a must for any PR maven."
—*Marketing Magazine*

THE BUSINESS OF EVENT PLANNING

Behind-the-Scenes Secrets of Successful Special Events

(ISBN: 978-0-470-83188-5)

"*The Business of Event Planning* is a must-read for those in the event planning business. Strategic in thought and design and user-friendly in presentation, it literally tells you the paths to follow and the pitfalls to avoid. Well told, with examples to follow and stories to relate to, it's the 'how-to' that's a 'must-do' for the meetings, incentive, and event planning industry."
—*Peggy Whitman, President, Society of Incentive & Travel Executives; and Western Regional Sales Director, Marriott Incentive Awards*

"Written for anyone who has to prepare dynamite meetings and special events, *The Business of Event Planning* is your bible and a must-have desktop reference. Thanks, Judy Allen! You saved the day!"

—Susan Fenner Ph.D., Manager, Education and Professional Development, International Association of Administrative Professionals (IAAP)

"Guidance for new planners, reminders for experienced ones, and useful tips for everyone. This book has it all! It's the key that unlocks the mystery behind event planning, and should be mandatory reading for planners everywhere."

—Leslie McNabb, Senior Manager Event Planning, Scotia Capital

EVENT PLANNING ETHICS AND ETIQUETTE

A Principled Approach to the Business of Special Event Management

(ISBN: 978-0-470-83260-8)

"This is a must-read not only for event professionals, but also for small-business people conceiving product introductions and conference appearances."

—Harvard Business School, Working Knowledge

"Judy Allen strikes again. The veteran event planner . . . writes with the voice of experience and offers readers guidelines for establishing ethical policies in the office and on-site at events . . . a good refresher, and excellent reading for novices who need to know how to keep personal and professional boundaries from being crossed."

—Corporate Meetings & Incentives Magazine

"This book contains invaluable information for anyone who handles events for their organization. A host of real-world stories from the field—the good, the bad, and the ugly—serve as examples of codes of conduct (or lack thereof) as well as cautionary tales of what can happen when ethics and etiquette fall to the wayside. Allen thoroughly examines many scenarios and provides practical advice that any planner would be foolish not to heed."

—Charity Village

MARKETING YOUR EVENT PLANNING BUSINESS

A Creative Approach to Gaining the Competitive Edge

(ISBN: 978-0-470-83387-2)

"For event planners who are tired of being a well-kept secret, *Marketing Your Event Planning Business* offers invaluable advice on targeting talents and targeting clients. It's a wonderful boost for event planners looking to expand their client base."
—Lisa Hurley, Editor, Special Events Magazine

"Judy Allen has crafted another meaningful book in her series on event practices. Every business owner must immediately add this treasure chest of useful ideas to their bookshelf."
—Richard Aaron, CMP, CSEP, President of BiZBash Media, NYC

"Judy Allen has given us the ultimate resource guide to event planning. It's everything you need to know to launch a successful company."
—Ramey Warren Black, Partner, Media-Savvy

TIME MANAGEMENT FOR EVENT PLANNERS

Expert Techniques and Time-Saving Tips for Organizing Your Workload, Prioritizing Your Day, and Taking Control of Your Schedule

(ISBN: 978-0-470-83626-2)

"She has done it again! Judy Allen has written an excellent, educational and user-friendly book, which is a priceless resource for planners worldwide. *Time Management* is an essential book for all planners, new or seasoned. Judy has provided the tools for managing your time which is one of the *most* important skills for event planners and all professionals."
—Ysabelle Allard, Meetings & Incentives Planner, Bilingual Meetings & Incentives

"At last, a time management book written by someone who knows what it is to juggle three programs, six clients, eighteen suppliers and a family in a pear tree! Using Judy Allen's tips have really made a difference!"
—Brigitte Mondor, CMP, Event Leader, Microsoft—Maritz Canada Inc.

"A very no-nonsense approach to the real problem of time management. Some excellent tips and strategies for the busy professional."
—Deborah Breiter, Associate Professor, Rosen College of Hospitality, Orlando, Florida

"As all experienced and inexperienced event managers will know, time is one of the main resources that has to be managed effectively for successful events. In this practical skills-based text, Judy Allen explores time management and provides techniques for event professionals to learn and apply to your work. From exploring your current use of time, through prioritising and action planning, to multi tasking, project management and balancing your personal and professional life, Judy provides hints and tips for making better, and the best, use of time, based on her years of experience in the events industry."
—Glenn A. J. Bowdin, Principal Lecturer, UK Centre for Events Management, Leeds Metropolitan University

THE EXECUTIVE'S GUIDE TO CORPORATE EVENTS AND BUSINESS ENTERTAINING

How to Choose and Use Corporate Functions to Increase Brand Awareness, Develop New Business, Nurture Customer Loyalty and Drive Growth

(ISBN: 978-0-470-83848-8)

"As usual, Judy Allen has written a valuable book filled with important information. She adds depth and breadth to the body of practical knowledge about the nuts and bolts of event strategy and tactics. This volume should at all times be on the desk of every planner and every business executive charged with planning an event."
—David Sorin, Esq., CEO, Management Mpowerment Associates, and Author of The Special Events Advisor: A Business and Legal Guide for Event Professionals

"Intelligent planning and thorough execution are the keys to success for any corporate function. Judy Allen outlines a succinct, practical methodology that will ensure your next event achieves its stated business objectives and creates a positive lasting impression."
—Zeke Adkins, Co-founder, Luggage Forward

"In today's competitive business climate, a 'business as usual' approach to corporate events and functions simply does not work. Judy Allen has compiled in one comprehensive guide everything today's successful executive needs to know to take this strategic function to the next level."
—Evans Gebhardt, Executive Vice President, Eos Airlines, Inc.

Event Planning

Second Edition

Event Planning

the ultimate guide to successful meetings, corporate events, fund-raising galas, conferences, incentives and other special events

Second Edition

Judy Allen

John Wiley & Sons Canada, Ltd.

Library and Archives Canada Cataloguing in Publication Data

Allen, Judy, 1952-

Event planning : the ultimate guide to successful meetings, corporate events, fund-raising galas, conferences, conventions, incentives and other special events / Judy Allen. — 2nd ed.

ISBN 978-0-470-15574-5

1. Meetings—Planning. 2. Congresses and conventions–Planning. 3. Special events—Planning. I. Title.

AS6.A44 2008 658.4'56 C2008-905630-2

Production Credits
Cover design: Ian Koo
Interior text design: Tegan Wallace
Typesetter: Thomson Digital
Printer: Courier Westford

John Wiley & Sons Canada, Ltd.
6045 Freemont Blvd.
Mississauga, Ontario
L5R 4J3

Printed in the United States

19 20 CRW 17 16

Dedication

This book is dedicated with much love to a very important person in my life, my 2jproductions business partner, mentor, dearest friend and so much more, Joe Thomas Shane, whose brilliant mind challenges me and whose incredible, continually growing and evolving spirit inspires me daily—personally, physically and professionally—to become my best (mind, body and soul) in order to do more, give more and be more; whose business acumen I hold in the greatest of respect; whose creativity sparks mine to greater heights; whose quick wit makes me smile and who is one of the very few people in the world who can easily make me laugh. Thank you for bringing new energy, purpose, passion and play into my life. I believe that our exciting new ventures, which will take event planning and special events in a very fresh and unique direction and add new dimensions, will have tremendous value in the world and I look forward to taking this step together with you. Meeting you—through the first edition of this book—has been life changing and I will always consider you one of my life's greatest blessings from God/the Universe.

Table of Contents

Preface **xiii**

Acknowledgments **xxiii**

Chapter 1: The First Steps: Initial Planning & Budgeting **1**

Determining Your Event Objectives 4

How Much Can You Spend? 5

Event Vision 7

Event Vision Q&A 17

Design Objectives of the Event Experience 24

Initial Planning 33

Visualization 38

Monitoring the Budget 41

Event Design Principles Checklist 45

Event Experience Design Objectives 45

Chapter 2: Organization and Timing **47**

Critical Path 47

Function Sheets 52

Timing 58

Date Selection 67

Critical Path Checklist 73

Charting Your Critical Path 74

Chapter 3: Location, Location, Location **80**

Site Selection 81

Location Requirements 90

Hotels and Convention Centers 93

Restaurants, Private Venues, Catering 98

Theaters 99

Tents 101

Gala Openings in New Venues 107

Contracts 108

Location Q&A 110

Move In Requirement Checklist 126
Event Suppliers' Setup Logistics Checklist 128
Event Suppliers' Teardown Checklist 131

Chapter 4: Transportation 133
By Air 136
By Land 140
Transportation Q&A 148
Transportation Checklist 164

Chapter 5: Guest Arrival 166
Guest Arrival Q&A 169
Fanfare 182
Fanfare Q&A 184
Registration: Guest Pass Security and Ticket Pickup 193
Registration Q&A 194
Guest Arrival Checklist 201

Chapter 6: Venue Requirements 202
Room Requirements 203
Room Requirements Q&A 203
Staging, Audiovisual, Lighting 208
Staging, Audiovisual, Lighting Q&A 213
Lighting-Specific Q&A 221
Venue and Event Supplier Checklist: Room, Venue and Supplier Requirements, and Contract Terms and Conditions 222

Chapter 7: Who's It All For? 226
Know Your Guest Demographics 226
The Guest List 230
Invitations 234
Media 240
Media Q&A 241
Children at Your Event 242
E-vites, CD and DVD Invitations 244
Event Websites and Event RSVP Websites 246

Chapter 8: Food and Beverage **247**
Examples of Texas Theme Parties with Different Energy 248
Food and Beverage Considerations 251
Menu Planning 255
Staffing 294
Charitable Donations 297

Chapter 9: Other Considerations **299**
Entertainment 299
Entertainment Q&A 301
Photographers and Videographers 308
Photographer Q&A 311
Themes and Programs 317
Final Touches 327
Staff, Supplier and Entertainment Work Permits 330
Event Risk Assessment 335

Conclusion **340**
It's a Wrap! 340
Applause! Applause! 349
Your Next Event 350

Appendix A: Sample Cost Sheets **352**
Appendix B: Sample Payment Schedules **376**
Appendix C: Sample Function Sheets **384**

Index **404**

For more resources, please visit us at www.wiley.ca/go/event_planning

Preface

The world of event planning has grown, evolved and changed since the year 2000 when *Event Planning: The Ultimate Guide* was first published. While the foundation of the first edition of this book—which introduces readers to basic event planning principles—is rock solid, I felt that the new growth areas that can be added in the second edition would make this book even more relevant in a rapidly changing world and event planning industry, which now includes professional event planning companies who handle corporate events, social events, nonprofit events and weddings (wedding planning has now grown into a multibillion-dollar industry and falls under the umbrella of professional event planning); incentive houses; meeting planners; independent planners; corporate in-house event planners and in-house nonprofit event planners, as well as corporate executives charged with producing company events that bring about a return on their corporation's investment of time, money and energy.

In terms of growth, many universities and colleges around the world have increased the number of event management courses available to students who are aspiring to become professional event planners or work in related industry fields and to those studying marketing, public relations, business and communications who know the tremendous value—and competitive edge—of being able to understand how to successfully execute and strategically use corporate events can be to them and the companies they will be working for.

The event planning/special events field has developed into a multibillion-dollar global industry with specialty niches that did not exist seven years ago. In the past, event planners worked for an incentive house, meeting planning company or communications firm, or in-house directly with the corporate client. Today, independent event and meeting planners have set up innovative boutique operations and are having great success working with clients who are looking to collaborate with those who are masters of creativity, have a history of successful event delivery and who may be able to offer more flexibility than larger firms and are no longer concerned with the size of the event planning company they are working with.

Many long-term event planning companies are now finding themselves competing for business with a flood of newcomers, and this is changing how business is being both sought and conducted (e.g., many are now working in partnership with hotels, resorts and venues and offering volume rates if a client will sign up for more than one event). And today, in many established larger firms, the number of employees that they house is often an illusion and clients are well aware of that. Many seemingly larger companies have opted—since 9/11 and then the SARS outbreak, when the event planning business came to an immediate stop in many parts of the world and was a time of major financial recovery for an industry very ill prepared to ride it out—to keep only a core creative permanent staff on hand and then bring in freelancers (who may work for many event planning companies over the course of the year and even handle the same corporate client but through a different division with another firm) when needed to handle planning, operations and on-site orchestration. In such instances, both sides must prepare for the major learning curves they will face, so that all flows smoothly and as per company standards.

In the past seven years, event planning has also evolved in many areas. It is now a proven means for a corporation to increase brand awareness, develop new business, nurture customer loyalty and drive growth, and corporate clients—both for profit and nonprofit (and sometimes a marriage between the two)—are looking for event planners who not only understand event design, strategic planning, logistics, timing and budget management, but are proficient in how events can be used to market and brand their company and set them apart from their competition. Being able to motivate their employees is no longer enough as clients are now aware of how events can be staged to meet multiple company objectives and are looking to align themselves with event planning companies who can help them acquire this skill.

The range of the types of events has grown as well and event planners must be able to not only craft traditional events but also to create, implement and execute a second tier of more advanced business functions. In the past, event planners were concerned with mastering primary business functions such as:

» Board meetings
» Business meetings
» Client appreciation events
» Conferences
» Conventions
» Corporate shows
» Employee appreciation events
» Trade shows

But now, they must be prepared to take their clients to the next level and elevate their event knowledge to include:

» Custom training seminars involving emotional and physical challenges
» Executive retreats
» Gala fund-raising events
» Incentive travel and premium programs
» Naming rights
» Product launches
» Product placement
» Special events
» Teleconferencing
» Webcasts

In addition, with some companies, event planners are now having to deal with not only a company's sales and marketing team but their procurement department, and that presents its own set of unique challenges that planners need to be aware of. Event planners can be of great value if they know what they can do to help their client's sales and marketing executive team to circumvent having to go that route.

Another growing area of concern in the industry is the escalating hard costs of preparing a client proposal with no guarantee of contracting the business. Many event planning companies have found themselves spending up to $15,000 on a proposal only to find that the company sent out the request for proposal (RFP) merely to fulfill company requirements of submitting three bids, while their intention was always to stay with their incumbent. Those kind of dollars are huge financial hits that no event planning company can afford to keep taking and stay in business. Ways for event planning companies to protect themselves will be outlined in this second edition. Just as the corporate client is looking for a return on their investment of time, energy and money, so must the event planning company, and there is a shift that must be made from positioning yourself or your event planning company as a service industry to marketing and selling your professional services, knowledge on how to design an event that produces results and meets company objectives, and event planning expertise.

Event security and airport security have all changed since 9/11 and that is affecting how participants travel, where they travel to and security requirements on-site at hotels, resorts and venues. This area now falls under event planning design, logistics and on-site requirements. Other major industry changes since 2000 also include technology, sophisticated multimedia presentations complete with storyboards, insurance and contract terms, conditions and concessions in terms of protecting a client's deposit and/or moving their event, for example in cases of disasters, such as New Orleans where a city's entire infrastructure disappeared, or in countries where recent murders of tourists have corporate clients and their guests wary of traveling to the area. Other areas of change include how corporate events are being played out in the headlines, with company executives—and those they did business with—being held personally responsible for breaches of company ethics, poor business etiquette and inappropriate event spending (e.g., Conrad Black charging back to his company some of the costs for his wife's birthday party in the South Pacific and for private jets).

My intent with the first edition was to design a book that would be used as a working tool, one that would contribute to successful event planning—whether the event is a premiere, tribute, meeting, corporate event, fund-raising gala, conference, convention, incentive, wedding or any other special event, and that has not changed with the second edition. Two of the tips in this book alone would have saved one gala fund-raiser several thousands of dollars in unexpected costs. In one instance, a nonprofit company had not properly researched the difference between holding its event at a convention center instead of a hotel, and had not determined what items would be provided free of charge and what would be provided at an additional cost. This led to an unexpected expense when guests took home centerpieces that belonged to the convention center, and the nonprofit company had to pay to replace them. A small note placed by the display thanking the convention center for the loan of the centerpieces would have avoided the charges the nonprofit company faced. This could have happened at any event held at a hotel, convention center, private venue or even your own home. Another tip in this book would have saved one event planning company the professional embarrassment and loss of a client and their reputation when they had to go back to them to let them know that they had made a $100,000-plus costing error in the calculation of union costs for a major move in, setup, rehearsal, day of, teardown and move out for their client, and that was only the tip of the iceberg of costs that were not properly researched.

Event Planning: The Ultimate Guide became so successful that it grew into a suite of books, each of which deals in details of a specific aspect of event planning. This best-selling series of books has been embraced as a valuable teaching tool and is being used around the world by event planning and related hospitality industry professionals, public relations and communication companies, nonprofit organizations, corporate business executives and universities and colleges for course adoption and required reading, and has been translated into five languages. Knowledge is the key to success and it is what will set you apart from your competition both personally and professionally.

What you do not know or do not know to ask can have a major impact on the success of your event and on your budget. In *Event Planning: The Ultimate Guide* I take you behind the scenes—from conception to on-site operations—to show you how to make your event as memorable as it can be, with as few surprises as possible at the end of the day. The magic begins in the detail, which through this book I will attempt to bring to you. Whatever your event may be, there is something in this book that will contribute to making it special. Creating memorable events without unexpected surprises and expenses is what I am most passionate about. This is what I want to bring to you.

To further help you with your event planning needs, visit our companion website. There you can access the sample forms in the appendices, as well as additional samples not included in the book. The website address is www.wiley.ca/go/event_planning.

For quick event planning logistical support reference, below is a brief overview of each of the companion books in the Event Planning series and in my Wedding Planning series, which, while written for the mass consumer, contains valuable event planning information for those event planners who are working in that market as well as for those handling corporate and social events.

The Business of Event Planning: Behind-the-Scenes Secrets of Successful Special Events (Wiley, 2002) takes event planning to the next level. Its comprehensive coverage includes strategic event design; how to prepare winning proposals and how to understand them if you're the client; how to determine management fees and negotiate contracts; guest safety and security issues that need to be taken into consideration; how to design events in multicultural settings; new technology that makes event operations more efficient; practical tools such as sample letters of agreement, sample layouts for client proposals, forms, tips and checklists; and a detailed case study that runs throughout the book—one company that is organizing two very different events. *The Business of Event Planning* will show you what behind-the-scenes tasks you need to take care of in your own event planning business before you even plan an event and how to take your event design and execution skills to the next level.

Event Planning Ethics and Etiquette: A Principled Approach to the Business of Special Event Management (Wiley, 2003) covers the business side of event planning ethics, etiquette, entertaining, acceptable codes of conduct and industry standards. The book provides event planners with the information they need to stay out of trouble, keep professional relationships healthy and profitable, avoid the riskier temptations of the lifestyle, and win business in a highly competitive market using ethical business practices. Harvard Business School said this book "is a must-read not only for event professionals, but also for small-business people conceiving product introductions and conference appearances."

Marketing Your Event Planning Business: A Creative Approach to Gaining the Competitive Edge (Wiley, 2004) takes readers through marketability, market development and marketing endeavors (business and personal). Topics covered include diversifying the client base, developing niche markets and areas of expertise, establishing a backup plan for use during downturns and finding innovative ways to solicit new sales.

Time Management for Event Planners: Expert Techniques and Time-Saving Tips for Organizing Your Workload, Prioritizing Your Day, and Taking Control of Your Schedule (Wiley, 2005) offers expert insight on time management as it relates specifically to the event planning and hospitality industry. Event planning is a high-pressure, around-the-clock job where planners juggle multiple tasks and work down to the wire against crushing deadlines and a mountain of obstacles. For smooth event implementation, and for business success, it is essential that planners manage their own time as expertly as they manage an event. This book will show you how to do just that.

The Executive's Guide to Corporate Events and Business Entertaining: How to Choose and Use Corporate Functions to Increase Brand Awareness, Develop New Business, Nurture Customer Loyalty and Drive Growth (Wiley, 2007) primarily focuses on the strategic event marketing thinking from a business objective perspective, not just an event planning one, and will give the business executives—who are now being held accountable for event results—insight on how to choose, design and use events to achieve business objectives and how to generate a return on their company's investment of time and money. As well, design elements and strategies found in this book will give event planners the tools they need to understand how the events they plan can better meet multiple layers of corporate objectives. This book will give event planners the ability to see the event from their client's perspective as well as from an event planning perspective. Executing events flawlessly does not mean that corporate goals are being met. This book shows not only how to plan and execute the perfect event, but also how, for best results, to closely tie it in to company strategy and objectives. Covered in detail are how to identify clear objectives for each event; which type of function is best suited to meeting your objectives; what you need to establish before forging ahead with organizing committees and reviewing or developing proposals; how to develop a realistic budget, and when to question expenses proposed by staff or professional event planners; the importance of sign offs; how to identify controversial spending and other red flag areas that could seriously damage the company's reputation, or even put it at financial or legal risk; how to establish spending guidelines and policies on employee conduct at company functions; and how to evaluate the success and results of your business functions.

Confessions of a Event Planner: Case Studies from the Real World of Events —How to Handle the Unexpected and How to Be a Master of Discretion (Wiley, 2009) a fictionalized case study that follows one corporate event planning company around the world. The book showcases fictionalized true-to-life scenarios that upcoming and seasoned event planners and corporate executives may encounter on the job during the actual event execution. This book will help establish and define company policies, procedures and protocol in the office and on-site (that can be signed off on by staff after review), which in turn will help to protect the individual, the event planning company, the corporate client and their guests from legal ramifications. Not knowing what to do when an event planning crisis occurs or steps to take to prevent one from happening can be costly—both personally and professionally—to those involved and to the corporations hosting and orchestrating the event.

Your Stress-Free Wedding Planner: Experts' Best Secrets to Creating the Wedding of Your Dreams (Sourcebooks, Inc., 2004) is a step-by-step approach to minimizing the complexity of planning the wedding day, broken down into the 10 stages used in successful, stress-free event execution.

Plan a Great Wedding in 3 Months or Less (Sourcebooks, Inc., 2007)

There may be many reasons why a couple opts for a short engagement or decides to move up their wedding date. These couples need a planner that helps them prioritize and move quickly to create a great wedding. This wedding planner shows couples how to:

» Find immediately available sites and choose the right officiant quickly.
» Prioritize wedding planning so nothing essential is missed or neglected.
» Explore such quick turnaround alternatives as destination wedding/honeymoon options and elopement.
» Save money as well as time on every aspect of the process.

Includes all the essential checklists, timelines, worksheets and resources that couples need.

Event planners around the world have asked me to share with them my creative ideas and I will now be able to do that through my upcoming television series and specials, website and other mediums in partnership with Joe Shane through our company 2jproductions (www.2jproductions.com) and Sensual Home Living™ (www.sensualhomeliving.com), building life experiences that will be a ongoing, valuable and creative resource of cutting edge—not cookie cutter—creative and innovative design, staging, custom ideas and life experiences.

Judy Allen

Acknowledgments

Over the course of seven years, due to reader response for the first edition of *Event Planning: The Ultimate Guide* and requests from planners-to-be, planners working in the field and business professionals for more event planning answers, *Event Planning: The Ultimate Guide* grew into a best-selling series of business books that are being used around the world by industry professionals and corporate executives as well as universities and colleges for course adoption and required reading. The books have now been translated into five languages. This well-received series of books then became the crossover platform for two mass-market consumer books—with more to come. My first wedding planner led the way in the wedding planning category sales and received media reviews deeming it to be one of the best wedding planners on the market because of its event planning focus.

Through the writing journey I have been on, I have been fortunate to work with one of the most respected publishers in the industry and to work with those who are masters of their craft. I would like to thank the outstanding team of professionals at John Wiley & Sons Canada, Ltd. for their contribution to the making of this book. I would like to express my appreciation to Robert Harris, General Manager; Bill Zerter, COO;

Jennifer Smith, Vice President and Publisher; Karen Milner, Executive Editor; Elizabeth McCurdy, Project Manager; Kimberly Rossetti, Editorial Assistant; Deborah Guichelaar, Publicist; Erin Kelly, Publicity Manager; Erika Zupko, Publicity Coordinator; Lucas Wilk, Marketing Manager; Thomson Digital; lan koo, Creative Services Director; Tegan Wallace, Publishing Services; Pam Vokey, Project Coordinator; Pauline Ricablanca, Project Coordinator; Meghan Brousseau, New Media and Rights Manager; Jessica Ting, Accounting and Royalty Manager; Stacey Clark, Corporate Sales Manager.

Working with Michelle Bullard once again on the structure and copyedit of my books is a pleasure. Michelle makes the process enjoyable. Her advice and direction are always on target.

I would also like to thank everyone who has reviewed my books and provided such positive comments and feedback. I greatly appreciate the time you have given both to me and to my *Event Planning: The Ultimate Guide* readers by reviewing this book. Your opinions are greatly valued by all of us.

I had the opportunity to write this second edition in the wonderful "active living" town of Collingwood, Ontario. I have to say thank-yous to some very special people who came into my life while living there: Sarah Applegarth MSc, CSCS, CSEP-CEP, SCS, Strength & Conditioning Coach, Active Life Conditioning, Inc. (www.activelifeconditioning.com), whose business is "Taking Care of What Matters Most—You." Active living, wellness, fitness and health is what Sarah professionally teaches, trains and lives by. Sarah is a world-class high-performance trainer and someone I was privileged enough to call my personal trainer. When I turned to her for expert help in an area that I had no knowledge in, I learned how to develop the physical, mental and emotional strength, stamina and flexibility athletes carry at their core to become their best so that they can do more, give more and bring their best to themselves, their family, their friends, their work (life purpose) and the world. Brianne Law, World Cup Coach for the Canadian Para-Alpine Ski Team (www.canski.org), who joined Sarah in training me this past summer and is an amazing trainer and teacher. Krista Campbell, Registered Massage Therapist, who is trained in Swedish massage techniques that have a therapeutic effect on the body by acting directly on the muscular, nervous, circulatory and lymphatic systems, promoting an overall feeling of health and well-being, and who has an amazing healing touch and had my muscles back to moving as they are meant to. Dr. Heather Munroe, Chiropractor, Mountain Chiropractic (www.mountainchiropractic.ca), who helps each individual achieve pain relief, injury prevention and personal enhancement through a drug-free, non-invasive approach to health care. In just one session, she was able to undo the damage a fall had done, and brought me back to pain-free alignment and then went on to release years of joint compression caused by years of sitting behind a computer, sitting in an airplane and sitting in meetings in boardrooms around the world. In my book *Time Management for Event Planners,* I shared the importance of having personal and professional balance in life and the value of taking part in all life experiences that present themselves in order to elevate your level of knowledge and creativity. I shared all that I had learned but did not address the area of physical well-being. It was a life-learning, life-challenging, life-changing and growing experience that was still to come and that came about from having a business partner, Joe Shane, who is a seven times Ironman, who honors his commitment to physical well-being, no matter where he is in the world or what his day personally and professionally demands, as do Sarah, Brianne, Krista and Heather (my "fit pit" team) their life partners. Living in an active living community for a year with people committed to health and well-being and surrounded by nature has been an incredible journey and one I am grateful to have experienced. I have learned that there is an amazing benefit to an active living lifestyle personally at home, at work and as you travel around the world on site inspections, fam trips and working programs on-site (and being fueled by nurturing and nourishing foods and fitness workouts, not just caffeine, and meals on the run when they can be fitted in between work deadlines and demands that can be intensive in this 24/7 industry)—and to bringing wellness, fitness and health lifestyle elements, not only into your everyday and work life, but to the programs that you design so that others can experience the benefits. As you will read later in this book, I feel this will be a very important emerging trend as corporate insurance costs continue to rise due to the effects of sedentary lifestyles, the rise in obesity due to unhealthy eating, and living practices and related illnesses around the world (in the *New York Times,* it was reported that in Japan, workers are required to keep their girth under prescribed limits: 33.5 inches for men and 35.4 inches for women and there is a high personal cost in respect to the quality of life lived professionally with regards to productivity. I share examples of how to introduce this new area, how to apply it by creating multi-tiered event programs and how it has been used successfully by one company to bring about a two-million-dollar yearly return on their $400,000 investment in a wellness incentive event program. This amazing team I worked out with—mind, body and soul—for over a year would be a great inclusion to any event introducing well-being principles to participants. I would also like to thank Judith Somborac, Personal Direction, Training and Coaching, my yoga and Pilates trainer; and Jackey Fox, Assistant Manager, A&P, Andrea at Collingwood Running Company and Tammy at Becker Shoes. Each played an important part in my fitness mission to counteract years of sitting at the computer. My personal "fit pit" team taught me about nutrition, stamina, strength and stretching—literally, not just physically—as a tool to push past discomfort in all areas of life. They shared their talents and expert knowledge with me, giving me new tools I can use every day for the rest of my life while taking on the world and the world of possibilities in front of me personally and professionally through my company, 2jproductions, with Joe Shane. I am excited to be bringing a new sense of purpose, passion and play to that—for me—which is bringing me closer to my personal, professional (life purpose) and creative best.

As always, I would like to thank my family—my parents, Walter and Ruth; my sister, Marilyn, and my brother-in-law, Hans; and my nieces and their partners, Natasha and her husband, Ed, and Jasmine and Rodney—and my friends for their continued love and support.

And again, I would like to say thank-you to my 2jproductions partner, Joe Shane. I look forward to working with you on taking event planning to an exciting, creative and innovative new level. There is no one I would want to take this journey with more than with you as together we bring Sensual Home Living™, Sensual Living for Two™, Sensual Suite(s)™, Wecation(s)™, and Welationship(s)™ to home, life and lifestyle design and world-class resorts around the world. The ultimate special event is your life and what you bring to it. Creating meaningful, memorable, and magical life experiences is what event planners strive for and those same event elements cross over to home, life and lifestyle—where work becomes play and play becomes work to be enjoyed 24/7, 365 days of the year, personally and professionally, and opens up a new world of possibilities.

1

The First Steps:
Initial Planning & Budgeting

Designing and producing an event—whether it be a meeting, corporate event, fund-raising gala, conference, convention, incentive or other special event—has been compared to directing a movie, but is actually more like a live stage production. It is a high-wire act without a safety net. Once your event starts there are no second chances. It's done in one take and there are no dress rehearsals. You can't yell "cut" and re-shoot the scene. You are simply not able to predict—as you can with a movie script—how your guests and suppliers will interact and react. But you can plan, prepare and then be ready for the unexpected. Never forget Murphy's Law: what can go wrong, will go wrong.

At one poorly planned event, the event planning decor, staging and lighting setup crew arrived days in advance to do an extensive setup for a poolside event complete with a dancing water light and music display at a privately owned venue. They found, to their horror, that the swimming pool had been filled in months ago but no one had notified the event planning company, and the event planning company and their suppliers had not been back since contracting to do a pre-event (pre-con) meeting, nor had they outlined swimming pool requirement stipulations in their vendor contract or event function sheets. Extensive decor and a lavish fireworks display—at great expense to the event planning company—had to be brought in at the last moment to create a new fantasy look that would appease their client, who did not need to have that added stress mere days before what had been a long-anticipated special event.

Although you are not creating an Oscar-winning movie, it is always important to remember that you are creating something that may be a lifetime memory for someone. Any event, whether it's for 50 or more than 2,000, needs to be as detailed and as scripted as any film production, and so does the budget. Budgets for meetings, corporate events, product launches, conferences, conventions, incentives and special events can go from tens of thousands to hundreds of thousands of dollars, and today it is very common to have them run in the millions of dollars. An event program is considered successful if it has no surprises on the day of the event and at final reconciliation and exceeds event objectives.

Before you begin designing your event, you need to first determine why you are having your event or taking part in an event. This is referred to as defining the event objectives, and there can be both primary and secondary objectives in each event. Event objectives will be discussed in more detail later in this chapter. Understanding *why* this event is being held will help you (and your client) to lay out the company or client objectives—both tangible (day of) and intangible (long-term) returns—so that you can then select the right style of event that will be capable of delivering them. Using a business convention as an example, a company can be an exhibitor at a convention, an attendee at a convention or an event sponsor; be represented by a company speaker; attend seminars; or host the gala farewell, a hospitality suite or an evening event for select conference attendees. Each of these event scenarios will bring different returns to a company on their investment of time, money and energy, and it is important to see which style of event will provide the most value and produce the best results in meeting the company's objectives. *The Executive's Guide to Corporate Events and Business Entertaining:* (Wiley,

2007) provides an in-depth look at key event styles and outlines in detail the company and event objectives each will return.

Examples of Different Event Styles

» *Board meetings*

» *Business meetings*

» *Client appreciation events*

» *Conferences*

» *Conventions*

» *Corporate shows*

» *Custom training seminars involving emotional and physical challenges*

» *Employee appreciation events*

» *Executive retreats*

» *Gala fund-raising events*

» *Incentive travel and premium programs*

» *Naming rights*

» *Product launches*

» *Product placement*

» *Special events*

» *Teleconferencing*

» *Trade shows*

» *Webcasts*

Once you have set your event objectives and determined the best event style to meet them, you will be able to strategically design an event that will be tailor-made to target those needs (you can find explicit strategic design principles I have created and strategic planning case studies in *The Business of Event Planning* [Wiley, 2002]). The next decision is to establish the scope of the event. Two criteria will determine this: money and objectives.

Determining Your Event Objectives

In order to design an event that delivers results and a return on the investment of time, money and energy the company hosting the event expends, the event must be crafted to meet guest expectations, as well as the company's. You want to create event anticipation, maximum guest attendance and full participation in embracing the primary and secondary purpose and message behind the event.

Event objectives can be both tangible and intangible and can be met pre-event (if a qualifying sales objective, for example, is required in the case of an incentive program), during the event, and post-event, and become the bridge, platform and positioning to meeting the next level of objectives for future events. An event objective must have value to the company holding the event, those taking part in the event, and cross over from professional to personal benefits and vice versa.

For example, one company had an objective of creating an event—or a series of events—that would result in having their staff become more productive, increase morale, reduce accidents in the workplace and bring down per employee health care costs. In order to do this they focused on an employee and work environment well-being theme with the top-level performers taking part in what would turn out to be a yearly three-day all-expenses-paid incentive program to climb a 14,000-foot peak in Colorado. This main event—one of many ongoing events tied to this event's objectives—centered on achieving specific individual fitness goals and has proven to be an outstanding success, with more employees qualifying every year. Their company's health care costs have been reduced to half the region's average—which is a savings to their company of $2,000,000 a year—and meeting this one event objective alone more than pays for their total event investment of $400,000 per year. In addition, over the years the company has been able to bring down their worker's compensation costs from $500,000 to $10,000, and they have created fitter workers, who are more productive and who now have a higher morale both personally and professionally.

How Much Can You Spend?

The first thing you need to do is to establish how much money you can set aside for the event. Even the smallest event requires a serious financial commitment. You may decide that you cannot afford an event at this time or may need to do something different to bring about the results you are looking for.

Remember, it is better to wait than to stage a shoddy event on a shoestring budget. And referring back to the conference example, you may decide that the event dollars that you have available would be better spent having company employees attend the conference as participants—where they are free to network by day and not be tied to an exhibit—and hosting an innovative, private, upscale dinner exclusively for the key people you want to spend quality one-on-one time with. Sponsoring what would be, due to limited event funds, a bare-bones budget "gala" dinner would give your company more visibility, but it may not reflect the company image you are trying to project. Spending the available event dollars to entertain 50-plus guests in the manner you know is required to impress your target audience, as opposed to trying to stretch those same dollars to cover decor, entertainment, food and beverage for 1,000 conference attendees, most of whom your company will not be doing business with, and in the end producing an event that is not in keeping with your company standards, would be the way to go.

One supplier did this so successfully that their dinner event—set on the stage of a well-known theater (which was closed to the public for the evening) with the stars of the show in attendance and putting on a private performance for them—was the talk of the conference the next day and really made their company stand out. Their invited guests had taken part in an event that made them feel like stars, while those who had not been invited aspired to be on the select guest list next year. They also hoped to make a business connection with the company employees at the conference, who (because they were there as attendees and not staffing an exhibit booth) had time to step out of the conference with prospective new clients and enjoy multiple coffee breaks, lunches, etc., with no time restraints. This company generated more industry buzz and secured future business in this two-tiered event approach than they would have had they spent the dollars they had available differently at this particular conference and time. When they assessed their company objectives—short- and long-term—they could easily see which style of event would best fit their event intentions.

It is important to always determine ahead of time how much you can spend so that you can then select the appropriate event style and plan the event to fit the budget. It is a good idea to do a rough estimate of anticipated costs and inclusions before anything else because, very often, budget approvals from the higher-ups are required before an event is given the green light.

By doing a preliminary budget based on your event vision wish list of inclusions, you will know what will be doable and what will not. For instance, if a company was planning an incentive program and their wish was for a seven-night stay in a specific destination, they would quickly be able to determine if the airfare used up the majority of the budget. If it did, they might have to decide if a three-night stay, which would keep them on budget, would also help them accomplish their goals. If it were determined that a seven-night stay was necessary, then concessions would need to be made. Perhaps they would have to choose a location closer to home, or they may need to devise a way to come up with more funding, such as by soliciting industry or supplier sponsorship of specific event elements.

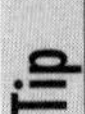

To obtain additional funding, consider approaching other industry members or the company's suppliers. Be aware, however, that you may not want to align yourself with one supplier over another, or to risk crossing business ethical lines. For more information on business ethics and business entertaining, refer to *Event Planning Ethics and Etiquette* (Wiley, 2003).

The company may need to look to other means to increase their event budget or look for other creative, cost-effective solutions that could involve partnering with another company and designing an event that creatively combined what each company could bring to the table to produce an event that would be a standout.

At one very upscale book launch celebrating glamour, millions and millions of dollars' of diamonds were brought in for guests to enjoy wearing and be photographed in while they were there. One woman was sporting more than 20 million dollars' in diamonds for her once-in-a-lifetime photo. The diamonds were brought in by Brinks trucks and 20 armed guards, and the event area was turned into a seemingly diamond-dazzling fortress (but remember Murphy's Law—two guests slipped out a side door that had not been secured to enjoy a private dinner in the hotel restaurant and caused the event organizers concern). But while the impact of the millions of dollars' of diamonds was major, the cost of having the diamonds on-site was not.

At midnight all the diamonds went back and the only hard costs for this very effective event element—where the objective was to project a glamorous experience—were insurance, Brinks trucks, armed guards and a professional photographer. And the luxury jewelry store that supplied the diamonds ended up selling some of the diamonds the next day to guests that had attended the event. For the store, it was a chance to present their diamonds to a very targeted audience and a marketing move that paid off handsomely in sales and in attracting new clients to their jewelry store. Their creative approach to getting attention for their store incurred very manageable hard costs. Minimum dollars were spent on creating a maximum one-of-a-kind event effect and it was a very effective event partnership for the book publisher, the author and the jewelry store.

Event Vision

In order to create an event designed to fulfill your client's objectives and be everything that they hoped it would be, it is important to begin with their initial event vision. This is where you will be able to determine what is most important to them. Event visualization—after event objectives have been set out—is your starting point for designing any event. Where you end up could be somewhere very different than you'd originally thought, but mapping out your event vision on a grid will help you to start laying out your event cost requirements. You can start to calculate backwards from the given budget to see if there is a fit or if flexibility in the budget or event needs to be found.

For example, one company had a budget of $4,500 for doing an outdoors luncheon event for 250 guests. The budget—they were told—would have to cover tenting, table, chair, linen, dishes, cutlery, food, beverage (wine, beer, etc.), entertainment and a small take-home gift. Their vision was to hold a New Orleans–style picnic. The reality of their budget was that they only had $18 a person to spend on all of the above. Tenting alone for 250 guests—including installation and teardown and permits and insurance—would more than exceed their entire budget. If staying with a New Orleans theme was deemed to be the most important element to help the company meet its event objectives (e.g., if they were launching an incentive program to New Orleans), a creative event option would be to take over a local jazz club on an exclusive basis and work with the facility to create decor, entertainment (taped or live), menu and an open-bar package inclusive of all taxes and service charges that would allow them to come in budget and keep the most important event elements. An inexpensive item like pralines—a traditional New Orleans treat—could be used to stay within budget and serve as a take-home gift.

My five event design principles that should be considered when visualizing an event are:

1. The Elements—All the Parts That Make Up the Event
2. The Essentials—Must-Haves
3. The Environment—Venue and Style
4. The Energy—Creating a Mood
5. The Emotion—Feelings

In-depth review of these event inclusions will be covered in later chapters, but for the purpose of designing your event vision blueprint for budgeting, here is an overview of the areas that you must consider:

The Elements—All the Parts That Make Up the Event

The first step when planning any event is to look at the big picture. Visualization must take place before you finalize your event date and even begin to look at venues. It is important to step back and take an overall look at the event requirements that carry hard costs and need to be part of your space request. The best way to do this is to lay out everything on a grid that focuses on the week of your event. More about how to use this grid will be covered in a later chapter dealing with location requirements.

Your event overview grid will provide you with valuable insight into your budgeting, event timing, logistics and orchestration, any of which could impact your final choices. It is a useful event planning tool that will evolve as your event unfolds and is the foundation upon which all your event elements will be built. Please be sure to work in pencil, as you will want to make adjustments as you move forward, or use a computer spreadsheet to construct your grid. You will want to make extra copies so that you can play with your initial event elements, arranging them in a variety of ways to find the best fit energywise to ensure you build to a grand finale and have your event end on a high note. Your event grid worksheet will lead you into event element inclusions and budget decision-making.

What you have to keep front of mind when planning your event is that each event element affects the next. If one area is overlooked, a domino effect can occur and place your event's success in jeopardy. Preparing an event overview grid right at the beginning, adapting it and adjusting it as you move forward with your plans, helps you to avoid crunch times and any unwanted surprises. By taking the time to plan in advance you will be poised to handle any last-minute changes with ease. Consideration must be given to the timing, logistics and orchestration of all the event elements that lead up to your actual event, the day of your event and the days following your event. These elements can include:

» Transportation of guests
» Accommodation of guests
» Shipping of items
» Advance move in and setup of the venue, including rental fees, labor costs, equipment rental, union costs, meals for crew, etc., in addition to the costs for event inclusions, staffing, security, permits, insurance, etc.
» Rehearsal space, including rental fees, labor costs, equipment rental, union costs, meals for crew, etc.
» Day-of-event elements, including rental fees, labor costs, equipment rental, union costs, meals for crew, etc., in addition to the costs for event inclusions, staffing, etc.
» Teardown and move out of the venue including rental fees, labor costs, equipment rental, union costs, meals for crew, etc., in addition to the costs for event inclusions, staffing, security, permits, insurance, etc.

Begin to pencil in, under the appropriate days, the schedule of event elements—your event show flow—as you are visualizing it now. At this point, you are not working with actual timing and logistics, but rather with an overview of how you see your event and pre- and post-event week unfolding. Make sure to have a calendar handy to check any critical dates that may be taking place around your selected event date, such as a major national or religious holiday or long weekend that could affect supplier delivery and guest attendance (see example grid on page xxx).

The Essentials—Must-Haves

Event "must-haves" are things that are, at the time of initial planning, nonnegotiable. They are determined by considering:

» Hard costs, such as airfare, hotel accommodation, space requirements (move in, setup, teardown and move out, as well as storage for suppliers, rehearsal space, on-site office space, etc., which is separate from actual main meeting/event function space), meeting/event function space requirements, meal requirements, activity requirements, etc., and all applicable taxes, service charges, permits, insurance, communication costs, staffing, and management fees (while these cost items can be negotiated and pricing concessions obtained, they need to be included regardless of the final event design and event inclusions)

» What would be meaningful to attendees
» What would make the event memorable to guests
» What would capture the magic of the message being delivered to participants

Some event must-haves are not based on the dollars and cents but on emotional currency and how they touch your senses. Some are easy to include and at minimal cost, while others require more thought, planning and money. It is important to identify the event's must-haves as you begin to visualize your event. Remember to think each decision through in terms of both economical and emotional currency, in meeting an event *need* not an event *want*. The event must-haves will become the core of your event design and your event elements will naturally unfold around them. At the same time you are compiling your list of event essentials, make a list of event enhancements that, budget permitting, could be considered to elevate your event to the next level.

The Environment—Venue and Style

Event Venue

Planners who rush off to choose a venue before they have visualized their event day from beginning to end, identified their client and their event's must-haves to decide what matters most to include, and determined where they stand financially, risk overlooking the venue that would have been the perfect fit for their event, one that meets all of their needs and their budget. Consider the earlier example of doing a tented New Orleans brunch versus doing a New Orleans jazz brunch utilizing a private facility with no additional tenting and rental charges to factor in when dealing with a budget of $18 a person.

The initial event vision and where you ultimately end up holding the event can be worlds apart from what you originally imagined. If you design your event around a venue just to lock up a date quickly, you may end up compromising what is important to the event and miss out on something very special. You will end up planning an event to fit the building, not designing one that will deliver the results your client is looking for.

We are living in a time when events are taking place in venues that are limited only by the event planner's imagination and budget parameters. Events today are held on land, on water, underwater (restaurants and spas in the Maldives, as an example), midair (on board aircraft), sitting on top of the world and in space.

Some examples of traditional venues include:

» Private mansions (rented or owned)
» Hotels
» Convention centers
» Museums
» Art galleries
» Country clubs
» Private yachts
» Wineries
» Private tents

But there is a world of options available to you. Events can and have taken place in theme parks, aquariums, entertainment complexes, roller-skating rinks, on theater stages, at private fly-fishing clubs, on golf courses, in tents in the middle of the desert, on swimming pools covered over for dining and dancing, in restaurants that have been taken over exclusively, on a soundstage, in converted barns, in plantation homes, on a catamaran, at a cottage retreat, at a country fair, in a retail store, on a mountaintop, in the middle of a forest, in a stadium, on a baseball field, on a rooftop, and in restaurants and nightclubs that have been closed exclusively for the client, have private rooms or areas that can be sectioned off just for you and your guests. Guests have been transported to event sites by private barges, classic cars, and snowmobiles; on wagons filled with hay; in double-decker buses and pedicabs; and by ferry, horseback, jeeps, motor coaches and limousines.

When looking for a place to hold your event—be it traditional or unique—you will need to consider seven key points when you are laying out your event vision. More location requirements will be detailed further on in this book.

1. **Location** (local, out of state, out of country)

   Your guest list will be a factor in deciding your event location. Where do most of the guests live and what transportation and accommodation costs will need to be included in your cost breakdown?

2. **Date**

   What national or religious holiday or other special event (e.g., sporting, election, etc.) could affect attendance or impact labor and other costs?

3. **Season**

   Even seasons play a part in venue selection. The same venue in different seasons can produce a different set of event logistical and budget considerations. Every season can have its own challenges depending on the type of venue you choose. For example, a tented event taking place in the height of summer, during the heat of the day, would require considering the cost of air-conditioning, backup generators or ceiling fans, while a heating system or freestanding heaters, flooring and lighting would be cost factors for a tented wedding held in early spring or late fall when it is considerably cooler during the day and night, the grass can be damp and chilly on guests' feet and it gets dark much earlier. The same applies to building sites. At one event a guest collapsed due to the heat in a quaint facility that did not have air-conditioning. At another event held in the same location, custom fans were handed out to guests as a way to combat the heat and became a lasting memento of the event.

4. Time of day

Time of day is an important factor. Will you be the only group holding an event in the venue or will multiple events be scheduled? If multiple events are being held, will you feel as though you are in an assembly line? What happens if the event that is scheduled to take place before yours gets a late start? What happens if their guests linger? How long will it take for your suppliers to set up, and for guests to have access to the room/venue? If you are the ones holding the earlier time slot, how will you ensure that guests depart on time so that the next event can set up? Will you feel rushed and harried, and would you be better served holding your event in a venue where you will be the only event in the facility or the only event using the room you have selected?

5. Whether you are planning an indoor or outdoor affair

You can place your event at risk if you plan to have it outdoors without having a bad-weather backup. For spring, summer and fall events, a tent or a private room at the same facility can be reserved for you in case of inclement weather. The same applies for outdoor winter events. Companies opting to do a ski event need to reserve space that they can move the event to if hazardous weather conditions occur,

Outdoor events require special setup and cost considerations. For example, if you are setting up a tent, depending on your requirements, move in and setup can take anywhere from two to three days to a week and could be delayed if it rains. Time also has to be factored in for the ground to dry. Teardown and move out can take a couple of days as well. Depending on where you are holding your event, you may have to factor in site rental charges for setup and teardown days, as the facility would not be able to rent that space to anyone else over that time period. You would also have to check labor costs for teardown on a Sunday because there may be additional charges. Other cost factors could include having the grounds cared for, or separate cooking tents for the caterers if the venue does not have a kitchen available or one that will meet your needs and security. Tents can and have blown away and having someone on hand to handle the situation immediately may help you to avert major problems. Also, there is the issue of making sure that rental items such as chairs, tables, decor, audiovisual equipment, etc., are secured overnight and during the move in, setup, teardown and move out days when people are coming and going.

6. **Whether the event is taking place in one or more than one location**

   If you are holding your event in two different facilities, you need to consider the travel time between the two venues, if your guests can easily travel between the two locations, and how you want to stage the arrival.

7. **Budget considerations**

   Not all venues are created equal when it comes to their terms and conditions. For example, what might be included at no additional cost in a hotel—tables, chairs, linens or specialty glasses such as martini glasses for a martini bar—is not necessarily included in the room rental cost in a convention center, museum, etc. These items may need to be brought in especially for your event and a rental fee may be charged.

Event Style

Your event style is the atmosphere or overall effect you are trying to achieve. Styles can be mixed and matched to create something new. Style is personalized. There are no "shoulds" in style and style is never about money. If your chosen event style or theme, for example, is romance, you can have an incredibly romantic event spending hundreds of dollars, thousands of dollars or hundreds of thousands of dollars. What you have to spend may limit your options but never the overlying theme or essence of your event style.

Your event style will influence the choice of invitations, venue, guest attire, flowers, decor, music, entertainment, food and beverages. Your end result will be layers of ambiance flowing together to create your event style.

The following are samples of different event styles:

» Traditional
» Classic
» Modern
» Country
» Cultural
» Formal elegance
» Casual elegance
» Romantic
» Fun
» Intimate
» Outdoor
» Themed
» Seasonal
» Holiday
» Beach
» Sports

The Energy—Creating a Mood

Every event gives off energy. The venue, the decor, the music, the food and drink, the activities and the guest mix all contribute to the energy in the room and the mood being set. The energy you bring to your event as a result of your event design can be good or bad. Poor design planning with regards to timing, logistical layout and included event elements can literally drain the energy from a room. This is the feeling you experience when things go flat, there is dead air, stilted conversation or awkward silences and the room becomes devoid of energy. Negative energy can fill a room when there are overlooked areas of congestion, long waits, hungry or tired guests, and insufficient seating. Choosing a room or a setting that is too big or too small for the size of the guest count can also bring down the energy in a room. Detailed information on how to stage a room for maximum effect and energy can be found in *The Business of Event Planning.*

The Emotion—Feelings

The event style you select will lend itself to conveying the emotion surrounding your event. For example, a romantic style may evoke feelings of tenderness, softness, intimacy, all wrapped up in love. An event that has a fun theme, depicting a playful nature, will give off a lighthearted warmth that is caring and affectionate with a dash of festivity. Give thought to the event style and the feelings that you want to bring out. Choose one that will capture the spirit of your event's objectives and the emotions that will make your event stand out.

Event Vision Q&A

The following questions will help you to create your event vision, determine what areas are most important to your client and guide you through budget considerations that you need to reflect on—those seemingly inconsequential items that can quickly add up to hundreds and even hundreds of thousands of dollars in unexpected costs, as in the case of the union labor costs for an extensive setup, if not factored into the very beginning stages of designing your event.

The questionnaire opens the door to discussion with your client, which will lead you into decision-making and determining what matters most to them and how it all fits into their event budget.

Event Date

- » *What year do I see the event taking place?*
- » *What time of year (season) do I visualize the event being held in?*
- » *How much event planning time will that give me?*
- » *What day of the week do I want our event to take place on?*
- » *What time of day would be my preference to have our event start?*
- » *Would the time of year, the month, date or time affect attendance?*

VIPs

- » *What VIPs will be part of our event? (This could mean adding in expenses for suites, limousines, etc., as a must-have budget inclusion.)*

Event Guests

- » *How many guests do I visualize attending the event?*
- » *Will attendees be invited to bring a guest?*
- » *What is the age range of the guests we will be inviting?*
- » *Do I see children being invited to our event?*
- » *Would any guests have any special needs, such as handicap accessibility?*
- » *Would any of the guests I would like to have at our event have to come in from out of town, state or country?*
- » *Would we be required to host out-of-town guests and entertain them pre, post and during the event?*

Invitations

- » *Am I open to invitation styles or do I have something particular in mind?*

Event

- » *Where do I see our event taking place?*
- » *Is the event taking place indoors or outdoors?*

- *Do I see our event being a formal, festive or informal event?*
- *What do I see the event participants wearing?*
- *Where is the event location in relation to where guests live?*

Event Decor

- *As the guests are arriving at the event, what do I envision they will see from the moment they arrive until they are seated? And will anything change as the event progresses?*

Event Music

- *What do I envision event guests will be listening to on arrival and during the event? (This will help you determine space requirements, e.g., do you need to accommodate a band setup, etc.?)*

Event Lighting

- *What ambiance does the lighting project?*
- *What mood do I want the room to convey?*
- *How will the event stage be lit?*

Event Arrival

- *How do I see the guests arriving at the event? Will they be making their own way there or have drivers assigned to them? Will they come by limousine or other transportation mode?*

Event Photographs

- *Will we be having professional photographs, videos or a live event webcast of our event?*
- *Who will be taking the event photographs, videos or event webcast?*
- *What backdrop would I like to see in my event photographs?*

Event Show Flow

- *What would be of utmost importance to me to have in our event?*
- *How do I see the event unfolding?*
- *How long do I see the event taking from beginning to end?*

Event Room Requirements

» *How do I see the room being laid out?*

» *Will it be a stand-up event with scattered seating?*

» *Will it be a sit-down affair with table seating for all guests?*

» *If we are including dinner, will seating be open or will we be having set seating/seating chart?*

» *Will there be food stations or buffet setups, or will food be passed or plated?*

» *Will bars be set up in the room or will beverages be served by waitstaff?*

» *Will a stage be required for speeches, the musicians, the DJ or the entertainment?*

» *Will there be dancing?*

» *Will there be any audiovisual requirements, such as rear-screen projection, plasma screens, etc., that need to be factored into the room size requirements?*

Event Audiovisual

» *Will there be speeches?*

» *Will a podium or microphones be required?*

» *Will we have any audiovisual requirements?*

Event Food and Beverage

» *What type of beverages will we be serving?*

» *Will it be a hosted bar or cash bar?*

» *What type of food do I see being served at our event?*

Event Departure

» *Will there be any special fanfare as we depart, or a grand finale?*

Pre Event and Post Event

» *What pre- and post-move in, setup, rehearsal, day of, teardown and move out expenses and space requirements do I need to factor in?*

Once you have completed your event vision and done an initial budget based on the must-haves it's time to make the key decisions that will enable you to design an event that may or may not be able to include enhancements that will bring your event to a higher enjoyment level. If you don't achieve this goal, you will still have an event that will stand on its own, designed around the essential event elements that will help you to meet set-out event objectives, including coming in on budget, or to know where to look for creative cost options for must-have inclusions to bring costs in line if need be, such as sponsorship, if appropriate.

For example, a new event budget, sponsorship and partnership consideration that is showing up more and more in event planning, has great corporate and public appeal and is becoming a must-have event inclusion is going green. At green meetings and events, the emissions are calculated—this can include duration, number of delegates, flights, number of rooms, electricity used, etc.—and then an offsetter (www.greenmeetingguide.com has a list of suggestions) that ties into your company or event can be turned into carbon offset sponsorship packages. This can bring goodwill and media coverage to the sponsoring company as well as the company hosting the event, or be factored into a company's event budget calculations if having a green meeting or event and being environmentally responsible is one of their company's objectives.

Ways to produce green meetings and events include:

» The use of USB keys over printed handouts, which cuts paper use, can include digital information from the company and sponsors and can be branded
» Moving from bottled water to providing reusable stainless steel water bottles that save money, cut landfill waste and are a healthier alternative (in response to health concerns regarding BPA, the main building block of polycarbonate plastic, leaching into the water) and can be logoed as well for corporate brand marketing purposes
» Green awards for recognition of company or personal green innovations and achievements

- » Team-building events that include green or corporate social responsibility (CSR) components, such as volunteer and community service projects like tree planting, or funding and building a home for Habitat for Humanity.

If green sponsorship dollars are received and sponsors are being recognized, it's important that they be recognized in a greener way than using signage. In the past, this was the most common way to recognize sponsors but it only contributes to more waste unless the signage is reusable. Greener ways to thank sponsors include using websites, showing a looping slideshow at the event, including green sponsors' names and logos in any recordings and speaking opportunities and, if promotional material with logos is produced, ensuring where possible that recycled materials are used.

Below is a sample of a preliminary budget that allows you to arrive at a very rough estimate of the main expenses for your event. More detailed budgets will be covered in Chapter 3.

Preliminary Cost Estimates

Generally, you can get written estimates from suppliers for the various items you are considering. These will be firmed up later after the preliminary budget is approved and event requirements are detailed. For example, a caterer would be able to give you an estimated cost for a basic five-course dinner versus a five-course gourmet dinner for budgeting purposes, but the actual dinner costs would be based on final menu selection.

Sample preliminary budgets should include main costs, such as:

- » Invitations
- » Accommodation
- » Transportation
- » Venue rentals
- » Rehearsal costs
- » Food
- » Staging
- » Audiovisual
- » Beverage
- » Floral arrangements
- » Decor
- » Music
- » Entertainment
- » Speakers
- » Security
- » Labor charges

- Lighting
- Special effects
- Photography
- Place cards
- Menus
- Gifts
- Print material
- Promotional material
- Insurance/risk assessment protection
- Power charges
- Promotional material
- Communication costs
- Translation
- Shipping and handling
- Customs
- Staffing
- Miscellaneous
- Taxes and service charges
- Event planning management fee

Make a detailed wish list that includes everything possible, regardless of cost, on a spreadsheet in Excel or other accounting software. Setting up your budget on the computer will allow you to quickly see where you are and make adjustments to costs as prices come in. You will be able to immediately see how your budget is affected when you add in and take out different event elements. Highlight the headings that absolutely must be included in your program. The remaining items are optional and can be factored in once you have established your preliminary budget. For example, if food and beverage may be a must-have but menus and place cards could be a nice event enhancement, budget permitting, or if menus and place cards are determined to be important to your company with regards to your company's presentation style, then you need to know that these costs will need to be factored into your preliminary budget in addition to food and beverage expenses.

If your preliminary cost estimates, including only the non-negotiable items, exceed your proposed budget, you will need to give serious consideration as to whether or not you should proceed with your planned event or look to where you could possibly make adjustments. For example, is choosing a basic menu but including the menus and place cards an option, or do you need to stay with a gourmet menu to fit the tone you want your event to set? If your preliminary cost estimates are well under your proposed budget figures you can then begin to factor in your optional items.

Design Objectives of the Event Experience

The next thing to consider is the objectives of the event. Why are you holding it? What are your event—not company—goals and intentions? What do you hope to achieve? In the case of the glamour book launch, the event objective and event elements had to deliver glamour while the publishing company's objectives was to get media coverage for their book and create sales interest. To meet these objectives, they had to create an event that would be deemed newsworthy to media (television entertainment shows, talk shows, news shows, newspapers, fashion magazines, Internet, etc.).

Be clear about all of your company and event objectives—each event can have multiple layers of external and internal company objectives that need to be met. It is important to prioritize them and to see how far-reaching they can be and how one event can become a strong foundation to build on another (which needs to be budgeted for in the future as well).

For example, a company planning a sales conference may be looking to include team-building event elements that will give their employees well-being tools they need to help them grow professionally and personally so that they can do more, be more and grow themselves as well as their company. They may have an added internal company objective for their sales conference event and team-building challenge, one that would extend back to the office: reducing health care, disability, sick-time costs, or recruitment and retention expenses.

One way of doing this would be to have the company CEO lead by example and sign on to compete in a CEO Challenge. CEO Challenges (www.ceochallenges.com) designs sports competitions exclusively for CEOs to find the world's best CEO in a number of different sports. They offer CEO

Ironman Challenges, CEO Triathlons, as well as CEO Golf, Cycling, Fishing, Sailing, Skiing, Driving, and Tennis Challenges. The company whose company and event objectives include promoting well-being and active living lifestyle, as a whole or in part, e.g., just the sales force, could get behind their company and their CEO taking part in a CEO Challenge. This could include a custom Employee Wellness Program designed and launched as a team-building training event—created to fit all fitness levels. This program could then continue back at the office, with a custom fitness facility being designed on-site for employees and the CEO to continue working towards their fitness and well-being goals. And, budget permitting, weighing cost versus long-term benefits, companies such as www.personalbest.ca can be brought in to work with corporations to create the perfect fitness training center in their workplace. Personal trainers can be hired to continue to work with the company employees to help them achieve maximum results, and mini events to keep the momentum going can be staged, as can a pre- and post-company CEO Challenge event should their company CEO qualify to take part in the World CEO Challenge.

Corporate clients and their participants are taking a step away from tired and traditional themed events and incentive programs to meet their corporate objectives—many of them now cookie-cutter and no longer cutting-edge—and opting instead for custom-designed events that raise consciousness and awareness, such as the green meetings mentioned earlier or events centered around personal, as well as professional development or giving. Such events are now becoming part of their corporate environment and branding and companies are moving towards more elevated events designed strategically to give their attendees tools that they can use to enhance their quality of life at home and at work, bring balance into their day and be of great value to the individual as well as the corporation. Companies are creating an event experience for attendees that will be one or more of the following:

» Educational
» Enlightening

» Engaging (connecting the company/group as a whole)
» Energizing
» Entertaining, but with a very exclusive educational twist

Enlightening

An example of an event built around enlightenment, bringing the mind, body and soul into alignment, and bringing balance into your life at home and at work could include building the event around yoga and bringing in a master such as Rodney Yee. Yee (www.yeeyoga.com) is one of America's premier yoga teachers and has been featured in *Time, People* and *USA Today*, and on the *Oprah Winfrey Show*. He travels across the country and around the world to destinations such as England, Bali, Australia and Mexico to conduct workshops and retreats. Yee is the host of more than 17 best-selling yoga DVDs and videos and author of *Moving Toward Balance: 8 Weeks of Yoga with Rodney Yee* (Rodale Books, 2004) and coauthor of *Yoga: The Poetry of the Body* (Yee and Zolotow, St. Martin's Griffin, 2002).

Corporations are realizing the benefits that training in yoga and meditation can make in both work and personal lives. Yoga is one of the greatest stress reducers, and meditation practices lead to greater creativity, better concentration and stronger relationships. The skills that participants learn will help them relate better to people and become more relaxed, present and productive in the workplace.

Yee recommends a weekend yoga retreat as the minimum time required to make a difference. The morning can begin with yoga and then move into the meeting portion of the day. Meditation can take place during the meeting on one of the breaks. This will keep attendees focused and enable them to come back refreshed and ready to begin the listening. Yoga can also be built into corporate events that have a sports element. Many top high-performance athletes—from football players to golfers—now cross-train, and yoga is a very important part of their strength, stamina, conditioning and flexibility training. A weekend corporate retreat can be built around a sports theme, such as a golf tournament, and include yoga and meditation skills to help them perform better in their game, at work and at home. Yoga and meditation help to restore the imbalance in the body, rhythm, breathing, concentration and bring awareness and show people how to live through this practice. During a yoga retreat, participants will be entertained, acquire learning and will be self-investing. Couples and family yoga is another element that can be built into a yoga workshop. Room gifts could include yoga mats, yoga balls, and Yee's DVDs and books, as well as yoga attire.

Another example of an enlightening experience that can benefit participants at home and at work is the Equine Experience at Miraval Life in Balance™ (www.miravalresort.com) run by Wyatt Webb. Webb is the founder and leader of the Equine Experience at Miraval Life in Balance™. Webb is the number one attraction at Miraval, which is the number one spa in America, and one of the top five in the world. Webb asks his clients to do a few simple tasks with horses that reveal to him what is going on in the clients' lives, as the interaction with the horse serves as a mirror to one's relationships with other human beings. Formerly the head of the juvenile program at the renowned Sierra Tucson Treatment Facility, Webb spent years studying different therapeutic modalities and then developed his own program that brings together horses and people. Webb is also the author of *It's Not About the Horse* (Hay House, 2002), *Five Steps to Overcoming Fear and Self Doubt* (Hay House, 2004) and *What To Do When You Don't Know What To Do: Common Horse Sense* (Hay House, 2006) and is one of the most sought-after therapists in the country.

Webb's Equine Experience brings consciousness to people, and teaches them how to pay attention and how to look at what they create in their lives and in their relationships. After taking these sessions, many have found that their relationships improve 100 percent and so does a company's bottom line, because they come away knowing how to listen and get out of their own way in order to be more successful. The Equine Experience elevates and benefits daily living. It becomes a personal experience where participants learn to become accountable. Barriers drop and they see who they truly are. After taking the course, they are able to assess how they have contributed to the stress in their home and work life. As they move through the course, they learn it is not about the work, just as it is not about the horses. The horse is internally focused and present in the moment, whereas people, unless they are taught consciousness, are externally focused. As attendees, the participants see how every move the body makes is a direct response to what they personally believe. They learn how to pay attention to what they feel, how to look at their behavior, and how to understand why they cannot live their life externally focused and why the switch to internal focus is of paramount importance to them in their personal and professional lives. They experience an emotional change and return passionate, enjoying the work they are doing.

Engaging

Events that engage the company as a whole can be designed as multitiered programs and have the added benefit of being able to be extended past the actual meeting or incentive. An event could launch the program and run over the course of a year—with mini events to keep the motivation going—culminating in a grand finale such as the CEO Challenge discussed earlier.

Energizing

Team building or group activities—held during a meeting, conference, incentive or stand-alone event—are now being focused on personal well-being and active living activities that are designed specifically to deliver an infusion of new energy and vitality to an individual, as part of an event's and company's objective that can benefit the individual both at home and at work and again can be multitiered. For example, in the winter, a day of play on the ski slopes (or snowshoeing or cross-country skiing) can be followed by a great "après" relaxation experience in the heart of nature at a facility such as Le Scandinave Spa Blue Mountain (www.ScandinaveBlue.com), as can a day of personal training, mountain biking, hiking or golf during the summer. A personalized logoed robe (initials and company or theme logo) or logoed stainless-steel water bottle (which adds a green element) that guests can use at home as well as during their visit to the spa can be the perfect gift to present participants with at arrival post-sports/active living event.

Educational/Entertaining

Providing memorable experiences with private performances has always been successful for corporate marketing and sales events. Real estate companies are now expanding on this and using celebrities to help them sell new properties by inviting selected guests—prospective clients—to an exclusive celebrity event. Corporations are now taking it a step further and creating celebrity travel events for their participants to enjoy. For example, guests can travel to Italy with a celebrity chef, shop in the markets with them and then come back to learn how to prepare healthy, wholesome meals with their celebrity chef by their side as they work together as a group to prepare that evening's meal. The same celebrity educational travel events can be built around fashion, wine appreciation, racing, tennis, golf, etc.

No matter what the "spin," the event's main objective should be significant, for example launching a major product like a new car, rewarding top sales performance or bringing down costs that influence the bottom line, such as those listed above, to justify the cost of the event. Don't use an event as an excuse to cover up internal strategies or to throw a personal party that is trying to pass as a business event. For example, staging a costly event to launch a minor product that has not sold well because of some defects will not only fail to solve your problems but also will add to them by wasting your money and tarnishing your company's reputation. Make sure the event is worth the expenditure of time, money and energy that will be spent on the planning, operations, execution and reconciliation of it, and the time, money and energy that will be required from your guests. Will they deem it to have been worthwhile and feel it was either educational, enlightening, engaging, energizing and entertaining, or meaningful, memorable and magical personally and/or professionally? Below are some examples of different objectives for various types of events.

Some Objectives for Different Types of Events

Meetings

» *Provide new information about your product or company*
» *Bring together people outside the office setting*
» *Exchange ideas*
» *Find solutions to existing problems*
» *Launch a new product*
» *Provide training*

Corporate Events

» *Appreciate employees*
» *Appreciate clients*
» *Appreciate suppliers*
» *Hand out awards*
» *Bring together suppliers and staff*
» *Launch products*
» *Support a fund-raising endeavor that the corporation advocates*
» *Raise public awareness*
» *Enhance brand-name recognition*
» *Celebrate milestones (50th anniversary, millionth customer or widget sold)*

Fund-Raisers

» *Raise funds for research*
» *Get media attention*
» *Raise public awareness*

- *Attract new sponsors*
- *Solicit new supporters and donations*
- *Increase number of volunteers*
- *Develop a mailing list for future events or sponsorship and donation requests*

Conferences

- *Bring a wide range of people together to exchange information and ideas*
- *Launch new products*
- *Recognize sales*

Incentives

- *Create one-of-a-kind events to recognize increase in sales*
- *Bring the top sales force together to discuss future strategy*
- *Get the top sales force and senior management together outside of the work environment*
- *Enlist the support of family and partners*

Special Events

- *Get media attention*
- *Raise public awareness*
- *Attract new clients*
- *Launch products*
- *Present awards*
- *Pay tributes*

Your event objectives will affect how you plan, set up and stage your event. If you are planning a client appreciation event where attendees at a conference may have several choices on the same evening, your objective would be to create something that will pique their interest, get them to your event, keep them there and get them interacting with your people.

For example, stockbrokers attending a conference flocked to an evening of fun, food and adventure at a brand-new entertainment complex. Motor coaches were waiting at their hotel to take them to the site and to bring them back. As guests boarded they were presented with a sealed package and told not to open it until they arrived at the private cocktail reception. Inside the kits were logoed golf towels that served a dual purpose: team designation and take-away gifts.

The first purpose of the golf towels was to divide the guests into six teams identified by different-colored towels. Each team was led by a senior member of the hosting company, allowing the company representative to spend quality time getting to know the team members. The golf towels easily clipped onto waistbands or purses and made each team member easily identifiable.

At the cocktail reception, guests were given instructions and then they set out on a two-hour adventure, taking part in something unique—a virtual-reality Olympics. Afterwards, they met for a "clock-in" dinner and an opportunity to share experiences. Scores were quickly calculated and prizes awarded. Then guests were free to stay and enjoy the facilities at their leisure, with the private area remaining if they wanted to relax and enjoy beverages, coffee and dessert. Shuttles left every half hour to take them back to the hotel if they chose to leave. Guests had such a great time that at the end of the evening most had not left. They had had an entertaining experience and the company's objectives had been met; they had spent quality time interacting and getting to know their guests.

The second purpose of the golf towels was as take-away gifts. Too often, such gifts are ill-considered, useless trinkets, but since many stockbrokers play golf, the towel was something they could actually use, and it would serve as a visual reminder of the event.

Had the event been planned as just a cocktail reception and dinner at the facility, people might still have had a good time, but the company's objectives would not have been met. Without the structure of the competing teams, there would not have been the same-quality interaction. If the guests had been left to explore the facility on their own they would have been too spread out, and with little to keep their interest they might have simply dropped in for a cocktail and a quick game before heading off to another event.

First Steps Questions

» *Should I hold an event?*

» *Do I have sufficient funds to stage an event?*

» *How much money can I set aside for the event?*

» *What is the purpose of the event?*

» *Does it justify the financial outlay?*

Initial Planning

A company or individual has decided to hold an event. After preparing an event vision and preliminary cost estimate, they have concluded that they have sufficient funds and have allocated a set amount for the event. They have defined the purpose of the event and decided that it would justify the financial outlay. They are now ready to begin the initial planning for the event. During this stage, if they do not have in-house event planners they will decide whether they need outside professional help and bring in an event planning company, hire an independent event planner to work with their internal team or have their internal team work with event suppliers directly to handle their event design; manage their budget, logistics, the timing and event execution; and orchestrate as well as help them to visualize the whole thing from top to bottom.

When planning major events too many people think in terms of dollars and cents, not sense. Clients—be they corporate, nonprofit, social or wedding—need to know when and where to bring in event planning professional assistance, including an expert in public relations, a creative director or a producer to handle event production from concept to completion. It is important that event planners do not present themselves to their clients as being a service industry—that is not the role they play—being perceived as merely order takers. Instead, they need to represent themselves, their company and the event planning industry as a valuable business sales and marketing tool that can help corporate clients, nonprofit organizations and individuals design, produce and deliver an event that has been custom created—not cookie-cutter—and strategically designed to meet and exceed their identified company, professional and personal objectives.

Event planners and event-related consultants should never be viewed as an added expense and a luxury. They can actually save money in the end, especially if they are brought in at the appropriate time. For example, a good public relations company can assist with your guest list and ensure that the *right* people are invited to your event; they can also help create press releases and press kits to get you national and international media exposure. A creative director or professional event designer works to provide you with a strategic conceptional overview of the event design, including planning, organizational, logistical and negotiating elements and the tiny details that make the magic.

Today, literally the sky—and beyond—is the limit when it comes to event planning, and professionals can expand the horizons of their clients. Space has now been used successfully to launch a new golf club, with an astronaut playing golf in space, to celebrate a magazine's anniversary celebration cover (an oversized mock-up was laid out in the desert and was designed to be seen by satellite from space); dinners (or breakfasts, lunch or cocktails) have been literally lifted to new heights by being served from a rented dining platform hanging 50 meters aboveground—held up by a crane—which can accommodate 22 guests, a chef, server and musician and be held anywhere in the world (permits permitting) or be used to have an orchestra or band play overhead of an event; and fashion shows have used the outside of buildings to walk—or rather rappel down face forward—to launch a new designer season and to create cutting-edge buzz and media exposure for the store that held the exclusive licensed rights to the brand. An event producer or event operations staff ensures that all that is visualized becomes reality and is responsible for confirming that fire and safety regulations are met, all appropriate permits are obtained and that the proper insurance is in place.

And the same applies to event planning companies. They need to know when to bring in expertise and where and how to use the services of freelancers in order to grow their company.

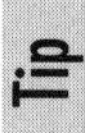

Bring event planners and event-related consultants in at the appropriate time and you can save money in the end.

Costly errors can occur when the professionals aren't brought in. Imagine the fire marshal standing at the front door about to close your event down because you don't have the proper permits, have too many guests for the size of the room or you haven't met all safety regulations. How costly is that? Or what is the cost if you hold a fabulous event and you need the momentum from positive press but nothing is done about it? How costly is it if you are not on top of what is new, fresh and exciting and the media report that people bolted for the doors before dessert was served? Companies need to know where and when to bring in the professionals. Will it be dollars and cents, or sense? Know where. Know when.

Corporate Event Committee or Team

When setting up or working with a corporate event committee or team—or both in the case of a company working in sponsorship partnership with a nonprofit organization—seek to match skills, areas of interest and time availability with areas of responsibility. For example, if a committee member's job function is sales and they are expected to continue producing results while assisting with event planning, they may not have time during the workday to be available to go on site inspections, review guest lists, etc., or be on call when month close-off is taking place and they are under the wire to close sales. Event planning time requirements are laid out—as are time-making and time-saving tips and techniques in *Time Management for Event Planners* (Wiley, 2005). You want to ensure that salesperson doesn't feel as though they are a deer caught in an oncoming car's headlights.

Remember to have one person from the corporation assigned to handle all communication with the event planning company or suppliers (if the company or organization is handling their event in-house). This ensures that suppliers are not receiving conflicting sets of instructions from a number of sources and that approval for expenditures is given to them by only those in a position to authorize them.

Type of Event

When determining the type of event, look at your targeted audience. Busy professionals may not take time out from their schedules to attend a symposium that will cut into their designated family time, but may attend if the event is designed to include their family members, such as a private showing in a theater or an exclusive booking of an entertainment center. The symposium could be held in the morning while their families are at play. They could then meet for a catered luncheon, with the balance of the day for them to enjoy the facility with their family members, or, in the case of a private showing in a theater or prime seating for an in-demand live show, the symposium could again be held earlier and a private pre- and post-meal function could anchor the entertainment element of the event. A company that was able to secure a private showing at the theater or seats at the hot, instant sell-out Hannah Montana live performance show would have no problem reaching maximum attendance at their symposium built around that family event, just as they would with a limited Cirque du Soleil performance. One company held an extremely successful private dinner under a tent with Cirque-style performers performing overhead and special effects.

A public event looking to create an event that will generate pre-show media exposure that will serve to bring clients to their doorstep may look to partner with a company or companies that will help them to achieve that goal. For example, a bridal show hoping to draw couples, their families and their wedding parties to their event featured a million-dollar wedding cake display. Again, as in the example of the glamour book launch, a jewelry company provided gems to be used to decorate a lavish wedding cake. The show, the jewelry company and the wedding cake designer all benefited from the publicity and, once again, the cost to produce a million-dollar wedding cake was minimal (security, insurance, labor on the wedding cake) but the return was maximal for all involved.

Time Requirements

In an ideal world you would have at least a year to plan your event, even though many details still would be undetermined. Yes, it is possible to put together major high-profile events for 1,000-plus in under six weeks, but there is always a cost. You run the risk of not being able to get the most sought-after locations and entertainment. Why settle for second best if you can plan ahead?

In deciding the amount of planning time required, list everything that you will need and assign a time frame to each item. Begin with the end in mind. What needs to be done for your event to be a success? Work backwards with your calendar and start to pencil in the proposed schedule of events. Remember to build in time buffers. Take the time to research in order to determine realistic timelines. *Time Management for Event Planners* will show you how to create and build in time buffers that will work in both your personal and professional life and eliminate deadline stress.

Plan ahead and you can avoid settling for second best.

Allow yourself sufficient time to achieve maximum results. What could stop you from meeting targeted deadlines, such as a conflicting deadline or your suppliers being closed for holidays? For example, printing companies traditionally close for vacation the last two weeks in July. Be sure to check with your suppliers and to factor this into your timelines. Summer is a bad time in general—even the media are away.

Will any key people be difficult to reach or out of the office at the time of prime planning and operations deadlines? Will year-end affect timing in any way?

One gala fund-raiser had a three-month timeline to secure a venue, obtain sponsors, arrange entertainment and printing and sell 5,000 tickets at $500 apiece. A flurry of meetings followed and the event was postponed after the company's planners concluded they would not succeed if they went ahead with their plans with just three months lead time. They would not be able to secure a quality venue or a desirable entertainer, nor would there be time to secure sponsorship dollars. The timing just could not be worked out, given obstacles such as the start of a new school year and the Jewish holidays. In the end, the plans were revised to allow for sufficient time to properly plan, secure sponsorship and contract big-name entertainment.

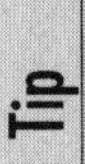

Don't be afraid to postpone your event if, when planning it, you realize it would do more harm than good to proceed with it. You may need more budget, more time, or a better location or date. Sometimes costs are not about dollars and cents; it can be very costly to proceed with an event if it doesn't make sense.

Visualization

Visualization is an important factor in ensuring a successful event; in fact, it is the next step after the initial event vision concept has been created. It is a process that walks you through your event in advance and allows you to see areas that could pose potential problems. It allows you to address these areas in the planning stages and not be surprised on the day of the actual event.

For example, if your guests will be arriving all at once and there is both an up and a down escalator leading to the ballroom, picture this in your mind. You may realize that you want to have both escalators set to go up to alleviate congestion and speed entry. (At the conclusion of the event the reverse is appropriate.) This could allow you to set up two separate registration desks at the foot of the escalators and help to lessen the waiting time in lineups. In addition, you may find that you could also use two separate coat check areas.

Visualizing such things in advance will help you determine the staffing you will need to greet and direct guests, sit at the registration desk and have both coat checks adequately operated. Visualization allows you to consider all your options and to see how they affect your budget before you finalize your plans.

Try to envision your event from beginning to end. You need to be able to do a complete preliminary visual walk-through in your mind. Here's a review of some of the key questions we've suggested you will have to ask (and answer):

- What is the purpose of your event?
- What time of year are you considering holding it?
- What will people be wearing? (Will a coat check be necessary?)
- What day of the week?
- What time of the day? (How will traffic and parking be?)
- Who will be attending? (Will it be individuals or couples? If couples, will they be arriving together or on their own—that factor could affect how many parking spaces you need to have available for your event.)
- What type of venue will be the best fit, the best setting, the best backdrop?
- Are you planning far enough in advance that the best sites will be available to you?

Remember, your event is a reflection of your company image. Keep in mind that what you do today sets the tone for tomorrow and can work both for and against you in building momentum for your next event. Of key importance will be the ambiance you create, the rhythm, the flow and the schedule of events from beginning to end.

This is just your starting point—we will cover detailed specifics in another section. Create a visual image of your event. List every element that you want to include. What are the priorities—the must-haves—that will make your event a success? Have you included one major "wow" factor in your event? What atmosphere are you looking to create? What take-away memories? What perception of your company or cause? Now walk through your event from start to finish in your mind to capture critical logistical event requirements that will need to be addressed and may need to be added to your budget.

One guest on a four-night incentive program in San Antonio said, "Each day was like Christmas. Each event was like opening up one exciting gift one after another." Events included a private golf course booked exclusively for the company's golfers. The golfers teed off in the morning and did not return until 6 p.m. Had any guests preferred basketball to golf, going one-on-one with a celebrity player could have been arranged.

Complete makeovers were provided for those who chose to be pampered instead. The salon was entirely theirs for the day. Appointments were scheduled and limousines shuttled guests from the hotel to the salon and back. Lunch was provided and most guests did not leave but chose instead to watch the other makeovers. The transformations were amazing. Professional photographs were taken and mailed to the guests. There were many requests for additional copies.

When the winning sales executives returned to work on Monday, their motivation was high, their enthusiasm contagious. The carefully designed and orchestrated incentive program had boosted the exact feelings the client was hoping to achieve—they had reached their objective. The San Antonio winners clearly felt taken care of from beginning to end, and their spouses were delighted as well. Every detail had been looked after and all their needs had been thought of in advance and attended to. And that all reflected directly back on the company and its image as one that took excellent care of its staff. The staff who had not met the targeted sales goals this time were motivated by the positive energy of the returning winners and were looking forward to the possibility of attending the next incentive program, which was announced at the farewell award dinner in San Antonio.

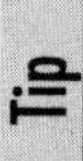

An important factor in incentive programs is that company sales targets are not excessive; they must be obtainable by all, and the number of participants who could attend the event must not be limited.

From the initial invitation to on-site operations, your event must be a true reflection of your company image. It will mirror how your business is run and your level of professionalism.

Monitoring the Budget

Cost Sheets

As you begin to plan your event, laying out your proposed budget on a cost sheet in Excel as mentioned earlier will allow you to clearly see what items can be included and still keep you within your budget. It will also show you how you are choosing to spend your money, enable you to look at alternate choices and see how they would work within your cost parameters. For example, once you have laid out your cost sheet and taken a look at where you stand in meeting your targeted budget, you may decide that for your centerpieces you can use simple candles (real or battery operated depending on the hotel and fire marshal regulations) supplied by the hotel at no cost as opposed to a more elaborate floral arrangement, and put the money saved towards the cocktail reception and doing something special. Your goal is to create a memorable event with the right event elements in it while staying in budget. You want to ensure that you have taken all possible steps to do so. Don't wait to find out at the end of your event that you have greatly exceeded your budget projections. Your event should be reconciled as you go forward—each time you receive new costs or make adjustments or changes, your budget needs to be updated so that there are no surprises.

Since each event will have different event inclusions, there is no set formula or format for a cost sheet. As you start to build your cost sheet, walk through your event from beginning to end and start to build the outline. Remember to add in move in, setup, rehearsal, teardown and move out. Then go back and fill in the costs. Remember to get all your estimates in writing. Never accept verbal quotes. Today, staff changes are the rule rather than the exception—people are here today and gone tomorrow. You need written confirmation of what is and is not included. Make sure that your suppliers spell it out. Have them be specific when it comes to items as seemingly unimportant as tipping—are gratuities calculated as a straight percentage of the total bill, or is tipping being taxed? That amount can add up, especially if it affects both food and beverage. Similarly, taxes on food and liquor can be different—don't assume.

Find out what additional costs may be added to the final bill and make sure you include them in your budget. Some venues will bill you for your actual usage of electricity. In those cases, for your costing purposes, ask for the figures from a recent similar event that can provide you with an estimate for your budget. With entertainment, royalties must be paid to the artist (ASCAP or BMI in the United States and SOCAN in Canada). Make sure that the company that is handling your entertainment needs has included royalty details in their written proposal. Computer spreadsheet programs allow you the flexibility to quickly see how your overall costs are affected if you have 750 or 1,000 guests. You can also easily add and remove items and see how that affects the bottom line.

As you update your budget as items are added and subtracted, save a new file. Date and number them (e.g., Revision 1, Revision 2). You need to stay on top of your budget so that you can make informed decisions on what to include. As bills come in, make sure nothing is paid out until they have been reviewed. Make sure that what is submitted is what had been agreed on, with no hidden surprises. Adjust your cost sheet accordingly. As each bill is received, record the actual amount on your cost sheet and compare it to your projected figures. Are they accurate? Are there any costs on the final billing that you had not included in your original estimate? Be particularly on the lookout for items that were charged for, but not contracted and signed off on. If an item has been miscalculated, you need to see immediately how it impacts your bottom line so that you can make budget adjustments in other areas to compensate for them before your event takes place. One planner underestimated the cost of shipping the invitation packages out to participants because the final package was oversize, not regulation size as originally budgeted for, resulting in a $15,000 unexpected charge.

Use a spreadsheet program such as Excel to track your budget elements and update them as necessary. This enables you to maintain relatively real-time files and share them with the appropriate people.

As you move from the creative planning stages of your event into the actual operation, the items you had originally decided to include may change. For example, you may decide to welcome your guests with a specialty drink that will require the rental of specific glassware, as opposed to your original plan for a standard open bar and available glassware. This would have an impact on your budget projections. Little by little, the cents add up to dollars, and the dollars can quickly escalate.

If you are not keeping your cost sheet updated, you could find that you have blown your budget. By constantly updating your cost sheets, your budget will be close to being reconciled as you go into your event. It will also allow you to make those last-minute additions that often come up, and knowing where you are financially allows you to make a responsible decision, such as whether you can afford to host the bar after dinner or if you'll have to set it up as a cash bar. Perhaps you now have sufficient funds left in the budget to include a farewell gift for your guests. See Appendix A for sample cost sheets. You can also visit our companion website at www.wiley.ca/go/event_planning to access these forms, as well as additional ones not included in the book.

Payment Schedule

Before you sign a contract you need to prepare a payment schedule to see if the due dates need to be adjusted. Hotels and other venues will work with you if payments need to be changed to match your client's check runs or cash flows.

Some corporate clients have asked event planning companies to finance their event. This is very risky business to engage in, so do what you can to avoid it.

Establishing payment schedules from the client and to suppliers is of paramount importance. Event planners need to advise their client at time of contracting of payment terms and conditions and lay out dates and amounts in the contract with time buffers built in. If there are any concerns with the payment schedule you need to know prior to signing contracts with suppliers—or having your client sign contracts with suppliers in the case of clients wanting their event financed so the event planning company does not place itself at financial risk—so that terms and conditions can be adjusted if need be and signed off on.

Your cost sheet is the base from which to create your payment schedule. Your payment schedule will need to be revised should the items you plan to include or number of expected guests change. Adjust amounts accordingly before sending the next payment off. Remember when creating your payment schedule to factor in supplier cancellation penalties. Should the event be cancelled at any point ensure that you have received sufficient payment to cover those cancellation charges, as well as your management fee. See Appendix B for a sample cost sheet and the payment schedule that has been created from it. Again, for access to these samples, as well as others not included in Appendix B, please visit our companion website at www.wiley.ca/go/event_planning.

Event Design Principles Checklist

Always consider the five event design principles when visualizing an event:

- ✓ *The elements—all the parts that make up the event*
- ✓ *The essentials—must-haves*
- ✓ *The environment—venue and style*
- ✓ *The energy—creating a mood*
- ✓ *The emotion—feelings*

Event Experience Design Objectives

The five event experience design objectives considerations are:

1. Educational
2. Enlightening
3. Engaging (connecting the company/group as a whole)
4. Energizing
5. Entertaining, but with a very exclusive educational twist

. . . and even a mixture of all of these event elements.

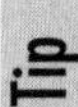

An event—corporate, or social used as a business investment—is used to drive sales, build awareness, create brand loyalty, motivate performance, raise productivity and increase profitability. When thinking about event design and how to create an event experience that will drive and deliver outstanding results, use the D.R.I.V.E. event design program I have created that is detailed in *The Executive's Guide to Corporate Events and Business Entertaining*.

D.R.I.V.E.

D *Define company and event objectives*

R *Research and develop your event vision*

I *Innovate and create a customized event experience using my design principles and event objectives*

V *Visualize your event step by step to capture all essential logistical event requirements and expenses*

E *Execute with detailed precision and timing*

2

Organization and Timing

There is a rhythm and a flow to every event that must be carefully orchestrated. All must be organized ahead of time—everything in its place and ready to go. Charting your critical path will take you to successful event execution, with the focus kept on what needs to be done right now and with the timing of the finishing touches and requirements factored in.

Critical Path

You have determined your company or your client objectives and established your event objectives, selected your event style, laid out your cost sheet and worked out a preliminary budget, put out your requests for quotes from suppliers and narrowed your choices down, updated your budget based on projected costs for your selected event elements and received contracts to review for terms, conditions and payment requirements before signing. Now is the time to begin to add contracted timing and logistical information to your schedule of events, which will now become the official master critical path that everyone involved—event planning staff, event planning corporate teams and suppliers—will be working from. As you move forward with event operations, changes will be made, event elements will be added or subtracted or upgraded, and unexpected time demands will develop, and you will have to continually update your critical path as the new information and supplier and venue requirements arise. Remember to always number and date each critical path revision—just the same as you will be doing for your cost sheet—so that you can easily know if everyone is on the same page.

Being organized and paying close attention to detail are two of the most important elements of running a successful event. Checking constantly that things are on schedule and moving forward as planned is essential. All involved—corporate clients, event planning staff and suppliers—need to adhere to the guidelines set out and contractually agreed upon. Taking two months to approve an item could result in poor event project management and lead to a stressful event where you are running right down to the wire. For instance, you could spend hours on a creative invitation design, but if it doesn't arrive at the printer's in sufficient time to make your mailing deadlines, it can have a disastrous effect on attendance. That's why creating a schedule of events that will become your working critical path should be one of your first steps after you have decided to go ahead with the event.

To create your critical path, take out your calendar and start working backwards from the date of your event, looking at what has to be done when. There are numerous horror stories of things nearly going wrong. At one event, the programs and signage required last-minute changes and barely arrived on time. At another event, inserts arrived after the programs had been distributed and, at a third, the logoed T-shirts arrived literally hot off the press—the boxes were steaming as they were opened! Each of these things sends a subtle signal of disorganization to those attending your event. Such missteps and near-disasters show that the event was poorly planned and coordinated.

There have to be strict cutoff times, or you will suddenly discover what the domino effect is all about. It is surprising how an apparently small thing can have a major impact. At one fund-raising event the "organizers" were changing the seating plans up until the very last minute and left themselves no time for a final review. This resulted in some embarrassing errors; one table had been assigned to two VIP sponsorship companies, which resulted in an additional table having to be set up at the final moment as the important guests stood and waited. There were no provisions made to have extra table coverings and centerpieces as backup, so the table could not be set up to match the others. By taking last-minute requests for table seating, they had not left themselves time to properly check the revisions that they had made to the seating plan.

Your goal is to have everything finalized well before your precons with clients, suppliers and on-site event planning staff—which are scheduled to take place well before move in and setup begins so that everyone involved can take the time to look after last-minute details and catch any last-minute glitches that should have been anticipated but slipped through logistical cracks. You want everyone to arrive the day of your event refreshed, at his or her best and giving their best, focused on every event element being successfully orchestrated and executed, not still scrambling to pull things together because time ran out.

Take each of your contracts and make sure that all key cutoff dates become a part of your critical path. Pay close attention to attrition and cancellation dates. These are the final dates when you are allowed to alter your attendance figures (attrition) or scrub the whole event (cancellation) without penalties or with minimal penalties. Often, you can lower the guaranteed guest count on food and beverage or the number of guestrooms booked at a hotel by a contracted percentage without incurring charges if the numbers are reduced by a certain date. Include the deadline and a time buffer date on your critical path to review it. Allow yourself time to make informed decisions. It could be a costly mistake if you miss an attrition date and a chance to reduce your guest numbers, as you would then be charged based on the original numbers of guests or guestrooms contracted.

Remember, as your event develops, it is imperative that you continue to update your critical path, cost sheet and payment schedule. Pay close attention to the language of the contract. For example, if final food and beverage guarantees have to be called in by a specific date, have your supplier give you in writing the actual date they are required, as opposed to *x* number of days before the event. To some companies, for example, 14 days before the event is 14 days prior to the event, while for others the 14 days prior to your event may be based on 14 working days—not actual days—before your event, which is very different. As you lay out your critical path make sure you give a description of each item, who is responsible for it and what the deadline is. Take the time to prepare your critical path and to put it into your personal schedule.

Below you will find sample critical path inclusions for invitations to an event scheduled to take place on November 1. This example takes you through some suggested timelines for the preparation of guest lists and invitations. These are the initial timeline items that would be added to the master critical path in date order and expanded upon as event operations progressed. In this example, a professional mailhouse was contracted to address the invitations, insert them into the envelopes and mail them out. This could also be done in-house, as long as you allow for additional time and staff to do this. If staff are handling the mailing in addition to their regular work, you could experience delays in meeting timelines. This outline includes key dates in the critical path. Of course, times will vary depending on your specific requirements, your suppliers' deadlines and the time of year.

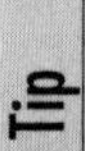

Whenever you are doing a mailing be sure to address one piece to yourself. This way you will know if there are any unexpected delays in delivery, and if you check the postage date stamp on the envelope you will know if the invitation actually went out on the scheduled date.

Critical Path Inclusions

Completion Date	Task	Person Responsible
May 1	Guest List Development Meeting	Michelle
May 1	Invitation Design Meeting	Rick
May 7	Mailhouse Contracted	Rick
May 15	Guest List Review and Sign Off	Michelle
July 12	First Review of Invitation Design	Rick
July 26	Second Review of Invitation and Sign Off	Rick
August 3	Invitations to Printer	Rick
August 3	Guest Name and Address Review	Michelle
August 5	Guest List Names and Addresses to Rick	Michelle
August 9	Envelopes and Guest List Sent to Mailhouse for Addressing	Rick
August 15	Invitations to Mailhouse for Packaging	Rick
August 23	Invitations Mailed to Guest List A	Rick and Michelle
September 13	VIP Passes Mailed to Guest List A RSVPs	Rick and Michelle
September 27	RSVP Cutoff to Guest List A	Rick and Michelle
September 27	Invitations Mailed to Guest List B (if applicable)	Rick and Michelle
September 27	RSVP Cutoff for Guest List B (if applicable)	Rick and Michelle
October 12	VIP Passes Mailed to Guest List B (if applicable)	Rick and Michelle

Function Sheets

Screenwriters have their scripts, songwriters their music sheets and event planners their function sheets. Each fulfills the same function. Like a good story, there is a beginning, a middle and an end. Each step of the way is scripted; each note is laid out exactly as it is meant to be played. Everyone is operating off the same page. Everything is clearly detailed. It lessens room for error and eliminates the "but I thought..." It reduces the gray areas and things that could slip through the cracks. From the detail comes the magic.

The function sheets become living and breathing things, and you are their creative director. They are the heart of your event, encompassing it from beginning to end. One person needs to be in charge of preparing them, to control all the information coming in, and that person must be the only one dealing with the suppliers and finalizing the plans. The creative director needs to know the event—every moment, every step, every detail—inside out, just like a conductor leading a symphony or a director making a movie. The leader can't be someone whose role it will be to host the event or to socialize. Each player needs to know what their part is and when to come in, but one person is in charge of the overall event. Make sure everyone knows their particular role. Don't have half a dozen people calling a supplier; that's a recipe for certain disaster, and it reflects badly on your professionalism and that of your organization.

As an event approaches, you will probably no longer need to refer to your function sheets because you know them by heart. You know—as a conductor does—when the wrong note has been played. One wedding planner booked a private estate for a celebrity wedding months in advance, and found out 10 days before the event that a large pond and hot tub had been constructed on the lawn where the couple had planned to say their vows. He was quoted as saying that the couple couldn't get married there unless they arranged to walk on water. For such a calamity to happen is unthinkable, and there are no excuses for not knowing about it until

10 days before. That is the purpose of the function sheets—to make sure that everything is in place, with no surprises. A solution was found, but at what cost to make the new layout work? Who needs to have that kind of stress and all the additional expenses? One event planning company ran an event at a $50,000 loss because of their poor event management; lost future business, referrals and their reputation; and had to deal with a very unhappy client wanting to take them to court because of the event planning company's unprofessional handling of their event. We live in a very litigious society and it is imperative today that event planning, operations and on-site execution be well documented to show that due diligence was taken in all areas. Your function sheets will give you that and help you to identify red flag areas in advance and in time to take appropriate action.

Attention to Detail

The function sheets are the information guide that tell your suppliers how *you* want your event to be handled. They set out exactly what has been contracted, and itemize the inclusions, the costs agreed upon and how you want the event elements handled in a manner that will fit your event style. They ensure nothing is left up to the supplier to decide. What if they choose to do what is easiest for them, not necessarily best for your event?

For example, say a hotel usually has a dessert and coffee station with the cups and saucers stacked separately. You may want the cup and saucer stacked together in a set for a more polished presentation that allows guests to pick up their cup and saucer in one motion. And in keeping with a more polished presentation style, you may wish the sugar, milk and cream to be in silver containers as opposed to plastic or paper, with a garbage can visible in the hopes that people will take the time to discard the wrappers and not leave them strewn about the table in unsightly disarray. You may also want the spoons to be placed on each saucer instead of providing plastic stir sticks.

You have to make sure that these event service requirements are spelled out in advance and not left to chance. And if you prefer sugar cubes, brown sugar or white sugar, or if you have negotiated and included in your cost sheet to have rock sugar on wooden sticks or chocolate-dipped spoons, these items—the quantity, the costs, the look, the manner in which they are to be presented—would be listed on your function sheets detailing the coffee and tea service portion at a meal or coffee break function at a particular date and time. The same applies to napkins. Is paper acceptable—and if so what quality, what color, what size and how do you want them presented—or does your event style require linen napkins to be laid out? The hotel needs to know this in advance—when they are preparing their quote and contract inclusions—so that they can advise the event planner if extra costs could apply for labor, rentals and special requests, and then these details need to be clearly indicated on the function sheets to ensure that the hotel directs their staff to change the setup. The above dessert and coffee station example is just one tiny aspect of an overall event—multiply that by, oh, maybe a million, and you see why event planners must be well prepared.

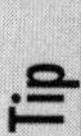

Always remember that the person with whom you negotiated contract terms and conditions may not be the same person that will be handling your event or even still be working there when your event takes place. Clearly, it is vitally important to have everything that has been agreed upon documented so there are no surprises.

Hotels, venues and event suppliers appreciate the detail. They may refer to your function sheets as a "book" at times—they can exceed 100 pages—but it is a book that they will read because they know everything must be in place come the day of the event. They can't say they didn't know about an issue, because it will have been presented to them in great detail. If the wiring on the twinkle lights is to be a specific color (green or brown as opposed to red, for example) to better blend in with the decor—and these terms and conditions have been indicated in your initial request for quote and agreed upon in your contract—this requirement needs to be stated in your function sheets.

Make it clear that on the day of the event what you have requested is what you expect to see. Anything else is simply unacceptable. If there is a problem with your request or your proposed layout, you need to know in advance and not on the day of your actual event. Suppliers will have ample time to advise you of any potential problems once they review and sign off on the first draft of function sheets, receive the amended function sheets and go through the pre-con with the event planning person leading the day-of-event orchestration. Let suppliers know that you will be assigning a staff member to advance or oversee each aspect of your event. Make note of who will be supervising each specific area and when they will be arriving to oversee setup to ensure that everything is going according to the plan set out in your function sheets. What is important when you are creating your function sheets is imagining the total visual effect. What will the camera see? What will the guests see? What is the impact? The ambiance created? Your function sheets are a step-by-step guide to creating the setting you want.

The function sheets are the working script. Every supplier and key player receives an initial copy in time to review it and make any necessary changes. Suppliers have often remarked that it is helpful for them to see the event laid out in its entirety. For example, it will help a tent rental company to know what the caterer is proposing to bring into the cooking tent and at what time they will be setting up so they can schedule their staff accordingly and have their people out of the way by the time the caterer is scheduled to arrive. This way the caterer is not off-loading their supplies and trying to work around the tenting staff. Ideally, you will have brought the tent supplier and the caterer together at the initial walk-through of the site, and the function sheets will be a review of what was discussed as well as the finalized plans. The function sheets will have laid out the proposed timing, logistical and legal requirements (such as fire marshal permits, insurance, etc.) for both sides. If the plans have not been finalized by this point, a review of the function sheets will send up red flags to you—as you are preparing them—or to the tenting supplier and caterer once they are presented with a detailed blueprint of what will be taking place.

Once your suppliers have had a chance to review your initial set of function sheets, and together you have fine-tuned any areas of concern, a revised copy is sent out to all. A pre-con meeting is set up to take place a few days before your actual event move in takes place. This is a meeting where all suppliers and key staff members review the final set of function sheets to make sure that there is a clear understanding of what is expected, and a final walk-through is done at this time. (These meetings were originally named to take place before (pre) a convention, but "pre-con" now refers to any advance planning meeting.) On the day of the event, each and every aspect is advanced by a member of the event planning staff, who will be on hand to supervise the setup and ensure that all is laid out exactly as outlined in the function sheets. They report any areas of concern back to the creative director, who will handle any problems.

Contact Sheets

Function sheets should begin with "contact sheets" that include all names, titles, company names, addresses, telephone, fax and cell numbers, e-mail addresses, text messaging address, emergency after-hour work numbers and, at times, home phone numbers. This serves two purposes. The first is that the creative director has all numbers in one central area. For example, if the creative director needs to reach a limousine driver who is transferring a VIP guest, he or she has that cell number immediately accessible to them. The second purpose is that with this list you have everything you need to be able to sit down after the event and write your thank-you letters; those contact sheets have all the information and serve as a checklist.

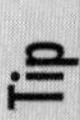

For those doing events for the first time, hotels and venues can supply a list of their preferred suppliers. In some cases, you are restricted to using only the suppliers they have recommended. Be sure to ask if you are permitted to bring in a supplier of your own choosing.

The information in your function sheets is confidential. Make sure your suppliers and all others receiving a copy are aware of that. Key staff will have their function sheets with them at the event—keeping them together in a binder works best—and must make sure that they are never left unattended. Each staff member is personally responsible for his or her copy. The sheets are also a good place for the staff member to write down any notes to be discussed later when they do the review of the event.

The function sheets are used to identify who will be doing what. And as you begin to complete the sheets, they will clearly show you how many people you will need to have on hand, their responsibilities, duties, and where they will need to be positioned and when. See Appendix C for sample function sheets. These samples can also be viewed on our companion website at www.wiley.ca/go/event_planning, along with others not included in Appendix C.

If you have assigned specific duties in your function sheets to volunteers at a fund-raiser, make sure they know the importance of being there on time on the day of the event.

At two separate fund-raisers there was a noticeable lack of volunteers—more than half had not shown up—and it impacted the success of the event because the remaining volunteers were not able to handle things smoothly. They had needed the extra hands. The problem was not the committee members; in general they were strongly committed to supporting their causes, giving endless time and energy.

It is extremely important that you tell volunteers how much you appreciate and need their support and how essential they are to the success of your event. Take the time to fill them in on the schedule of events and the part they will play. Let them know what will be expected from them (dress code, protocol, hours). Don't have them show up on the day of the event uninformed; make sure that you have assigned a member of the event planning committee to review their responsibilities with them and oversee the volunteers during your event. They will need to have someone they can report to exclusively.

With more and more corporate clients becoming sponsors of nonprofit events, meeting the standards and needs of your corporate clients, potential new ones and the nonprofit organization can become a juggling act. When a corporate client aligns his company name and brand to an event, it is important to remember that they have the funds to bring in trained staff to run their event. They are used to events being executed with professional precision and their event expectations will be the same for a function that may use volunteers to reduce the cost of staffing.

Timing

Deciding on an appropriate date is a major factor in the success of your event. Along with ensuring that most of your invitees will attend, there are other factors to consider when selecting a date. For example, what else will be going on around the time of your event? If you are thinking of inviting families with children, a school night would not be a good idea. Guests would not stay late because both parents and children would need to get up early the next day for work and school. Moving the event to the weekend would be more appealing and would reduce the possibility of having to take two cars per family to get there if one or both parents are coming from work. If you still decide to go ahead with a weeknight, do you know if it is before or during exam time? This could have an impact on your event.

One company was considering having their gala opening, one that would involve children and teens, on a school night immediately following Halloween. It was suggested that this would be a mistake—which it would have been—because with two consecutive busy nights, both filled with excitement, young children could be overtired and fretful at the second event and attendance could be affected should parents choose not to have their children out late two nights in a row.

It is always important to know what other key events may be taking place at the same time or even in the same venue. Imagine arriving at a hotel one Saturday night in June for your black-tie gala reception and dinner to find police stationed in the halls and a school prom going on in the next ballroom. One major event had that happen. Their guests arrived to commotion and confusion, with the fire department and an ambulance arriving just as they did. Someone attending the prom had passed out and needed medical attention. Holding your event next door to a school prom is definitely something you wish to avoid, so be sure you ask what else is scheduled to take place at your venue during your event.

Consider the seasons before you finalize your plans. For example, May and June are traditionally peak months for weddings and proms, and November and December are packed with holiday festivities. Ask the venue if there are any possible areas of concern that you need to be made aware of. For example, one hotel had two major competitors booked to launch their new products at the same time and both were vying for the same guests to attend their function and not the other.

Climate is another area that needs to be discussed. With all the changes that are occurring due to global warming, it is no longer predicable, and climate history needs to be reviewed. Find out if it is the time of year when the destination you are considering traveling to tends to have major electrical storms, tornadoes or flash floods. Ascertain whether or not they have a hurricane season. Ask if there are any roads that are consistently unpassable because of major snowstorms at a certain time of year. This could affect meetings being held in ski resorts.

Today, risk assessment plays a very important part in event planning, from timing to contract negotiations and cancellation protection clauses to event cancellation insurance for "Impossibility," also known as "Force Majeure," which protects both parties from events outside of

(continued)

either party's control that make it impossible to use the hotel or venue for an event. Impossibility is what was in effect in New Orleans as a result of Hurricane Katrina, where the rebuilding of an entire city's infrastructure was required, and in Indonesia and Thailand—popular incentive destinations—where a devastating tsunami took place that affected 11 countries on December 26, 2004, and killed 225,000 people. One event planner was informed that the hotel in New Orleans where they were to hold their event in just a matter of weeks no longer existed, and when they moved their event to Florida, that area was hit with a major hurricane as well.

The Executive's Guide to Corporate Events and Business Entertaining *covers event cancellation insurance and event risk assessment (weather, health advisories and other key risk assessment considerations, and guest safety and security) in great detail; later on this book will cover other critical event risk assessment areas as well. Along with risk assessment demands of today comes the development of new guest safety and security procedures for all involved, which need to be included in function sheets.*

The first step in planning *when* to hold your event is establishing the year, and just as you have done with regards to determining budget, start to work backwards to select the time of the year, the week and the day of the week. Include move in, setup, rehearsals, day of, teardown and move out requirements, and then lay out your event timing and logistical requirements on your critical path to see if you have sufficient planning and preparation time allocated.

Time of Year

Give careful thought to the time of year you are planning to hold your event. Are there any holidays or national events such as an election that might interfere with event fulfillment, require additional costs to be factored in or affect attendance? If your event is being held in another country, you need to consider local as well as international holidays that could have an impact on your event. For example, in Malaysia, there is an event called Eid Festival—Hari Raya Puasa, which is a celebration of the conclusion of a month of fasting and abstinence, and it is a very special occasion for Muslims. It involves two days, which are considered public holidays, and most businesses are closed for the duration. If your event is in Kuala Lumpur, you need to know this and factor it into your program. And while it can be a memorable part of your participants' stay for them to see local celebrations, such as the candlelight parade through the streets that occurs in Mexico on the Anniversary of the Virgin of Guadalupe (December 12), make sure that you know in advance how and where it could affect your events. Consider how local events could affect your activities and plan accordingly.

Be aware that in our secular culture, we often forget the enormous impact religion has in other parts of the world. When I was in Morocco doing a location inspection, traveling the country by limousine, I saw firsthand how religion can have a bearing on your planned itinerary of events. Our limousine driver was Islamic and answered the call to prayer five times a day. We were able to schedule our appointments around these halts and respect the beliefs of not only our driver but also our suppliers. Not planning for this could have been disastrous.

Make sure that your event does not overlap any long holiday or celebrations such as Mother's Day or Father's Day, which are typically times when families get together. Spring break can be a problem (times vary), and in summer it often seems that virtually everyone you have to talk to is out of town. This can impact timing with regards to sign off from company officials, etc., and need to be taken into account when you are laying out your critical path (which will include your to-dos as well as what is contractually due). *Time Management for Event Planners* breaks down the event planning critical path's to-dos and dues and teaches you how to organize your day to be most effective—using right brain (creative) and left brain (logistical) thinking—and get more done in your day.

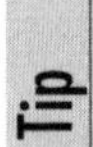

Look at the reasons why the time of year you are considering would work best to help you succeed in meeting your company and event objectives. Is this the right time for your event, or is there another time that could be a better fit or produce better results?

For each type of event, here are special considerations you should keep in mind when planning the "when."

Meetings, Conferences, Conventions

Traditionally, new-car launches take place in the fall. This is a time when car dealers expect to get together with manufacturers to see the new product line. What you want to make sure of is that the time between launching the new car—where you build anticipation and excitement—and it arriving in the dealerships is not too long.

One car manufacturer found that by switching their car launch, from their traditional June date to late Fall, when more of their cars would be available, they were able to keep with the rest of their industry's timing and were in a better place to get a jump on their competition. In addition, they added an incentive program, which gave them the opportunity they were seeking to connect closely with their top dealers early in the season and begin to talk up their new line. This move delivered outstanding sales success. They were able to develop close relations with them, introduce product and get them excited and talking about what was coming to their customers. They were able to take advance orders, then reconnect with their dealers in the Fall to deliver their product and their sales message with no major lag time between the dealers seeing their actual product and then having them in their store. When they had held their product launch in June, by the time the actual product hit the dealer's showroom in the late Fall, the enthusiasm for their product had lessened as the dealers were returning from other car manufacturers' launches, excited about their offerings, while theirs had long been forgotten.

You want to keep the momentum high. Keeping up the momentum applies to any product, as well as policies or procedures. Don't introduce new company policies or procedures at a meeting or conference and not be prepared to implement them in the near future.

Fund-Raising Galas

Is this a time of year when the people and support you are trying to attract will be in town? If your event is a society event, remember that your intended guests could be out of the country for an extended period of time over the winter months.

Will your event be overshadowed by another major ongoing event, such as a film or music festival? What will you be competing with? Check local newspapers, magazines, and tourist and convention offices to see what's going on when. There are also companies that specialize in providing information on upcoming events to their membership. Ask your tourist and visitor office to see if one exists in your area.

Incentives

Will the time that you have chosen work well for the company as well as the intended guests? Are you taking everyone away from traditional family time, such as the summer holidays or over long holiday weekends?

Will the destination hold maximum appeal at the time of year you are considering travel? Sunny Barbados as an incentive during cold winter months has major appeal, but less so in summer. Are there any weather concerns at the time of year you are planning to go? Hurricane season? Monsoon rains? Check with local tourist boards to obtain past weather history.

> ***"Need Dates"***
>
> *Are there any price advantages to moving the date to when hotels and venues need business? For example, for foreigners, times such as Memorial Day, Thanksgiving and election week in the United States have*

(continued)

proven to provide excellent rates and availability at top U.S. hotels. The savings on the hotel accommodation can then be applied towards expanding the program.

When looking at dates when hotels have high vacancy rate, some areas that can be successfully negotiated are:

- » *Complimentary welcome check-in reception*
- » *Complimentary room amenities or gifts*
- » *Complimentary spa/health club admission*
- » *Early check-in*
- » *Late checkout*
- » *Foreign currency accepted at par*
- » *Complimentary breakfasts*
- » *Upgraded rooms*
- » *Complimentary welcome cocktail reception*
- » *Additional VIP suites*
- » *Special rates for additional nights*

Time of Day and Day of Week

The day of the week you are considering holding your event can have an impact on meeting your objective, as can the time of day. You need to take into consideration where your participants will be coming from. It may be better to have an early morning start to your meeting and serve light refreshments than to schedule your meeting to begin later. This minimizes the risk of your participants being tied up in rush-hour traffic or getting caught up in work if they decide to go in early to get some work done before heading out to attend your meeting. If you have planned your event to take place on a Friday during the day, by mid-afternoon your participants' thoughts will be turning to how they can best beat the weekend traffic, to their personal plans and to how fast can they make their escape. They will not be tempted to linger and discuss the events of the day.

Meetings, Conferences, Conventions, Incentives

Anyone who has attended a meeting, conference, convention or incentive has seen the long lines at the telephone booths, people talking quietly into their cell phones during break, sending messages on their BlackBerrys or slipping out quietly to take care of pending business, never to return. Are you scheduling your event over a particularly busy time period when your participants' minds are going to be elsewhere? For example, at the close of a sales period, your sales force needs to be out signing contracts, not in a ballroom. Would midweek work better than scheduling your event on a Monday, or is your industry traditionally quieter on Thursdays and Fridays? If your event is taking place far away, you need to take into consideration travel time, costs (airfares are lower if you are staying over a Saturday night), overnight stays en route to the final destination and how the company will be handling requests for extensions. Do you need staff back and ready to work in the office Monday, or is there any flexibility?

Corporate Events, Fund-Raisers, Special Events

For corporate events, fund-raisers and special events, either midweek or a Saturday night is the most successful for achieving maximum attendance. Scheduling an event on a Friday night could limit attendance for those for whom it is a religious day and for those who want to get away for the weekend. Many things come into play in selecting the perfect date for your event. Consideration should be given to:

» Whether it should be a daytime or evening event
» What time it would start and end
» Whether it would be formal or informal dress
» If guests would have time to change clothes if coming to/from work
» If volunteers would have sufficient time to leave work and have everything ready well before your guests arrive

For most of these events, your guests may be invited to bring their partners. If the event is planned to take place during the day midweek, it could be difficult for one of the partners to attend, and an evening event may be a better choice. Or you could look at moving it to the weekend when both may have more flexibility.

Where will your guests be coming from? Take this into consideration as you plan your start time. Will they be coming directly from work? When does their workday typically end? If they are bringing a guest, will this work for them as well? Could they be caught in traffic? Are you bringing them from uptown to downtown? How late will your event go? Is the next day a business day, when both partners may need to get up early? Partners may arrive independently, in separate cars. Is there enough parking?

If the event is black tie, will your guests have time to go home to change, or will they need to bring a change of clothes to work? Will they be in a position to leave work early?

Will timing affect the availability or pricing of any of your event elements?

Several years ago, a private gala dinner celebration was planned in Los Angeles. It was deliberately timed to coincide with the Academy Awards and included a themed Oscar-night party. All guests were from out of town, and this was their farewell event. The magic of Hollywood was in full swing and star sightings were everywhere. For their L.A.-arrival party, a film set was taken over, and the guests had the opportunity to film their own "movie" complete with scripts, makeup artists and costumes. Their Oscar party was going to be taking place away from their hotel, and they would require transportation. Twenty-five stretch limousines were reserved well in advance, contracted and deposited on long before others began to think about Oscar night. As you can imagine, limousines would be at an absolute premium around Oscar night, but advanced planning ensured that the guests would have them at their disposal for the evening. After the party ended, the guests headed out to their waiting limousines to experience Los Angeles on a night that is like no other.

It was a memorable event and is still talked about to this day. Had the timing of the event and the need to secure the limousines not been anticipated, contracted and deposited on—giving the limousine companies no out or opportunity to raise their prices—their event would not have ended on such a high note.

Will limousines be a factor in your event? Will weddings and school proms be in full swing at the same time, which could affect availability? What timing with regards to securing your desired event elements or locations could have an impact on the success of your event?

Date Selection

Although we touched on it briefly in the last chapter, before finalizing your date, take out your calendar and fully investigate the following seven areas and look at the impact they could have on your event:

1. Major Holidays
2. Religious Observations
3. School Breaks
4. Long Weekends
5. Sports Events
6. Other Special Events
7. Other Considerations

Major Holidays

Check to see if there are any major holidays around your event when guests may have their own personal plans and attendance at outside functions could be limited.

There are some areas where, with proper planning, holidays can work in your favor. For example, silent auction fund-raisers held before the holiday season can be extremely successful when guests use the occasion

(continued)

to purchase gifts and donate to charity at the same time. One Saturday afternoon fund-raiser had all that potential and wasted it. The organizers held a silent auction right before the holiday season, but sales were disappointing because the invitation failed to mention the auction. Guests were delighted with the quality of merchandise, but most had already completed their holiday shopping and others had not brought cash, credit cards or checks. The idea was excellent, the guest list impressive and the timing was in their favor. But the silent auction required advance notice on the invitation. The invitation should have announced that a silent auction was to be one of the main attractions and possibly include a list of some of the items available.

Religious Observances

Is the date in conflict with any religious observances, such as Friday night for Orthodox Jews or Sunday for practicing Christians? Holding a gala fund-raising on such a day would limit attendance by excluding religious individuals.

Black-tie galas (corporate or fund-raising) work well on a Saturday night, especially if the event has been geared to couples. Saturday is generally considered the middle of the traditional weekend and allows couples to leisurely dress and prepare for the occasion. They can avoid taking two cars to an event, which is not always the case if both parties are coming directly from work. Guests can enjoy themselves more fully as they are not concerned with having to get up early for work the next day.

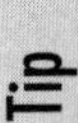

If you are scheduling an out-of-town event and feel that some of your guests may wish to attend local church or synagogue services, the hotel concierge desk can assist them with location and times. If you feel this could apply to a majority of your participants, consider the group activities you are planning for this time period so that these guests are not excluded from events of major importance.

School Breaks

Is the date in conflict with any of the major school breaks? Guests could conceivably be out of country, and attendance could be low. School breaks vary from country to country and even region to region. If your event is scheduled to take place over one of the school breaks (times and schedules may vary from originating destination and final destination), you may want to give special consideration to your choice of location. If the break is taking place at home, you may get a poor turnout, and if it is scheduled at your destination you may have problems booking accommodations and activities. For example, don't try to go anywhere in Latin America around Easter or on the fifth of May. Traveling to certain locations at less-peak times often makes good sense. For example, Orlando is more enjoyable when lineups are shorter. We have all heard the stories about Daytona and other beach destinations popular with college and university students over Spring break and how the town is transformed for the duration of their stay. You may prefer to choose to travel at a time that may be more appropriate for your needs and requirements.

Long Weekends

Are you considering scheduling your event on a Monday or Tuesday or a Thursday night around a long weekend? Guests may have chosen to extend their time off and this could also affect attendance at your event.

Long weekends are eagerly anticipated, and often plans are made well in advance. The Thursday night before a long weekend is frequently used to get an early start on a drive to the cottage or for final preparations—shopping, food preparation, cleaning—for the weekend ahead. Similarly, the evenings immediately following a long weekend can be used for personal catch-up after being away.

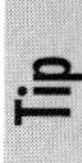

The days before, during or following a long weekend are not considered the most favorable for achieving maximum attendance at your event. People's energies and focus will be elsewhere.

Sports Events

Are there any major sports events going on at the same time as your event?

One corporate client chose to hold an out-of-country special event on the same dates as the World Series. The company was fully prepared to hire a private plane to bring their guests back home for the day to see the final game if their local team made it all the way. Do not underestimate the importance of sporting events—particularly play-offs—when considering the date of your event. Check all possibilities and record your findings.

Another gala corporate sit-down dinner is a cautionary tale. The company had planned their client appreciation banquet, selected a beautiful menu and taken great care with their presentations. The company had taken pains with most of the details—all except one. Obviously, none of the event planners was a sports fan, and they had not done their homework. The dinner was scheduled for the same evening as a major baseball play-off game. The planners had received RSVPs and had signed guarantees to the hotel for cocktails and dinner. Of the 150 guests invited only 45 showed up, but the company was on the hook for all 150 dinners. Even if guests called on the day of the event to cancel, it still would have been too late to adjust the numbers. The attendees looked lost in the room set for 150. Some invited guests were at the game, others at home watching it on TV and some chose not to venture downtown because the dinner was being held close to where the big game and other major events were going on, and they didn't want to get tied up in traffic. Game time and the start of the reception overlapped.

Had the event planners realized the conflict in dates before finalizing things, they might have still salvaged their event even if they had no flexibility in dates. They could have moved the event out of the hotel in the center core and to a place that had a little more appeal, which would have enhanced their objective of promoting their destination as a possible incentive site. The host company had the choice of many beautiful and exclusive restaurants and private clubs, any of which could be taken over in whole or in part for a private dinner and presentation. That may have pulled more people in, especially if they were away from the downtown congestion with ample parking nearby.

Another possibility had they realized the conflict in time would have been to set up a private sports bar theme event with large-screen TVs. An even better idea might have been to take private boxes at the stadium and hold the event there. If it is something exclusive, fun and out of the ordinary, people will battle traffic without a second thought.

Other Special Events

Is there anything else scheduled for the same day as your event? Take the time to do a blitz of the city. Are there any theater openings or movie premieres scheduled for that day? Are any new performances coming into town? Are there any conflicting events such as jazz festivals, fireworks displays or major special happenings such as the Academy Awards? Pay attention to other fund-raisers, galas and special events similar to your own that could affect attendance or cause event disruption. For example, a charity/fund-raiser run that closes roads or re-routes traffic could cause timing delays for guests, suppliers and staff, and solutions need to be found in advance and not on the day of the event or move in and setup.

As mentioned previously, there are companies you can subscribe to that track events in the city. They will register your event and let you know what could be in conflict. Check with your local tourist/convention board to see if there is such a company in your area.

Take a close look at your targeted audience—who will make up your guest list? Will your event be competing with any others that will be inviting the same people?

Other Considerations

What else could be taking place over your selected dates that could impact your event? What could be at a premium? Limited availability often leads to surcharges and other increases in costs at peak times. In the Los Angeles example, not only were limousines at a premium, weekend hotel accommodation was significantly higher during the Oscars compared with alternate dates in March and April. As well, reservations at top restaurants were difficult to get and the waits longer.

Is your event—whether you are holding your event locally, out of town or out of country—scheduled to take place at a time or location when there could be health, security or guest safety concerns that would limit attendance? In today's world, these are very valid concerns. In the past, participants were eager to travel the world and experience all that there was. But we have witnessed events such as 9/11, the SARS outbreak, Hurricane Katrina, the devastation of a tsunami and the war in Iraq. Advancements in technology and the Internet have brought world events nonstop into our living rooms, computers, cell phones or BlackBerrys as they are happening. Technology and world events have also changed how people travel (e.g., increased airport security and new carry-on regulations), what they are willing to do and where they are open to going. As a result, Web conferencing has become a new event planning element and employees are happily taking part in meetings without leaving the comfort of their office or even their own home, as more and more companies have opened the door to having their employees working from both the office and from home. In the past, business took place face-to-face, but in today's world, face-to-face meetings can mean virtually through a webcam and can become a time-saver.

Critical Path Checklist

Your critical path is going to turn your event vision into your event reality. And successful event execution depends on how detailed and accurate your critical path is and how strictly you adhere to the timelines. Your critical path is a master to-do list where you will began to plot in the timelines, delivery schedules, confirmation dates and supplier and venue requirements that you and your event team—from clients to suppliers—need to be on top of. You will see clearly what has to be done and by when; where you will have personal, professional and event planning crunch periods; and what tasks you need to begin to bring others in on. You already have the majority of information you need to start, outlined in your various contracts, correspondence and budget cost summary breakdown.

You can set up your critical path manually or on your computer. Using your computer is more efficient because it is easier to add and subtract items in sequential order and print out revised copies for everyone involved. To begin to prepare your critical path, you will need:

- ✓ *A new calendar to be used only for your event details; choose one that has space to write in the date and choose a calendar that begins on a Monday not a Sunday, so you can see the weekend as a block of time in which to focus on event timing operations requirements*
- ✓ *A set of colored highlighters*
- ✓ *Pencils with good erasers*
- ✓ *All your supplier contracts*
- ✓ *All your correspondence from your selected venues and suppliers*
- ✓ *Your revised event vision overview grid and outline*
- ✓ *Your revised event budget cost summary breakdown*
- ✓ *A paper punch (this is the time when you will also be sorting through your signed contracts and quotes and pulling essential hard copy material to file in your event planning operations binder)*

Charting Your Critical Path

1. Begin your critical path by laying out as headings the months from contracting to your actual event date. Break down into weeks the two months prior to the start of the event. At the top of the calendar pages, make note of contract business-day cutoff dates so they will continue to stand out in your mind and be easily identifiable. Remember, it is business days prior to when your supplier contract fulfillment begins. Most hotel and supplier contracts stipulate business days (Monday to Friday) for cut-off, attrition and cancellation dates. The contract start date for a supplier is not necessarily your event date, e.g., if your decor company's setup begins a day or more prior to your event date, that—not your event date—is their start date and the same would apply for your venue, as they would be contracted to allow an early move in). You are calculating for contract guarantee cutoff dates, not the actual number of days prior. It's conceivable you could have 21 different business cutoff dates for various suppliers. List them in sequential order as well. For example:

   February—begin event planning
   March
   April
   May
   June
   July
   August
   September
   October
   November
   December
   January
   February
   March

April—12 weeks prior to event

60 business days prior guarantee (date/supplier)

May—8 weeks prior to event

45 business days prior guarantee (date/supplier)

May—6 weeks prior to event

30 business days prior guarantee (date/supplier)

June—4 weeks prior to event

21 business days prior guarantee date (date/supplier)

21 business days prior guarantee date (date/supplier)

21 business days prior guarantee date (date/supplier)

Three weeks prior to event—14 business days prior guarantee (date/supplier)

Two weeks prior to event—5 business days prior guarantee (date/supplier)

One week prior to event

Six days prior to event

Five days prior to event

Four days prior to event

Three days prior to event

Two days prior to event—move in and setup

One day prior to event—rehearsal morning

One day prior to event—rehearsal afternoon

One day prior to event—rehearsal evening

Event—morning

Event—afternoon

Event—two hours prior

Event—one hour prior

Event—show flow

Event—teardown and move out

Under the applicable month, fill in all major holidays when offices will be closed and you will be unable to reach people.

2. Add in known times when you, your key staff, and decision-making/ sign off clients will be unavailable because of business or personal travel. Put these and all the following dates in sequential order.
3. Note professional or personal time crunches when your workload is heavy.
4. Check to see if any of your main event venue and supplier contacts know when they will be away from the office.
5. Pulling details from your contracts, list your payment dates, attrition dates, food and beverage guarantee dates and other guarantee dates.
6. Pulling details from all your suppliers' policies, terms and conditions, and general information brochures, list any cutoff dates that could affect your event and your event suppliers.
7. List the dates by which copies of all permits and insurance must be in to your venue or fire marshal.
8. Record the dates by which you must receive copies of all permits and insurance from your suppliers.
9. Pulling details from your supplier quotes and budget cost summary breakdown, start determining applicable timelines, e.g., dates on which copy for the invitations must be in, first proof of the invitation is due, song list must go to musicians, the photographer requires the master event photo-shoot list, etc. Remember to keep listing all entries in sequential order.
10. Fill in cutoff dates that you are aware of, e.g., when invitations for Guest List A will need to be mailed, RSVP date for Guest List A, when Guest List B invitations will go out, seating chart to be finalized, etc.
11. List all supplier site inspection dates and scheduled meetings.
12. Schedule in times for budget updates—this can be daily or weekly as prices are finalized.

Once everything is laid out in month and date order, it is easy to see where you will be facing event operations overload and where your personal and business timelines will be colliding with deadlines. What you have before you at this moment is only your critical path guideline. Now you must begin to schedule your critical path backwards and build in time buffers and deadlines to allow you to have breathing space. These dates must remain listed where they are in date order on your critical path so that you are always aware of them and have them handy if you have to do some juggling down the road. Leave them as they are, but with your calendar in hand back up their due date by three or more days—pick a day of the week that is appropriate, fits in with your schedule, is not a holiday—and enter your deadlines in sequential order. You have to give yourself leeway, e.g., your food and beverage guarantee should not be scheduled to be called in the same day as your expected RSVP from Guest List A or B, as you will need time to figure out if the final count will also affect the number of tables you need, room layout, etc. As well, if you are falling under the guaranteed minimum when you've received all your RSVPs, you need time to consider your options before calling in your final numbers. Building in time buffers is essential. Do this for the balance of supplier and venue deadlines.

Pay careful attention to the last month before your event. Your goal is to clear as much as possible from that month and move any items possible to an earlier due date. Keep the last two weeks before your event entirely clear of outstanding event operation issues—there is no need to be planning right down to the wire. For example, your musicians may need your song list one month before your event, but if you can give it to them two or three months earlier than they require it you are freeing yourself up to do other things. You want to get as much as possible out of the way as early as you can so that you can finalize your event function sheets, but you must be realistic. By laying out all your upcoming commitments and deadlines—personal, professional and event—in month and date order, you know early on what is in front of you. If your critical path shows that your year-end at work is coming exactly at the time you need to be verifying the correct spelling of names and addresses for your guest list, you know that's something you have to move up. The invitations can be sitting, stuffed and sealed, waiting to be mailed, if you have a specific date you want to mail them on.

Do as much as possible immediately upon contracting. Continue to touch base with suppliers on a regular basis, checking in to see if anything needs to be updated. Call in and follow up in writing with guarantee numbers when needed, but if the bulk of the work is done early on you can be on to your next project with your critical path keeping you on track. Your critical path will remain fluid, as you add in new items and finalize timing and logistics with your suppliers. Remember to cross off or mark in some way, e.g. highlight—not entirely delete—what has been done on your critical path. It will serve as a reminder that it has been looked after and what remains to be done will stand out and draw in your attention. If you make changes, date them and print out a revised critical path; otherwise, it will be confusing. Keep old copies but move them out of your event binder into a separate "dead" file. They are there for reference only. Keep in your event binder only what you are currently working on.

Clearly seeing what is in front of you allows you to be proactive and prepare for it. You have removed the unknown and are in possession of an action plan that will work for you, your clients and your suppliers. If you do not take the time to lay out everything in the very beginning, you are setting yourself up for the domino effect to kick in. One missed deadline affects not just the next one after that, but also your costs and possibly those of your other suppliers. Once you have signed your contracts, updated your budget cost summary breakdown, revised your event flow overview, prepared your critical path, reviewed your dates, built in time buffers and moved as much as possible out of your final month of planning, you will find that you are in total control of your event elements, know them inside out and are knowledgeable about all the terms and conditions you have to meet.

If you just prepare your critical path without building in your personal and other professional (work) commitments, you will not be able to foresee problem areas and take appropriate action to diffuse them by pulling in help and moving due dates to a better (earlier) time. This also allows you to prepare your clients by giving them advance notice of when, where and how you will need their help and decision-making so that they can make any necessary adjustments to their personal and work schedules. The earlier you can finalize details with your suppliers, the better it is for them as well. They are juggling a number of special events and the more organized you are, the better they will be able to service you and help you create your event vision.

The onus is fully on the event planning company for meeting payment dates and calling in guarantees. Do not look to your suppliers to call you and remind you that a deadline is approaching; that seldom occurs and their contract waives them of any obligation to do so. It will be your responsibility to be on top of your timelines, guarantees and commitments. Once your critical path is in place, it's very easy to do. The time and effort you put into designing the critical path will be well spent and it will prove to be of great value to you in the end, serving a dual purpose by becoming the layout and timing for your event function sheets.

3

Location, Location, Location

Having laid out the framework of your event vision and knowing all your function space requirements—including supplier move in, setup, rehearsal, day of, teardown and move out space needs and what to look for—finding the perfect event venue is much easier. You will feel a strong emotional connection when locale is exactly the right fit. It will come across as an inner, intuitive knowing that grows with experience that you have found what you were looking for. As soon as you walk into the indoor or outdoor site you're exploring for your event, you will be able to rule out venues that will compromise your event vision. Such venues won't feel right.

By creating a strong event vision, laying out your event grid (which will serve as a blueprint for you to build your event from), becoming deeply familiar with your space, event and supplier requirements before you start to look for a venue, you have ensured that what is best for you meets your list of event must-haves firmly imprinted in your mind. It will not matter to you how wonderful the architecture of the building may be, how charming a balcony may be or how great a group picture could look posing by that column if the rest of the elements that you have identified as event must-haves are not in place.

Site Selection

As they say in real estate, location is everything. The selection of the site where you will be holding your event is of primary importance; it can make or break your event.

Consider an exhibition for seniors that was being held in a large convention center that has two separate areas—a north wing and a south wing. The north wing is older but has good access to the ballroom. Parking is conveniently close by. The south wing is newer but is more than a 20-minute walk from the parking area. In this particular case, the south wing was chosen as the site of the exhibition, but considering the targeted audience—seniors—the north wing would have been better. The south wing was also the site for a large garden show, where guests could purchase plants of all sizes. Again, it wasn't the most convenient choice for the guests and exhibitors, who had to walk from the parking area to the ballroom and back again carrying heavy purchases or boxes, especially since a convention center does not offer bellman assistance with boxes like a hotel does. The lesson can be physically exhausting to both attendees and exhibitors, as well as costly to exhibitors. It resulted in low attendance and in this case low sales of plants because they were too heavy for most guests to trek back to their cars with no help. Make sure that you match your site to type of event. Look for ways to make it as accessible as possible for your guests.

There is one large specialty show that comes to Toronto twice a year. It is extremely well attended. The location of the show offers underground parking—those attending can leave their coats in the car, take the escalator up and be right at the site. The show organizers provide carts to make shopping easier. Aisles are wide and there is room to maneuver between them. Purchases can be dropped off at a parcel-pickup area located by the main doors if your cart or your hands become too full. Assistance is provided if you require help getting your purchases to the car. There is plenty of scattered seating. There are also several refreshment areas, right down to water stations, catering to different budgets. The venue also offers excellent washroom facilities and a diaper-changing room complete with supplies, and the building is handicapped accessible. It has everything for a comfortable experience and people eagerly anticipate going to the show, knowing they will have a stress-free experience, with all their needs attended to.

You are not limited to hotels, convention centers or restaurants when it comes to site selection. Chic boutiques will allow you to take over their facilities for a private cocktail reception and dinner, followed by a fashion show introducing their new lineup of clothes. Some even have cooking facilities attached to the store, making it easy for caterers to set up and serve. You can take over yachts, roller-skating rinks, airport hangars or hold a gala in an armory, museum or art gallery. You can tent a parking lot or do a catered affair on a covered tennis court or even on a hotel rooftop. Private clubs, restaurants or empty warehouse space can be taken over and completely transformed.

You are limited only by your imagination and your budget. You may have to pay a premium or surcharge to have the venue closed to the public, and you must take this into account when you are considering your site options. You may decide that it is cost prohibitive and instead look for a venue that has a private room that will accommodate your guests, as opposed to taking over a facility exclusively. What is most important is finding the right fit. For example, one restaurant that can be taken over exclusively offers spectacular 30-foot ceilings and four massive fireplaces as the perfect site for a candlelit winter or festive Christmas-themed wedding, where the service can be conducted in the mezzanine overlooking the dining area.

Skilled event planners can develop a sixth sense when it comes to knowing they have found the right location, one that radiates the event energy they are looking for and meets all of their event elements' needs and logistical requirements. They can see it, feel it and visualize it as soon as they step into the space. There is a sense of inner knowing that they have found the perfect fit—it feels, as Goldilocks once said, "just right." She didn't settle for second best; she wanted what was just right for her. And that is what you must look for when you plan your special events.

Whenever and wherever possible, try to get out of the ballroom. When it was decided to hold Disney's worldwide theatrical opening gala for Beauty and the Beast *at one of Toronto's most popular restaurants, Mövenpick Marché, the Marché had never closed to the public before.*

It is one thing to feed 1,000 customers over the course of the day and another to feed 1,000 guests arriving en masse, but Mövenpick Marché felt "just right" for this event. So many elements from the stage production were already there, such as the fountain and the enchanted forest, which was enhanced for the evening, and the market village scene, where the food stations were renamed after the various characters from the play: Lumiere's Flaming Grill, Mrs. Pott's Tea & Coffee Bar, Le Fou's Tossed Salads, the Silly Girl's Sushi Bar, Gaston's Bar, Cogsworth's Seafood Buffet, Marie's Baguettes, Babette's Desserts and Madame de la Grande Bouche's Rosti & Pasta. It was a perfect fit. Of course, it could have been re-created in a ballroom, but why go to that considerable expense when something wonderful already exists and can be turned into something memorable and magical with a little event planning innovation and creativity.

Not only did having the event at Mövenpick Marché add a much more exclusive feel than having it in a ballroom, but holding it there was doing something that had not been done before—another first.

In many parts of the world it is common practice for top restaurants to close for private events, but some restaurants are still not open to the idea, and you could run into resistance. The restaurants' greatest fears are that guests once turned away will never return. The following are suggestions that could help overcome any concerns. These are areas of negotiation with the restaurant, as there are costs involved. The restaurant may pick up some of the charges and you may be responsible for others. You need to find out in advance what will be covered, have it listed in the contract and add to your cost sheet the costs for which you will be responsible.

» Post signs announcing the closing well in advance.
» Have reminder table toppers during the week of the event.
» Post "Private Party" signs on the day of the event.
» Advise the concierges at local hotels that the restaurant will be closed for the day.
» Hand out coupons for complimentary beverages or appetizers to any turned-away walk-in customers as a thank-you for their understanding.
» Advise neighboring restaurants so that they can be prepared to handle additional walk-in customers.
» Set up a transportation shuttle to another restaurant.
» Have staff positioned at underground parking to advise guests before they park that the restaurant is closed.

Aside from these courtesies and goodwill gestures, there are many other things that have to be taken care of in planning an event in a restaurant:

» If the restaurant is in a mall, make sure that you obtain permission from mall management and find out what restrictions could apply regarding your event. A number of malls operate on a percentage rent basis where they receive a percentage of what the store takes in, and an event could provide them with extra revenue if you are holding your event on a night that is traditionally quiet. If your event will have a high profile in the media, it could bring the mall added publicity. As a gesture of goodwill, invite top mall officials to the party if agreeable to your client.

» Inform the mall tenants that a special event will be taking place so that they can plan accordingly. You will find most quite understanding as this is an opportunity for them to bask in the reflected glow of the publicity. Also, the location is being introduced to clientele who may not have visited it before.

» If the restaurant is freestanding, check with local fire and police authorities to see what concerns they may have and legal issues you need to be aware of. If the location is in a mall, check with the management of both the mall and the restaurant so that you are not violating any lease agreements or fire and safety rules and regulations.

» If you have negotiated for the restaurant to close after breakfast or lunch, have staff on-site well before this to make sure that this is carried out. Don't allow late arrivals to be seated and have their service rushed as you begin setup. They will be unhappy, and so will you. This also applies when you are closing down a single section for your guests. Always be ready well in advance, and be very clear with management about what time you will require the room or section closed. Guests are usually understanding and amenable to being reseated when offered an explanation and a complimentary beverage.

Always know specifically what is taking place before your event. Make sure that the contracted access time for setup and decor is clear and that you have it in writing. For example, there is a fabulous venue that is often used for special events. It is also very popular for weddings. You need to know what is scheduled to go on before your move in and make sure that there is an adequate time buffer built in. Here, you could run into a wedding rehearsal scheduled to take place just before your move in. Wedding rehearsals are notorious for not beginning on time and/or running late, resulting in time delays. You want to be aware of this in advance and you want to ensure that the wedding party is well aware of the time of your move in so that there are no misunderstandings. They must know the importance of keeping to a schedule so that they can do their rehearsal without being rushed at the end.

I can remember going up and down the coast of a Caribbean island in torrential rains one October (even the cows were huddled under the bus shelters) looking for the perfect venue for a farewell gala that would take place in January. I found myself knee deep in water and mud at times. One word of caution: be wary of dropping by restaurants before they are opened—I was met at one by two very efficient and effective guard dogs.

Local agents had suggested many places, but none of them felt "just right." I had a very clear picture of what I was trying to achieve that night. This particular island is very dear to my heart as a destination; it feels like a second home. I have very happy memories of being there both on vacations and for work. I wanted to make sure that the participants came away experiencing the full beauty of the island and I was not stopping until I found the "just right" setting.

The restaurant selected was exactly right for that event. It was a magical evening—row after row of all-white limousines took guests from their hotel to the site, which was exclusively theirs for the evening. There they enjoyed cocktails as the sun slipped into the sea, scattering brilliant bands of gold, red and orange across shimmering waters. Tables were set with white on white, soft candlelight glowed, a private performance was put on by one of the island's premier performers, and guests danced under a canopy of twinkling stars. It was absolutely picturesque. It was pleasing to the eye. It was a perfect farewell event.

It is always worth the effort to take the time to find what would be just right for your event and to do everything possible to make sure the experience is flawless. If you are doing an outdoor event, investigate and know when the sun will be setting, and time the cocktails appropriately. There is no additional charge for a spectacular sunset. And don't forget to look at the weather history—are you considering holding an outdoor event in the middle of the rainy season?

Each season brings with it its own set of considerations and items that should be factored in when considering both your choice of location and your budget. The one thing we know for sure is that we cannot predict the weather, but we can be prepared. What is crucial is your guests' comfort and first impressions.

With meetings in other countries, some of the best values can be in off-season. Before you book, consider the impact the weather will have on your program if it is less than ideal. You don't want to be in the Caribbean or Florida during the hurricane season or in Arizona when typically there are flash floods and electrical storms. Check with local tourist boards to find out past weather history—temperature, precipitation and humidity—before you make your final decision. Ask to receive the official weather history statistics—they are available. Do not simply accept a verbal report. And even if it has never rained or snowed before during the time period when you are planning to hold your event, secure weather backup for outdoor events—it has snowed in June in Banff—and be prepared. Weather patterns have changed with global warming and can no longer be predicted as accurately as before. Extreme weather conditions are becoming more frequent, and we have witnessed how ill prepared some cities have been when disaster has struck. Make sure you are familiar with your location's safety and security procedures as well as event cancellation clauses. Review contract cancellation clauses with a fine-tooth comb. Make sure that your clients are aware of all charges that could apply should an event be canceled at the last moment because of an unforeseen circumstance, be it weather or the fear of infectious diseases in the area, e.g., SARS. Today it is of utmost importance that event planners not only be aware of cancellation charges but also be able to anticipate the financial risks that unexpected occurrences represent to their client. They must be able to prepare a thorough risk assessment plan with an appropriate plan of action and provide their clients with event cancellation insurance options.

When planning an outdoor event, always make sure that you have weather backup on hold. On the day of the event (or earlier, depending on event setup requirements), if the weather looks uncertain, there will be a time when you will have to make a call on where to commence setup. Find out at what specific time you or your client will have to make a final decision on where to hold your event.

With some destinations, high temperatures are not a problem. In Las Vegas, temperatures can soar to well over 100 degrees Fahrenheit and not affect the program. Guests are picked up in air-conditioned motor coaches or limousines and whisked to their air-conditioned hotels. During the day they are comfortable in their meetings or out by the pool and in the evening the temperature drops, and they can enjoy a very pleasant walk along the Strip. Anyway, the hotels and casinos are all very close together and have been designed to make you want to stay inside. Any excursions are usually just a matter of going from air-conditioned hotel to air-conditioned bus to air-conditioned venue and back again. The heat is not a major factor.

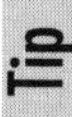

When guests are flying in winter weather and they need to make connecting flights, try to fly them as far south as possible. For example, if a group is flying out of Toronto in winter and have a choice of connecting flights through Chicago or Dallas, choose Dallas because the chances of weather delays there would not be as great as in Chicago.

Weather also affects water temperatures and what can be found swimming in it. For those planning a program down south during the summer months, in certain areas you may find more jellyfish than during the winter season when the waters are a little cooler. For those planning a meeting aboard a cruise ship, find out how weather will affect your sailing—is there a time when the seas will be calmer? For day and evening cruises on private yacht charters, find out how much shade and how much shelter the boat provides for guests. Can everyone be comfortably accommodated inside should a sudden rainstorm occur, and is there sufficient protection from the sun?

Remember that weather can have an impact on your event almost anywhere. Be prepared.

When planning open-air events, weather backup is a must, particularly in cooler climates. Another consideration for outdoor events is heaters. A number of evening outdoor gala events are held on the cliffs overlooking the ocean in southern California, and freestanding heaters make guests extremely comfortable. The setting here is so dramatic—imagine listening to the strains of a classical guitarist as silver moonbeams dance on the gentle waves below. That kind of magical setting can't be re-created in a ballroom but, as magical as it is, the setting would not be just right for a gala fund-raiser that included a silent auction where items would be on display, or if you were looking to include audiovisual, staging or speeches. What is essential is that the site be a match for your event and for your guests.

Location and Your Budget

Location selection and cost considerations can apply to a physical building or setting location or a destination. If you are doing an out-of-country event, some key location considerations are:

» Will overnight airport accommodation need to be included in your budget?

» Are there direct nonstop flights to your destination?

» If your guests will be required to change aircraft, will they have a long wait in the connecting city?

» Does the total travel time justify the length of stay? For example, North American companies considering holding a meeting in Hawaii or the Orient should look at a seven- rather than a three-night stay, unless all guests will be departing from the west coast, because you are looking at two full days of travel and jet lag.

- » How long a trip is it from the airport to the hotel?
- » Does the hotel and the destination meet all of your needs?
- » What concessions will you need to factor into your program to allow for time change and jet lag? For example, upon their arrival, your guests may enjoy a light repast in their rooms and time to settle in and adjust to the time change, with the welcome festivities taking place the next night when they aren't too tired to fully appreciate them.

Location Requirements

When you start to plan, begin with an overview of your event and start to map out your requirements on a grid similar to the one on page 91. This will enable you to establish in your mind the initial flow of events and an overall picture of what needs to be included. Your grid can then be sent to the different venues you are considering using to see if they can accommodate all of your needs. Remember to include move in, setup, rehearsal, teardown and move out requirements, especially timing and logistics.

Do a visual walk-through of the event to determine the appropriate space requirements. Start to investigate availability and begin to prepare your cost sheet. Be very specific. If you need to have a 20-foot ceiling to accommodate your audiovisual and staging, you need to make note of it on your grid. Include advance setup and rehearsal space as well. If you need to have a ballroom on a 24-hour hold so that your setup remains in place until the day of your event, list this as well. If you will require dressing rooms for entertainers, offices for your staff or an area to prepare or set up displays, make sure that you advise the venue from the onset so that they can secure appropriate space for you. It is easier to release space and scale down than to try and work with inadequate space once you have signed the contract.

Program Outline	Day 1	Day 2	Day 3	Day 4	Day 5	Special Notes
Breakfast						
Morning Activities						
Lunch						
Afternoon Activities						
Cocktail Reception						
Evening Activities						

In order to prepare an accurate budget, you need to look at all aspects of your event to make sure that you include as many costs as possible. As you work through this section you will find mention of different areas that need to be included in your costs, such as street permits, off-duty police officers and so on, where to include them and why. Keep updating the costing as you go along, adding and subtracting items as changes are made. As mentioned earlier, it is important to know where you are at all times in your proposed spending so that you can make adjustments as you go along and ensure that you have the funds you require for the essential event elements that will help you to meet your company and event objectives—and the right location can play a part in delivering them.

For example, one of your event location objectives could be to provide the setting to do something extravagant and produce an event that will be talked about in the years to come, such as a symphony under the stars in the desert with a well-known performer to entertain your guests exclusively. You could have your guests arriving at sunset by hot air balloon, with champagne served when they land. Along with the creative aspects of your events, you also need to factor in the practical cost realities of your location, such as backup transportation in case weather conditions or the winds are not right for the hot air balloons to take off; transportation costs to the event for guests that may choose to travel by balloon chase car as opposed to riding in the hot air balloon; return transportation—hot air balloons do not travel after dark; a clear plastic tent (for visibility) as weather backup; a cooking tent; porta-potties; the cost to have everything transferred to the desert; medical assistance on standby; security; lighting; heaters; electricity and backup generators; and someone to handle any curious critters that may decide your event requires closer inspection. Once all of these costs have been added to your budget, you may decide that holding that particular event in the middle of the desert is cost prohibitive and that you need to consider a different idea or look to your cost sheet to see where else needed dollars can come from to fund your original idea. Knowing exactly where you stand financially at any given time allows you to make informed decisions and run an event with no final reconciliation "surprises" that in reality could have been addressed and managed in the planning and operations stages. Know all your costs ahead of time so that you can make responsible decisions.

Hotels and Convention Centers

The differences between hotels and convention centers will affect your budget. Both facilities can be wonderful, but make sure that you know where they differ and what needs to be included in your cost breakdown.

If you will require guestrooms as well as function space, holding your event at a hotel may be a more cost-effective way to go. Because the hotel will be receiving revenue on the guestrooms, in addition to the food and beverage, there could be concessions made for such things as room rental charges for setup and rehearsal time. Generally, hotels do not charge a room rental fee for the time the event is actually scheduled to take place if they are receiving food and beverage revenue. This, of course, will depend on the total dollars being spent at the hotel.

Holding your event at a hotel will mean that your guests will be able to easily walk to the meeting rooms, eliminating costs for additional transportation if they were staying at a hotel and attending a meeting at a convention center that is not within walking distance.

Not all convention centers have agreements with nearby hotels for special guestroom rates, and you will probably be negotiating with the hotel and the convention center separately. You may want to do a cost comparison to see how they differ in price. In addition to room rental charges, there are other cost factors to consider.

Most hotels will allow your setup people to pull up and off-load their vehicles, and will ensure they have staff on hand to assist with transporting the items. (Remember to include dollars for tipping in your budget.) Hotels usually do not charge for tables and chairs for registration or display, and they can often provide most specialty glasses, such as martini glasses for a special martini bar as part of your event, at no additional cost, depending on numbers. Hotel ballrooms are usually carpeted, so there is no additional expense to bring in carpeting, and there is usually no additional charge for room cleanup. Hotels can generally provide you with locked storage areas and are frequently willing to replace lost keys at no additional charge.

For hotel-based events that are only running one day or over the course of several days but no guestrooms are required, day rooms or change rooms can be negotiated for setup staff and VIPs. If your event is running over the course of several days and guestrooms are part of your requirements, suites, upgraded rooms, early check-in, late checkout, one in *x* number of rooms to be complimentary and special rates for staff are areas of negotiation and cost concession. If additional charges will apply in any of these areas on top of room rates and taxes, they need to be included in your cost sheet, as will any other hotel fees that will be added to participants at checkout. These add-on fees must be factored into your budget—or negotiated with the hotel—at contract time so that you have a clear understanding of total room costs.

Add-on fees could include:

» Daily resort fees
» Daily health club fee
» Daily hospitality fee
» Daily groundskeeping fee
» Hotel telephone fees
» Internet and cable fees
» Wi-Fi fees
» Towel fees
» In-room safe fee
» Fee for opening the minibar
» Turndown service fee
» Daily bellman and maid fee
» Mandatory valet parking fee
» Newspaper delivery fee
» Fee for beverages such as orange juice served at complimentary breakfast (non-exclusive group function)
» Room delivery charges of room gifts, invitations, etc.
» Business office fees
» Energy surcharges

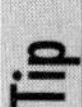

Always check to see if there will be a cell phone activation fee when traveling with your cell phone to another country. Some countries have the ability to put a block on using your cell phone in their country unless an activation fee is paid to them. You may need to investigate renting local cell phones etc. from the hotel or your ground operator.

Hotels provide many services, including stocking minibars with personal requests, dry cleaning, laundry, faxing, typing, photocopying, providing extension cords through their in-house audiovisual suppliers, cell phone rentals, walkie-talkies, telephone hook-up at your registration desk, the installation of banners (this one can be surprisingly expensive) and allowing the use of their computers for the middle-of-the-night changes to speeches that always seem to occur the night before a presentation if the client has opted not to bring theirs along and you need access to yours to manage your event. But beware, there can be a charge for each of the above-mentioned services.

Always find out in advance any charges for add-ons, and ensure that you authorize all expenses posted to the master account. Make sure you note clearly on your copy exactly what the charge was for so that you can include it on your reconciliations and get sign off on it from the person who was authorized to add on this expense.

While it may be less expensive to go to the local copy center to make copies or send a fax, is it worth your time to do so when you are in the middle of running an event? That's dollars and sense. Hotels will provide you with a list of the services they provide, along with applicable costs. Include these costs in your budget wherever you can. For example, if you know you will want telephones at your hospitality desk, you need to include the costs for hookups and the charges for local calls (which will vary from hotel to hotel; at some hotels there is no charge and at others it could be more than $1.00 per call). Estimate this number and include it in your costs, because the dollars can quickly add up and throw your budget out the window.

These and other add-on fees can also have mandatory taxes and service charges that need to be calculated and added on top of the actual add-on fee. Function space rental and private food and beverage functions can also have add-on charges that may not be spelled out in your contract but referenced simply as all applicable charges outlined in different hotel material, e.g., group catering menus that may list terms and conditions in the back, such as fees for chefs, add-on surcharges if guaranteed guest count decreases and you wish to utilize the same room (note that the hotel does reserve the right to move your group), add-on power drop charges for any extra power used by your audiovisual company, or union fees in the case of function space rental. Before you sign the hotel contract, you need to know exactly what charges could conceivably apply, have them put in writing and look at how they will affect your total budget.

With convention centers, none of this necessarily applies. There can be labor charges for off-loading of goods, and in some instances you could be looking at three- or four-hour minimums or overtime costs as well as union fees. There can be charges for tables, draping and skirting. Convention centers may not have specialty glasses on hand, and it will cost you extra to bring them in. One company that advertised a martini bar at their event was holding their event at a convention center as opposed to a hotel for the very first time. They encountered rental fees for martini glasses of more than $6,000! Exhibit space is not necessarily carpeted, and rental carpet is another additional cost. There can be extra costs to cut keys and for vacuuming done at a trade show exhibit. Find out in detail—and in writing—what is or is not included, where there's room for negotiation and what add-on costs will apply on top of basic costs.

If you have done your cost comparisons, you will know whether the hotel or the convention center is the more cost-effective venue for your event, and you can address specific issues with the venue. The convention center may be able to waive certain rental charges, as can the hotel, but before they can do so they need to know exactly how much you will be spending at their facility in terms of guestrooms, food and beverage. At both hotels and convention centers, be prepared to have rental charges increase should your numbers decrease. This will be laid out in their contract. Pay special attention to this area as it can have a major impact on your budget.

Find out before signing any contract what additional charges may be applicable, by asking such questions as:

» Are there any charges for tables and chairs?
» Does anything need to be brought in for your event that will be a cost to you?
» Are there charges for cleanup?
» What overtime charges could apply?
» Are there specific firms you must work with?
» What are the charges for electrical power?

Request that all additional charges be itemized on your contract and include these in your budget. You cannot afford surprises at the end of the day, especially if you are working with limited funds.

Tip

With any facility you need to ask:

» Are staff union or nonunion?
» How will this affect your labor and other costs?
» When are contracts and wage negotiations coming due?
» Are renovations being planned and, if so, what impact will they have on your event?

You don't want to have your event taking place in the middle of labor negotiations or under the threat of a possible strike. You need to know in advance what renovations are planned. How major will they be, and what impact will they have on service, on the state of the facility and on what your guests will see and experience during their stay?

Hotels and convention centers each have their strengths and weaknesses. What matters most is finding the facility that best meets the needs of your particular event and making sure that you are fully aware of all possible charges that need to be included in your budget.

Restaurants, Private Venues, Catering

You may decide to take your event out of a traditional ballroom setting and find something just a little different. A better fit might be a museum, art gallery, theater of the performing arts, private estate home, heritage building, exclusive restaurant, airport hangar, yacht club, racetrack, local attraction and entertainment center, elite nightclub, skating rink, enclosed tennis court, indoor volleyball facility, golf club, retail store, aquarium, converted warehouse, armory, film studio, boat charter, luxury car dealership, garden, the desert or the beach. Even the ocean has been used as the facility in which to host a white-glove-service cocktail reception and dinner, with guests being seated at tables in their bathing suits (the waitstaff were in formal attire) in the middle of the South Pacific. The list of location options is limited only by your imagination and your budget.

Ask your facility where else they have exclusive rights to cater off-property events. One hotel owned an incredible private home with breathtaking gardens that they could make available for special events to groups staying at their property. The hotel still received the revenue dollars for rental, food and beverage, and the guests had the opportunity to experience a very special setting outside of the hotel.

As with any hotel or convention center rental facility, you need to find out and include all applicable and logistical charges in your cost sheet summary from the onset when considering holding your event in non-traditional event locations. To accurately do this, remember to visualize every aspect of your event, from beginning to end, to capture every single event element cost that will be required, e.g., the porta-potties in the desert setting.

Theaters

There are many ways theaters—both movie and stage theaters—can be utilized for special events. Some of the newer theaters have space you can rent for your function and some will even allow you to hold your cocktail reception or sit-down dinner right onstage as mentioned previously. You might decide to hold your entire event under the theater's roof, or you may want to do the opening event at the theater followed by a reception at another site. Alternatively, you could start with dinner at another location, provide transportation to the theater and return to the original site for cigars, coffee, liqueurs and desserts.

When you are considering holding your event at a theater, make sure you do a complete walk-through. Find out the true capacity—how many seats are obstructed, broken or otherwise unusable? Go behind the scenes. Make sure the fire exits are completely cleared. You might be surprised to find they aren't. Although you would be even more surprised when the fire marshal closes down your event because you forgot to check. One event planner opened the fire exit doors and found garbage piled sky high, blocking both the exits. Staff were using the laneway to throw garbage away in the winter months instead of disposing of it properly. Not only was the laneway a fire hazard, it was needed for move in. At the event planner's request, the garbage was cleaned away and the theater powerwashed the walkway to the street to get rid of the smell and stains.

As with all facilities, find out if the theater—whether it is live theater or a movie theater—is unionized, what rules and regulations must be followed, and what costs will apply and where. Find out when the theater is accessible for you to set up. What costs are involved in theater rental, staffing and bringing in a cleanup crew?

If you are previewing a film, do a run-through before the event to make sure all is in working order. Find out what the costs are to bring in a projectionist the day before the event to screen the film, and make sure to include them in your budget. When one film was previewed it was found to have 10 minutes of dead air in the middle. The film was originally meant to have an intermission, but this time it was to run without a break. The reel had to be cut and spliced. Other reasons to preview are to check the film quality and to screen it for dirt and tears.

If a film is arriving from out of country, make sure that you allow sufficient time for it to clear customs. It is better to have it in your hands well in advance than to risk it being tied up in customs the day of your event. Check with the individual film companies regarding their film rights and applicable charges. Some companies have local representation, and they can assist you with bringing the film in. Theater management can also provide you with contact names and phone numbers.

Other ways to help ensure a successful film event include changing the marquee, rolling out the red carpet (or whatever may be most appropriate—today "red" carpets can run the gambit in colors and custom design), and having existing carpets cleaned and floors washed. Have beverage cups and popcorn bags with custom logos. Think about the arrival. Are people coming with tickets and invitations or not? Set up two lineups to avoid congestion and unnecessary waiting. What signage will you need? Do you need to bring in registration tables, draping and skirting, or tables for the beverages?

Everyone will arrive at once. Do you know how long it will take to pop popcorn for 700 people, package it, place those bags in miniature shopping bags with other handouts, and place all that on each theater seat? Don't wait until the day of the event to find out. Discuss the beverage setup and distribution. Do you need to remove candy displays or have them filled with a specific product? Do you need ropes and stanchions? Do you have a "private party" sign? How will you handle movie regulars? If you are putting the name of the movie up on the marquee, do you have someone to field the phone calls that will come in? Will you require crowd control? Searchlights? Are there any special theme or entertainment giveaways?

Are you providing transportation to have guests shuttled between more than one location? Do you need to add in traffic control if all guests are arriving, departing and going on to a secondary location at one time? Give thought to congestion and lineups and how to avoid both in all areas. Will the theater be open to the public for a later movie or theater seating, or will it be yours all night? If the theater is doing a late seating, you need to discuss where the people that are purchasing tickets for the late show will be able to wait. You want the lobby area and bathrooms held clear until all your guests have departed. Make sure that it is included in the contract prior to signing that no others will be allowed in until your event has ended, and the theater has been cleared. And, last but certainly not least, make sure all costs are factored into your budget.

Tents

If you are considering holding your special event in a tent, you should watch *Betsy's Wedding* so that you can fully appreciate the importance of including certain elements in your budget. In the film, the tent they rented had patches in the roof, and small tears quickly became large tears when rain poured heavily. The roof on their tent was unable to support the weight of the water and partly collapsed. The grass floor became a sea of mud.

Tents can be used to create a main venue, or provide additional space and serve as a second area. For example, if you were considering doing a wedding or a special event, you could use the main area to greet guests and hold a reception, and then move guests into the tent for a sit-down dinner. Or, you could do your entire event in a tent from beginning to end. A tent can provide shade—important for sporting events—as well as being a backup space in case of inclement weather. If you are doing an event where smoking is not permitted inside the building, such as a historical home, you could even set up a smoking tent adjacent to the main area.

Allow 20 square feet of floor space per person when calculating the size of tent you need. This will give everyone breathing room, especially if bad weather forces all of the guests indoors.

You need to give consideration to the type of tent that will best suit your requirements. Pole tents have the high, peaked ceilings like those found in a circus, while framed tents generally have higher installation costs but provide more structure.

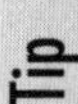

Contact your local tent rental companies and make sure that you see actual samples of the quality of tents they supply. All have catalogs, but ask to see firsthand what the company has to offer. A clear sidewall may look great in the catalog picture but turn out to be cloudy and full of cracks in real life. Take the time to do a site inspection at suppliers' places of business so you can determine the quality as well as the options offered. Do you want a solid color or a striped tent? What type of sides do you want? To ensure that the tent they install does not have scratches, cracks, tears or visible repairs and is installed in pristine condition, note these items on your contract. Be specific. A tent with dirty sidewalls is not acceptable and must be scrubbed clean. State it on your contract, and note it on your function sheets. Be specific about when this must be completed. At one event, tent installers were seen cleaning the tent walls as guests were arriving.

Have your contracted tent supplier do a site inspection with you at the venue to determine the tent that will best fit your needs. It doesn't matter how pretty a tent looks in a picture; what is important is that the tent design works with your location and your specific needs. The tent rental company will need to decide if the tent can be set in the ground or if it will need to be anchored, and what additional costs could be incurred. For example, if you were covering a parking lot, you could not set the tent into the ground without damaging the surface of the lot; in this case the tent would need to be firmly anchored. If you were setting the tent in a field, then you could look at a design that could be set in the ground. If the tent is covering an area where there are permanent trees, you will need to ensure that the ceiling on the tent will be high enough above them. And the reverse applies if there are any low-hanging wires. Are you considering setting up the tent in an area that could be a potential wind tunnel?

You need to know what type of tent will best suit the site and not what simply looks good. Never sign a contract without having done a site inspection with all involved. Have the tent rental company, the caterers and the people who are supplying the tables and chairs all present at your site inspection. Don't assume anything. Accurate measurements will need to be taken. The proposed site must be measured off to see if the chosen tent is workable.

There are other considerations, too. The caterers will need to advise you of their needs. Will you need a separate cooking tent where the caterers can set up and prepare the meal out of sight? If they will be cooking inside a tent, it will need to be well ventilated. What are their lighting and electrical needs? Is the site covered in uneven patches of land? A floor may not be an option but a necessity. You also need to check the fire regulations regarding how close the tent can be to existing buildings.

Who owns the land on which you are planning to set up your tent? Whose permission and what permits will be required? Will you need a tent permit? A building permit? Will you need a land permit? What other permits could come into play? You could be setting up a tent on restaurant grounds, and the restaurant has the land permit and owns the right to your putting your tent on their property. Or if your event is being held in a park, you will have to obtain permission and the land permit from the local parks and recreation department. Will you need a hydro permit? Are you planning to be hooked up to electricity and have access to running water, or will you be bringing in generators? What you decide to include in your event will affect the permits you will require. Who will obtain them? Each case is different; there is no standard rule. Check, check and double-check. Spell out in the contract who is responsible for obtaining each specific permit, and insist on receiving a copy of each well in advance of your event. And on the day of the event, make sure that you have all permits in hand in case inspectors drop by, and have an additional copy in your files.

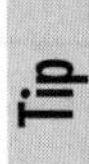

Always anchor your tent. They can and have blown away. The day before one gala event in Los Angeles, the tent actually did blow away and another one had to be flown in—there were none large enough left in LA.

How many days will setup and installation involve? A car dealership was planning to tent their display area for a private event until they found out that it was going to take two days to set up the tent prior to the event, which meant moving their cars off the lot for a total of three business days. As this would drastically affect their business sales, an alternate venue was found. They had originally anticipated having the cars off the lot for only one day.

What steps do you need to take to obtain a liquor license? Always check with company lawyers for social host responsibility and liability issues and required insurance to protect the client as well as your company. What will you need to do to conform to it? In some areas, alcoholic beverages may be served only in an enclosed area. How will your tent need to be set up to conform to the regulations? Does the tent rental company have fire exit signs or will you need to provide them? Will you need to set up portable bathrooms? Check regulations on how many are required (your event could be closed down should you not comply with regulations).

A good rule of thumb is to have approximately one bathroom for every 75 guests.

Budget permitting, provide separate bathroom facilities for the men and the women. Upscale bathroom trailers, complete with a sink and running water, are available for rent for gala events; you are no longer limited to those porta-potties that you find on construction sites. Staffing must be assigned to make sure that the facilities are kept refreshed.

When you are holding a tent event, build into your budget the extra cost of security for the tent overnight between setup and the actual event. This will ensure three things: that the tables and chairs that have been set up are secured overnight; that unexpected guests do not "camp out" under your tent; and that the tent is still standing the day of the event. Other items to factor into your budget will be the rental of tables, chairs, china, silverware, linens, napkins, decor, caterers and other related items such as the caterer's cooking tent and electrical needs. And remember, inclement weather could delay installation of the tent. Make sure that this is taken into account when you are scheduling deliveries and calculating total preparation and setup time. Be sure to find out what cleanup charges apply before and after the event to the site the tent is being set up on. Will you need to have the area cleaned? The grass cut? The area sprayed?

These are all items that need to be factored into your budget, as well as flooring, lighting, generators, air-conditioning or heaters for the main tent area, the catering tent, smoking area and any other required tent setups. Many consider tent flooring optional, but unless you are working with an absolute bare-bones budget, consider it essential if you are setting your tent up in a grassy area. With tents taking up to two days to install, you have to plan ahead if you're going to beat Mother Nature. If the ground is wet and doesn't have time to dry out, without flooring you will find tables and chairs sinking into the ground at odd angles.

As guests struggle to get out of their sinking chairs, they will grab onto the tables, which then are driven even farther into the ground. That could spell disaster for the centerpieces, the place settings and the whole food and beverage service. And, what if it's black-tie and women are in heels? Or it's nighttime and the air has cooled and the grass is damp under your feet? Flooring will ensure your guests' comfort and safety.

If you are looking at having your tented event in early spring or late fall be sure to include heat in your budget, in addition to flooring and lighting (for evening events). In cooler seasons, heaters ensure your guests' comfort. Remember, heat rises, so use ceiling fans to push warm air back down from the roof of the tent. Heaters will also equalize temperatures. For example, if you are looking at having cocktails served in a main venue—such as a house—and using a tent to serve the main meal, you want your guests to remain comfortable when they move into the tent.

There are also many different sidewalls you can consider. You can have sidewalls installed that can be rolled up if the day is warm, with a lining of mesh to keep insects out. The sidewalls can be lowered if the weather turns inclement. And if you are having any special effects, such as indoor fireworks, you may need to cost in an exhaust system as well.

If you were doing an event that offers both indoor and outdoor facilities, you should look at tenting as both a weather backup in case of rain or hot sun and as a separate venue. And if total capacity and the number of invited guests has been based on using both the outdoor and indoor area in entirety, tenting becomes much more than an area to handle the overflow comfortably; it becomes a critical part of your event. You need to make sure that guests will move out into this area and spend time there so that the indoor area does not get too crowded.

One way to do this is to serve the main meal in the tent to pull the guests to the outside area. Make sure that the tent has adequate seating, a buffet dinner setup and music or other entertainment, otherwise there will be nothing to keep guests there. Rather than a full buffet, finger foods and hot and cold hors d'oeuvres could be passed around, allowing more room for additional tables and chairs. Tables can then be smaller in size, making the area less like a banquet and more like a nightclub. You have then created two areas of high energy and atmosphere, as opposed to one main room with the tent being merely the overflow area, devoid of *any* atmosphere. If guests encounter dead air (no music or entertainment), a lack of ambiance and just some food stations and a few seats, your tent will appear bleak and uninviting, especially if you have created an atmosphere of high energy in the other area. Providing these things in the tent will draw guests out and keep them there.

When you are spending major dollars, as you can on virtually any type of special event, it makes no sense to skimp on the arrangements for your tent. With a high-energy band in the tent, specialty lighting or a laser show, you can create another area of excitement and fun. Remember to ensure that the laser show is put on by experts so no eye damage occurs through too much light intensity in an enclosed space.

Gala Openings in New Venues

Doing event planning for venues that are just opening to the public brings new elements to be aware of, ones that can play a major part in determining whether the opening can proceed as planned. Below are two very different examples of what to look out for:

A gala opening event with more than 2,000 guests was almost placed in jeopardy because building contractors had not been paid, and there were still items in dispute. The contractors were on hand on opening night and were preparing to remove fixtures or even close down the event. Make sure that you are familiar with the terms and conditions of any contracting work and that any disputes have been resolved prior to opening night.

One major gala restaurant opening almost did not occur. They had neglected to obtain final clearance from the fire marshal and building officials to open to the public. One hour before guests were due to arrive, the restaurant was told to stop food preparations and to begin to take down fixtures from the wall. Make sure that you know what needs to be done before opening to the public. Find out from city officials what permits are required and what needs to be done to meet all safety and fire regulations.

In both cases planners were fortunately able to scramble around and work out an agreeable last-minute solution, but you can't count on that kind of luck. Plan ahead and try to consider every eventuality.

Many event planners hold off on doing events in new venues until they have been up and running for at least six months. With new venues, always make provisions for risk-assessment insurance in case the building does not open in time.

Contracts

In addition to having copies of all permits with you on-site, always make sure to bring with you a copy of all signed original contracts and key correspondence in case there are any areas of dispute regarding contracted locations or other event elements. Having your paperwork with you allows you to deal immediately with any concerns.

On an incentive program in Mexico, one client was very explicit about which guestrooms she was requesting for her group and did a walk-through of each and every one—beachfront rooms, the best on the property. During the pre-con it was discovered that the hotel was trying to put the client into other, less desirable rooms. After the event planning company had signed the contract, the hotel had changed the names of all the room types and categories. The function sheets had always referred to the rooms by name and type in addition to the specific room numbers that had been contracted. They showed the event planner their new map. The event planner showed them their old map with the signed contract detailing the room categories. They said others had now signed contracts for the beachfront rooms and nothing could be done. The event planner disagreed. One of the first rules of event planning is not to accept no *for an answer. They ended up calling the vice-president of the hotel chain, who quickly resolved the matter, and the client received every room originally contracted.*

It was of utmost importance that they had the original contract and map with them, and that in all of their correspondence the room categories had been detailed from the very beginning. Because of that they were able to act quickly and have everything resolved before the client and guests arrived, as it was proven that the other company holding the desired rooms had signed their contract after the event planning company had signed theirs.

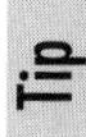

Make sure when you are negotiating changes and concessions to your contract that you are speaking with someone who does have the authority to say *yes*. You may need to go higher.

When you are doing an event, particularly one out of country, arrive well in advance of the group to ensure that everything is ready. Always make sure that you do a final review of contracts and function sheets with the hotel and all suppliers involved in any aspect of your event.

A pre-con can involve anywhere from three people to a cast of thousands depending on how intricate the program is. Everyone's actions must be in sync. They must be orchestrated to come together perfectly layer after layer. It is like a relay team, each person passing the baton to the next at precisely the right moment. If someone drops the baton, someone else must be ready to pick it up and run with it without missing a beat.

By reviewing your contracts and function sheets with all those involved, you are ensuring that nothing that has been contracted for has dropped through the cracks or been overlooked. Your goal is to ensure that all involved are operating from the same page and that all that has been agreed upon is in place.

In another instance, an incentive group was on a Caribbean cruise. I was flying to each port of call in advance of the group to set up special events in preparation for their arrival. In the final port of call we had planned to hold the farewell gala away from the ship. When I arrived late Friday night I noticed a number of large, unsightly construction trucks in the parking lot outside of the main entrance to the venue where we were holding our farewell. Visually, the trucks greatly detracted from the impact of the site. In all contracts and correspondence it had been noted that this area was to remain clear. The owners of the trucks had left them to be parked over the weekend. Because it had been specified in the contract, and I had copies with me, I was able to get them to trace down the company that owned the trucks and have them moved.

When assessing locations as to whether or not they will be right for your event, there are many more event location elements that need to be taken under consideration than just the facility's size and layout. By addressing them, you can better estimate and control your event's costs and determine the location's suitability for the staging of your event.

Location Q&A

Q&A

What time would you have access to the facility?

Be very clear about exclusive access time to the facility and make sure that it is noted in the contract so that there is no room for misunderstandings at a later date. Keep in mind that the person you are working with now may not be there at a later date, and in the event planning process you may have been passed on from the sales department to their operations department to their on-site day-of-event scheduled staff, so get everything in writing from day one and as you move forward with your event.

Q&A

Is that enough time to set up?

If you require more time for setup than the venue is prepared to give in exchange for the realized dollars from your event for food and beverage, you may need to negotiate a flat rate with them for additional setup time. Remember, although they are receiving revenue for your event, asking them to close for an extensive amount of time will cost them additional dollars in lost food and beverage sales. They may agree to a longer setup in exchange for additional compensation. In addition to knowing your setup requirements, you also need to find out what else will be taking place in your facility on your move in, setup and rehearsal days that could impede your timing.

At one facility, being considered for a car product launch, it was discovered that the room they would need to move the cars through in order to be able to get them into their blocked function space had been reserved for someone else's event. The other event was switched to another room and a 24-hour hold was put on the room whose availability was necessary to facilitate the move in and move out of the cars (because of the size of the width of the doors). The time to discover this key logistical requirement is before contract and not the day of move in.

Make sure that your contract stipulates the time the room will be guaranteed to be available to you and that it will be cleaned after its previous use and back to its agreed-upon state.

Q&A

Will any furniture or fixtures need to be removed?

When looking at space, do not be limited by the furniture or fixtures in it. Most facilities will agree to moving out furniture and fixtures—such as a hanging chandelier that may not fit the theme decor or block or interfere with audiovisual sight lines or lighting requirements—and having them stored elsewhere in order to accommodate more guests. In your contract, be specific as to which items you will want removed and what costs you will be responsible for.

Q & A

What extra costs could be related to that?

You could be looking at additional cost to bring staff in to move the furniture and fixtures out, as well as union requirement fees (such as a meal being provided for crew, minimum-hour charges, etc.) depending on the venue. If the facility does not have accessible storage space it may be necessary to utilize moving vans and store the unwanted furniture and fixtures overnight or longer depending on the time required for setup, move in, rehearsals, day of, teardown and move out. You may also need to factor in the cost for staff and other applicable logistical costs to move in and set up the furniture and fixtures before the start of business the day following your move out. Make sure that you have proper insurance for the furniture and fixtures in case of damage or loss, and that all involved are covered for injury. Another area you may need to look at is street parking permits for the time supply trucks need to load and off-load.

Q & A

Will you need to provide a cleaning crew before, during and after the event?

Do not assume that this will be provided by the venue at no additional cost. It is an item that can often be negotiated but you need to know this before signing the contract.

Q & A

What is the legal room capacity?

The importance of knowing the room capacity and adhering to it cannot be stressed enough. Sometimes the solution to maximizing the number of guests is to issue invitations with two or more specific times, such as separate morning, afternoon and evening functions. In these cases it is essential that there is an official beginning and end to each event, and all guests are gone before the next event begins. This can be tricky because there is no way you can control when guests leave if there are not very specific and separate events.

One high-society event planner tried a different tactic that ended up with the fire department and police being called in for

Q & A

crowd control and almost being closed down. They told their client that their elite guests would understand "it is a social attitude" and would comply with the terms of the invitation sent to them and their family members, which included children. The first invitation read 6 p.m.–10 p.m. for Group A and the second invitation read 8 p.m.–12 a.m. for Group B. What happened was easily predicted by more experienced planners. Group A did not want to leave as their children were having a marvelous time. When the party is in full swing and guests are having a good time, how are you going to force Group A to leave at 10 p.m? Even if you use "visible" ID so you know who is in each group, do you really want to put yourself in the position of asking your invited guests to leave if they have extended their stay?

It is important to honor the legal capacity of the room or hold two or more separate events not only to protect your guests' safety and security and be in compliance with the law, but also to protect your client, your company and yourself from being sued should anything happen and it is discovered that capacity was exceeded. It *has* happened. A nightclub rented for a private event caught fire and many were killed. A ballroom floor collapsed from excess weight and resulted in many deaths and injuries. A private boat charter tipped over and many lives were lost because there were too many people onboard and the boat simply could not handle it.

There are many creative ways to increase capacity, which can sometimes be governed by the number of washroom facilities available to guests. If the venue is attached to an office tower, for example, it may be possible to open up additional facilities by using additional security staff. Upscale portable bathroom facilities are also available for rent. Check out your creative options with local authorities. It is much better to work hand in hand with them than to have them show up at your event and close it down because you violated regulations.

Your guests' comfort should also be of primary concern. They will not be comfortable if they are packed in like sardines or if they have to line up forever to use the bathroom facilities. They will simply leave your event in frustration.

One fund-raiser was held at a private venue where there were hundreds of invited guests. They were down to just one working bathroom, as the facility was slated for major renovations the day following the event. This event was to be a send-off to a famous room that would be totally remodeled. The size of the room was fine, but there was no way it would have passed inspection with only one bathroom. Had inspectors dropped by—as they can and do without notice—the event would have been immediately closed down. And, as could be anticipated, the bathroom was out of commission well before the event was scheduled to end but guests departed far before that in search of bathroom facilities that had not been stopped up, flooded and rendered unusable.

Q & A

What is the zoning? Are there any restrictions or regulations that should concern you?

Find out what can and what cannot be done. You need to check with local authorities—fire, health, police and city officials. If your event involves tethered hot air balloons, for example, you need to check with nearby airports to obtain written clearance from them, as these could be potential flight hazards. One company wanted to do a boat team-building event on the water and needed approval from the harbor police. Rescue boats, staff and standby medical care needed to be built into the program and budget in order for the event to be able to take place.

Q & A

Are there any noise restrictions?

If the facility is in the middle of a residential area there may be noise restrictions, which could affect how late your event can be open and how loudly and where music can be played. For example, there is an amazing castle with beautiful outdoors grounds that is perfect for an outdoors summer event, but because it is set in a residential location no music—live or recorded—is allowed to play past 10 p.m. in the gardens. Inside, the sound must be kept at a specific volume level. Resorts can have noise restrictions for private outdoor functions as well, as they want to make sure that their other guests are not inconvenienced by bands playing late into the night.

What insurance do you need to protect your guests, your client, your company and yourself?

Make sure that you have investigated insurance requirements with your facility and your suppliers and discussed your findings with your client, their company lawyers and your company event planning lawyers to ensure that everything is covered and everybody is protected should anything go amiss. Ensure that you follow all protection procedures. For example, in the case of team-building corporate events, it is necessary to obtain a signed waiver from guests.

Remember, if guests are taking part in any physical activities and you are serving alcohol, serve it after the event, not before. For example, a fun team-building event can be a car rally with various refreshment checkpoints along the route, e.g., sampling of local ice cream, etc. One of these stops could be lunch, but it should be a non-alcoholic one. Drinking and driving don't mix. You can serve alcohol back at the hotel at the end of the rally at a check-in party, where guests gather and discuss their day over a drink. Or, if you want to have the check-in party at the luncheon location and want to include alcohol, have motor coaches waiting to transfer your guests back to their hotel, and arrange for the cars to be ferried back to the rental agency.

Safety must go beyond insurance concerns; a participant was killed at one of these road rally events in Europe. If you are considering a road rally in a country such as Barbados, where the driving is on the opposite side, there are ways around the problem rather than to risk guests becoming confused. For example, you could turn the rally into a GPS scavenger hunt and have guests driven around in limos, Mini Mokes or minivans by a professional driver. Clues could be given in the local dialect and with a contest

Q & A

to create a limerick using the new words they have learned. An added twist in a location such as Mexico could be that guide drivers are instructed to speak only Spanish.

Whatever event you undertake, consider guest safety and security and find out what legal requirements you need to meet and how much insurance your client, your suppliers and your company will need to take out to make sure everyone is covered should anything ever happen. Some hotels and venues are making client and supplier insurance clauses contractually mandatory, i.e., you will be required to make sure that your suppliers have *x* million dollars' worth of event insurance, and it will be up to you to obtain copies of the policy to make sure that they have obtained it and submit it to the facility, making sure to keep a copy for your records as well.

Q & A

What restrictions would you need to work around?

Historical buildings, museums, art galleries and other locations have some very specific guidelines about what can and cannot take place there. Ask to see a copy of their rental agreement. It will outline what specifically applies to the venue—there is no standard form. The restrictions that could apply are as varied as the venues. You may not be able to smoke in a historical building, even though you are holding a private event (in some venues even if smoking is not allowed when they are open to the public, you may be allowed to smoke at a private event where you have exclusive use of the building or to set up a smoking tent nearby). You may not be able to attach anything to the walls.

You need to know what you can and can't do. In museums, you may need to pay for additional security. Guests may not be permitted to enter certain restricted areas. At an art gallery, guests may be able to look but not touch, and areas might be roped off. You may not be able to serve food or beverages in certain rooms. In one car museum, you are not allowed to serve certain beverages because they might damage the paint finish if splashed on a vintage car. If you have rented a private estate, are you renting just the grounds, or will guests have full access to the house?

Find out all restrictions that could apply before you sign the contract. If there are additional charges, such as security, they must be included in your cost sheet so that you can calculate the effect they will have on your budget.

What will you need to bring in?

Some venues can be perfect with just a few additions; others need to be virtually transformed.

One of the first things to look at is lighting. Lighting adds interest and adds ambiance. It can be dramatic. It can be romantic. It helps to create a mood. It can add energy and with today's technology add great special effects for minimum dollars.

You may want to bring in additional greenery or rented furniture to enhance what is already there, or, as mentioned earlier, empty the facility and bring everything in.

Prop houses are an excellent source of a large variety of items to rent. Meet with local decor companies, and do a walk-through of their inventory to see what ideas it may trigger for your event. Another option, budget permitting, is to have furniture and props custom made. These items can then be sold to the venue or decor companies to recoup some of the costs to the client.

How are the sight lines?

If you are considering having speeches or audiovisual presentations, you need to pay particular attention to the sight lines. If there is a pillar or anything hanging from the ceiling blocking the view, it needs to be removed for your event and if so, remember to include any applicable labor costs to take them down in whole or in part. One event planning company determined that the chandelier in their function space did not detract from screen visibility and opted to leave it hanging. What they had neglected to pay attention to was the distracting tinkling sound the crystal chandelier made when the fans were turned on; it was so loud that it drowned out the guest speakers onstage. The planners needed to have the facility show them the room as it would be in full operation, not dark.

Q&A

When planners are doing their site inspection, they need to visualize what the guests will see, feel, hear and smell, and the quality of what they will experience. For instance, if you were doing an audiovisual presentation in a room that has floor-to-ceiling windows, planners would need to determine whether or not the room should be completely darkened to provide a better visual image presentation. In many restaurants you cannot do this, and you would need to look at bringing in pipe and draping—freestanding fixtures on which material is hung—to cover the windows or to divide up the room.

Q&A

Where are the kitchens and how many can they service?

How will the food get to your guests? What other areas does the kitchen service? Is the same kitchen used to prepare food for restaurant guests, for example in a hotel, in addition to private functions? How many functions will be going on at the same time? How many can the kitchen comfortably serve at one time?

One particular restaurant has one kitchen servicing two entirely different areas physically separated by a walkway. But in order to service the other side, it is necessary for the waiters to take the food orders through the main section of the restaurant. They can do this discreetly, but you should know this in advance and decide if it is appropriate. If you had exclusive rights to the private room it may not be a concern, but if you are holding your event in the main room that would be entirely different. You do not want to be surprised on the night of the event.

Q&A

How large are the kitchens and how are they set up?

Find out the capacity. If you are having your event catered at a private venue, plan to meet at the site with the caterers or on-property kitchen staff so that you are aware of all of their needs and any areas of concern. It is essential that caterers do a site inspection—they need to be familiar with the layout, capacity and any potential problem areas from the standpoint of food

Q & A

preparation and service. This includes such seemingly minor points as, will the caterer's cooking pans fit into the venue's oven, fridge or freezer? Will their dishes—if oversize, which many of today's tableware can be—fit into the facility's dishwasher or microwave? How many electrical outlets will they require? Where are they located? Will extension cords be required? Will additional or backup generators be needed? What will they need with regard to parking and off-loading of equipment and food? Do they have any special requirements, such as a separate cooking tent? Ask where food will be prepared—off-site and finished at your venue or fully prepared on-site?

Tip

Accept quotes from caterers only in writing. Make sure your quotes include menu selection, quantity, price, taxes, delivery and the number of experienced staff they will be providing. Have them detail the number of hours they have been contracted for, including preparation, arrival time and cleanup. Make sure that they lay out what their staff will be responsible for. Will they be taking and serving drink orders at the tables? Will their staff be replenishing and clearing the tables? Will they be taking care of cleanup and dishwashing?

Q & A

Are there enough glasses, dinnerware and cutlery, and enough staff to replenish them?

The last thing you need at an event is your guests standing around waiting for glasses, dinnerware and cutlery to be replenished. At one restaurant food-tasting fund-raiser with just under 1,000 guests, this is exactly what happened. More than 25 top restaurants were offering assorted food tastings to the invited guests. What had not been anticipated was that some of the restaurants were using the facility's wineglasses for their desserts, which caused a shortage. In addition, guests were going to each station and picking up clean plates and cutlery. Once finished, they would lay them down wherever they could find space and proceed to the next food station, and begin the procedure all over again. Needless to say, 1,000 guests went through an enormous number of plates,

Q & A

knives and forks in minutes. The dirty dishes were everywhere in unsightly, dangerous, precariously towering piles. Clearing staff had not been provided in sufficient numbers to handle the situation, and there were only three people in the kitchen to handle the onslaught of incoming dirty dishes. It was not enough. The number of staff required to clear the dishes, clean and stack them in the dishwasher, unload it and bring the clean utensils back out needs to be reviewed in great detail when you are planning your event. You also need to know how fast the dishwasher turnaround is.

Another gala fund-raiser faced the same situation as above but handled it differently and successfully limited the number of utensils used. As guests arrived, they were presented with the wineglass, plate and cutlery that were theirs "for the evening." The hostess made it very clear that they were meant to keep them for the whole food tasting. The wineglass was attached to the plate with a clip, making it very easy for guests to keep track of their glasses, and cutlery was wrapped together in a napkin. For some events, this solution may be acceptable, but for an upscale gourmet food tasting it would not be and provision would need to be made to have multiple sets of glassware, tableware and cutlery available to each guest and sufficient staff on hand to handle all of the logistical turnaround elements (clearing, cleaning and replenishing supplies quickly, where and when needed).

Tip

If you are planning a gourmet food tasting where your guests will use a number of different plates, glasses and cutlery, make sure that you have sufficient quantities. Also, find out whether there are any specific requirements, such as specialty glassware. Include the cost of professional, experienced help in your budget, and use your in-house staff or volunteers in other ways.

Q & A

What are the dishes, glassware and cutlery like at the venue?

Make sure that you actually see the utensils that will be used. Well before the event, do a walk-through to make sure that all is in readiness and up to standard. A walk-through at a location before

Q & A

a client's breakfast meeting revealed that the glasses that had been put out for breakfast were cloudy, spotted and still had orange pulp clinging to them from their last use. They were disgraceful, but because the event planner held the walk-through well before the scheduled meeting, there was time to replace them.

At an event on a quality property in the Caribbean, the walk-through showed a number of the dishes that had been put out for dinner were chipped and totally unacceptable. They had to be pulled from the table and the table reset.

At an afternoon social event, which was held in a private venue, the dishes used were completely wrong for the event. They were chunky, heavy, standard truck-stop diner restaurantware, but the event was meant to be light and elegant, with fine china and silverware. Proper planning and a site inspection before signing the contract and having the contract clearly state what would be used might have avoided this problem. Better-quality utensils would have added to the event and raised the level of the experience.

Q & A

Have you considered hiring professional help and included the cost in your budget?

At any event, be it a corporate gala or fund-raiser, some corporations or nonprofit organizations look to save dollars on professional help by using in-house staff or volunteers for additional on-site support. But what happens—and it does happen—if some of the volunteers are no-shows? Or what transpires if assigned employees are pulled away to mingle with the guests? Considering that the additional costs for professional help amount to only pennies per guest, do you really want to have your event appear unprofessional or unpolished to save a few dollars? What is key is the perception of the event and how well it reflects the company's image. Guests will be looking for polish and finesse.

Give thought to how you want your event to be handled. Plan for it, right down to the number of staff clearing the plates and in the kitchen. Make it as polished and as professional as you can.

Q & A

How many bathrooms are there?

How many of them are there and what state are they in? Do they require any touch-ups? How will they be refreshed on the night of your event? Will bathroom attendants be provided?

One restaurant holding an event seemed to do an outstanding job—everything was gleaming. The only thing that was not up to snuff was that in one of the bathrooms a piece of wallpaper was missing. It was a small thing, but it took away from the total effect. It had not been missing during the site inspection or the pre-con meeting—it had been damaged just recently and the restaurant had not had the opportunity to have it fixed. Knowing how important this was to us, they immediately contacted the designer, who brought over a piece of the wallpaper and put up a temporary bandage.

Q & A

How will you be handling bathroom attendants?

Some upscale restaurants have in place bathroom attendants who expect a tip for providing you with a hand towel. At a special event, guests may have to pay for their own parking and coat check (a sign is usually posted), but it is tacky to expect them to tip for any other service such as a bathroom attendant.

Discuss tipping with the facility management, and make it clear how you will handle tips and such. You can provide for them in your budget and have this added to your bill, or you can distribute tip envelopes at the end of the evening, as you are personally thanking those involved in making your event a success. It is perfectly acceptable to let both guests and staff know that their tips have been taken care of. Make sure that a tip plate is never left out, and instruct staff that if a tip is offered they should say that the service is being provided by their host for the evening. If perfume is offered, it must be complimentary. Make sure that you have someone review these policies with the staff on the night of the event.

Q & A

Is there a separate area away from the event where the staff can take their breaks?

Think about where their staff—not the event planning staff—will take their breaks. If you don't want them gathered around a front entrance smoking, where do you want them to be? It is important to take good care of the staff and for more than just humanitarian reasons. If they are exhausted, hungry or thirsty the level of service and your whole event could be affected. Make sure that refreshments are made available to them—food, juice and soft drinks. Find out if separate washrooms for the staff can be arranged. This is important to know for the comfort of both guests and staff. If you are hosting a gala event you want to be sure that your guests are not kept waiting in the bathroom line longer than need be, that their conversations are kept private and that they are not subject to the personal conversations of the staff. The staff should be comfortable and looked after as well, not delayed unnecessarily from their tasks.

Q & A

How experienced are the staff?

You want to make sure that you have the best, most experienced and professional staff. Take time to go to the facility and observe it—see if there are any areas of concern. Will it be acceptable if the waiters have earrings, lip rings, colorful hair? What is the host's company image? Is this in keeping with their profile? Discuss all areas of protocol with senior management. Be clear on the tone you want to set. Do you want the staff to be friendly and upbeat or more reserved? Management can then pass the word to their staff.

Ensure that you make note of everything in your function sheets. If you can't guarantee that the staff's appearance will be in keeping with the client's image, you may have to book another venue. On the night of the event, prior to final setup, have the management address their staff for one final review of the evening's expectations, and have them introduce their staff to the main contact person, usually the event planner. This would be the perfect opportunity to thank them as a group for their efforts and for all they have done and are about to do in making this event a success.

Q & A

Have they handled events of this nature before? How large?

Ask for references and also speak to suppliers who have worked at the facility before. Ask what went well and what could have been better. What is the maximum number of people they have handled at one time, not over the course of a day, but at a private event? What level of experience do they bring to you? Ask for proof. Have them be specific. Who have they worked with, and what have they done in the past? Get names and phone numbers from both past clients and suppliers.

Q & A

Have you, the special events planner, handled events of this nature before and at this type of facility?

What personal experience do you or your company bring? If you have handled only smaller events in the past, look at who you may need to bring in to handle a large event of, say, over 2,000. Don't put your event at risk by trying to bluff your way through. It is better to work and learn from someone who has done it successfully before than to get in over your head. Creative directors can be brought in on a project basis and provide you with creative design and logistics, work with your event planning team and share their knowledge with you.

A restaurant that normally did not do private catering handled a fund-raising event at another location, and while their service at the restaurant was absolutely five-star, at the event it was not up to par. Catering staff are trained to look for different things than regular restaurant staff. They are used to circulating, looking for empty glasses and plates wherever they may be laid down. This can be especially important if the event logistics were not properly planned. If insufficient thought is given to where used items are to be placed at a stand-up reception, left to their own devices, people can be very creative. Catering staff know instinctively when to remove a glass or offer a napkin, and such finesse and proper protocol are essential elements to the success of your event.

Tip

A restaurant that has a separate catering company works extremely well for stand-up receptions with food stations. You may want to bring in catering staff to handle the VIP areas.

Q & A

Are there any things that should be put away?

If there are items normally offered for sale at the venue that you are taking over exclusively, have them removed and put out of sight or you may find yourself charged for items guests may have "assumed" were part of the evening's events. At one fund-raiser, shelves were stripped bare of merchandise guests thought was being offered as free samples.

Q & A

What are the fire and safety regulations? What permits do you need, and what permits would the facility need to obtain?

It is imperative to know the regulations and who is responsible for obtaining which permit. Do not assume that the facilities will provide all that you will require. You may need to obtain a special liquor license; a permit to extend bar closing time, which can be obtained for special occasions; or a tent permit. Ask for copies of every permit for your files.

You will also need to know the maximum capacity the fire marshal will allow in the venue and how it could be affected if you removed some of the furnishings or brought in additional washroom facilities. Remember, it is your responsibility, not the facility's, to make sure you do not exceed capacity. Which doors have to remain clear and unlocked for fire safety? Will you have to clearly post exit signs?

Discovering new venues and creating one-of-a-kind events is how you create unforgettable occasions. You want everyone to go away feeling as though they have attended the event of the year each and every time. Don't be afraid to try something new, but be prepared to do your homework, plan and prepare, and bring in the experts where you need to. You can take events out of the ballroom and make magical memories, but be prepared to be involved in all aspects of planning and operations. Remember, no detail is too small. Will the rugs in the venue need to be sent out to be cleaned for your event.? Is the bathroom up to par? How is the paint? the wallpaper? Give all areas your full attention. It is worth it. Create events that guests could not duplicate on their own. Look for ways to make them special.

The following farewell event was held at a private villa. The look, the feel and the energy of that very special night could not have been duplicated inside the ballroom (but that being said, the ballroom was put on hold as weather backup, something always important to have with outdoor events):

Imagine holding a private dinner poolside in the villa where they filmed the movie 10. *The white cabanas you see in the movie were carried up to the villa and scrubbed spotless, providing a dramatic backdrop, serving as the bar stations. The back garden wall was freshly whitewashed, the grass was cut and sprayed, the pool was cleaned. The villa was immaculate. Everything was white on white in keeping with the mood of the resort. There was fine dining under the stars. Softly glowing candlelight, beautiful fragrant florals and soft music set the mood, and the sky filled with fireworks at the end of the evening. That evening—a perfect* 10. *The mood—magical and memorable. And that is what the "just right" location should always deliver.*

Move In Requirement Checklist

✓ *Will there be anyone else moving in or moving out at the same time our event suppliers require move in access time? If so are there any logistical move in challenges or additional expenses that we need to be aware of, e.g., blocking the service elevator exclusively for our move in at specific times, etc.?*

- ✓ *What legal and financial responsibility is the venue prepared to undertake contractually if their other client's teardown and move out causes ours to be delayed?*
- ✓ *What are the parking facilities like for our suppliers' vehicles with regards to availability and access (e.g., large trucks, small trucks, or cars)?*
- ✓ *What kind of delivery access to the site and special arrangements do each of our event suppliers need, e.g., secure storage or holding areas, water, refrigeration (florists, wine, food)?*
- ✓ *Can the venue handle a multitude of suppliers making deliveries over the course of several days or all day long on one specific day, or will other scheduling arrangements need to be made?*
- ✓ *Will our event suppliers be bringing in any large, heavy or awkward-to-carry items?*
- ✓ *Will our event suppliers require special equipment to be brought in, with an additional cost to off-load and move in these items?*
- ✓ *Will our event suppliers require a venue that has a ramp or loading dock to make move in easier? Will our client require this as well, e.g., car product launch with cars being displayed inside the venue?*
- ✓ *Could our event suppliers' move in crews encounter any difficulties with the location we are proposing to contract?*
- ✓ *Will the event planning move in crews be able to maneuver through the doors, make their way through the aisles, and go up, down and around staircases?*
- ✓ *What would facilitate an easy move in (e.g., service elevators, service corridors being cleared)?*
- ✓ *What type of items and in what kinds of quantity will we be having delivered to the event site?*
- ✓ *Will the site layout and timing of the move in require our event suppliers to bring in extra staff, at additional cost, to facilitate a faster move in?*
- ✓ *What are our client's move in requirements and what do we need to ensure is in place for them? How will their timing affect our event suppliers' move in?*

Event Suppliers' Setup Logistics Checklist

- ✓ *Do we know which of our event suppliers will require move in and setup access to our event venue the week prior, several days ahead, or the day before our event? (Remember, tenting can require several days to set up, as can an extensive stage and audiovisual production.)*
- ✓ *Will we need to put a 24-hour hold on any of the spaces we are reserving for setup?*
- ✓ *Have we received all of our event suppliers' timing and logistical requirements for setting up before and on the day of the event?*
- ✓ *How does the timing of each suppliers' move in and setup impact our other event suppliers? Are there any areas of logistical conflict or potential timing problems?*
- ✓ *Have we prepared our critical path outlining the sequential order in which our event suppliers need our move in and setup to occur?*
- ✓ *Is there anything else taking place at the venue or otherwise that could cause our event suppliers' move in or setup to be delayed (e.g., construction, renovations or labor contract disputes)?*
- ✓ *Will our event suppliers be focused on our event move in and setup, or juggling multiple setups and events on the same day that could result in timing difficulties for us? How tightly are their services booked?*
- ✓ *What prep work will be required in advance of our event supplier move in? For example, tent installations may require that cable lines, gas lines, hydro lines and water lines be identified and marked before installation can begin. In addition, the lawn may need grooming, floors may need vacuuming, insect prevention may be required, tree branches may need to be tied back or raised, and sprinkler systems may need to be turned off before move in and setup can occur.*
- ✓ *Will any of our event suppliers require a locked storage area? If so, how large would it need to be to hold the proposed items?*

- ✓ *How long could our event suppliers conceivably require the storage space? Will they need it from move in, setup, during our reception and possibly afterwards, or until teardown and move out can take place?*
- ✓ *Will any of our event suppliers have any special requirements that we need to be aware of and make sure are available to them (such as access to running water, refrigeration, etc.)?*
- ✓ *Do we know what electrical power each of our event suppliers requires?*
- ✓ *Do we have a blueprint mapped out of electrical outlets and where they are located in relation to supplier requirements and room layout?*
- ✓ *Will our proposed layout result in visible wires showing that will need to be covered or secured (taped so that guests do not trip) or require that extension cords be brought in?*
- ✓ *Have we alerted the venue as to how much total power will be used by all of our suppliers and reviewed with the venue whether the facility can safely accommodate this (or if backup generators will be required)?*
- ✓ *Do we need to bring in an electrical technician to confirm that the suppliers' needs can be safely met or advise us whether or not we need to consider a backup generator to ensure there are no power blackouts?*
- ✓ *Does the venue have on-site security to ensure there is no theft or damage to event supplier goods between move in, setup and our event, or will we be required to provide it?*
- ✓ *Does the facility have any noise restrictions that we need to make our suppliers aware of, such as noise related to building of any custom items, how loud the music can be played and if there are noise curfews or permits required?*
- ✓ *Do we know the venue's rules regarding use of tacks or any other fastenings for walls, chairs, tables, etc., so that we can advise our suppliers?*

- ✓ *To make sure that our event suppliers are aware of and will adhere to our event venue's policies, do we need to add an addendum to their contracts so that we don't incur any charges for damage?*
- ✓ *Do we know what type of insurance and coverage amount will be required by the venue from us and our event suppliers?*
- ✓ *Do we know if there are any special permits or licenses we or our suppliers will be required to obtain (e.g., fire marshal permit for any special effects, liquor license, building permit)?*
- ✓ *Do we know the venue and fire marshal rulings and regulations regarding items such as having candlelight or votives with open flames?*
- ✓ *Will open flames be permitted or will we need to look at an alternative such as Candle Safe, which is a battery-operated candle that comes in a variety of colors, shapes and scents?*
- ✓ *If the venue only has one parking lot and space is limited, and setup is taking place on the day of our event, do we need to look at alternate parking spots for our suppliers so that our guests are not inconvenienced?*
- ✓ *Could anything else be going on at our event site at the same time as our move in and setup that could inconvenience or delay our event suppliers, such as having to be quiet while another event is in progress?*
- ✓ *Does the type of venue we are looking at lend itself to multiple events taking place at the same time?*
- ✓ *Could this impact the timing and logistics for move in and setup of our event suppliers, inconvenience our guests or interrupt our event in any manner?*
- ✓ *Will our event suppliers need early access to the event site on the day of the event?*
- ✓ *Can the facility accommodate early access and are there any additional charges we need to be aware of to do this (e.g., the venue bringing in additional staffing, security, etc., in order to meet our event suppliers' needs)?*

✓ *Will our event suppliers still be on-site when the guests arrive and is there a separate parking area for them?*

✓ *Are the venue or any of our suppliers unionized?*

✓ *What special provisions do we need to make available to them during move in and setup (e.g., meals for crew) and what are all applicable move in and setup union costs that we could be incurring?*

✓ *What are our client's move in requirements, what do we need to ensure is in place for them and how will their timing affect our event suppliers' setup?*

Event Suppliers' Teardown Checklist

✓ *What are our client's teardown and move out requirements and what do we need to ensure is in place for them?*

✓ *Will any of our event suppliers be tearing down and moving out decor, staging, lighting, etc., after our event has taken place and guests have departed?*

✓ *How much time will they require?*

✓ *Could our event suppliers' teardown and move out be extensive?*

✓ *Will we require extra time from the venue to allow them to move out the same day or night, or could additional time be required with teardown and move out taking place the next day and the days followings?*

✓ *Could our event suppliers conceivably require storage space after the event?*

✓ *Will there be another event or event party moving in as our event suppliers are moving out? How much time do they have to tear down our event site and move out?*

✓ *How does that impact our event suppliers with regards to timing and logistics? Will they be required to bring in extra staff to tear down and move out quickly to accommodate the other event's move in and setup?*

- ✓ *Do we need to extend the time we have blocked to accommodate our event suppliers' teardown and move out?*
- ✓ *Are there any possible overtime charges or other costs that could apply that we need to budget for?*
- ✓ *What legal ramifications and expenses are we liable for if our event suppliers cause a delay on teardown and move out that will impact another event's move in and setup and what can we do to protect ourselves and our client from additional expenses?*
- ✓ *What are our client's teardown and move out requirements and what do we need to ensure is in place for them?*

4

Transportation

Transportation is as much a part of your event as the other elements are and creativity needs to be employed to make sure that getting to the event site is an enjoyable experience, whether it be by air, land, water or even a combination of all of them, which is possible in some destinations and venues. Always look for ways to make the experience as pleasant as possible and not just a means to an end.

Events that involve moving guests from one location to another can be a creative challenge. For example, at an event in Singapore, guests were transported from one location to another in a unique manner; they were greeted by a line of rickshaws waiting outside. Themed T-shirts on the runners designated the rickshaws that had been provided for each guest. The return trip was made by more prosaic motor coaches.

There are times when you may need to be inventive with parking and transportation. Where else can you park in the area? Are there nearby shopping malls or other places with larger parking facilities that you can rent? Shuttles to ferry your guests to and fro will solve all parking problems. You can make them fun—double-decker buses, school buses or, in some places, chartered ferry or yachts. In Key West, you can use open-air "conch" trains to transport guests from one place to another during "progressive" dinners, where you have cocktails at one location, dinner at another, and finally a lively nightspot. But always let your guests know what to expect in advance. Make sure that they receive detailed instructions with their invitations.

Event transportation can include air—private jets, private air charter, commercial airplanes, helicopter, hot air balloons; land—limousines, private cars (road rally), motor coaches, private trains; and water—private boat charters, private barges.

Private boat charters and barges can be used to transport guests to a private venue, such as a waterfront restaurant with a landing dock, In San Antonio, Texas, you can rent private barges—with entertainment—to take guests from their hotel to a riverfront site for an exclusive event (as opposed to the yacht being the actual event, as in a whale-watching dinner cruise).

Care and consideration should always be given to the mode of transportation, as well as to how many times you are physically moving your participants and when. For example, if you have guests arriving from a long flight, transferring to their hotel via limousine or motor coach, they may not be anxious to step into another vehicle the same evening to be transferred to the site of their arrival dinner. That would be too much movement in one day. A better option would be to have a casual welcome event at the hotel and allow guests the option of retiring early so they can wake up refreshed and ready to partake in their program in a relaxed frame of mind. You can save those dollars to put them into the next night's dinner and have that become their official welcome celebration. If that's not an option, a more soothing option than being stuck back in traffic just to be transported again in a motor vehicle would be to look at alternative modes of moving your attendees to their event. One event planner did this by chartering a yacht to transport guests directly from their waterfront hotel to an exclusively reserved restaurant that their yacht could pull right up to. They timed the yacht transfer to sunset and turned it into a sunset cocktail reception, and it was a pleasant and pleasing beginning to their program. Motor coaches were used for the return transfers but at that point, guests were relaxed and ready to just return to their guestrooms and retire for the night.

Transportation requirements can also play an important part in choosing the best site in which to hold your event if it is being held locally and your guests will be making their own way there. It is important to look at where it make the most logistical sense to hold your event. For instance, If you are hosting a client appreciation event and your clients are located in the suburbs, does your choice of venue warrant bringing them downtown? Will all of your guests be arriving by car? When considering a location, in addition to parking, you also need to look at ways your participants will get there. Is public transportation available? How accessible is it, and how late does it run? You may need to change your schedule of events to coincide with transportation schedules. For example, if one of your objectives is to address your guests after dinner, and the last commuter train departs at 9 p.m., how many guests will leave immediately after dinner to catch that train?

Whatever the mode of transportation used, it's important to view the transfer as an event inclusion, give the same care and detail to guest enjoyment of the transfer as you would to the actual event and capture all applicable costs in your budget. Just as there can be hidden costs in accommodation, there can be in transportation as well. You could be hit with "barn to barn" charges, which is the cost of getting your transportation from where it is housed to your pickup location and back to their housing location, and this can apply to a limousine, a motor coach, a boat or even a moving van (for storage). Or, you could incur minimum rental charges, e.g., minimum four-hour rental as well as charges for gas, insurance, detailing, staffing and more.

By Air

Many corporations hold their company incentives or company events at destinations out of state and out of country. It is critical that getting to the location be perceived by the winning participants or attendees as a pleasurable part of the event, not an endurance test in stress.

Destinations for incentive programs, meetings, conferences and other events have come under close scrutiny by participants since the occurrence of 9/11, SARS, Hurricane Katrina, the tsunamis, the war in Iraq and news of violent outbreaks, murders and kidnappings in certain cities and countries. Corporate clients are choosing their destinations and which events they will take part in with more care and concern. They are considering what they can expect in emergency situations—how prepared the infrastructure is in handling disasters, both natural and man-made—and how difficult will it be to get home to loved ones in the event of a major catastrophe, and deciding whether or not a destination will pose or be perceived by their attendees as a great safety and security risk and therefore limit attendance. With the added passenger safety and security demands at airports now in effect, many participants no longer view flying off to an exotic locale an adventure but rather an endurance race to get through.

Event planners are now looking for ways to ease travel stress and build more creative air travel elements into their program and into their budgets. Airports in Europe and Asia are starting to cater to their passengers' rising new needs to de-stress pre-boarding—whether checking in or transiting—that have come about as a direct result of travelers anticipating or having previously experienced trying times and lengthy delays checking in due to heightened security demands. Their response has been to add elements of relaxation to their environment to make the experience as pleasurable as possible. Airports around the world can now be found with entertaining features such as spas, beauty salons, massage centers, gyms, swimming pools, rooms rented by the hour (perfect to shower and freshen up in), movie theaters, casinos and upscale shopping. One airport even runs a nearby golf course to help their passengers unwind.

Savvy planners know that their client's participants' trip starts the moment they leave their home—not at the arrival at their selected destination—and that the more they can do to make their group's check-in, in-transit and arrival experience pleasurable, the better their client is deemed to be taking care of those taking part on their trip. Whether the trip is business (meetings) or a combination of business and pleasure (incentives), such handling often leads directly back to repeat business and referrals.

Advance seat selection and Web check-in are two ways event planners are working with airlines to reduce the time that their group has to stand in line. Each airline has its own procedures. At the time of group airfare negotiation—not post-contract—find out what can be done to ease the way at check-in for the group. With some airlines, it has been possible to have someone check in the entire group and print boarding passes in advance, with copies of passports obtained and distributed to the lead travel director, along with the number of bags each individual intends to check.

To ensure smooth, stress-free security checks, planners are now making sure that participants are receiving detailed information in their pre-trip material, such as itinerary booklets. Attendees need to be informed of:

» What is allowed in carry-on
» What is not allowed in carry-on
» What is allowed in checked baggage
» Maximum weight restrictions for baggage
» Additional baggage charges
» Proper airport etiquette when interacting with airport staff and airport security

» What to expect on each leg of the journey—e.g., where they will be met, what they need to be aware of upon arrival, baggage claim procedures (whether they will be required to present their claim checks)—so there are no surprises

Airline VIP lounge passes can be negotiated or purchased for a group and are another stress-reducing option event planners can investigate. Planners should always try to negotiate VIP passes as part of a group concession. And access to VIP lounges does not have to be limited to departures. Remember to research what can be done en route as well as in transit to airports. In certain cities, you can pre-purchase access to VIP lounges for a fee.

A new service, one that offers your clients' participants the utmost in care and convenience and that can be added easily to the group's budget as a program enhancement consideration (depending on the destination and country travel regulations), is arranging to have their luggage picked up from their home or office, shipped directly to their hotel and delivered to their guestroom upon check-in. There is a new industry of luggage shipping companies that has sprung up to meet this demand in addition to major courier companies who may offer this service as well. The luggage and sports equipment would still be required to be packed as it would be for standard airline check-in. For luggage traveling internationally, the luggage shipping companies collect information about the clients' trip and the contents of their suitcase. Using this information, the luggage shipping companies prepare the necessary customs documentation on a country-specific basis and then oversee the customs clearance process on behalf of the client. They work closely with many leading hotels and resorts around the world. Each property has their own procedure for receiving forwarded luggage, and the luggage shipping company works directly with the hotel staff in the necessary manner to ensure that luggage that is received before a client checks in is held in a secure place until being delivered directly to their guestroom. Similar for shipments from a hotel, the luggage shipping company works with the concierge and bellman to coordinate the collection of the bag(s) for the return trip. Luggage Forward (www.luggageforward.com) is one of the leading luggage shipping companies, shipping luggage to more than 200 countries around the world. They have an exclusive agreement with Starwood's Luxury Collection and W Hotels.

Stress-reducing benefits to the traveler include:

» Not having to transport their luggage to and from the airport.
» Being able to bypass long check-in lines by going directly to the departure gate.
» Attendees not being subject to airport excess baggage charges, which can in some cases be hundreds of dollars.
» Having their luggage handled by a company that specializes in transporting luggage not people, which is the airline's priority.
» No waiting for their luggage at baggage claims.
» Having their luggage waiting for them in their destination location when they arrive.
» For groups, special rates negotiated, with group discounts based on the number of bookings and service level used.

If your client has the budget, consider the possible return—motivational impact and desire payback—of having them charter their own private aircraft (company policy permitting *x* number of employees to travel on the same flights) and fly their participants as part of a select group aboard a luxury airline, complete with pampering and pleasure-filled touches guaranteed to reduce flight stress. Private charter options are a growing business trend for meetings and incentives and can be presented as a program enhancement cost consideration and return on investment comparison option (to scheduled air).

Of course, if money is not a concern, some airlines, such as Singapore Airlines—who are known for their exceptional service—are now offering personal luxury suites on their A 380 aircraft that feature a private bedroom, office, and cinema and dining area, which could be a once-in-a-lifetime experience for top incentive winners and their partners that would create motivational desire.

By Land

Land transfers can be formal, fun or innovative. There are many enjoyable things you can do to make your land transport part of the event and a memorable experience. For example, as an alternate to traditional limousine transfers to an upscale event, classic cars, convertibles or exotic luxury cars can be arranged, with their owners as designated drivers. Contact local specialty automobile clubs to see what can be arranged. Horse-drawn carriages, sleighs, rickshaws, gondolas, barges, helicopters, horses, camels, elephants, outrigger canoes, hot air balloons, jeeps and all-terrain vehicles have been used successfully around the world.

Look at how you can incorporate what is special to the region. On an incentive trip to Holland, one company was transferring their guests to an afternoon event by a motor coach that "broke down" right by a bicycle rental company so guests could bike to their final destination. The recommended dress code for the event ensured that participants were dressed appropriately to get on a bicycle and ride. Of course, the motor coach was "repaired" for those who chose not to ride the bicycles. The guests got to experience the typical mode of transportation in the region.

Make sure you have proper insurance and waivers signed for any less conventional transportation, such as biking, horseback or hot air ballooning. Always check with company lawyers to see what they require.

Remember that weather can cause more than flight delays when you are considering your transportation timing and logistics. Roads can be closed during severe storms in certain destinations, and this can affect transfers, as can roads under repair and construction. Find out in advance what can be done should any of these elements occur during the time your event will take place. For example, if roads become closed down due to weather when airport pickup has been scheduled are there airport hotels? Depending on the length of the transfer, are there other hotels en route should the roads become impassable? Are you prepared to pick up the cost for each member of the party should something unforeseen take place, e.g., weather, vehicle breakdown, etc?

Limousines

Make sure the limousine fits the occasion and the client. Some people are uncomfortable stepping into a limousine that seems as long as a city block; others revel in it. Know your client and their needs.

If you are hiring a number of limousines, think about visual presentation. Do you want a row of gleaming white stretch limos pulling up one after another, or does it matter? It may be more important to have all of them similar in style rather than color.

Think protocol. In some countries, it is essential that the president's limousine reflect his exalted status. The same is often true in companies. It may not be acceptable to have two limousines of similar quality. Handle this matter discreetly by checking with the president's personal assistant. Do not put your client in an awkward position by asking him or her directly. He or she may not be comfortable telling you that they would prefer a super-stretch limousine with all the amenities just for themselves. Others may prefer a less showy arrival and something a little more subdued. You can offer gentle guidance. For example, it would not be appropriate at a fund-raiser for the committee members to arrive in extravagant rental limousines unless they are personally paying for them or the limousines have been donated, a detail that should be displayed prominently in the program. Limousines could lead guests to wonder how the money being raised is spent. The same would apply if a company has recently undergone major downsizing.

What extras should be included in the limo? Should you include favorite beverages, snacks, magazines or newspapers?

Be attentive to detail. Although the beverages can be alcoholic, they do not necessarily have to be. Having fresh Florida orange juice on ice when in that state is always a nice touch; in fact, including local specialties is always a good idea. Look for what is produced in the area. Are there any items they are known as or considered to be regional favorites? New Zealand has a wonderful bottled water (Fiji Water), the Caribbean offers an array of tropical fruit beverages and in Hawaii, fresh pineapple juice would be a natural choice. The same applies to snacks as well. Do something that has a little flair.

Find out the configuration of the limousine. How many will it comfortably hold? How are the seats positioned? Some limousines have seats that pull down to provide additional seating, and while this may be acceptable for a short distance, it will not be desirable for long drives. Is there another layout that will work better? Depending on your numbers and your budget, you may want to look at the cost of renting two smaller limos rather than one large one and make sure that everyone enjoys a comfortable ride. If the limousine is rented for a gala event, will the seating allow for a graceful exit from the car? This is especially important if media will be present.

What happens if the limousine breaks down? Does the company have backup? Always book with an operation that has more than one car, and find out how quickly they can respond to an emergency situation.

If limousines are to be a part of your event, you have to know how many you will need to supply and which VIP guests will be coming with their own limousines. You will need to know all this so that you can arrange for parking permits, parking spaces or a holding area for them. This would apply whether your limousine transfer is being used to pick up attendees at the airport to take them to their hotel and the same on the return, being used to transfer them to a function at a specific location or being used as part of an activity, e.g., a limousine road rally.

At an informal gala that may have guests arriving in their own limousines, drivers may simply park on nearby side streets and wait until the guests call for the car to be brought around. However, if limousines are being used for a formal group event or a private function where you have major celebrities and VIPs attending who are providing their own transportation, you may be required to secure reserved parking for their limousines as well as your own fleet of limousines to ensure all flows smoothly.

When contracting limousines for your event, you will need to know the number of limousines your participants will be arriving in and whether they are regular sedans, stretches or super-stretch limos so that you can secure the proper space. Remember when blocking your limousines that the capacity of the limousines does not determine the number of arriving guests, since a super-stretch limo may have just one or two in it while you can have half a dozen in a regular sedan. You also need to make sure to factor in additional time to drop off and pick up people if more limos are being used. It depends on the effect the company is trying to achieve. For an incentive program, one company opted to have one stretch limo, filled with pampering touches, per couple, as opposed to having them share their limo to cut costs. If limousines will be a major consideration at your event, you need to take this into account during your site inspections before you finalize the venue. Where can the limos be parked? Will street permits be required? How many limousines can be accommodated?

The caliber of limousines and drivers varies from company to company. Ask for referrals. Where possible, go and look at the company's operations, and compare the quality and condition of the cars. See how the drivers are dressed and how attentive they are. If you want a particularly good limousine driver, find out his or her name and ask for them each time you book. As you begin to develop a long-term working relationship you'll know what to expect and how your clients will be looked after.

The limousine should arrive spotless, fully gassed and 15 minutes early. Obtain each driver's cell phone number and keep it handy on the night of your event.

When booking your required number of limousines, you need to determine how tight each limousine schedule is. You need to find out whether or not each limousine is being booked to be somewhere else just before your pickup time. Contractually you need to know what happens if delays due to air or ground traffic, immigration processing or missing baggage throw off your scheduled arrival time and complicate the pickup for limousines being used in airport arrival transfers. You need to know if the limousine you are reserving has to be somewhere else immediately after your airport pickup or pickup and transfer to your event. You need to determine a course of action if there is a possibility your event could go on longer than planned, and decide whether or not you need to budget for buffer time at the beginning or end of your event.

Compare the cost to have the limousine be at your disposal for the entire evening as opposed to booking it strictly for pickup and drop-off, with the limousine going on to other calls during your event, and running the risk of delays should the transfer they are doing before yours run into overtime.

Remember that if you do not have the driver and car booked for the entire evening, you will not be able to leave anything behind in the car. And if you are booking two one-way limousine transfers, you need to find out if the return trip will be made by the same driver and car. If not, the new driver will probably not be familiar with the exact location where you were dropped off, and neither of you will know what the other looks like. In a large gala event with a number of guests exiting at the same time to waiting limos, having the same driver and car for both drop-off and pickup is strongly recommended.

If you are having guests met at the airport, provide the limousine driver with appropriate signs—showing the name of the event and *not* the guest. Some guests, especially celebrities, will not want their names held up on display. You want their arrival to be handled quietly, quickly and with finesse. If they prefer publicity, that is a different matter—make sure that you respect their preferences.

Motor Coaches

Motor coaches come in many shapes and sizes. You can rent anything from a standard bus to a motor coach with a custom interior complete with sofas, entertainment centers and no company logo painted on the side—those often used at weddings.

The first step is to decide what your needs are. On a long transfer, you may want to make sure that the motor coach is equipped with a TV and DVD. The transfer time can then be used to view a corporate message, to watch a motivational speaker or to simply enjoy a movie to help the time pass more quickly.

Companies doing a team event may want to keep the preassigned teams together on the transfer, allowing them to spend quality time with one another, the purpose of the teams in the first place. This could mean having to hire additional motor coaches, since keeping the teams intact may mean that each vehicle is not filled to capacity.

Figure out the total number of people you will be transferring. Will some guests be making their own way to the site rather than taking the motor coach? Will that be an option?

Consider the length of time your guests will be in transit. Double-decker buses, school buses, streetcars and trolley cars can all be privately rented should you be looking for a less traditional means of transportation. A classic motor coach would provide more comfort than a school bus for long transfers, whereas a double-decker bus or school bus could be a fun way to shuttle guests from the parking area to the venue.

Always check to see where motor coach parking is located, how many coaches can be accommodated and how much parking costs, and be sure to include that amount in your budget. Check to see if there are any obstacles, such as ceiling height, to contend with. Can the bus drop guests directly at the front door or will they need to use the side entrance because the bus cannot fit under the front overhang? Motor coaches should arrive at your event spotlessly clean and fully gassed at least a half hour before the event to allow one of your staff to do a walk through to make sure everything is in order.

When renting vehicles, find out what is included in the cost. In some areas a "barn to barn" cost needs to be factored into your budget. As mentioned earlier, barn-to-barn charges mean that you are billed for the motor coaches from the moment they leave their garages, not from when they arrive at your pickup point, until they return to the garages, and this can apply to all modes of transportation.

You need to be very clear if you want the buses to remain at your disposal for a certain number of hours or if you simply want two one-way transfers. As with limousines, find out where the buses will be before and after your event. If you are concerned about tight schedules or time buffers, you will need to add in additional hours especially if there is the possibility that your event could extend past the expected departure time.

Motor coaches do break down. How quickly can the company send a replacement if this happens? Always have a backup plan. Once, during a conference on an airport return shuttle, the last returning bus broke down. It was better to send the remaining guests on to the airport by taxi than to chance missed connections while waiting for a replacement bus to arrive. In case such situations arise, it is best to carry either plenty of cash, a credit card or taxi vouchers. It is also a good idea to have an agreement with the hotel or facility to have taxi charges billed to the master account. Get the bus dispatchers' phone number or the bus drivers' cell phone numbers, and make sure they know how to reach you in case of an emergency or delays.

Where are the motor coaches coming from? On an incentive program to Ocho Rios, Jamaica, the return airport transfers were scheduled for very early in the morning. Since the buses were coming from Montego Bay, which was two and a half hours away depending on traffic conditions, it was decided to bring in the buses the night before. The drivers were given a room for the night and breakfast the next morning at the hotel. The additional cost was minimal, but the peace of mind was invaluable. No one had to worry that the motor coaches might be delayed by early morning rush-hour traffic. It allowed time to leisurely load up the luggage and stock the motor coaches with refreshments.

Self-Drive—Parking

If your guests are responsible for their own transportation, parking—both its accessibility and its availability—will play a part in the success of your event, which, when you think of it, actually begins and ends in the parking lot. Who doesn't have a parking horror story to tell? Don't let your guests arrive to find a parking lot full because of construction or a major sporting event. Don't leave them circulating the lot getting more and more frustrated. The last thing you want is your guests arriving at (or departing from) your event frazzled and frustrated. With research and planning this can be avoided.

What time does the parking lot close, and why is this important to know? Say a parking lot closes just after midnight. There is a sign to that effect, but it is so small that most people miss it. Nevertheless, the gate is closed, and cars are locked in. To add insult to injury, guests have to pay overnight parking charges in addition to the normal parking charges. Put this together with the expense and inconvenience of finding alternative transportation home and then back the next morning, and you can expect some unhappy campers. That is not how you want your guests' evening to end. But there is a solution. You can arrange to have the lot's hours extended for an additional cost, which would need to be factored into your budget.

Some events are multitiered and held at two or more locations. For, say, a product launch or a private film screening, often the first part of the evening takes place in a theater with the reception following elsewhere. If transportation is not being provided, and guests are to make their own way to the reception, you need to keep in mind that they will all be departing the theater and arriving at the second location at the same time, which can lead to a congestion problem. Remember that hotels reserve the majority of the parking for their own overnight guests, which could limit the space available for your guests. Find out what other options are available. For example, one hotel that is often used for special events has limited parking and, although there is additional parking nearby, the hotel does not have a sign out front announcing that its parking is full and directing patrons to the other lot. This leads to massive confusion and frustration, which is complicated by local traffic patterns, such as one-way streets and left-hand turns. By having an off-duty police officer directing traffic and uniformed hotel staff guiding guests to the alternate parking, the wrinkles could be smoothed out, making everyone happy.

If it is at all possible, leave the cars parked in the original parking lot, and set up a shuttle between the theater and the second venue. This way, guests are inconvenienced as little as possible—they don't have to park and pay twice. Remember the extra costs to factor in, such as the police officer to direct traffic, and street parking permits for the motor coaches or limousines.

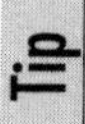

Always have your street permits with you on the day of the event, and keep a copy in your files.

Transportation Q&A

When and where will provided transportation be required for each event element?

Take the time to look at all your event transportation requirements so that you can look at where, when and how you can mix up the modes of conveying your event guests from one location to another to make their transfer part of the event experience as opposed to merely a means of getting from A to B.

Q & A

What are my various transfer options?

Look at conventional, convenience modes of transportation and consider all your creative transfer options as well. There is a time and place for each. For example, sunrise horseback ride (with jeep transfer for non riders) for a desert cookout breakfast could be a fun experience, but the return transfer could be via jeeps for a more comfortable and relaxing return. The same applies to a riverboat transfer for an evening event in San Antonio with a motor coach return after guests have spent the evening drinking and boarding the riverboats safely could be a concern.

What are my route choices?

There is a time to choose the scenic route and a time to select the fastest route possible. For example, the scenic route can become part of the event, e.g., providing a slice of island life to a group arriving in a tropical location on their way to their resort while taking the highway on the return journey back to their hotel after a group night out when guests are anxious to get back to their guestroom would be a better choice.

How can I enhance the transfer experience?

Look at transportation enhancements (cool cloths, food, beverages, entertainment, etc.) that will elevate the journey and help to set the mood and build anticipation for the upcoming event. For airport transfers, consider all that can be done to lessen stress, reduce time spent in lineups, etc.

For each transfer what needs to be done to ease individual and group arrival and departure?

It is important to look at how your guests will be arriving at the point for transfer, what they could be facing, e.g., parking, line-ups, overnight airport stays, etc., and determine how best you can reduce their stress, lessen confusion and make their departure from the transfer point as seamless and as easy as possible. For

Q & A

example, for group departures from a hotel for an evening event, weigh the options of having the guests meet in a crowded lobby for a front-door departure against a quieter, more contained side-door entrance.

Where will most of your guests be coming from?

You must consider where the majority of your guests will be coming from, and what could affect their arrival time. If you're having an evening function, guests may be coming from work, or fighting rush-hour traffic, and fighting rush-hour traffic applies to out-of-town events, as well and to transfer timing and logistics. This must be factored into the start time of your event. If participants will be making their own way to the facility, consider the cost of parking and compare that to the cost of renting vehicles. Does it make more sense to have your guests leave their cars and be transported as a group? Remember, many motor coaches have facilities that allow you to show a company message or entertainment video. Transferring guests as a group works well for employee appreciation events as well.

No matter what type of event you are holding, you will have to consider where the motor coaches or limousines will park, whether you will need street permits and what other charges will apply. For example, if you were looking at taking your employees to a sporting event such as a car race, will your buses need any parking passes or permits to obtain a designated parking spot at the facility?

Q & A

What is the estimated number of cars or arriving vehicles (limousines and other forms of transportation)? Will guests arrive as couples or individuals?

For local events, if your event is for couples and on a weeknight, anticipate two separate arrival times and twice as many cars to park because both individuals are likely coming from separate locations. If you are including vouchers for complimentary parking, take this into consideration when you are arranging the printing

Q & A

of the vouchers. This will also affect the number of staff required if you are including valet parking. Base your budget costs on the maximum number of cars.

For group arrivals—which can still be done as individuals and couples, as well as group—at out-of-town events you still need to assess the number of cars, limousines, motor coaches or other modes of transportation that will be required.

Q & A

Will factors other than rush-hour traffic have an impact when considering start time?

In addition to standard rush-hour traffic, another factor that can hold people up is other major events that are taking place at the same time. This can include a variety of things such as concerts, sporting events, road repairs, street festivals, movies being filmed, local parades, fund-raising runs and marches, protests and weather. Remember to conduct proper research and take all these into consideration.

Q & A

Where is the closest parking?

Physically check out the available parking. How far is it from the venue where you are considering holding your event? Is there an attendant? Will your guests be required to bring change for parking? How many parking spots are available? Are there any under construction or not able to be used in any way?

A trade show at a local convention center ran into problems when it was discovered that most of the parking spaces were under construction and that there wasn't access from the garage to the convention center from all floors. Exhibitors with bulky items had a particularly difficult time getting through. They had not been advised about the problem with parking and the difficulty in getting to the elevators. Had they known in advance, they could have arranged to have the material delivered directly to their booths.

Q&A

Who does the parking lot belong to? Is it owned by the venue or is it public parking? How secure is it?

Find out who owns the parking lot and how safe it is. Have they had any problems with break-ins or thefts? Is it well lit? Do they have security, or is the lot left unattended? Are there any special concerns with regard to parking and security? For example, if you are doing a car launch it is sometimes necessary to store the cars in a designated area where they can be prepped and detailed before bringing them into the display area. It is important that the cars be secure and that they be away from public view. You can make arrangements for special security for the cars while they are in most hotel parking lots, but it is essential to know if the facility has had any problems such as theft or vandalism. In extreme temperatures in Las Vegas, cars have been known to explode due to intense heat building up inside. The secret is to dissipate the heat by leaving a window open a crack, something that would be rather important to know in advance.

Q&A

What time does the parking lot open and close?

You need to know this in advance. If you have access to the venue at 5 a.m. to start setting decor, staging and lighting, you need to know that the parking lot will be open to accommodate your suppliers. You may need to make special arrangements to have it opened early. You need to speak directly with the owners of the parking lot and make any necessary arrangements directly with them. The same applies to closing time. It usually costs only a minimal amount to extend parking hours. A main objective of any event is to bring people together, and you want to make sure that they can relax, mingle and engage in conversation without worrying about their car being locked in overnight. Even worse would be guests not realizing that the parking lot closes early and ending up carless at the end of their evening. If you are not extending the parking hours at the very least make sure that parking attendants inform arriving guests about the early closing.

One high-powered event was filled with very influential guests. There was an abundance of food and drink, and budget was not a concern, but one detail had been overlooked—extending the parking lot hours because it was scheduled to close early. The company's presentation had started quite late, leaving guests with only a limited amount of time to enjoy the lavish display and have conversations with other guests. People dashing off to rescue their cars put quite a damper on the whole evening.

Q & A

What is the capacity of the parking lot?

When you speak with the parking authorities be specific regarding the day and the time of your event. Find out the capacity, the general availability at that day and time and how many spaces are reserved for monthly pass holders. If you are holding your event at a hotel you need to take into consideration that a majority of space could be utilized by hotel guests.

Q & A

Who uses the parking lot?

If it is the prime parking area for major sporting events, for example, that could limit access for your guests, and your guests could be left circling the block looking for parking, which would not only delay their arrival at your event but also leave them in a less than festive mood. For one client appreciation evening where timing was critical—the client had chosen to do a reception and sit-down dinner before the opening of a new theatrical show in the downtown core—guests who were driving into the city were advised in advance and then reminded personally the day before the event that a ball game would be going on as well and that traffic could be heavier than usual and parking limited.

Q&A

What is the cost for parking?

If you are competing with a special event, keep in mind that in addition to parking being limited, parking costs are usually increased for the night. If you are picking up the cost of parking for your guests, you need to factor those increases into your budget.

Q&A

Can a block of space be sectioned off for the attending guests?

Check to see if this can be made available for your guests. You will probably be required to prepay or, in the case of hotel parking, have it billed to the master account, for the number of designated spots that you wish reserved. You may need to add in the cost of additional parking staff to monitor this and direct your guests to the designated parking area.

Q&A

Can parking be prepaid?

If you are doing a special event at a hotel, generally the cost for parking can be added to the total bill if you are picking up the cost of parking for your guests. The hotel may also have agreements with nearby parking facilities. Most other parking facilities are also open to prepaid parking or having their lots exclusively taken over for the evening.

You can also look to prepaying parking spaces in order to set up a prominent display in the parking area. For example, a company launching a new product might wish to set up a dazzling display in the parking lot to greet its guests and to introduce the product to the public.

Q&A

How will prepaid parking be designated?

Custom parking vouchers can be included with the invitations. This way, the vouchers can be handed in, providing you with an accurate count for payment. These can be professionally printed with theme logos or simply done up on a personal computer.

Q & A

Are there special rates that can be negotiated for attending guests if the parking is not prepaid?

This is another area that you can negotiate prior to contracting your event. Arrangements can be made to have special rates for your guests. Guests showing their invitation could receive a flat rate as opposed to the standard hourly charge. This could be one area that you negotiate with a hotel or at a public venue, but the amount of concession you get will depend on how much money you are spending at the facility.

Q & A

Does the facility have any complimentary parking passes for key guests or staff?

This can be negotiated in advance as well. Check to see if the facility can provide parking passes for staff and key VIPs. These should be negotiated up front, especially if you need a substantial number.

Q & A

Is the parking lot fully wheelchair accessible? If not, how many accessible spaces are available? Are there fully automatic doors or buttons to activate them?

Many parking facilities claim to be wheelchair accessible but are not. There may be ramps to the elevators, but these are not much good if doors don't open automatically or at the push of a button. Doors that open only manually could present difficulties to physically challenged guests arriving on their own.

Also important is the location and size of the parking spaces. Many converted vans require extra-wide spaces to allow wheelchairs to be lowered.

Also make sure that there are no lips or other obstacles on entrance doorways and that the doors are wide enough to allow for wheelchair access.

Q & A

How many parking lot attendants will be on duty for both arrival and departure?

Let the parking lot management know what will be happening. What could be a typically slow night for the parking lot with only minimum staffing could be the cause of major delays and lengthy lineups when 400 cars show up at the same time for your event. Inform lot managers well in advance how many cars are coming and when so that they can arrange to have adequate staff. If your guests are arriving for their evening out as people are leaving from work, make sure that there are extra people on duty to handle everyone with maximum efficiency.

Q & A

When are shift changes and breaks scheduled?

Let the parking people know your timing so that they can schedule shift changes and breaks.

If you're planning a split program where guests will be driving their own cars to a second location, make sure that parking staff have been advised. You don't want 800 guests arriving back in the parking lot at 9 p.m. to find that everyone has gone on break!

Q & A

Is there a "lot full" sign? Where is it positioned?

The location of a "lot full" sign is key. You want guests to see it before they turn in, and thereby avoid any unnecessary delays. If the parking lot does not have a sign, have one made up. Consider hiring professional staff to direct the parking and to advise you when the lot is full.

Tip

If making a "lot full" sign, ensure that the sign has been made with aircuts—cuts in the signboard or banner that allow wind to blow through it instead of knocking it over or tearing it. Have the sign frame built so that it can be weighed down with sandbags to ensure that it won't be knocked over. Make sure the sign is large enough to be seen clearly by someone sitting inside a car. You want guests to know when the lot is full so that they do not waste time turning in or circling the parking lot.

Q&A

Do you need shuttles to transfer guests from the parking lots to the venue?

Is parking within walking distance, or will you need transportation? Give thought to things such as weather and what people will be wearing. If it is a dressy affair, is the distance from the parking lot easily walkable in heels? Do your parking attendants need to advise guests that they may wish to drop off their passengers for their convenience and comfort?

One event was just beginning when a sudden, heavy rainstorm struck. Disaster loomed, but good planning prevailed. Attendants with huge umbrellas waited in central locations in the parking lots to escort guests indoors, and others waited street-side for passengers being dropped off. A lone saxophonist played in the outside covered stairwell greeting guests. The planners had taken great care with their event, and you could tell that before you even got in the door. They had thought of their guests' comfort, and it showed. The heavy rain and the music merely ended up adding to the atmosphere.

Q&A

You can make parking shuttles fun. Use horse-drawn carriages in Montreal, Niagara-on-the-Lake, Nassau, Bermuda, New York or New Orleans; Mini Mokes in Barbados; rickshaws in Singapore; outrigger canoes in Hawaii; or covered stagecoaches with drivers in western garb in Arizona. In winter, use horse-drawn covered sleighs with carolers to greet guests at the entrance (depending on weather temperatures—performing in the cold is difficult for singers). As they disembark, provide hot roasted chestnuts and hot chocolate to warm them.

Q&A

Is there an area for VIP limousines and cars to park? How many will it accommodate?

You may wish to make arrangements with the hotel for the president and other top VIPs to have their cars valet parked or parked

Q&A

immediately out front so that these individuals are not kept waiting when it is time to leave. It is a good idea to know the license plate numbers of VIP vehicles to ensure they are positioned directly out front. Most hotels are able to come to terms with this request.

For black-tie galas, where you know you will have a number of limousine arrivals, you can make special arrangements to ensure that there is parking available for your VIPs and celebrities. Obtain street parking permits and hire off-duty police officers to oversee this. The officers must have a list of key guests and their license plate numbers so that they can secure the spaces reserved for those guests.

Q&A

Who is responsible for obtaining permits?

Will you be arranging the street permits, or will the facility be getting them on your behalf? Keep several copies of the permits with you, and make sure that all key staff members, including those designated to oversee the parking, have copies.

Q&A

Where do you get these permits and what do they cost?

Check with the police in the area where the event is taking place. Procedures can vary from area to area, even within the same city, so never assume that what applies to one region applies to another. Most police divisions have someone handling special events and assigning off-duty officers. They can advise you where to go and who to contact. The cost of permits varies from location to location. Make sure that you include that cost in your budget. Street permits may be required for a variety of reasons. For instance, you will need to obtain one for any display areas or if you are including searchlights and the like.

Q&A

How much time do permits take to process? Will a site inspection be required?

Check to find out how much time will be required for the appropriate organization to process your permit. Often it is necessary to meet with officials and do a walk-through of your event with them before your permit can be processed. They will want to see exactly what you have planned—where guests will be arriving and where the transportation will be stationed. They will look at how your event could obstruct traffic; they may permit this, but usually with the provision that an off-duty police officer be responsible for directing traffic and ensuring the safety of guests. They will also advise you of which street vendors have a license to be there, as well as designated taxi areas and bus stops that may need to be re-routed.

Will parking meters need to be bagged?

If there is metered parking right out in front of the venue where preferred space for limousines would be, the meters need to be bagged to reserve them. Ask police what time works best. These spots have to be reserved before the end of rush hour even though your event may not start until much later. For example, if no parking at meters is allowed during evening rush hour from 4 p.m. to 6 p.m., you would need to have the meters bagged by 5 p.m. with a police officer on duty to oversee and enforce. To try to bag these meters after 6 p.m. would be impossible.

Will any orange cones be required to designate the area?

Orange cones are recommended because they clearly mark your designated area and are quite visible. They are very effective in keeping drivers away from your designated area and can be set out and removed just before your guests are due to arrive. Your local police department can provide names of suppliers and, although the cones are available at minimal cost, that should be included in your budget.

Do any licensed street vendors need to be informed? Will they cause any congestion? Can they be temporarily relocated? Is there a cost for doing so?

This will be one of the areas you will cover when you do your site inspection of the area. You need to know who the licensed vendors are and where they are located so that you can avoid these areas of congestion. You would need to speak with them and the authorities

Q&A

about the possibility of relocating them for the evening. Generally, street vendors are very helpful and cooperative, particularly if you are willing to compensate them for lost revenue.

Q&A

Are there any authorized taxi stands stationed right out front that could hinder the arrival of your guests? Can these be temporarily relocated? Is there a cost involved?

Again, this is another area that should be covered on your site inspection. You will need to speak to both the authorities and the head of the taxi association to see what can be negotiated for the benefit of all.

Q&A

If the media are attending, is there a location where their trucks and cables can be situated?

This is important and needs to be factored in if you want media coverage of your event. Find out their needs. What equipment will they be bringing? What time will they be setting up? How will this impact your event? You don't want your guests tripping over an assortment of cables at the entrance.

Q&A

Are additional paid off-duty police required for crowd control, traffic direction and security?

Look to see where you might need assistance. Paid off-duty police can be in uniform, which is advisable for traffic control, or dressed in suits when more subtle security is called for, such as at gala, black-tie events. You may wish to have some on horseback or in full dress uniform for added effect. Police are usually wonderful to work with and excellent on-site.

Q&A

Does the area that will be blocked off interfere with any public transportation such as bus stops and subway entrances? Can they be temporarily re-routed?

Look at where the bus stops are located. Are there any areas of congestion? Review this during your walk-through, and discuss

Q&A

options with the proper authorities. At one area where motor coach shuttles were in competition with public transportation, an off-duty police officer was all that was required to see to the safety of both the guests and those using public transportation. Visit the location at the day and time you are planning to hold your event to see exactly what you will be dealing with. If you must visit the site during the day, but your event is at night, remember that what you see during the day could change at night. Will cars and limousines be contending with extra public buses put on to handle the rush-hour crowds or for local events? How busy is the street? Be familiar with how the traffic moves at that time of day.

Q&A

Are there any concerns with traffic flow? What else is going on in the area at the same time—sporting events, theater, major concerts that could cause delays? What time would they begin and end?

Know what other events are going on around you, and know what is going on during the same time period. Know the times they start and finish and what effect this usually has on the traffic in the surrounding area.

At one venue the entrance to the subway is located inside the building. During the day this area is quite congested, with a steady stream of commuters that would present a barrier to guests arriving for an event in the venue. At night after rush hour, the place is nearly deserted unless there is another special event at the same time.

Q&A

Are there any movies being filmed in the area during your event that could cause traffic and accessibility to be obstructed?

Depending on the season and the number of movies being filmed, this is another area that can affect your event. Find out if there is any filming going on in your area. Again, check with the local

Q & A

police division. They are generally on hand overseeing this area as well. Find out if any streets have been blocked off. Will there be any trailers obstructing traffic flow? What can you do to work around this? Ask if they will be filming in your facility either directly before or directly after your event. If they run into any delays in filming, your start time for your setup could be affected.

Q & A

Can private valet parking be arranged?

Valet parking is a wonderful touch—budget permitting—for any special occasion. It adds an element of elegance and finesse to your event and takes looking after the comfort of your guests to the next level. It can be arranged at specific hotels and convention centers as well as private venues. Check with your facility to see if this is something that could be offered for consideration. You want to make sure that the company handling the valet parking is familiar with the site. Check to see who has worked on their premises before. Get references, and talk to someone who has worked with them. Were they pleased? Was service efficient? Was it professional? Check with both the event planner and the facility where the event was held. Something that could have looked fine on the surface could have had some areas that you need to be made aware of behind the scenes.

Q & A

What does valet parking cost? Is tipping included?

Find out what needs to be factored into your budget. Consider how you will handle tipping. Do you want it leave it to the guest's discretion, or have the tipping picked up by the host? If the tipping is being included, make sure that the attendants are told and that they inform the guest that the host has taken care of all gratuities.

Q & A

What ratio of attendants to cars will you need?

The number of attendants to handle a specific number of cars will vary from location to location depending on loading area, drop-off lanes, separate access, distance to parking area, length of time and other factors. You will need to schedule a site inspection

Q & A

and do a walk-through of your requirements in order to obtain an accurate cost.

Q & A

How will the attendants be dressed?

Generally, valet attendants will be dressed in black pants and white shirts, but for something fun and casual you could have them dressed in custom-themed shirts, if it is appropriate and in your budget. How they are dressed must be in keeping with the tone of the event.

Q & A

What insurance does the private valet parking company have?

Have the valet company outline in writing their insurance coverage, both automotive and general. Check with your insurance agent to see if you need additional coverage. This is extremely important. You must know what insurance the parking company has. How is their record? Do they have any claims?

Q & A

Does the valet company have an upcoming event where you can see them at work?

If you can see the valet company at work that is always advisable. But keep your distance. Be respectful of the event that is in progress. You would not want uninvited guests at your event, and you need to be mindful of that for others. Check to see how efficiently the valets are managing the cars, how they greet the guests and how long guests are kept waiting.

Tip

It is possible to take over parking lots exclusively to use them as part of test-drive programs for launches of new cars, motorcycles or bicycles. Parking lots can also be transformed into party venues with tents, carpeting, decor, staging and lighting.

Be creative when it comes to utilizing existing space. Hollywood premiere parties have been held in parking lots, and a hotel in Mexico uses theirs regularly to hold their Mexican fiesta. Budget permitting, parking lots can be totally transformed.

Q & A

What arrangements can be made for parking your shuttle buses at airport pickups and drop-offs?

For out-of-country meetings where you are having your guests met at the airport and transferred to the hotel, check with local ground handlers to see if anything can be done to ensure that your buses can be positioned as close to the airport entrance as possible for your guests' convenience.

At an airport, two major competitors were arriving at the same time. The buses for one group were lined up all in a row right outside the front doors and bore their company logo. This group felt well looked after. The second group was grumbling as they walked past the long row of their competitor's motor coaches to finally reach theirs.

Q & A

Where will staff be parking?

Is there a separate area for staff parking? Can your own staff and suppliers park there as well? If not, where can they park? While you obviously want to make sure that primary parking is reserved for your guests, you also need to give consideration to where designated staff parking will be. Remember, they will be arriving earlier and leaving much later than your guests and not necessarily as a group. Make sure that the vehicles are parked in a safe, well-lit area. Once the guests have left, your staff may want to move their cars closer to the entrance before cleanup begins. This will also make it easier if you are transporting any materials back to the cars.

Transportation Checklist

✓ *Assess all event transportation requirements*

✓ *Look at where conventional and creative transportation options are appropriate*

- ✓ *Determine the number of vehicles required per transfer*
- ✓ *Consider what can be done to elevate the transfer to becoming a part of the event experience and as comfortable, convenient and stress free as possible in order to set the event tone*
- ✓ *Choose the route—scenic or fastest—that is appropriate for the outbound and the return*
- ✓ *Know all your costs. For example, will the charges be barn-to-barn, do parking permit costs have to be factored in, etc.*
- ✓ *Decide how group departure and drop-off can be made more convenient*

5

Guest Arrival

Guest arrival sets the anticipatory tone for the event ahead. Your event does not start the moment the guests step into the venue but the moment they arrive on its doorstep or in the designated parking drop-off point. You have to plan and prepare for weather they could encounter stepping out of the vehicle, the appearance of the walkway to the venue and what they will see to tell them visually they have "arrived" at the event. Arrival can take the form of fanfare, special meet-and-greet touches that can range from simple—but still showing care and attention to detail and setting the mood—to sensational and filled with special effects. Each of the event guest arrival elements comes with timing and logistical requirements—venue, supplier and guest—and involves cost and creative thought as well. They apply to airport arrivals, hotel and resort arrivals and arrivals at an event or each event for a multitiered event program, such as an incentive or a conference.

Give some thought to creating energy in the arrival area. How do you want it to look and feel? You want to create a buildup of anticipation, not a dull, flat and listless entrance. You want your guests to feel they have arrived somewhere special, that there is excitement in the air. You can create energy by touching guests' senses in as many ways as possible. One event planning company effectively used inexpensive lighting to create movement with moving custom gobos to lead the way into the main room. (A gobo is a silhouette pattern cut from metal or glass and used to project images from a light fixture [spotlight] onto any surface—could be the wall, dance floor, ceiling or drape, and they can be static [stationary] or dynamic and move around the room). Music, entertainment and special effects are other ways you can add a feeling of expectancy that something wonderful is about to unfold.

When you hold special events in other countries or regions, take particular effort in greeting the guests as they step off the plane. Check with local tourist boards to see what can be done for minimal cost or possibly as part of the board's own promotional budget. Often they can supply a local band to greet guests as they are waiting to check through immigration. A welcome banner can be displayed and a local beverage provided.

But greeting arriving guests is not the first step—the first step takes place at the originating airport where guests are departing and includes things as discussed earlier, such as arranging for a private group check-in, having someone provide luggage carts for your guests' convenience and perhaps setting up a private room with refreshments reserved for your group if airport regulations permit it. When and where possible, it is also a good idea to arrange pre-boarding and group seating so that your guests can all sit together. This is actually a plus for the other passengers, too, as they are not being disturbed throughout the flight by people talking across one another.

On board the aircraft, there are other things that can be done. These include welcome-aboard announcements, custom-printed headrest covers, food and beverage vouchers and movie and headset vouchers. And, depending on the numbers and availability, groups can sometimes be upgraded as well. If the whole group cannot be upgraded, you may choose to decline the offer. One incentive group did a random draw to see who would be upgraded to first class, as there were only a limited number of seats available. Keep in mind that guests will need to be dressed appropriately. Many VIPs do not like to sit in first class themselves when the balance of the group is in coach. VIPs who favor first-class travel will often book on a separate airline and arrive in the destination in advance of their guests. Some items can be negotiated with the airlines prior to signing the contract or be made available at minimal cost. Perhaps it is a birthday cake presented on board to celebrate a very special sixteenth birthday or visits to the cockpit for younger children. What can and can't be done is in a constant state of change since 9/11. It is important to review individual airport and aircraft policies and procedures for each leg of your trip at time of booking your group, note them in your function sheets and review them before the group departs.

When guests arrive at the destination, it's important that they be offered a touch of local culture. It is a nice beginning to be welcomed to Hawaii with a lei, or to Jamaica or Barbados with the sounds of steel drums and with fruit punch (with or without rum) or local beers such as Red Stripe or Banks. On the shuttle have refreshments and cool towels, and at the hotel have a private group check-in set up exclusively for them. Here, packets containing keys to their rooms and the minibars, as well as general hotel information and express checkout forms, should be waiting for them. Credit card imprints to cover incidentals can be taken at this time. This arrangement ensures that they do not have to wait in line with other arriving guests.

In a hot climate, it is helpful to have ice-cold water, fresh lemonade and iced tea waiting when guests first arrive. In the Caribbean, many hotels hand out ice-cold cloths along with refreshments to arriving guests. The hotel staff can dip clean facecloths in lemon water, wring them out thoroughly and slip them into individual plastic bags to freeze before transporting them to the airport in coolers.

Hotels around the world swear that they cannot do private group check-ins, but they can and do. Be persistent. It is simply not acceptable to have travel-weary guests standing in huge lineups to check in, when they could just as simply wait in a private room with refreshments and a private check-in.

If the flight has arrived too early for their rooms to be ready (other guests have not checked out as yet), it is a simple matter to arrange for a day room so that clients can change, leave their carry-on luggage in a safe, secure area and go out to enjoy the hotel's facilities. (Their checked luggage will be handled separately by the bellstaff and be sent directly to their rooms once the rooms have been assigned.) Make sure that you arrange for a security staff member to oversee the guest day room and the guests' possessions. A hospitality desk can be set up in this room.

The event planner must do everything to make sure that the guestrooms are available as quickly as possible—request extra maid service in advance, provide the hotel with an arrival schedule well ahead of time so that the rooms can be assigned in order of flight arrival and request early check-in wherever possible. If the budget allows, you can book the rooms for the evening before your group arrives so that they are available for immediate check-in. If that is not possible, sit down with the rooms manager the night before the group arrives to see how many rooms are vacant and how many you can start to pre-assign. Don't wait to begin the next day.

Guest Arrival Q&A

Q & A

What is the arrival area like?

Visualize your guests' first impression as they arrive at the venue. What will they see, smell, hear and feel? For example, if you are doing an evening charter cruise, don't just think about the appearance of the ship—which of course is important—but take a look at the area surrounding the pier as well. Is it clean? Is there a clear path to the boat? Do guests have to step over piles of freight and other unpleasant things? Are there any unsightly messes that must be cleared away so as not to spoil your guests' first impressions? Is the area covered? What is the area like concerning safety and security? These same questions apply to any

Q & A

land location as well—be it a venue or a resort—anywhere in the world. One beautiful new resort was opened in an area that would be a fitting locale for the property many years in the future when existing run-down and abandoned buildings had been demolished and new boutique shops had moved in. As it was now, the resort had a problem with the homeless, had gated the pool and beach area and had tight security measures in place, which could raise the safety concerns of guests coming from out of town.

At the launching of a new ship, guests were put off even before they got on board. The cleanliness of the area where the boat was docked left much to be desired and, to top it all, the crew forgot the gangplank. Arriving guests had to jump from the pier to the ship, which was a little daunting for those in heels. Apprehension increased after the evening's cruise and drinks. Despite the fact that they sailed around all evening, there was still no gangplank by the time they docked—and this evening was supposed to showcase the company's newest yacht to potential clients!

Remember, the ship you inspect may not be moored at the pier from which it usually sails. Find out where it will be sailing from and check out the condition of the surrounding area. This would also apply if you were to arrange for an alternate pickup location (you would need to budget for the cost to transfer the vessel from one location to another). Take the time to check out the area and make arrangements to have it cleared of any debris before the day of your charter. Find out what, if any, restrictions could apply and what needs to be put in place in case of inclement weather.

Q & A

How do you arrive at your venue? Is there a unique or picturesque way to approach it?

Sometimes it's not just the entrance but how you arrive at your destination that can set the tone of your event. If you were staying on the west coast of Barbados, there are two ways to get to your hotel.

You can take the fast route through the center of the island, or you can take the East Coast Road, which follows the coastline and offers guests wonderful views of the beautiful blue Caribbean waters, although it does take a little longer to drive. Depending on the time your flight arrives—such as an evening arrival when the ocean is not as visible—you may choose to take the faster route to the hotel, and use the picturesque East Coast Road route when returning to the airport, allowing your guests one last look at the island before they depart. If you are arriving early in the day, do the reverse. Or take the East Coast Road both ways if you are not in a hurry.

In some areas of the world, such as Holland, you can even choose to arrive at your hotel by boat instead of by bus. You may need to use buses to take the guests to the canals or a central spot first, but this will provide them with a relaxing introduction to the city. International flights arriving in Holland (as well as many other overseas destinations) may arrive too early for the standard hotel check-in time of 3 p.m. Including a canal tour as part of their transfer allows guests to adjust to the time difference, enjoy local specialties—coffee and pastries—and have their first view of their destination at a leisurely pace. Make every step of your event as enjoyable and as visually memorable as possible. You could do something similar in London and Windsor as well. Of course, budget permitting, you could pay for an additional night at the hotel and have the rooms available for immediate occupancy, or negotiate early check-in for your guests depending on the season. It is not a good idea to put guests on a bus tour as soon as they step off the plane. They will be tired from the trip and because of the time difference they will not fully take in everything. Also, coming directly off the plane, they may not be dressed for a tour. But being on the water is always soothing and relaxing.

Q&A

Is there a convenient drop-off point at the venue?

Take the time during your site inspection to review the main doors your guests or your suppliers will be using to enter your venue. Whether it's suppliers dropping off materials, guests choosing to

Q & A

drop off their passengers at the front door for a gala event, or motor coaches or limousines off-loading guests and luggage, the convenience of the drop-off point is important. You want to make sure that access into the area where you are holding your event is easy and suitable for everyone's particular needs.

If your guests are dropping their passengers off at the front door because of inclement weather, and they are exiting into busy rush-hour traffic, they are going to need to proceed with caution as they open their doors. You may want to consider having someone to control traffic.

If it is volunteers dropping items off for a silent auction at a convention center where there are no doormen, bellboys or staff on hand to assist with the off-loading and transfer of items to the display area, you need to make sure that there are enough hands on deck to assist them.

If you are transferring a group by bus, you need to know whether or not the vehicle can come right up to the main doors or if its height prevents it from doing so. There is one hotel in Arizona where the motor coach will not fit under the roof and the passengers and luggage are generally off-loaded at the side door. It's a bit of a disappointment, especially given the impressive panorama of the hotel lobby seen when entering through the main doors. One solution is to have the guests disembark and walk through the spectacular main doors. The bus would then pull around to the side door and off-load the luggage. On the return trip to the airport guests can board the motor coaches at the side door so they can identify their luggage. After all, they'd have already been wowed by the entrance on arrival.

Q & A

Is the entrance covered?

Find out whether or not the entrance is covered at the time of year you will be holding your event. Consider whether or not you will need to have umbrellas ready in bad weather for those guests who are being picked up or dropped off. No matter what the location, you have to figure out how to get your guests from A to B without getting wet.

In the middle of an unexpected torrential tropical downpour, arriving guests were met at the airport with souvenir umbrellas, theirs to keep. They were going on a luxury cruise, and the walkway between the bus and the gangplank was not covered. The cost of the umbrellas was minimal, but it demonstrated the event planner's commitment to the comfort and care of each participant. Everyone arrived on board the ship happy and dry—a wonderful beginning to their week.

Q & A

There is one resort in the Caribbean that had wonderful, huge, logoed umbrellas that were part of the gifts for arriving guests. The umbrellas were tastefully done, well-made and useful. They were the perfect gift because the walkways from the villas to the main restaurants were not covered and therefore guests could get drenched if it rained. They also served as great promotional items long after the vacation.

If you are doing a program in the Caribbean, make sure that the hotel or your program directors have access to several of the larger varieties of umbrellas in case they are needed to help escort guests from one uncovered area to another. Don't wait until it starts to rain to go in search of them. Downpours in the Caribbean can be very sudden and very heavy at times. The rainy season traditionally takes place in, but is not limited to, the summer months.

Disney World has great, bright-yellow rain ponchos in all its stores. Whenever it rains, the park is quickly transformed in a sea of bright yellow, with thousands upon thousands of Mickeys staring at you from the backs of the ponchos. They keep you absolutely dry and your hands are left free to hold onto little hands, cameras or bags. They fold up to nothing.

If you are doing an event at a destination where your guests will be out and about walking and exploring, consider doing something similar, with a custom company logo in place of Mickey. The ponchos are inexpensive, easy to pack and because of this utility are great advertising pieces. They can be handed out as weather backup at guest arrival for outdoor fun events such as a group visit to an outdoor theme park.

Q & A

Who will be available throughout the event to ensure walkways are kept clear of snow, ice and slush in winter, or of slippery rain puddles and mud in summer?

You want to make sure that the walkway and the entranceway are kept clear of hazards. If you are doing an event in winter, one of the areas you need to review is who will be responsible for shoveling the walkways, keeping them salted and cleaning up snow brought in on people's boots at the front entrance. Does the venue have all necessary supplies on hand? Make sure that they don't wait for the day of the event to be out searching for bags of salt or additional snow shovels. Also, find out who maintains the parking area and when you can expect it to be cleared.

A front entrance of pure marble or other tile can be extremely slippery when wet. If non-slip carpeting needs to be laid down in front, make sure that it is anchored firmly in place. Depending on weather conditions, you could require more than one carpet; you may need to have it replaced if it becomes too wet. Do you have insurance coverage in case anyone slips, falls and injures themselves? Don't depend on the venue to have sufficient coverage—get your own insurance. Remember Murphy's Law? At one fund-raising social, not only were there both ice and snow to deal with but also a broken water pipe next door that flooded the street with water, quickly turning it icy.

Tip

If budget permits, custom table runners could be a weather option or added decor option. The Original Runner Co. (www.originalrunners.com) designs custom runners for weddings and other events. After the event, the runners—which could have the company logo or theme on them—can be made into throw pillows or framed as event or wedding mementos.

Not all events are black-tie galas with ball gowns and tuxedos. What if your meeting takes place somewhere more rural—for example, a visit to a plantation in the Caribbean where guests are taken out into fields to see something that is relevant to the work they do?

One particular incentive program included an agricultural farm conference that was taking place in the actual fields. Guests had been advised to bring tall rubber boots with them. What do you do with a busload of delegates wearing muddy knee-high boots back at the hotel? The planner's solution was to greet them at the hotel entrance with inexpensive slip-on terry slippers (you could also provide custom-logoed spa-style slippers, depending on available dollars), and have staff on hand to handle, remove, clean and return the boots to the guestrooms. That way delegates did not have to worry about trekking mud through the hotel and into their rooms.

Q & A

Which services are supplied and which cost extra?

Find out what is available and what needs to be brought in. In some five-star hotels, shoe cleaning is part of the service they offer. Ask what is provided at no additional charge and what needs to be factored into your budget. In a case such as the one above, there could be extra dollars involved to bring in additional staff to handle that number of muddy boots upon the guests' arrival back at the hotel. Remember when negotiating costs for something of this nature that it is in the hotel's best interest to not have to clean up behind the guests' muddy boots.

Q & A

Is the entrance fully wheelchair accessible?

Find out if the main entrance is fully wheelchair accessible; if it is not, find one that is. The next question is, which public rooms and facilities are wheelchair accessible? Be familiar with their location. Make sure there is sufficient room to easily maneuver in. Some hotels have whole rooms adapted for guests in wheelchairs. Be sure to request this when making your booking.

At one hotel, the front entrance is not wheelchair accessible, but there is one entrance nearby that is, and it is located right next to the elevators. Knowing that in advance prevents the added inconvenience of going to one area, only to be redirected to another.

Q&A

An important consideration is the width of the door. Can the wheelchair be easily accommodated? Find out the required width in advance—not all wheelchairs are the same width. Some models have wheels that can be popped off in cases of extreme necessity.

In addition to accessible rooms, guests in wheelchairs may want someone nearby in a connecting room if they require assistance. Ask in advance if this is possible.

Q&A

Are doormen provided?

Whenever and wherever possible, have the venue's professional security staff or, if they are not available, paid off-duty police staffing your doors. Do not rely on corporate staff or volunteers if the event is nonprofit. As guests are arriving it is too easy for the corporate staff or volunteers to be called away, and you really need to have someone stationed permanently at the entrance, with specific people designated to relieve them during breaks. Professional staff are trained to handle difficult situations. If at all possible, it is always good to have them equipped with walkie-talkies in case of an emergency.

At one event, the singer engaged for the evening had invited some local couples—who were considering hiring her to sing at their wedding—to drop in and to see her perform. Unfortunately, it was a private event; they were not on the guest list and they were inappropriately dressed. The couples were very unhappy and very vocal about not being let into the event. The situation was handled swiftly and with discretion. Assistance was called for and the couples were escorted away from the main doors.

Q&A

In the downtown core, it is not unusual to see, at the front doors of a restaurant—even very upscale ones—homeless people appear to act as doormen in the hopes of tips. And as soon as one is asked to leave, another appears, unless someone official staffs

Q&A

the doors for the duration of the event. This is another good reason to have the doors staffed by professionals.

Q&A

What does a front entrance attendant cost? Has tipping been included, or do you need to budget for it?

This is an area you may be able to negotiate in your contract. The venue may be able to provide a doorman at no additional cost to you, but you will probably have to budget for gratuities. Always remember, you may be using a facility more than once, and you want to make sure that all staff have been looked after adequately. Find out the appropriate amount to tip the doorman, and add it into your budget. Tipping procedures and amounts vary around the world and are ever-changing. If you are doing an out-of-country event, your hotel and most other venues will advise you what amount will be posted to the master account for doormen and others. You can use these rates as guidelines at other venues.

Q&A

How will the doorman be dressed?

Find out how the doorman will be dressed. At an informal event, you may want him to be wearing a themed T-shirt or dress shirt for the evening, but for a more formal affair, you might wish to consider renting a traditional doorman uniform complete with top hat to add a little more splash.

Q&A

Is there a sign announcing that the event is a private party?

It is always a good idea to have a "private party" sign at the entrance. On your initial walk–through, examine the entrance and consider where and how the sign will be displayed. Does the venue have its own easels or frames, and, if so, are they suitable? Do they need to be polished? Are there any missing or broken parts? You may decide to bring your own frames. Restaurants often have menu displays under glass outside, and you can have a sign made to size for your private party.

Q & A

Where is the coat check in relationship to the entrance? Are there any problems that could cause congestion?

Always keep traffic flow patterns in mind when laying out the room.

At one event, the venue had a very small coat check area, but the room beyond was open concept. The planners positioned a food station extremely close to the coat check area, and the two lineups intersected and caused noticeable problems and delays. The food station could easily have been on the other side of the room, where it would have provided better flow and would have had the added advantage of drawing people into the room. You also need to keep traffic flow in mind when considering the position of your registration tables.

Q & A

What is the capacity of the coat check? Does it have enough racks and hangers?

How many coats can it handle and how quickly? How many staff will be required to staff the coat check to provide optimum speed and efficiency? Is it effectively laid out? How much more would it cost for more racks, hangers or staff? It is always better to have too many than not enough.

At one fund-raiser the volunteers staffing the coat check were inexperienced, there were not enough coat racks and hangers and it was in the dead of winter—everyone wore a coat. Coats—many of them very expensive—ended up being piled one on top of the other, and the resulting confusion was horrific. Guests were kept waiting, some well over half an hour, to retrieve their coats. It projected an image of total disorganization and rank amateurism.

Q & A

What types of hangers are there? Will flimsy wire hangers handle the weight of heavy winter coats?

At gala events you often have a number of fur or faux-fur coats, and using wire hangers is asking for trouble; expensive coats do not belong on the floor.

Q & A

What provision is there for umbrellas, boots, briefcases and other items? For example, in Bermuda, coat checks have room for motorbike helmets.

At special event evenings held directly after work, guests can arrive with their briefcases or laptops in hand, and be looking to you for a safe and secure place to have them stored while they enjoy their evening out. If none is provided, you could be left literally holding the bag, which you do not have time to do during an event. Nor do you wish to assume responsibility for contents. One corporate client who enjoyed holding theater evenings after work that featured a private dinner at one location and guests being transferred to the theater as a group and returning to the dinner site for dessert, coffee, liqueurs and cigars started realizing the value of adding in the cost for security to staff a secure room in which to hold their guests' briefcases and laptops when they saw how encumbered the guests were. Guests did know that they were leaving their items in a secure area but also were advised—verbally and by signage—before leaving their goods that the host and the venue were not responsible for any losses and they were doing so at their own risk.

Q & A

How many people are staffing the coat check at arrival and at departure?

Find out how many staff will be on duty at arrival and at departure. How far in advance of opening will they be arriving? If the evening is extended—which can sometimes happen—will staff be able to stay on later than originally planned?

Q & A

Who are your most experienced staff? How experienced are they? Can they be scheduled to work during your event?

The arrival is absolutely crucial because first impressions are lasting. How professionally guests' needs are looked after sets the tone for your event. Find out about the staff. Make sure the most experienced staff are assigned to your event.

Q & A

Are there any additional costs for staffing, coat check and tipping, or are they included?

Is the cost of the coat check included in your overall bill, or will there be a separate charge? Will you be hosting—paying on behalf of the guests—the coat check, or will it be at the guests' own expense? Will you be picking up the cost for gratuities? Be very clear about how you want to handle the issue of tipping. If you are hosting the coat check, you do not want to see any tip plates left out for tipping. Make sure the staff knows this.

Q & A

How secure are the coats?

Are the coats kept in a safe place, or are they left at guests' own risk? If the latter, are there signs to that effect? If not, make your own sign and have it clearly posted advising guests that they are leaving items at their own risk. In the long run, it is better to budget for additional staff and make sure that the coat check area is secure and adequately staffed at all times. Find out if the coats are insured or if your client will require additional insurance to be purchased, in case there is a mishap.

Q & A

What is the staff break schedule during the event?

Review your schedule of the event with them so that they are aware of timing. Make sure that breaks are scheduled after all guests have arrived and are finished before guests begin to leave. Remember that there could be a staggered departure, with the majority most

Q & A

likely leaving as a group. You do not want your guests to arrive to see a group of employees standing around, having a smoking break by your event entrance.

Q & A

If there is a site emergency, who will be on duty throughout the event to attend to it? Is the site prepared?

Make sure that you know in advance how an unexpected "emergency," such as slippery floors from rain or snow, or flooding bathrooms, will be handled. You do not want to have it left to the actual day of the event to find out that there are no provisions on hand. At one event at a venue that is not used frequently, staff had to go out to buy mops and a bucket while the event was in progress as there was no one assigned to handle the potentially dangerous situation of slippery wet floors at the entranceway to the event.

You need to know who to you call in an emergency. Find out who is responsible in case of an emergency, and make certain that you have a phone number where they can be reached throughout the event and during setup and teardown. At one gala event held in a convention center, the main bathroom flooded and there was water everywhere. You want to make sure that you can reach the proper people quickly and that any areas of concern are dealt with quickly, efficiently and as discreetly as possible—from group arrival to group departure.

Q & A

At arrival, does any special notice need to be in place or special handling have to take place with regards to cell phones ringing during the event or pictures being taken by cell phones or cameras at the event?

Cell phones and cell phone cameras are a very real concern at events. The ringing of the phones and people taking calls can be disruptive. You may decide you need to have someone stationed near the entrance doors at group arrival to remind people to turn off their cell phones or turn them to vibrate, and advise guests that if a call comes in they should step into the hallway to take it so that they do not interrupt the event or disturb other attendees with their

Q & A

personal calls. At live stage productions, some actors have been known to stop the show until phones are turned off.

You need to consider how ringing cell phones will impact your event, decide in advance how you and the event host want cell phones handled, e.g., announcement from the stage, and set up the means to do so and note them in your function sheets. At events, some corporate clients have asked that cell phones be turned off, while others have required them to be checked in at the coat check, which can delay check-in procedures. As their way of stopping annoying cell phone rings, some venues have installed blocking devices—which may not be legal—so that no calls can come through. Unfortunately, this also affects the cell phones used by event planning staff.

Another concern with cell phones is their ability to take pictures and videos and send them around the world in a matter of minutes. There are guest privacy issues to consider here, with legal ramifications if their photo is taken without their permission at a private function or a video is taken of their actions or antics after a couple of drinks and posted on YouTube and broadcast for the world to see. Company lawyers—both for the event planning company and the event host—should weigh in on company policy and procedures in this area and advise how they want this issue treated and what steps need to be in place to legally protect their company, your company and their invited guests.

Fanfare

Simply stated, fanfare is more than the blare of trumpets; it is anything that plays a part in the arrival atmosphere. The carpet has been rolled out (and it is no longer just red), searchlights sweep the sky, excitement fills the air. Everything is in place and you are ready to go...or is it? Have you covered all your bases? Have you informed proper channels that searchlights are being used? Have you received clearance in writing? Local airports will need to know about anything that could affect their flight patterns and the safety of their arrivals and departures. The same applies to events involving hot air balloons, the release of helium balloons into the sky and even kites.

A festive summer event taking place on Toronto Island planned to give custom-logoed kites as their take-away gifts. But there is an airport on the island. The event planners reviewed the proposal with airport authorities and received clearance for the kites to be flown on the island with the provision that the kite strings not exceed 30 feet. The lesson is to plan ahead and act early. The last thing you should ever be doing is dealing with the authorities as your event is about to start. Never assume anything. Dot your i's and cross your t's.

And what about that carpet? Did you receive clearance from the city to have it there? Is it securely in place? Have you met all safety regulations? What happens if someone trips and breaks a leg on the carpeting—who is responsible? Are you insured? Ask the questions. Avoid the surprises. Do you know the dent it can put in your budget to have a union team remove helium balloons from the ceiling with a cherry picker? You probably don't want to know, but you have to.

One fund-raiser was using helium balloons for a "balloon burst," a type of silent auction where the name of a donated prize is inserted into the balloons. Guests purchase a balloon, are given a pin with which to pop it and can then pick up their gift at a designated table. The proceeds from the sale of the balloon go to the charity. But helium is tricky stuff, and a lot of the balloons escaped. In addition to the extreme added expense of rescuing fugitive balloons—it was at a union facility with a set minimum of hours that had to be paid for in addition to the rental charges for the cherry picker—planners were unable to auction off all of the prizes, as there was no way of knowing which prize was in each balloon that had escaped. This could have been avoided had they implemented a numbered system so that they could track the balloons. An escaped balloon could have been replaced. Another consideration in such situations is knowing the ceiling height you are working with and making sure that the strings attached to the balloons are long enough so that they can be retrieved.

Fanfare Q&A

Q & A

Will you be planning any special arrival activities?

Once guests arrive in their rooms it is always a nice touch to have a welcoming phone message and a small gift waiting. In Hawaii, it can be something as simple as tropical juices on ice and freshly baked pineapple bread. In the Orient, it can be a hot pot of tea with an assortment of local fruit. (Be careful in choosing the fruit—in Singapore there is one fruit that at first glance looks like a large spider in your fruit bowl. You don't want to scare your guests!) In Morocco, exotic juices and a plate of local delicacies or a huge bowl of fresh Moroccan oranges are always tempting and visually pleasing. And the local long-stem roses are unusual in color, exquisite and relatively inexpensive. Now is not the time to bring in the snake charmers, the animal acts and the local artisans. Save those for later in the program. Guests will be tired from traveling and will want to be looked after and pampered. Look for ways to make their arrival anything but ordinary.

Tip

Special note: In Las Vegas, always make sure to note in your contract that the rooms are to be cleaned before being assigned. Some hotels have been known to assign "dirty" rooms, allowing the guest to go up and drop off their luggage and usually head down to the casino to wait and perhaps play, which was the hotel's intent.

Q & A

At your special events will there be searchlights, displays, carpets, crowd control, staging, special effects, lighting, audiovisuals, lasers, fireworks?

Before you begin to plan, do a walk-through of the area. This is called a site inspection, and may reveal whether or not your fabulous idea will work logistically. Before you spend your time and energy (and that of your suppliers), take the time to do an initial inspection on your own to get a feel of the facility. The next step would be

Q & A

to return at a later date to do a planning site inspection with the suppliers you are considering working with. It is always a good idea to have your key suppliers meet at the site at the same time beforehand, so that on the day of the event you will all be coming together and operating as a team. That way, your caterers can talk directly to the person who is installing the cooking tent to ensure all of their needs will be met, and you are not losing time continually going back and forth over issues that could have been resolved with one joint meeting. All the key players have to be operating off the same page. The more they know about the event in advance, the better they can meet your needs and offer recommendations based on their past experiences. Once you have decided what you want to do, the next step is making sure that your plans fall under the proper rules and regulations, and that you are fully aware of what will need to be done, including all permits and requirements, such as safety and fire regulations.

Q & A

How much setup time is required?

You will need to find out from each supplier how much setup time they will require, and begin to plan the order of each sequence. For example, the stage and the band equipment would need to be set up before moving in the banquet tables. You will need the area clear to bring in that equipment as well as lighting, audiovisual and decor—rather than trying to maneuver between the tables. Then the tables can be moved into place. If you are providing special lighting, such as pin-spotting that highlights each table, the lighting crew will need to know when the tables have been moved into their final position so they can make any necessary adjustments. Look at the total time each area requires. Does it all fall within the time parameters you are working within? Do you need to request earlier access to the room? All these items are key because each could affect both your budget and whether the site is feasible or not. If you do need earlier access to the room, you will probably have to pay additional rental charges if that means the facility is losing revenue.

Q&A

In addition to finding out from the facility what time you can move in, you also need to know what else is happening just before you set up. Could there be any delays? Find out if it is a simple breakfast or luncheon setup that will take place just before you move in, or something much more complex. Try to anticipate anything that means the preceding event might not be out of the room on time. If it is going to be touch-and-go to pull everything off and you cannot get earlier access to the room, this might not be the right venue for you unless you are willing to change your setup. Find out how much time you will need *before* you sign the contract.

At one fashion fund-raiser, the venue's earlier clients were still cleaning up when the fund-raiser guests were arriving at the main doors. Guests had to repeatedly step aside for the workers. The planners had not taken into consideration what else was going on in the room and, once the food and food stations were set up, they found that there was no adequate room left for the guests let alone a runway! Obviously the planners had not thought this through.

Q&A

Is there any special equipment that specifically needs to be brought in to handle guest arrival and any theatrical special effects requirements? What will this cost? Have you factored in labor costs, such as overtime? Is the facility union or nonunion?

At one poolside event, guests were greeted with a mesmerizing dancing water show to give them a taste of what was to come. Dancing Waters (www.dancingwaters.com) entertainment involves a program of colorful cascading fountains of water choreographed to move to the beat of high-energy music or orchestrated to keep time to the classical sounds of a symphony. A trained Dancing Waters technician plays solo or with your musicians all night long—from pop to rock to classic—lighting up your night with spectacular entertainment.

This magical display of water, multicolored lighting effects and lasers can be set up in five hours. Portable theatrical fountains are available for rent for corporate product launches, society galas, weddings or other special events.

Along with dancing waters, there are bubblewalls, waterwalls, waterfalls and numerous other special effects incorporating water that can be used to create stunning visual experiences for guest arrival as well as in the actual venue. Many special effects incorporating water can also be set up in private homes.

Every event that you plan—whether it is in a private home, a ballroom or onstage—is in a sense a live production. And like on Broadway, you will want to set out to dazzle your audience with at least one "wow" element by including some theatrical touches. Guest arrival might be the ideal time to do a special display. Doing so can be relatively inexpensive. The key is in knowing where to look in the event flow with regards to timing and with an eye to your arrival layout as to when and where to add in the "wow" element for the most effect. (For example, if guests are arriving via multiple entrances you would need to do something at all of them, and you would want to choose an effect that all can enjoy, not just the early arrivals. Also, you will want to consider what will have the most impact for the dollars you have available to spend on guest arrival.

For example, Le Flame is a simulated flame—created by light, airflow and fabric—that provides instant ambiance in a room, entranceway, garden or pool area. Le Flame is set in a 14-inch matte black bowl and can be hung from a chain, mounted into a wall or incorporated into your decor in a variety of other ways. It has been said that it is virtually impossible to differentiate the effect of Le Flame from a real flame. Visualize the mystical feeling of walking into a guest arrival area set with low lights, fog and walls of flickering flames tying into a theme party that would incorporate those elements.

For a more dramatic guest arrival effect, you can light up the night with a walkway of pillars of flame (propane flames)—6-foot pillars with flames burning up to 48 inches high. Picture these standing by an entranceway or lined up along a red carpet! Not only will they have visual impact, but they can also work well to take the chill off the night air. And yes, you will require the services of a licensed and insured professional in order to create this special effect. The dollars for added drama do increase, but depending on the number of guests attending your event, when the cost is averaged it can be surprisingly affordable.

Find out in advance what equipment you'll need to handle any installation requirements for guest arrival and for the actual main event setting (there can be different needs because of ceiling heights, etc.), as well as safety regulations that have to be met. For example, will you be doing ceiling decor or special lighting at the entranceway and require the use of cherry pickers? They may not be required inside the actual room, but they could be necessary if the guest arrival is in an atrium setting with soaring ceilings. Have all of your suppliers factored in what they will need in both setups? What does the facility have, and what will you need to bring in? Will the facility charge you for the use of their equipment? Make sure that you build these costs into your budget.

It is also very important to find out if the venue is union or nonunion, because this can have an enormous impact on costs. If the facility is union, ask them to provide you—in writing—with a list of everything that could affect your costs. For example, you could budget installing a banner at one hour but end up paying for a three- or four-hour minimum. Also, find out when their contracts are up for renewal. If it is around the time of your event, how could this affect your event? Do you need to build into your budget an anticipated increase in labor rates? Union costs are often estimated subject to the "prevailing" rate, so check your contract and build in a buffer if necessary. Have the venue provide estimated union costs in writing based upon your requirements. Ensure the union has factored in any overtime costs, any required crew meals and any necessary other costs. At one union hotel, rigging was required for a Cirque-style performance. The entertainment company had their professional riggers installing the ropes, but at this facility it was necessary to have one union staff member work with each company rigger. And the cost for this applied for not just setup but rehearsals, day of and teardown.

Q & A

What are the access routes in and out of the building like? Will freight elevators be required, and can they be booked for specific times? Are there any charges?

The same logistics that apply to your main event setup also apply to guest arrival. Don't focus only on the needs of the main event but on all the event elements from arrival to departure (as they could conceivably be in different locations for multitiered events). Find out where and how items will be moved in. Where are the loading docks? Are there any height restrictions? If there are freight elevators, what are the dimensions? How wide are the hallways? Are they cluttered or are they clear? Are there weight restrictions you should be aware of if you will be moving in something bulky like a car display? Do the freight elevators work? How often are they out of service for repair (you might be surprised by the answer at some facilities)? When do you have access to them? Can you book specific times?

Q & A

Does the facility have any particular requirements or restrictions as to what can be done with regards to guest arrival installations in public and private space?

For example, suppose you are doing a fund-raiser that's offering a new-car giveaway or lease as a prize. You will want to have the car on display where your guests arrive, especially if the car manufacturer is one of the lead sponsors of your event. Find out what the facility requires you to do to move the car. You might have to lay down plastic runners on the carpet and have the car rolled into place by hand. If so, who supplies the plastic runners—the facility, the car manufacturer or you? Will there be a cost involved? Perhaps they will want you to "diaper" the car to ensure no oil drips onto their carpets and floors. If these are damaged, could you be charged? Do you need to have insurance to protect you? Discuss with venue managers in detail when you will be arriving, what they can assist you with and where you need to bring in additional help. How do you arrange for that help? Are

Q&A

you limited to specific suppliers? Do you hire the help or does the union? What perks, such as meals for the crew, are part of their contract agreements and need to be included in your budget? Find out everything that needs to be done. One event planning company underestimated union costs for a major move in and setup at a hotel by $100,000. That is a hard and very costly learning lesson, and a very sure way to lose your client and your personal and company's reputation.

Be aware that today, some venues have been named after a specific sponsor, and in such cases there could be limitations as to what competing products can be displayed in these venues' common areas or even in private function space. This could be an issue in the case of the car being set up at the guest arrival registration area, if a competing car company was one of the building's main sponsors with regards to naming rights or other sponsorship areas.

Q&A

What are your electrical requirements to produce the impact you desire for your guests' arrival?

Know your electrical needs in advance. At one fund-raiser, organizers decided to set up their silent auction in the guest arrival area—an area that had not been factored into event logistics and total electrical requirements. At setup, they wasted countless hours running to buy extension cords and changing the layout to fit their electrical needs. Figure out in advance what has to be plugged in and where the plugs are located in the arrival, registration or the main event areas.

Will there be enough power? Do you need backup generators? Do you need to hire a professional electrician? Does the venue have one? Are you limited to using specific companies that have been approved by the facility?

And when you are doing events out of country, find out in advance what voltage they use and how their plugs are configured. North American equipment will not work in Europe, for example. Don't assume that you can simply bring your own props and decor with you. Lava lamps for your '70s theme party may not work everywhere. Check and double-check. With the technology demands and uses today, it is important to know all of your electrical requirements to not only meet the needs of your event inclusions but guests attending.

What will your power costs be?

What costs, such as labor for installation, will you know upfront, and what costs should you budget for that will be billed back at the end of your event based on actual usage? Read the fine print on your contracts. They may say that power charges will be billed based on the amount used during your event. Ask the facility to provide you with an estimate based on similar events; you will need to include it in your budget projections. To get an accurate estimate you will need to know where, when and how many cables or power bars you will need.

Are there any additional costs that you need to budget for?

The key here is to ask around. If you are using special effects such as indoor or outdoor fireworks, lasers, confetti or snow bursts, what costs could apply? What insurance do you need to cover attendees as well as potential property damage? Are there any charges for cleanup or key personnel? For example, if you're using fireworks, who pays for a fire marshal or someone on fire watch? (Note: Consider this position absolutely essential!)

What permits will be needed for delivery, setup and teardown for your suppliers?

These need to be factored into your budget as well. Drop-off locations may be different from the parking for the limousines, and you may need permits for both. You may also have to bring in additional traffic control—separate from what you may require for your event—if suppliers will be dropping off items during peak traffic times. For example, you may be removing existing furniture

Q & A

from a venue and storing it in a moving van parked nearby. You may need a permit for this and another for the area where suppliers pull up their trucks and off-load their material. This, of course, depends on the venue and accessibility.

Q & A

Are there any safety or fire regulations that must be followed?

Make sure you know all regulations that apply both inside and outside the building.

At one high-profile celebrity event, many media were on hand to cover guests' arrivals and, because there was danger of them stepping farther into the traffic as they sought to capture the perfect shot from their designated area, police had to be hired and barriers erected to create a buffer between the media and the oncoming traffic. The traffic barrier was one of the conditions of the street permits.

Q & A

Are there any zoning, noise, time or other restrictions that will affect your event?

Do local bylaws and other regulations restrict you in any way? Do regulations apply outside the venue and inside? Are there any time restrictions? Can music be played outside the venue to greet guests? How late can the band play? How loud can the music be? Is any type of music allowed—hard rock but not classical? At hotels, if you are considering doing a party poolside, you may not be able to have it continue past a designated time, as it could disturb other guests. What can and cannot be displayed? You may not be permitted to display banners or company products outside the venue. Certain facilities named after corporations may not allow competitors access, and they may also have a permanent display of their products.

Registration: Guest Pass Security and Ticket Pickup

Your guests have arrived and been welcomed to your event. All the cars, limos or buses have been parked. People are standing by, directing guests to the coat check and restrooms. Staff is easy to identify by uniform colors or with visible ID such as name tags or logoed security passes that can be worn around the neck. The next stop is guest check-in. Here they'll display their event tickets or VIP identification passes, have their names checked off a guest list and pick up tickets or hotel room registration at a private check-in with refreshments where appropriate.

If your event is a fund-raising auction, there may also be a table set up for guests to register their credit cards for bidding. If the table is not staffed adequately by professional, well-briefed people who are knowledgeable about the event, you can have confusion and congestion. The same applies for those registering for their hotel rooms for a meeting or convention. A credit card imprint is generally required for personal incidentals, taxes and porterage, the main charges going to the master account. This is generally handled by the hotel staff at a satellite check-in set up exclusively for the group.

As you start to plan your event, consider what will be needed at arrival. How many tables will be required, and will they have to be draped and skirted? What about chairs? Will you need electrical outlets and phone lines for computers or credit card processing? Will there be display tables requiring outlets as well? How many extension cords will be required, what length should they be and will the facility supply them?

At one fund-raiser, event planners apparently overlooked the fact that there were two entrance points. Guests arriving from one went directly into the ballroom without registering, and there was no one positioned to direct guests to the check-in table. This is something you definitely want to avoid.

Is there a charge or are they free? Do you need to bring your own? Is the area well lit? Is there more than one access point?

Once guests have checked in, will they be receiving programs, floor plans, a seating plan or information kits? Do you need a table to display these on and store extras underneath? Will you need display easels for signs? Will you be using banners? Do you require telephones, outlets for computers or tables for media kits or take-home gifts? Can tables serve a dual purpose? For example, once all guests have arrived can the registration tables be used to display the take-home gifts? Not all facilities are created equal. Not all have sufficient quantities of tables and chairs and other equipment on hand. And not all will set them up for you at no cost and have the staff on hand to assist you on the day of your event if not requested in advance.

Registration Q&A

Q & A

What is the ideal layout of the tables and chairs, the stage and the other elements for the needs of the event and the dimensions of the room?

Work from a blueprint or room layout chart, which you can usually obtain from the facility, either reduced to manageable size or sent electronically at no charge.

Tip

If you need to work from actual blueprints, there are reproduction houses that can shrink blueprints down to a more manageable size. Make sure that you make several copies—for yourself and your suppliers—as you begin to sketch out proposed room layouts.

Q & A

Some venues, such as hotels and convention centers, can provide you with plans showing the actual placement of the tables, staging and so on as you have laid them out. This will help you to see things more clearly. For example, you may want to have the stage moved to a more central location, set up three staging areas or hang a large screen with live video coverage so everyone can see what is happening onstage.

Tip

Avoid having the stage at one end of the room, such that the guests in the back are unable to see.

Q & A

Seeing everything laid out on paper will help you to decide which design will best meet your needs. As you start to look at your proposed requirements, make sure that they will all fit into the space provided. What you ideally want and what will actually fit are not always the same thing. Think about how the area can best be laid out to avoid congestion. How many tables will be required, and will they be six- or eight-foot, long or round? How many chairs will you need?

Q & A

Are the tables, chairs and such provided free of charge?

Facilities do not have unlimited tables and chairs and not all facilities provide them for free. Make sure that you ask if there is a maximum number you can request and if there is a fee, and reserve what you need in advance. Make sure they are in good condition.

Q & A

Is draping and skirting provided for all the tables free of charge? (Draping covers the top, and skirting covers the legs.)

Not all facilities provide draping and skirting—they may provide only draping, leaving the table legs exposed—and even when they do there may be an additional charge. If you are bringing in your own draping and skirting, the facility may have regulations on how it may be attached—no pins, nails or tape. You will need to find out the depth of the table top to make sure that the proper-size clips are ordered and used, because if the tables are damaged you could find yourself charged. Do you need insurance coverage to protect you against damage at the venue—if a chair breaks, a display item is chipped or the silk wallpaper damaged?

Q&A

Do you have any choice in the colors for the drapes and skirts?

If the facility does provide draping and skirting, find out what colors are available. Sometimes you will be able to use the hosting company's corporate colors or the event's theme colors to tie in at no additional charge. One company's colors were red, white and blue and the hotel had all three colors available in draping and skirting. It brightened the room and tied in perfectly with all of the print material and banners at no additional cost.

Q&A

Are the table covers in good condition?

Whether they are owned by the facility or rented, you want to ensure that the draping and skirting does not have any cigarette burns, stains or visible mending. Be very specific about this in the function sheet you send outlining your requests. As you are doing your site inspection, take note of the condition of the table coverings that they are using. If you are not satisfied with the quality and condition, you may demand they be replaced or rent replacements from another establishment. This would have to be added to your budget. Another possibility is to place colorful overlays or runners on top of the existing table draping as accent pieces. Overlays are contrasting pieces of material laid on top of the tablecloth, and runners are strips of material placed on the tabletop. For example, with a black and gold theme you could have black draping with a gold lamé runner over top.

Q&A

How many chairs will you require? Are they provided free, or is there a cost involved?

In your planning estimates, carefully calculate how many chairs you will need. Does the facility offer standard banquet chairs, or only heavy, bulky chairs that are difficult to move? Heavy chairs could be a problem at the registration table where you need to be able to move around quickly.

Again, don't assume that every facility has a surplus of chairs or that the ones they have would be acceptable to be out on display. A theater, for example, may only have a few chairs for the

Q&A

manager and the ushers to use for their breaks. They may simply not have enough to set up a registration desk, and the ones that they do have may be mismatched and in disrepair, particularly if you are using an older facility.

Q&A

How many easels or sign holders will you require?

Your signage is an important aspect of your event. How many signs or posters will you be having made up? Will they all require easels or sign holders or will any be freestanding? Will any need to be hung? Will they be standard size or will there be a variety of sizes and shapes?

Q&A

Are sign holders provided free, or is there a charge? Is there a maximum number that can be reserved? What about flip charts?

Find out in advance the number of sign holders and flip charts available. Will the venue have any other events going on simultaneously that may use up the venue's supplies? Are the holders provided free and, if not, what is the cost? Do you have to arrange to rent sign holders from an outside supplier?

At registration and for meetings, flip charts are commonly used. There can be rental charges for the flip charts, the pads of paper and the markers. Factor these into your budget.

Q&A

In what condition are the sign holders?

Are they all similar, or are they mismatched? Are they beat up and battered, with missing pieces? Do they just need a little loving attention, or are they in such poor condition that it would be more efficient to bring in good ones? Do the dimensions of the holders match your signs?

Q&A

Will there be banners? Can they be displayed? What is the cost to have them installed and taken down?

It can be very expensive to have a banner put up and taken down if doing so involves cherry pickers and three- or four-hour

Q & A

minimum labor charges. Find out the cost in advance and budget for it. What are the dimensions of the banner, and where can it be hung? Will the banner require aircuts to let the wind blow through? Will it require grommets? Are these banners that you want to use again, or are they single-use throwaways? Will the banners be hung inside or outside? Do they need to be weather resistant? It will make a difference in the material you use.

Q & A

Does anything need to be attached to the walls, and will the facility allow you to do so?

It's important to ask the venue if anything can be attached to the walls. In five-star hotels, exclusive restaurants and private venues, the answer very likely will be no, and you will need to come up with creative ways to display your material. At art exhibits, paintings are often hung on chains that are attached to the ceiling or on moldings with the use of S-hooks, on large wooden easels or set on pieces of furniture that lend themselves to the type of artwork and enhance the painting. Signs can be made to be freestanding, furniture or props can be rented, and walls can be completely draped, which would allow you to change the look of a venue and affix any items you needed displayed. For an artistic theme, for example, signs could be made up to fit into ornate picture frames—flea market finds that have been spray-painted—that could be propped up against a wall. Light refreshments could include an assortment of dips in different colors set out on artist's palettes, with a can of used brushes, their tips painted in matching colors, set out beside them. Do something a little bit different that will draw people's eyes.

Q & A

Does the facility have extension cords, and is there a rental charge for them? Are there any restrictions on installing electrical cords?

These are not always available free of charge. You will need to know the length and number you will require, and how they can

Q & A

be best laid out. Be sure to test them in advance of your event. Tape the cords down to avoid having anyone trip over them. Try to get tape that blends in with the carpet and is not unsightly. Find out if the facility has any objections to tape or has other specific requirements. For insurance purposes, the venue may need to have their staff install and tape all electrical cords to ensure that it is done to their standards.

Q & A

What will be your communications requirements with regard to telephones, cell phones, BlackBerrys and walkie-talkies?

You may need to have telephone lines installed. Never depend solely on cell phones, BlackBerrys or walkie-talkies because you may find that they do not work inside the building. Always test your cell phones and walkie-talkies in all areas you will be using them. And even though you may have tested them previously and they worked, you may find that when you need them they will be affected by other events near yours. If possible, try a few different models to see which works best where.

Make sure you have fully charged backup batteries that will last from setup to teardown, often 24 hours or more. And know, just know, that if one person sees you using a cell phone, there will soon be a lineup waiting to use it for "only a moment" or "a quick call"—and there goes your battery! People will ask to use your phone even if they have their own, as they may be wanting to conserve their batteries or minutes. So, bring lots of spares or practice saying *no* a lot. Take note of where the public phones are, and have a supply of change on hand—it is less expensive than having guests use your cell phone. Tell them nicely that your batteries are low, but the public phones are just over there and if they don't have change, you do. (Unlike hotels with gift shops and check-out counters, other venues, such as convention centers, may not have areas where you can quickly obtain change.)

Q & A

What are the costs for telephone installation, long distance, cell phones, walkie-talkies and batteries; daily charges; and charge per local call? How much notice is required to install the telephones?

Most hotels and convention centers do charge for telephone installation. The telephones can be set up for local calls only, limiting the damage if guests manage to get hold of your phone. Most phones can be unplugged and stored out of sight if you need to be away from the table, and can be stored in a secure room if you will be away for an extended period of time. Find out if there is a charge per local call and what that is, and if there is a charge build in to your budget an estimated cost per day.

Q & A

Will you have any special electrical requirements such as outlets and modems for computers?

List all areas where you will need access to electrical outlets. Know exactly where you are going to need them and how many you will need in total. On your floor plan be sure to make note of where electrical outlets are located. Go through your event elements one by one to determine your requirements. Will the musicians playing at the reception require outlets? Will the photographer need one for lighting or other equipment? Will the bartender be serving frozen beverages, and if so, how many blenders will be used? Will you be bringing in an ice cream machine, for example? Where will it be stationed? Is there an outlet there? How many outlets will each person need? Don't wait to find out on the day of the event that there are not enough outlets to go around.

Once you know all your electrical needs, the next thing you need to know is if the facility can handle all your power requirements if everything is taking place at the same time. And, if they can handle not just your event needs but the electrical needs of any other events taking place at the same time in the location. You may have all the electrical outlets you need to power up your event, but can the venue handle the capacity? You'll need to know this at the planning stages—not on the day of the event. Has the facility ever experienced blackouts? How have they handled them? Is there a backup generator? Do you need to bring one in? Have your venue professionally assessed as to power capacity. If you are holding your event in a private home, do they have a supply of fuses, candles and flashlights on hand?

At one resort in the Caribbean, when they had an unexpected blackout, their staff sprang into action. Within a matter of minutes, they had candles lit everywhere, and they had enough on hand to give some to guests making their own way back to their guestrooms. The staff was fully prepared; they had a plan of action in place to tell them what to do should such an event occur.

Guest Arrival Checklist

- ✓ *Assess all guest arrival transportation and parking requirements and options for both individual and group arrival at the actual time of day of the guest arrival*
- ✓ *Decide if there are there any weather backup or other legal considerations that need to be in place, e.g., tenting of entranceway, shoveling of snow, permits, crowd control, off-duty police to direct traffic, etc., from the parking or drop-off area to the entranceway*
- ✓ *Determine how many entrances will need to be covered and whether or not there will be one main registration area or multiple entrance check-ins and how guest check-in will be controlled*
- ✓ *Design an arrival that is welcoming and sets the tone for the event ahead*
- ✓ *Find out what will be required by suppliers, e.g., electrical requirements, setup and teardown timing, logistical, permits and legal considerations, etc.*

6

Venue Requirements

It is essential that you know all of your event requirements before starting to check the availability of venues. What may seem initially to be the perfect fit may turn out to be inadequate once you take into account all of your needs. Go in with your wish list and know where you are willing to compromise and where you are not. Keep in mind the feeling you are going for. You want your event to have a vibrant energy, and you won't get that if the room is too small or when people are too close together, too hot and uncomfortable. Remember to keep in mind wheelchair accessibility as well.

Your main focus is always going to be on the room or rooms you are holding your event in, but you also have to keep in mind your suppliers' (decor, entertainment, caterers, florists) move in, setup, rehearsal, teardown and move out timing and logistical requirements as well, so the venue itself has to be a fit as well as the selected event room. For example, if you were doing an intensive stage and audiovisual show your audiovisual and staging company might need the adjacent room for move in and setup but not during the actual event, and you would need to find out availability and block off that space as well from the onset. Or, your selected entertainment may require a venue that has extensive storage space for props, two or more dressing room areas complete with access to water and mirrors, riggings in the ceiling and provision for special flooring to be brought in, for instance in the case of hiring a Cirque-style act to perform.

Room Requirements

When you are selecting the room to hold your event you have to consider:

» what is on the floors, walls, ceiling, back entrance,

» width of the doors, ceiling height,

» sight lines

» if using airwalls that need to be opened and, if so, how do they operate and how long does it take for them to open,

» soundproofing, room acoustics,

» room capacity and fire marshal rules and regulations

» the venue's terms and conditions and insurance requirements

» the suppliers' room requirements on the day of the event and on move in, setup, rehearsal, teardown and move out days

Before you can begin to look at venues and the rooms they have available, you need to know all of your possible space and room requirements from your clients, your suppliers and your guests as well as service staff and your own staff needs (e.g., separate dining area for event planning staff, etc.).

Room Requirements Q&A

Q&A

Is the room carpeted? Will it require carpeting? What are other options?

Do not assume that all function space in all hotels and convention centers is carpeted, because this is not always the case. Check when you are inquiring about space. You can rent carpeting, but you need to know in advance how this could affect your budget—it is not cheap. For very special theme parties, you can order custom carpets that will tie in with the decor. For example, one car launch considered having the ballroom carpet transformed into a highway

Q&A

(black carpeting with highway markings on it) and having their new cars displayed in various scenes you would find along the highway. For a beach theme party in a production studio or even a ballroom, you can lay down plastic over existing carpeting and cover with sand. Specialty lighting can also transform carpeting.

Q&A

Will you be having a dance floor?

If you plan on having a dance floor how large does it need to be? How many does it need to accommodate? Will everyone be up dancing at once or just about half at a time? Then, allow three square feet per person for the dance floor and 20 square feet per instrument for the band, who move around more than the dancers.

For very special events or theme parties custom-designed dance floors are available. You can have them hand painted to match the motif and pick up on the decor. For instance, for a wedding you could have the couple's initials displayed, a company's logo could be shone on the dance floor through specially cut gobos or the floor could be made into a giant board game with the participants becoming the playing pieces. It could even be a colorful, plastic uplit floor for a disco theme party. You are limited only by imagination and budget.

Q&A

Does the facility you are considering have a permanent dance floor?

Just because you don't see it, don't assume that it isn't there. Sometimes a built-in dance floor is hidden under a section of carpeting that can be lifted. Check to see how many the floor will accommodate and what it looks like. Is it in good condition?

Q&A

Is there a rental charge for the dance floor and a labor charge for installation and teardown?

Find out if any charges will apply. You will need to include any rental and labor charges in your budget. Also, if the dance floor must be installed, you will need to coordinate the timing with the installation of the staging, audiovisual and lighting.

Q&A

Will you be setting up any major displays in the room, such as a car (which is sometimes done at fund-raisers)? Is there a clear passageway from the loading docks to the display area for large items?

Make sure that you work with the floor plans to avoid any areas of congestion. Are you leaving a clear path for the waitstaff? Will they be able to easily make their way around any items on display? Check the width and the height of all passageways. Are they free of clutter? Will all display items fit comfortably through?

Q&A

Are the ballroom doors wide enough to accommodate large items, such as a car?

If you run into any areas of difficulty here, ballroom doors can be removed, but there is usually a labor charge involved. Find out how much that would be, how long it will take and any other constraints. To move larger items into place, you sometimes need to take them through sections of a ballroom that you may not be using for your event. You need to know when these areas will be available, and you need to find out when it is best to have large items moved in so that they will not be in the way of the staging, audiovisual and lighting setup.

Q&A

Will the floor hold the weight of something as heavy as a car?

Ask the management if the floor will take the weight. For example, a covered-over orchestra pit by the permanent stage could present a problem. The area may not stand the weight of a car on it. Find out if there are any areas such as this that you need to be concerned about.

Q&A

What are the fire and safety regulations regarding room layout?

Where are the fire exit doors? Are they clearly accessible? Are they hidden by pipe and draping? If so, you will need to obtain

Q & A

and clearly post exit signs. Make sure that you adhere to all fire and safety regulations or you may be shut down by the authorities or have problems getting insurance.

Q & A

Will airwalls be in place? Will you need them opened at any point?

At times you may be holding one part of your event in one section of the room and a second in another section. If these areas are adjacent, you need to know if the airwalls—room dividers—are manual or automatic and, if you are having them opened to allow your guests to move easily from one area to the next, how long do they take to open and close? Who will be operating the walls—can you or your staff do it, or must it be done by facility staff? Are there union rules involved? Discuss this with the account manager who has been assigned to handle your booking.

Q & A

Are you considering any special effects?

Are there any restrictions on indoor fireworks, lasers, dry ice or other special effects? Do any items need to be fireproofed? What insurance do you need? Will all of the proposed items fall under the fire and safety rulings? Will any permits be required? Speak to management at the facility, the local fire marshal and the company that will be handling the special effects. Do not accept just one opinion. Do your homework. Know all that has been attended to and what you and your suppliers will be required to do, and ensure it has been done in advance and meets fire marshal standards. One event planning decor company sent fabric away for a special fire retardant application and had the paperwork with them as verification that they had spent thousands of dollars to have 10 bolts of fabric treated for an event they were doing. When the fire marshal tested the fabric as they were beginning event setup, it exploded into flames and they were in tears. The last 1/4 of a bolt that had not been treated was tested and nothing would make it burn. The fire marshal could have closed the event down, but luckily simply said, "Just do the show and be careful;

Q & A

keep your staff close by, and never use that company to do any fireproofing again."

At another event, miniature Christmas-tree centerpieces were stopped from entering the site as they were being unloaded when a fire marshal told the decor company that flammable material couldn't enter the building. When they protested and insisted the trees were not flammable—but had no proof of them being treated—the fire marshal pulled out a lighter and set one ablaze. In this case, the fire marshal did not permit the centerpieces to be used at the event.

Q & A

What are the entertainers' requirements with regard to electrical outlets, rehearsal time, sound checks, dressing rooms, and rooms for meals and breaks?

Avoid day-of potential pitfalls by making sure that everything has been tested in advance and meets safety and insurance requirements. Are the acoustics in the room good? Make sure that space is set aside to accommodate the entertainers' needs, and that you have included all these costs in your budget.

Q & A

How will the room be set up?

Will food be passed or served at buffets, food stations or plated? Will people be standing or sitting? Will there be scattered seating? Will the events take place in one room or several? Will there be smoking or not? Will you set aside a separate smoking area? Are cigar rooms permitted? Are the room and the facilities as a whole wheelchair accessible?

Q & A

Is there anything scheduled to take place at the same time you are holding your event?

What other events are taking place at the same time as your event? What time are they scheduled to begin and end? Will they be having any breaks that could cause noise, disruption or congestion for your event? Where will these other events be held? Will their move in and teardown be going on while your event is in progress?

Q & A

You don't need hammering and sawing as a background for your presentation, or someone else's coffee break stationed right outside your doors, or worse, both of you breaking at the exact same time. This could cause congestion and long lineups in nearby washrooms. Will anyone else be moving in and setting up at the same time as you are? Will you both require access to the freight elevators and other equipment the facility may have? Have you checked to see how soundproof the rooms are? Are there any competing events, or are any of your competitors holding events at the same time? Ask management to keep you informed.

At one new-product launch, competitors who were staying at the same hotel tried to sneak a peak at the new product that was being revealed in the hotel ballroom. But the ballroom doors had been secured while setup was going on and security had been posted by the main doors, ensuring only authorized personnel with security passes got in.

Staging, Audiovisual, Lighting

Before you can find the ideal location for your event, you need to consider all of your room and venue requirements. For example, if you were planning for 1,000 guests and were considering a ballroom with a capacity of 1,000 for a sit-down dinner but wanted to have a rear-screen projection (which has a clean, professional look), you would need extra space. You need a minimum of 18 to 26 feet behind the screen for projection equipment, which means that you lose seating for about 250 guests. In this case, you would have to cancel the rear-screen projection idea, reduce the number of guests or get a larger room. Do your plans include any front-of-room setup by the audiovisual company? Do you need sound booths, translation booths, staging or a dance floor? All these will take away more seating space, as will your some of your food, beverage and entertaining requirements. For example, will your food and beverage setup include food stations—double sided for better access—or bar stations in the room, and will your entertainment need any special handling, like rigging points in the ceiling for Cirque-style effects?

It is better to seat eight comfortably at tables that can accommodate 10 (10 at tables for 12) and have breathing room than to cram everyone in elbow to elbow to save a few dollars. Make sure that tables are not too close together and that people can maneuver between them with ease. But you don't want the other extreme—where a few tables are lost in a massive space. Once again, you will have lost the energy of the room. You want the room to be comfortably filled, vibrant and alive. In one way, you are better off with too much room rather than too little, because you can always reduce the size of the room with decorating, lighting and special effect tricks, but why spend unnecessary dollars if you do not have to or can spend those dollars on lighting and special effect tricks to instead enhance the event experience?

Lighting can be used effectively to create mood or even change moods throughout the course of your event. Lighting can be used to add drama. Strategically placed low lights and professional-looking, battery-operated candles or open-flame candles (if permitted) can create ambiance at very limited cost. Splash lights with colored gels and mirrored balls are inexpensive and simple effects that can provide visual impact.

Lighting effects are only limited by your budget. You can opt for a full laser show as a grand finale to your event, pinspot the tables, have your room bathed in changing color, have custom gobos shine a message, or display your event message or corporate name on a wall or dance floor and be static or dance around the room. For one event, the ceiling was softly draped with fabric and lit with twinkling mini lights to produce a canopy of stars overhead for a special lighting effect. There are many imaginative options available to you. One company used moving gobos to create an innovative visual display at guest arrival. Gobos are an inexpensive, interesting and dramatic specialty lighting effect. As mentioned earlier, a gobo is a silhouette pattern cut from metal or glass and used to project images from a light fixture (spotlight) onto any surface (could be the wall, dance floor, ceiling or drape). You can use them in static lekos (remains stationary), which will be very inexpensive, or use them in intelligent lighting fixtures (moves around the room), which is of course more expensive, or on the pathway leading to the ballroom, which is what this company did. The effect was showstopping but at minimal cost. Lighting can add a feel of extravagance without the cost and can be changed throughout the night to transform the room dynamics and take your event from day to night throughout the course of your evening.

If you will be requiring staging for a dance band, specialty lighting and audiovisual equipment, always make sure to get your staging, lighting and audiovisual technical directors involved in venue choice before contracting. Room height, location of pillars, chandeliers, loading dock access, size of elevator, etc., can all affect costs. Your staging, lighting and audiovisual suppliers can offer budget-saving solutions and creative options if they obtain staging knowledge of the room well in advance.

Space Requirements

Type of Event	**Space Required**
Cocktail Reception	8 square feet per person
Cocktails with Food Stations	12–15 square feet per person
Seated Dinner	20 square feet per person
Dance Floor	3 square feet per person
	20 square feet per instrument for the band (room to move around)

Consider not only all your space requirements but also your time requirements. Before you proceed, consider how much time is required for staging, audiovisual and lighting to move in, set up, perform sound checks, rehearse and tear down, and how the timing will work with your decor, catering and other suppliers' move in and setups as well as teardown and move out.

Make sure that you consider what space will be needed by all the event elements involved. Will the musicians need a change room or a room for breaks? Do you or any of your suppliers need any storage space? Look at the total picture before you sign a contract and find that you have neither enough space nor time in which to work.

And don't forget that if you are considering holding your event at a hotel or convention center, you must find out who is booked in before you. Then start a discussion that includes these questions:

- When are they tearing down and moving out?
- What are they tearing down and moving out?
- Could they run into any delays?
- When do you have access to the room?
- Who else is moving in and setting up the same day?
- Are there any conflicts with the timing or with competitors or competing events?
- What else is scheduled to take place at the same time you are holding your event? What time are they scheduled to begin and end?
- Will the other events be having any breaks that could cause noise, disruption or congestion to your event? You will need to adjust your timing accordingly.

If you are using only a section of the ballroom, schedule your site inspection at a time when the whole room is empty. Request that the airwall be put into place. Have someone go into the adjoining section and test the soundproofing. In one five-star luxury hotel, the test of the dividing wall revealed that you could hear every word that was being said in the next section of the ballroom. As a result, the contract stipulated that the adjacent section of ballroom remain unused during the event, ensuring no music, speeches or noise from the next room. This is not a common problem in many hotels, but the one time you don't take the time to check can't be undone.

Are there any noise factors to consider? Remember the earlier example of a car launch in a Las Vegas theater, in which the air-conditioning vents needed to be redirected or the chandelier removed so that the tinkling sound of the crystal chandelier did not distract from the speeches? Are you working with any noise obstacles?

What about sight lines, ceiling heights, pillars or hanging chandeliers that will block views? Can they be raised or removed, and what will it cost? Can the lights be dimmed? Are there window drapes, and can they black out the room if an audiovisual presentation is taking place?

Where are the fire exit doors? These have to remain accessible and cannot be blocked or locked. If they are covered with draping you may be required by fire marshal ruling and fire permit requirements to ensure that an exit sign is clearly posted and that there is a part in the draping that will allow easy access to the doors.

How is the layout? Can staging be set up so that there are no bad seats in the house? Can TV monitors or large screens be hung in the room so that everyone, no matter how far away, can see what is taking place onstage or in the audience with live video coverage? Can live video cameras be stationed to project what is happening onto the TV monitors or screens that have been positioned around the room? This is what you see on award shows where the cameras pan the audience to show the winner make his or her way to the stage. Can lighting be hung? Can projectors be suspended from the ceiling? Are there hanging points in the ceiling from which this can be done? These are all things to consider when you are selecting your venue.

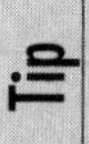

If you are doing live video coverage at your event, it is essential that those operating the cameras know where the VIP guests are seated. Prepare a seating chart and a detailed schedule of events occurring onstage so that the camera operators know when and where to focus their cameras.

It bears repeating that you should always work with a detailed floor plan. Have the venue provide a layout based on your needs. If they do not have a floor plan, work with a copy of the original blueprints reduced to a more manageable size.

And keep an eye on labor costs. Are there minimum charges, such as a three- or four-hour minimum call? A minimum call means that you will be charged for a minimum of three or four hours no matter how little work they actually do. Keep overtime in mind, too. Will anything be taking place over a holiday or on a Sunday when overtime might apply? Is the standard overtime time and a half or something else? All of these costs need to be factored into your budget.

Staging, Audiovisual, Lighting Q&A

Q&A

Is the facility unionized or not? How will this affect your program? What additional costs should you budget for? If the facility is unionized, when do the contracts expire?

Always find out the impact the labor situation will have on all areas of your program. How does it affect costs? What regulations do you need to adhere to? Make sure that you have a meeting with union officials to discuss your program so that you do not incur unexpected costs that should have been budgeted for in the beginning. Before you submit your costing or proposal, take all labor charges into account. What would happen if you based your labor costs on regular hourly rates and did not take into account minimum call times, overtime costs and meals for the crew? It can make thousands and thousands of dollars' difference to your bottom line, or $100,000 as the one event planning company found out.

Tell the union officials what you will be doing, and have them submit an estimate, including how many people and hours are involved and what it will cost, including crew meals, etc. All of this must be detailed in writing to you in a formal quote. Ensure that the audiovisual company that you hire has a technical director who has worked with union facilities before and can monitor the

Q&A

schedule, ensuring that all breaks are taken and that everyone starts and leaves on time for four-hour calls. Otherwise, you could be billed for extra overtime hours. Add a buffer of 10 percent to your initial budget. For non-union facilities, review your program in depth with management, asking them to put in writing all additional charges that could apply.

Q&A

How high is the ceiling in the facility?

Ceiling height will make a big difference in all your staging, audiovisual and lighting calculations. For example, the recommended minimum ceiling height for rear-screen projection is 22 feet. You will need to set up a site inspection with your staging, audiovisual and lighting suppliers to together decide the best layout for the room based on all your requirements.

Q&A

How are the sight lines?

Check out the room from all angles. Are there any obstacles such as support pillars or hanging chandeliers? Will all guests be able to see the stage or screen clearly? Can the chandeliers be raised or removed? In many cases this can be done, but you need to know what labor costs are involved. How much time will it take, how many people will be involved and ultimately, how much will it cost?

Q&A

Will you be having one stage or more?

You need to know where the staging will be set up and how many staging areas you will be having in total, as they can eat up a lot of space in your room and affect the total number of tables or guests you will be able to accommodate.

Q&A

How large or how high does the stage need to be?

What will be taking place onstage? How many people does the stage need to accommodate? Will the musicians be set up on the main stage or off to one side? Is the height of the stage one that works well if guests are seated at tables or theater style?

It is possible to include elevated seating? Sections of the room can be built up and carpeted, transforming your ballroom into a nightclub or restaurant. You need not have everyone seated at one level, but bear in mind that elevated seating is not cheap, and the cost will depend on the room layout and any obstacles, such as pillars, that will have to be worked around. It also depends on the number of people attending. Amortized over a large number of guests the cost may be acceptable, but that's not likely the case for a smaller group.

Does the facility have a permanent stage?

Have them provide you with floor plans of the stage, including the backstage area. Find out if there are any existing dressing rooms, an area to off-load and move in equipment, how wide the aisles are and so on. Will the stage meet all of your needs and requirements?

Does the facility have any special effects that you can use?

One of the nice things about doing a product launch in a Las Vegas theater is being able to use existing props and staging to enhance your presentation. Revolving stages, elevators that will raise your product from below for a dramatic onstage unveiling of your new product line—all the special effects are already there. You have to work around show times and rehearsals, but it can be done. Find out when the theaters will be dark (no shows going on) and see if a schedule can be worked around that. Restaurants and private clubs may also have special lighting effects, laser shows or bubble machines.

What costs do you need to include in your budget for staging?

Will you need any special effects built into your staging, and will they be simple or elaborate? For example, will one of your stages need to revolve, or will you require special ramps or runways? If you are doing a fashion show, will you need to include pipe and

Q&A

draping behind the staging or off to one side to provide change areas for the models? Take the time to think of all the elements that need to be included in your budget.

Q&A

Will there be decor (props, greenery) onstage?

Will your stage sets be fairly simple, or will they rival those seen on television award shows? How much or how little will be included? How will they work with what will be taking place onstage? If you are not working with a full production house that can provide both the staging and decor, you will need to bring all your suppliers together to best determine your staging needs.

Q&A

Will the stage area require draping?

What will be behind the stage? What will you need as a backdrop? Will it be simply the existing back wall, the more polished look that draping provides or an intricate stage setting? All of these items need to be considered so that you can accurately project your costs.

Q&A

Will there be audiovisual presentations?

If you are including audiovisual, will it be rear-screen or front-screen projection? How many screens do you envision? Does the room have the space (in depth and height) for rear-screen projection?

Q&A

Will the presentation be in more than one language and/or sign language?

Will translation booths need to be factored into both the budget and the room layout? If so, you will need to think about where the booths will go and also about an area where the headsets can be distributed. This can be either inside or directly outside the meeting room. Will you need to provide bilingual (or multilingual) staff to help hand out the headsets and explain how they work? Will you need to ensure that bilingual staff are available throughout the program? Make sure that you count the number of headsets received and have adequate numbers of staff to collect them at the end of the meeting before guests leave the room. You could have

Q&A

guests sign for the headsets, but that could cause congestion. Take care in the location of the sign-out table to make sure that it does not block the entrances. Have you included the costs to have the translator there for rehearsals?

Q&A

Will there be any front-of-room setup required by the audiovisual company?

Find out the needs of your audiovisual company. Do they have equipment, such as teleprompters or live video cameras, that they need to position on or in front of the stage?

Q&A

How much rehearsal time will be required?

Find out when and how much rehearsal time will be needed. Make sure that rehearsal space has been requested, is available and the time has been blocked off for you. Dancers may need to practice their routines, speakers may need to recite their speeches and the client will need to review video presentations. Everything that will be happening onstage needs to be finely choreographed, just like any live theatrical stage production. Find out what additional charges for such things as room rental, labor and crew meals will have to be included in your budget.

Q&A

Are there additional charges for cleaning the room?

Once everything is set up you may need to have the room thoroughly vacuumed before the actual event. Some venues will supply people and equipment at no additional cost; others will not. For example, if you are setting up a display in an exhibit hall at a convention center, you might need to book this service in advance, and there will be a cost involved. Check to see if this needs to be scheduled, and if there will be any additional charges.

Q&A

What sort of access will there be on and off the stage?

How will all those who are involved in the program be getting up onto the stage? Will you need to have stairs leading up from the audience to the stage, or will access be only from backstage? Will it be one or the other or both?

Is there an additional cost to rent the stairs, and are there any applicable labor or insurance charges regarding insuring guest safety in getting on and off the stage?

If you are using an existing stage, the facility may have stairs that you can use at no charge, but if you have a custom-designed stage, the cost for the stairs needs to be included in your staging budget.

Are the stairs lit?

Strip lighting that runs across the edge of each step can be installed to make each individual stair more visible. If the room will be in darkness when people are getting up on the stage, you may wish to consider adding this type of lighting, or have the stairs lit from the sides.

Will a ramp or lift be required for wheelchair access to the stage from the audience?

Ramp requirements need to be specific because ramps take a fair amount of space and will affect the layout of the room. Find out how much space will be needed. Some facilities have lifts to raise the wheelchairs onto the stage. When you are positioning the lift, you need to keep in mind what else will be on the stage and ensure that sufficient room is available to maneuver. What additional costs are involved in a lift or ramp?

How much time will be required to move in and set up the staging and how much to tear down and move out?

You need to know how much time is involved in these activities to see how all elements will interact and so you can begin to lay out your initial schedule of events based on the time requirements of all your suppliers. You need to ensure that you have allowed

Q&A

sufficient time for move in. Depending on how elaborate your set is, you could require anywhere from a few hours to two days or more. Then you need to add to this the time you will require for rehearsals and other preparations. If you need more time for setup, expect to pay more for site rental and labor, and factor these into your budget. Doing something as elaborate as a large car launch can require over a week of setup and rehearsal time.

Q&A

Are there any special requirements or equipment needed for the off-loading of material and the setup of the stage?

Make sure that everything is done to facilitate the move in, which needs to be done as efficiently as possible, with all necessary equipment ready, passageways cleared and the room empty and ready for the setup to begin. Avoid any delays that could result in additional costs. For example, make sure that the facility is not just beginning to move tables and chairs out of the way as your setup crews arrive. Have staff on hand well in advance of the move in to ensure that preparations are well under way.

Q&A

Have you included in your budget crew meals and breaks during setup, rehearsals, the event day and teardown? Do you need to have the breaks set up in a separate room, or will they be set up in the room? What other suppliers could be setting up in the room at this time? And will you interfere with their setup?

Find out what you are responsible for, and make provisions to have this billed to the master account. Do you have to pay the crew for meals and meal time when they are setting up? Will meals for the crew be a separate charge that needs to be budgeted for, or has it been included in the supplier's written estimate to you? In some cases you do not have to pay for this. Find out.

Will the crew need a separate room for meals and breaks? If so, has the space been reserved, and is it located close to the setup area? Will you, as the event planner, need to make the

Q & A

arrangements to book this space, or will your contracted supplier be handling this? Will you be charged for that extra room rental?

Who will be making the meal arrangements for the stage crew—you or your supplier? You can work with the facility to have them create menus that will fall within your budget guidelines. Do you need to set up meals for your own staff as well? Will you require additional space for them? If you are using different suppliers, you will need to account for meal and break time for all suppliers. Schedules could differ, for example, between the staging crew and lighting crew. Find out who will be responsible for making all arrangements and overseeing this area.

Q & A

How much time will be required to move in and set up audiovisual requirements? How much time to tear them down?

If you are working with two different suppliers, one that is handling the staging and another the audiovisual, you need to make each aware of the other's schedule and timelines so there are no areas of conflict. Ideally, the company that is designing the staging that will also be handling your audiovisual setup, lighting and stage decor. Look for companies that are full production houses that can handle all of your needs. However, compare the costs for full production houses versus individual contractors. You may need just a simple stage but an audiovisual and light show that has the intensity of a rock concert. Or you may need an elaborate stage with simple audiovisual and lighting. Find out if the production house owns their own equipment or will rent it based on your requirements. You want to make sure that you have access to what best fits your needs and not what is simply on hand.

Q & A

Are there any special requirements or equipment needed for the off-loading of material and the setup of audiovisual equipment?

Are there any arrangements that need to be made before the audiovisual crew arrives? For example, do any chandeliers need to be removed or air vents turned off to reduce excess noise? Have you made sure that everything is ready to make the move in as easy as possible? What do you need to have for the audiovisual crew so that they can maximize the time available to them? You do not want crew sitting around waiting for rooms or passageways to be cleared or waiting for generators if you find out late in the game that your facility cannot handle all your electrical requirements. You need to be on-site prior to their arrival to ensure that all has been prepared for them.

What additional costs should you budget for?

Find out any and all additional charges that could apply. For example, could charges for labor or power be posted to the master account based on actual usage, or are they firm? Include estimates in your budget from their past events, and build in a 10 percent buffer. It is better to come in under budget than over. Make sure that you receive written estimates of costs.

Lighting-Specific Q&A

How much time will be required to move in and set up lighting and to tear down?

Ideally you will have a single contractor for staging, audiovisual and lighting but, if not, you need to work with each one to determine who needs to be in first and what needs to be completed before the next step can begin. Find out what can be done simultaneously.

Are there any special requirements or equipment needed for the off-loading of material and the setup of lighting equipment, move in timing or logistical dock conflicts?

Each area of staging, audiovisual and lighting has its own specific requirements and needs. Make sure you review each with the particular supplier so that all is prepared. Will one cherry picker be enough, or will two need to be brought in? Are there any areas of overlap?

Q & A

Have crew meals and breaks for lighting setup, rehearsals, day of the event and teardown been included in their budget to you?

Again, as with staging and audiovisual, make sure that you have covered this area with the suppliers and, if necessary, the union.

Q & A

Will the lighting move in, setup and rehearsals have any special requirements that need to be met?

When working with staging, lighting, audiovisual and decor companies as well as the venue, you have to visualize the sequence of events that each supplier needs. For example, lighting crews may need the tables already in position in order to pinspot them, while staging may need the tables out of the way until their setup is in place so that the area is clear. Tables could require final placement, and it is best to do that before the tables are set.

Tip

For any changes to the costs for staging, audiovisual or lighting, make sure that a revised written estimate is submitted and that all parties approve each change and cost. Never give or receive approval verbally. Doing so can turn out to be a very costly mistake. Remember that the person who gave their verbal approval may not be there the next day, week, month or year.

Venue and Event Supplier Checklist: Room, Venue and Supplier Requirements, and Contract Terms and Conditions

- ✓ *Legal room capacity*
- ✓ *Electrical requirements and venue and room capacity, backup capabilities and charges (up front and at final reconciliation, e.g., power charges)*
- ✓ *Fire marshal rulings to be aware of and required permits*

- ✓ *Required permits to be obtained, e.g., liquor licenses, host and supplier liability insurance*
- ✓ *Supplier-required access time for move in, setup, rehearsals, day of, teardown and move out, plus any related charges (e.g., labor, equipment, security, insurance, etc.)*
- ✓ *Venue and room access times for move in, setup, rehearsals, day of, teardown and move out and any related charges (e.g., labor, equipment, security, insurance, etc.)*
- ✓ *Potential timing and logistical conflicts with regards to move ins, setups, actual events, teardowns and move outs, and how they could affect your event, e.g., noise, blocked access for move in, etc.*
- ✓ *Supplier timelines and commitments pre and post your event, e.g., are the suppliers handling only your event or rushing to or from another event?*
- ✓ *Written quote, laid out in menu format, with all applicable taxes, service charges and tipping (and how they are calculated), and any other charges that will be billed at final reconciliation*
- ✓ *If the venue or an event supplier is unionized, obtain written confirmation of all applicable charges, terms and conditions from the union*
- ✓ *Sample contract to review*
- ✓ *Sample payment schedule to review*
- ✓ *Attrition dates (dates you can reduce quantities, guest numbers, food and beverage guarantees, without penalty)*
- ✓ *Number guarantee dates*
- ✓ *Cancellation charges*
- ✓ *Terms and conditions*
- ✓ *Policies and procedures*
- ✓ *General information/general catering information*

Your contract will refer to the fact that their policies outlined in their general information literature—these are usually stand-alone brochures or handouts with their full sales kit that should be presented with your other catering information—will be applicable, as are any related charges, terms and conditions. It is essential that you know what they are and what they will mean to your event. For example, in many General Catering Information booklets, it is stated that function rooms are assigned according to the guaranteed minimum number of persons anticipated and that the venue reserves the right to relocate your event to a more appropriate space should your guest's expected number change. You can lose the space that was the perfect setting for your event or be forced to pay a room surcharge in order to secure the space.

Should you not take the time to review the contract terms and conditions and related material, you may also see hidden charges show up on your final reconciliation that you may not have anticipated. For example, in the General Catering Information it may state that a cake-cutting fee of $3.50 per person plus applicable taxes, service charges and gratuities will be charged should you select your own baker; that seemingly small cost can add up depending on your guest count.

Or, you may find a clause that says round tables of 8 or 10 are customary and the venue reserves the right to adjust the table size in the event the number of guests has changed. (This could affect your seating chart and table assignments as well as tabletop decor, linens, etc., requirement and charges.)

These are critical areas that must be reviewed as they affect your costs, staff requirements, timing and logistics, but are ones that may not be listed specifically in your contract.

Many of the clauses listed under General Information can be waived, reduced, amended or adjusted if you make them part of your contract negotiations, but first you must do your homework and request necessary changes to contract terms and conditions. Your contract must clearly define all terms and conditions you are agreeing to. Do not hesitate to ask any of your venues or suppliers to prepare a revised contract or a written amendment. Never sign a contract until the changes you have requested have been made.

Once you have received concessions on various items, have the changes and amendments clearly spelled out in your contract and properly signed off on by someone who is an authorized signing officer of the company. Once you have signed the contract you will have lost your negotiating advantage and will be legally bound to their terms and conditions.

7

Who's It All For?

Know Your Guest Demographics

It is important to fully understand exactly who will be in the room or attending the event so that you can tailor your event inclusions and event style to meet their needs, tastes and event expectations.

For example, consider the target audience that would be a fit for each of the following festive corporate holiday theme events (or end-of-year celebrations, as some companies are choosing to refer to holiday events, to be politically correct and inclusive), both in and outside the office:

Jingle Bell Rock

In Jingle Bell Rock, office holiday parties combine fantasy, fun and the spirit of the season with team building. During the day, staff members form bands, choose their instruments and learn to play one or two classic holiday songs with a rock-and-roll edge. Air bands with choreographed moves—in place of instruments—is another option. Later in the day, staff come together, perform their songs in front of one another and have the office rocking as they jam together, taking celebrating the season to a new level. Suggested Jingle Bell Rock party menu: mini burgers (beef and veggie), hot dogs, French fries, milk shakes and create-your-own ice cream sundae bars.

Cool Yule

Guests are invited to step into Jack Frost's frozen winter wonderland. Snowfall light boxes simulate a cascade of snow falling as the venue doors open. For added drama, dry ice would produce a magical special effect—Jack Frost blowing frosty air when staff members enter—as would a laser show reproducing the northern lights. Oversize icicles and snowflakes are hung from the ceiling. Ice penguins and polar bears frolic on iceberg sets. Further room treatment could include blue mini lights, ice shards and full-size ice snowmen. Serving tables—featuring a stepped raw oyster and seafood bar—could be covered in frosty sparkle organza. Tall cocktail tables, when covered from top to bottom in white spandex and uplit, give off an icy glow. Added decor touches could include snowflakes in chipped-ice rectangles, ice candle snowball globes and ice vases filled with yuletide bonsai on ice pillars. Drinks such as a "Polar Ice Cap," as a true icebreaker, could be served in glasses carved from ice from an actual ice luge—guests' drinks will slide right down into a sparkling Swarovski-crystal martini glass. The Glass Orchestra providing ethereal percussion and performance ice sculptors would have guests spellbound. Take-home gift ideas: miniature snowglobes by Christopher Radko, which when shaken produce a wonderland of snow, or a set of Waterford's red crystal flutes with clear carved snowflakes and a bottle of champagne to celebrate the upcoming new year.

Holiday Fun Do

Gather the office for an informal catered holiday "fun do"—a fondue party featuring thinly sliced meat and vegetables (eggplant, mushrooms, etc.), breads and fruit. Guests can sample a heartwarming fare of meat and vegetables simmered in an assortment of savory broth, dip cubed bread and fresh vegetables in melted Kirsch-seasoned Swiss Emmental and

Gruyère cheese, and for a sensational finish, swirl fruit, pound cake and marshmallows in melted chocolate. Fondues are making a comeback, add a touch of nostalgia to the holiday season and provide a melting pot of memories. Holiday Fun Do can also be incorporated into an office ice skating, sledding or cross-country skiing party theme. Special note: Fondues cater to non-vegetarians, pure vegans (vegetables and vegetable broth) and lacto-vegetarians whose choices allow cheese, those looking for no carbs, as well as people who want to indulge. There is something for everyone.

Holiday Magic

Alternate theme name: Mistletoe Magic (if spouse/partner is invited)

It is the perfect season to conjure up a celebration that includes a sleigh(t) of hand, merriment and magic. Close-up magicians (both male and female) can entertain guests by mingling, mixing with them during the reception and performing a customized parlor magic and mentalism show. The magic acts can be tied to the season or, as a finale, to a corporate message. Take-home gift idea: an award-winning, mind-bending collection of parlor puzzles that capture the magical theme, set in a custom-designed box (www.parlorpuzzles.com).

Festive Frolic

Alternate theme name: Nutcracker Sweet

Step through candy cane arches—guarded by six-foot nutcrackers—into a childhood vision of the holiday season. The room is filled with prelit miniature evergreen trees, which twinkle and beckon guests in. A flame in a full-size ice-fireplace bar is warming three-foot-high candy mittens. Festive holiday sprites flit around the fireplace with glasses of world-famous Frrrozen Hot Chocolate for guests to sample, or cups of cheer in the form of a winter warmer along with old-fashioned finger food. A 20-foot ice sleigh is filled with snow cones in festive tones capturing the season's playful spirit. Oversize holiday props bring back the feeling of being little and having stepped back in time into the magical world of make-believe. Decadent chocolate-caramel candy apples made merry with marzipan decorations, giant lollipops, pretzels dipped in chocolate and covered in peppermint sprinkles, cheesecake pops, tempting cupcakes, over-the-top custom candy creations and nostalgic favorites such as Pez are among the tantalizing treats displayed on iridescent crushed velvet. Interactive childhood games, train sets, cookie-decorating areas, candy picture frame stations and candy jewelry–making tables can be set up around the room to bring out the kid in all of us. In the course of the celebration, an improvisational painter will capture the merry mood and create a lasting office memento. Take-home gift idea: candy cane–monogrammed scarves—winter warmers—packaged in brightly wrapped gift boxes with licorice ribbon and sugared candy, or festive fiber-optic holiday stockings filled with holiday treats.

Knowing your audience will tell you if they are open to a festive and fun event style or if they would prefer a more classic holiday event. Knowing who your target audience is and what the company and event objectives are will help you to create an event with style and substance. Just as your client has event expectations that have to be met, so does the attendee. And if your event lacks audience appeal, perhaps because you proposed Jingle Bell Rock to guests who would have enjoyed more classic holiday fare and been more comfortable listening to entertainment and perhaps joining in (caroling) than being forced to be the main entertainment, then attendance and interest will be compromised and not viewed with event anticipation. At one corporate event, guests were asked to wear fake tattoos and women were asked to wear theirs on their lower back, dress permitting. A tattoo in this location is often referred to as a "tramp stamp." It caused guests to be uncomfortable, as did the pole dancing that had been set up for guests to take part in and entertain their fellow employees.

The Guest List

Who is your targeted audience? Who will make up your guest list? Who are you inviting? The reasons why you are choosing to invite these individuals can be as varied as the types of events that can be held. For an in-depth review of how to choose the right event to meet corporate and guest objectives, please refer to *The Executive's Guide to Corporate Events and Business Entertaining.*

With any event, you want to ensure that the "right" people are there and that it is not just a roomful of people. If you send an invitation to a specific person, make sure that you state on the invitation whether it is transferable. In some cases it may be acceptable to have someone else come in the place of your invitee. In other cases you may have a limited number of spots and you want to prioritize your guests. Therefore, those on Guest List A who cannot attend will be replaced by the next person on Guest List B. In this scenario you don't really want someone you don't even know coming in place of the original invitee.

Who needs to be there? If it is an event where you are seeking media attention, how many journalists are you inviting? Are government officials being asked? Corporate staff or clients? Suppliers? What kind of energy will be generated if you mix different groups? For example, if a hotel chain does a client appreciation event, it may or may not be appropriate to bring potential corporate clients together with sales staff from competing companies. The potential corporate clients could end up feeling like they have been thrown into a feeding frenzy as sales executives vie for their attention, and sales executives may never leave their side, hoping to keep their competitors at bay. Instead, the hotel could do two different events—one for the potential clients and one for the sales executives. Or, if it wanted to showcase its talents, the hotel could do one splashy event for all. What is key is that the hotel knows how the guests could interact with one another and make their decision on who to invite based on the objectives of the proposed event.

How Many?

As discussed earlier, before you can begin to look for space for your event you need to know the number of guests that will be attending and some idea of what your event will include.

You need to take into consideration all of your event requirements in order to know the number of guests you can accommodate and fit budgetwise:

» Will you need overnight accommodation? For how many?

» Will the number of rooms be based on single or double occupancy?

» Will you require any suites for VIPs?

» If it is a day event, will you need any accommodation for guests to change in or use for private meetings?

» Will you require any early or late checkouts?

» How many participants will your meeting room need to hold?

» What room setup are you considering? Will it be theater style, rounds of eight, U-shaped, a hollow square? Will it have display areas? How will the food be presented? Will you need to allow space to set up buffet tables or food stations?

» Will you be having rear-screen projection, a stage or translation booths?

» Will you be requiring breakout rooms where guests attending meetings in the main room may break into smaller meetings? For how many? For how long? What will be the room setup in each? Will any audiovisual equipment be involved?

» Will you be requiring separate rooms for meals or coffee breaks? How many will be attending? Will they be stand-up or sit-down?

» Will you require any rooms or offices for your staff to work from?

» Will you require a private area for setup? How many people does it need to accommodate?

» What sort of event will you be having? For example, will you be having a silent auction? How many tables will you require?

» Will your reception be stand-up with some scattered seating? Does it need to be held in a separate area?
» Will your dinner be plated—served at the table—or a stand-up buffet?
» If your dinner is sit-down, will the tables be round, seating 8 or 10, or perhaps rectangles?
» Will you require a stage, room for a dance band or a dance floor?

All of these logistical and budget requirements can help you determine the number of guests that you will be able to invite to the event.

Guest Profile: Who?

» What are the age demographics?
» Will guests be coming as couples or singles? Is this a corporate event without spouses? Are the corporate sponsors attending a fund-raising gala, purchasing individual tickets, tables of 10 or tickets for family and friends? Who will make up your guest list? Will it be corporate only, social—family and friends—or mixed?
» Will children or teenagers be attending? Will they be accompanied by adults or not? Keep in mind the legal drinking age and the liability of the host to check ID.
» How will guests be handling transportation? Will they all be arriving on their own, by private car or limo, or will accessibility to public transportation need to be a consideration?

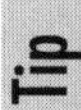

It is important to know what event elements are a must for maximum guest attendance. For example, for a multimedia event by a major corporate sponsor for 3,000 guests aged 19 to 24, having accessible public transportation was a key factor in venue selection. Had the venue for this event been located in an area that was perceived as being difficult, time consuming or expensive to get to, then it would not have had targeted guest appeal nor met guests' needs, which included access to public transportation.

Guest List Checklist

List Development *6 Months Before Event*

Allow a minimum of eight weeks for the preparation of the guest list to ensure that addresses are current and have been cross-referenced.

Guest List A

Keep in mind maximum room capacity set by fire regulations.

Your event can be closed down if you ignore fire regulations on capacity, fire exits, bathrooms and signage. But remember that there are ways of increasing capacity, such as outdoor tents, bringing in additional bathroom facilities and the like if your proposed guest list count requires that you look at other options to comply with fire regulations.

Watch timing of mail delivery and RSVP date.

Will guests be out of the country for school breaks, or will holidays such as Christmas, New Year's, Passover or Easter interfere with the success of your event?

Guest List B

Backup to replace guests from Guest List A who are unable to attend.

Again, pay attention to timing of invitations for mailing and RSVP date.

For the attendee, every event begins with the invitation. And unless the event is mandatory attendance, such as a company function, what the invited guest holds in their hands—or inbox in the case of e-vites, or viewed on their screen with CD or DVD invitations—is their initial reaction to the event. The invitation style, delivery and timing of its arrival (if it arrives days before the event, they will assume they were on the B or even D list of invitees) can influence greatly whether they will choose to take part or give the event a pass. The invitation, as all event elements, must be a match for the intended guests as well as for the individual, company or sponsors hosting the event.

Invitations

If your event is taking place during a busy social season, you may wish to consider sending save-the-date teaser cards. If the event is being held out of country, send postcards showing the location, with a printed message saying that you are looking forward to meeting with them there, the date of the event and other pertinent information. Another idea is a letter or teaser invitation, such as a snow scraper with the message "Don't be left out in the cold" sent to participants of an incentive program to spur on their sales. These should include details such as date and time. Location and dress information can follow at a later date. This works well for all special events, including meetings, conferences, conventions and incentives. It builds a "buzz" of anticipation around your event.

If you state in your save-the-date card or letter that invitations will be forthcoming by a certain date, make certain that they are. It will demonstrate to others how your company does business—you deliver on time. When you receive an invitation a month later than the date stated in the save-the-date letter, it demonstrates a lack of professionalism. If the message is going out under your president's signature, ensure that you deliver what it says.

When placing your printing order, allow for one invitation per couple and one place card and menu per person. Make sure that you order more than you need and that you have allowed adequate time for printing. For some reason, printers always seem to want a minimum of four weeks unless you want to incur rush order charges, which would need to be included in your budget breakdown. Of course, you will have checked with them to see if they can handle your order and deliver the appropriate quality and quantity of items on time. Make sure that you have all camera-ready artwork ready when needed and know the exact Pantone color to be used for company logos. Have your envelopes printed first so that you can begin to address them and, if you can afford it, hire a calligrapher. People generally open hand-written invitations first, making them much more effective than those printed on labels or envelopes.

Print Invitation Quote Requirements

» *Your timelines—the dates you will require your print material by*

» *Type of print material you will be requiring (e.g., invitations, RSVP cards, enclosures, etc.)*

» *Quantities of each type required*

» *Quality of paper—you may be looking for stock or specialty paper such as handmade, Japanese, vellum, watermark, torn edges (deckle edge), die cut (specialty shapes) and/or decorative envelope linings*

» *Type of printing—embossed (raised print), thermography (raised print that is similar in appearance to engraved printing, but less expensive and is adhered only to the surface with no impression; the back of the paper is smooth), engraved (formal, leaves an impression on the back of the paper), letterpress (more expensive), etc.*

» *Colors*

» *Fonts (typeface)*

» *Graphics*

Whether you are mailing the invitations yourself or using a mail house, always send an invitation to yourself to gauge if you are going to run into any problems. When it does arrive, check to see when it actually went out. If you contracted a mail house to mail the invitations by a specific date, and your invitation's postmark shows they didn't do so, you will need proof when you discuss the matter with them. If your invitation does not arrive by a certain date, you will need to start phoning guests to see if they have received theirs. There could be a problem with delivery, or they could still be sitting on someone's desk. If guests receive their invitation just a couple of days before an event, it makes it difficult to change established plans and could result in a very poor turnout. Not only will it have the effect of making your guests feel as though they were on Guest List Z, it also makes your job of planning the event nearly impossible.

In order to call in food and beverage guarantees and to do a revised costing based on accurate numbers, you must request that your guests RSVP by a specific date and have staff follow up with phone calls to confirm attendance. The phone follow-up is a good time to confirm any name or address changes.

If security passes—visual event ID that guests wear at celebrity events—or tickets to the actual event are being mailed out once the invitation has been received and the RSVP called in, make sure that you have allowed sufficient time for the guest to receive them. At some events it is necessary to show your security pass, invitation or ticket to gain admittance, and while there will be an official guest list at the front door in case any guests forget to bring theirs, there will be less congestion and the lineups will move faster if all guests have received theirs in time.

» Check mail delivery schedules for first-class mail. What are the minimum and maximum number of days for your area? Keep in mind that these times can change without notice and the time of year could have an impact as well. If your invitation is going out over the holiday season, there could be delays. Check with your local post office as you start to plan your event. Check both local and international delivery schedules if applicable.
» Check postage rates for first-class mail. Out-of-country mail has a different rate than local. Make sure that mail is separated and the correct postage applied. Oversize and odd-shaped envelopes will require additional postage that needs to be added to your budget, and it can run into the tens of thousands of dollars as one event planner

found out. It is always best to bring a sample invitation to the local post office to ensure it does not exceed the standard size or weight, and if it does, find out what the cost will be for mailing and courier (depending on what else is being sent with the invitation).

» Check mail delivery schedules for third-class mail. What are the minimum and maximum number of days, and what are the postal rates?

Check both local and international delivery schedules if applicable. Adjust timelines accordingly to accommodate the third-class mail delivery schedule if you decide to use this route. You usually have to send a minimum number of pieces to be eligible for third-class mail. Again, out-of-country and oversize, heavy and odd-shaped envelopes will require extra postage. Again, it is always best to bring a sample to the local post office to make sure the invitation does not exceed size or weight standards.

Never use third-class mail for corporate events. Third-class mail is generally associated with bulk or "junk" mail and is not appropriate for elegant events.

Invitation Checklist

Invitation Design — 6 Months Before Event

Issues to Decide:

» Maximum number of guests to attend per invitation.

Things to be Included on the Invitation:

» Number of Guests Invited
» Event Name
» Event Description
» Date
» Time (Beginning/Ending/Schedule of Events)
» Venue
» Directions
» Parking Details
» Dress Code

(continued)

- RSVP Address, Telephone and Fax Number
- Ticket Order Form (if applicable)
- Return Reply Envelope (optional)

Details to Designer 16 Weeks Prior to Event

- Make sure you have advised designers of your proposed timelines well in advance so they are prepared to handle your order.
- Check to see when they and printers will be closed for holidays.
- Will they require additional time for special orders such as custom paper?
- What will they require from you? Will they want camera-ready artwork? Decide what their needs are and incorporate them into your Critical Path so that you will have everything available to them on time.

Mail House Booked 16 Weeks Prior to Event

- Make sure you have advised mail house of your proposed timelines well in advance so they are prepared to handle your order.
- You may wish to handle mailing in-house for more hands-on control.

First Review of Invitation Design 14 Weeks Prior to Event

Second Review of Invitation Design (if required) 13 Weeks Prior to Event

Invitations to Printer 12 Weeks Prior to Event

Envelopes to Mail House 10 Weeks Prior to Event

- Envelopes to be addressed, stuffed and stamped. Allow a minimum of one week for processing. Check their recommended timelines, which could change based on whatever else they may be handling over the same time period.

Invitations Mailed to Guest List A 7 Weeks Prior to Event

- This will vary depending on your area's delivery schedule and where invitations are being sent. A teaser could be sent out earlier letting guests know to hold the event date open, with the invitation to follow.

RSVP Cutoff for Guest List A 5 Weeks Prior to Event

VIP Guest Passes Mailed to Guest List A 5 Weeks Prior to Event

(If applicable—guest passes are generally used as a visible means of security control, and they can be worn around the neck, clipped onto purses or belts or worn around the wrist. At some events there can be two types of guest security passes—one designated "all access" and others that have a more limited access to VIP rooms, etc.)

Invitations Mailed to Guest List B	5 Weeks Prior to Event
RSVP Cutoff for Guest List B	3 Weeks Prior to Event
VIP Guest Passes Mailed to Guest List B (if applicable)	3 Weeks Prior to Event

These timelines are based on everything being received and completed on time. Dates should be backed up at least one week if you have any concerns about artwork being received on time, imputing of addresses, delivery schedules and such. What you least expect may happen—mail strikes, computer breakdown—so, whenever you can, prepare as far ahead as possible.

Invitation Overview

Guest List Development	6 Months Before Event
Invitation Design	6 Months Before Event
Details to Designer	16 Weeks Prior to Event
Mail House Booked	16 Weeks Prior to Event
First Review of Invitation Design	14 Weeks Prior to Event
Second Review of Invitation Design (if required)	13 Weeks Prior to Event
Invitations to Printer	12 Weeks Prior to Event
Envelopes to Mail House	10 Weeks Prior to Event
Invitations Mailed to Guest List A	7 Weeks Prior to Event
VIP Guest Passes Mailed to Guest List A (if applicable)	5 Weeks Prior to Event
Invitations Mailed to Guest List B	5 Weeks Prior to Event
RSVP Cutoff for Guest List B	3 Weeks Prior to Event
VIP Guest Passes Mailed to Guest List B (if applicable)	3 Weeks Prior to Event

* Depending on local delivery and busy holiday schedules. Keep in mind that over the holiday season, school breaks and summer vacations, guests could be out of town and you schedule accordingly to ensure that Guest List A have sufficient time to respond.

Media

If you are inviting media to your event, you need to look at how and when they will attend. Will they be treated as invited guests? If so, you need to factor them into your food and beverage count. Are you thinking of doing a separate press conference? What are their requirements? It is in your best interest to find out what they need and to do everything possible to make sure that those needs are met. They may need an area to park their film crew's truck, places to run their cables or have a media feed that they can plug into. They could be doing live coverage and need to have a specific interview at a designated time. Take the time to ask what they need. Even better, anticipate what they need. Assign staff to work with the media exclusively to ensure that they have access to the right people for interviews. Make sure that press kits are prepared for them in advance and accommodate their photo shoot list by prearranging the time and the setting with people who will be required to be photographed together. At one high-profile event held in a ballroom, a separate side room was set up exclusively for the press in a quiet, contained, private environment, complete with refreshments, press kits, etc. An assigned staff member brought in key people to be interviewed and posed together, as opposed to having it take place in the actual event when people could be engaged in important conversations.

Media people are very busy. Respect their time and never forget what they contribute to the successful coverage of your event. Look for ways you can work together so that both of you come out ahead. They may need access to a room where they can conduct private interviews or have people pose for pictures. It is important to remember that media have numerous events to choose from and if you want them to consider your invitation, you will have to make the experience pleasurable. Work with them. Together you are building working relationships. One thing to always bear in mind, though, is that they can be called away on a breaking hard-news story at any time.

Media Q&A

Q & A

Will media coverage be a part of your event?

Decide when and where media will be included in your event. You may choose to hold a press conference beforehand or set up separate media interviews. Consider where these will be best held and if you will need a separate room.

Q & A

Will media be at your event as invited guests?

Have you included them in your food and beverage count? If you are having a cocktail reception followed by dinner, will they be seated at a separate press table or with your guests? At one fund-raiser where media were invited, tables were provided for them but no food. Needless to say, they were not pleased. Imagine the coverage that fund-raiser got, not to mention future relations between the media and the charity and the event planning committee. If you have invited media to be there as guests, treat them as such. If they are invited only to cover a certain segment, be very clear about that in your invitation so that they know what to expect. If, for security reasons, media are admitted only one at a time to meet key celebrities, a separate media room (with ample refreshments) should be set up for them.

Q & A

Are there any special requirements for media that need to be included, such as a separate media room, media feeds or parking for their equipment trucks?

Find out when the media are coming and what they are bringing. What would they ideally like to see happen? What would make their job easier for them? Don't be caught off guard. You don't want a media news team showing up to go live with no news to report. It is a waste of everyone's time if media arrive too far ahead of the celebrities/guests/entertainment and before the event has truly begun. It is your job to tell the media the best time for them to show up so that the energy of the room comes across on the screen

Q & A

or in pictures. On the other hand, keep media deadlines in mind when planning your schedules. For example, if you want coverage of your president's speech on the 11 p.m. news, you have to give the media cameras and editors enough time to prepare the story. To maximize your coverage, you need to work with media wherever possible. That way you both end up winning, and they will remember you at your next event.

Q & A

What is the purpose of press kits?

Press kits should include any information that will make it easier for media to report their stories. You need to consider the focus of the story and the message that you want the reporters to deliver. Include, where applicable, biographies of any of the attendees or background information on the event or its sponsors. Know how many kits you will need and make sure that you have added the cost for these into your budget. You need to take into consideration who will be responsible for preparing them, and where, how and by whom they will be distributed. You need to decide if you will be setting up a separate registration table for media so that they can sign in and receive their media kit, as opposed to waiting until they have concluded their interviews and photo shoots to get the kit. By doing a separate media registration desk, you will be able to see who has arrived and assign representatives to show them important areas and introduce them to key people. Also, you can keep track of media no-shows, follow up with a phone call and mail them a press kit.

Children at Your Event

If children will be attending your event there are some wonderful properties that seem to be designed just for them. Many cruise ships and hotels have excellent supervised activities. Meals can be arranged at separate times and locations, away from the adults, and experienced babysitters can be arranged. Separate theme parties can be held for adults and children. There are a number of activities for children, such as private excursions, or they can receive expert sports instruction—private beach Olympics can be geared to the children's ages and abilities.

Menus are designed to delight young palates, with small portions that are easily manageable and fun being the order of the day. Entertainment can include acrobats, costumed characters or clowns, face painters, jugglers, magicians, puppet shows or storytellers.

Sample theme parties that you can set up at the venue of your choice include:

- Carnival with games and prizes for all. Photo booths and sticker machines (each child's face is put on stickers) can also be rented. Also available are machines for popcorn, candy floss, candy apples, waffles, snow cones, hot dogs, nachos, pretzels, donuts, ice cream and candy.
- Miniature golf with lessons from the "pros." Older children can actually have lessons on the greens either out on a mini golf course or with simulated golf holes rented and set up at your venue.
- Arcade games can include virtual reality and big-screen interactive videos, driving simulators, ski and snowboard simulators, wave runners, foosball, air hockey and skill cranes filled with stuffed animals of your choice.
- Pool tables with "pool sharks" on hand to teach older children trick shots. (This can also be used for an adult cocktail party theme.) Pool tables can be rented and set up at the venue of your choice.
- Giant inflatables that can include the sticky Olympics (with Velcro body suits and Velcro obstacles), megamountains to climb, bungee runs, sports games and giant slides and obstacle courses.

If children are taking part in active games, it is advisable to have parents give their written permission. You will need to know if there are any medical problems such as food allergies, and have professional staff on hand in sufficient numbers to provide proper care.

Make sure that you know how to contact the parents in case of an emergency. Remember, children and parents do not necessarily have the same last names. Make sure you have all pertinent information.

Security is also important. You want to make sure that children are in a safe, protected area. You can also arrange security ID. Make sure that children are accompanied to the bathroom by staff of the same sex so that they can assist them if needed. Name tags on sweaters and jackets do not work, as children are prone to take them off and they also allows strangers to call them by name. A wristband ID might be a better solution.

E-vites, CD and DVD Invitations

Today invitations come in many forms. For casual get-togethers, people are personally using free e-vites that are available online to send out invitations to family and friends. In business, however, companies that want to be viewed as cutting edge are using custom interactive CD and DVD invitations in addition to print invitations, if their event and event style suggests that an imaginative high-tech invite may be the way to go.

There are companies who can create custom CD-ROM invitations for events that can stand—and stand out—on their own as the formal invitation, be used as a hold-the-date teaser, or act as supplement to their print invitation.

Just as they must with traditional invitations, event planners will need to have event logistics, such as the event date, location, times, RSVP information, etc., in place before they can place their order. Costs can be comparable to paper invitations.

Planners have several options available to them. They can use existing templates and include video inviting their guests to the event (or just provide text if preferred) or create a personalized CD-ROM that can include edited video (sent on VHS or MiniDV or, if digitized, as an AVI, MPG, MOV or WMV file) anywhere from 90 seconds to 2 minutes in duration, and the photos and images that will be incorporated into their invitation.

For a custom wedding invitation, for example, couples can share the story of how they met, how their courtship evolved and how they became engaged, in addition to inviting guests to come and be a part of a very special day in their lives. They can include on their custom wedding invitation CD-ROM everything from childhood photos to photographs of their first date, engagement party and them standing in front of the church where they are to be married (and even include family and friends in it). Couples end up with an invitation that uniquely reflects them as a couple and contains all of their special memories. For example, a couple whose shared passion is a love of skydiving can have their whole CD-ROM reflect this and they can have their skydiving pictures and experiences built into their personalized wedding invitation. Custom verse as well as music can be added to their CD-ROM. The front of the CD-ROM can feature a picture of the couple and the couple's names set against the backdrop of their choice. This same application can be done for corporate, social and nonprofit event invitations.

The process usually takes anywhere from two to four weeks depending on which package is chosen and the nature of the invitation inclusions. Planners will have an opportunity to preview the final CD-ROM before it is shipped. What is important, from a logistical standpoint, is to keep in mind the invitation mailing date—not the event date—and work backwards from there to set your timelines as to when everything has to be submitted. You will need to factor in shipping times as well. Remember to build in a time buffer. Estimate to have everything in to the company creating your custom CD invitation at least 60 days prior to your mailing date. The video and pictures that are being used may not be returned, so it will also be important to ensure that enough time is scheduled in to have duplicates made. If RSVP cards or traditional invitations are also being included, remember to coordinate their timing so there are no mailing delays. Rush orders can be accommodated but there will be surcharges.

Custom envelopes can be ordered and addressed in advance so that that everything is ready to go once the wedding invitation CD-ROMs are received. Once the invitations are packaged, it will be important to take them to the post office to make sure that appropriate postage is affixed and have them hand stamped.

Event Websites and Event RSVP Websites

Print, CD and DVD invitations are all using custom—password-accessible only—event websites for RSVPs as well as pre- and post-event information and event management. Event planning companies now have the capacity to create websites that are exclusively for a specific event. They can be set up so that there are private areas available only to the event planning company, but provisions can be made so that the client can have access to review specific areas such as guest list RSVP. Guests—using an assigned password—can also view certain unrestricted areas of the event website to review event inclusions, dress codes, etc. Post event, with the event planning company's and event host company's legal approval, pictures of the event may be posted. There may be certain provisions that have to be adhered to with regards to posting pictures of people attending the event.

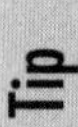

When sending CD or DVD invitations and requesting RSVPs via website or using the event website for other purposes, such as media presentations and podcasts. keep in mind your guest list and whether or not they have computer access, optimal Internet speed, proper media player installation, etc.

8

Food and Beverage

Food and beverage at an event can be the main focus, such as at a gourmet wine- and food-tasting theme party, or can become creative eye candy, an enticing edible centerpiece, an interactive icebreaker and even a sweet, tempting take-home gift. Picture, for example, red tablecloths with centerpiece platters made of bright, shiny, red candy apples that are covered in M&Ms for a festive feel—one that will be pleasing to both kids and kids at heart. Or, apples that have been covered in thick, creamy, gooey caramel and drizzled with milk and white chocolate, set out as part of your centerpiece display on deep, rich brown linens for a fall event. You will find when using items such as tempting candy apples instead of floral arrangements at your next party, your centerpiece will become edible artwork at the end of the evening. Clear cellophane bags can be distributed at each place setting and your guests can take home a sweet reminder of the evening to enjoy at their leisure.

Food, beverage and how they are served, as well as room layout, also play an important part in strategic planning on how to meet certain company and event objectives (strategic planning is covered extensively in *The Business of Event Planning*). Food stations can be set up to deliberately draw people into a room and get them moving around, mixing and mingling, as opposed to staying in one spot and having drinks and appetizers passed to them by waitstaff. There is a time and a place for both and you need to look at food and beverage style and service as staging tools that can be used to orchestrate and bring about a specific guest response targeted to meet a company and event objective. Consider the different event energy that food and beverage and how you present them can bring to your event.

For example, people tend to congregate at the bar during events when drink service is not provided and standing in one spot when strategic planning is not part of the mix. You need to create icebreakers that will draw people into the room, and set up action food stations, beverage stations and entertainment staging to get people interacting.

Don't be afraid to try something new, like setting up a Glenlivet "tasting" station (Glenlivet, French Oak Finish [aged 12 years], American Oak Finish [aged 12 years], Glenlivet Archive [aged 21 years]) as an icebreaker to get your guests talking and sharing their thoughts as opposed to a standard wine-tasting event element. It can be entertaining, enlightening and educational and bring people together.

Examples of Texas Theme Parties with Different Energy

Taste of Texas and Diamond & Denim

You can have fun with the invitations! For a casual, country-western "Taste of Texas" theme, you could design "wanted" posters (with familiar faces) and have them done up in sepia tone. Or if you want to do something a little more ritzy, consider a "Diamond and Denim" theme, and go all out with the invitations and invite guests to come dressed in denim and "diamonds" (real or faux, only they will know).

You could begin your evening or event with a strumming cowboy to greet your guests at the door and serenade your guests.

Icebreakers can include card sharks (sleight-of-hand card tricks by magicians dressed in western garb), trick ropers or even a friendly game of horseshoes. You can also rent a jukebox filled with classic western tunes.

Budget and space allowing, you could even consider bringing in some midway games.

Appetizers featuring crab cakes with roasted red-pepper sauce, boiled Texas Gulf shrimp, hickory-smoked salmon or cornbread-crusted oysters can be passed among your guests.

Cowboy Cocktails, such as Jack and Seven, also known as Seven and Seven in the South (Jack Daniel's Old No. 7 and 7UP), Texas Comfort (Southern Comfort and Ginger Ale), Texas Tea (Jack Daniel's and Pepsi, among other ingredients), whiskey/bourbon on the rocks or straight up, and whiskey sours may find their way on to your beverage menu. Beers—Lone Star and Shiner Bock—served in the bottle, not a glass, could become a staple part of your function. Chardonnay and Cabernet by Llano would be much-enjoyed wines. For sodas—an assortment of root beer, Pepsi and Slice sodas are in keeping with the Texas theme, as are pitchers of iced tea and lemonade.

You'll want to include traditional Texan eats on your supper menu. Think of tantalizing T's—sizzling T-bone steaks hot off the grill, tender beef tenderloins served smothered in your guests' choice of steak toppers—sautéed garlic mushrooms, caramelized onions (cooked with butter and balsamic vinegar) or, as they do in Texas, a combination of both.

If you are serving a Texas Hill Country Buffet, you might want to include hickory-smoked, barbecued back ribs, mesquite grilled chicken or grilled whitewings—chicken breast stuffed with a jalapeño pepper, marinated and wrapped with bacon—(originally created by Don Strange, Catering by Don Strange of San Antonio, using dove breast), pecan-crusted chops, Texas burgers or a big ol' hot dog with all the fixings (mushrooms, onions, bacon, cheese, avocado, chili and hot peppers). For those wishing a touch of the more exotic, you could include fried alligator tail, rattlesnake, smoked buffalo sausage, Rocky Mountain oysters (don't ask), game and fish.

Texas fare is hearty. Side dishes could include a selection of fluffy baked potatoes with sour cream, cheese and chili; red skin or garlic mashed potatoes; baked beans; coleslaw; potato salad; corn on the cob; chuckwagon salad; Texas chili (suggestion—you could make this vegetarian) and fresh baked rolls with creamy butter.

For dessert, keep it simple—rich chocolate brownies, apple cobbler à la mode and caramel, chocolate and pecan (Texas state tree) cheesecake and coffee and tea.

For the decor—with a country-casual theme—you could go with gingham in red or blue tones for the tablecloth and napkins—and ideally use enamel tableware.

With the Diamond and Denim theme—denim tablecloths—with handfuls of sparkling "diamonds" shimmering across the tabletop catching the candlelight. More "diamonds" can adorn the napkins, pulling in the theme.

A suggestion: as part of a Diamond and Denim theme party for a gala fund-raiser, sell chances at $100-plus apiece to make a "diamond mine." Proceeds benefit the charity. One diamond (donated) will be real and the others will be cubic zirconia. Or, another alternative as a fund-raising item would be to have Stetsons available (donated/sponsored) for sale, and have them custom steam fitted and sized at your event to each individual guest.

It goes without saying, the yellow rose of Texas would be the perfect floral choice. Or floral arrangements in blue tones in honor of the bluebonnet—Texas's state flower.

Following cocktails and supper, you may want to work off your dinner by dancing. Professional instructors can come to your event for an hour or so and teach your guests the Texas Two-Step, the latest line dance or even lead them through a square dance.

Be prepared to pass the bourbon and cigars at your party, but give a pass on any suggestions for old-fashioned shoot-outs or quick-draw competitions. In a western theme party in the past this may have been one of the entertainment elements, but not today—we only have to think back to a past Halloween when an actor attending a private party was killed when his costume included a toy gun that was mistaken for real.

Now, if you'd like to add a little spice to your event, with a few simple adjustments you can inject a Tex-Mex feel to your party.

Appetizers can include items from above and a selection of Mexican specialties, such as smoked chicken quesadillas, nachos, salsa, sour cream and guacamole.

The buffet can have an array of tempting southwest Mexican favorites—tortilla soup, fajitas, Spanish rice, tacos, enchiladas, refried beans, jalapeño poppers and pollo a la diabla (chicken breast sautéed in butter, chili, garlic, onion and mushrooms, served with a spicy Mexican salsa).

Add Corona or Tecate to your selection of beer and sangria to your choice of wine, and offer margaritas or tequila sunrises as part of your signature beverages.

A Mexican guitarist can greet your guests and the balance of the evening's entertainment can be mixed. And with your decor you would want to introduce a little more vibrancy.

Texas is known for and takes pride in doing things up "big," so don't be afraid to go over the top.

Cattle Baron Ball & Texas Black-Tie and Boots Ball

For a more formal Texas theme event, the "Cattle Baron Ball" and "Texas Black-Tie and Boots Ball" are two traditional theme parties that would have an entirely different feel and food and beverage menu.

Food and Beverage Considerations

Whether your event is a stand-up reception or a formal sit-down dinner, do not feel that you are limited to the menus you are offered. Most hotels, restaurants and caterers are willing to work with you to come up with a creative menu that will work within your budget. At one event, the dessert was ice cream fruits—ice cream in the shape, color and flavor of various fruits. Guests left talking about it, and many called the next day inquiring about them. The actual cost of the ice cream fruits was minimal, but the effect was maximal. That is the sort of inspired creativity you are looking for. For example, a well-known caterer does a wonderful fortune cookie cake that contains customized messages. Look for what is different. What can you do that shows flair, creativity, imagination and style?

Give thought to the type of food you will be serving. Remember to always include vegetarian selections. On your registration forms, be sure to include an area that asks about special meal requests and food allergies to help you in planning menus. You will need to know in advance how many guests are vegetarian, how many have allergies to seafood, peanuts and so on. Special meals can usually be arranged to meet their specific requirements.

If you are doing a stand-up reception with hot and cold hors d'oeuvres passed around, make sure that they are bite-size and can be handled easily—no bones or dripping sauces. Will people be eating them while holding just a napkin, or will there be plates? Does the facility have enough plates for several courses, or will there be delays as the plates are cleaned and brought back out again? The same applies to glasses for specialty drinks. Does the venue have sufficient glasses on hand or do glasses have to be brought in and budgeted for? You need to ensure that you ask the questions and are comfortable with the answers. Advertising a martini bar as part of your event loses something in the presentation if you find out the day before your event that the facility does not have martini glasses in stock. You could be scrambling to find rentals at the last minute and paying premium prices. It would play havoc with your budget projections as well.

You will have to tell the caterers exactly how many dinners to prepare in advance. This is known as a food guarantee and it can be a tricky business. If you guarantee 100 dinners and only 50 people show up, you will have to pay for all 100 meals and will have 50 very expensive doggie bags. Late RSVPs and no-shows make the guarantee a juggling act. In addition to no-shows, you might suffer the opposite problem—unexpected guests. That is where "overage" comes into play. With overage you still have to guarantee a certain number of meals, but the facility will prepare extras in case of last-minute changes. You may be able to cut your guarantee by 5 to 10 percent. You will be charged on the actual numbers, but should you have last-minute cancellations or no-shows, you may be able to save some dollars.

Decide who are included as guests and need to be included in the food guarantee. Are staff, staging and lighting crew, entertainment, photographers, and media included as invited guests, or will separate arrangements need to be made? If you are feeding them, make sure you have included these costs in your projected budget.

Perhaps the first rule of special events is to always have enough bartenders. And, if so, the second rule is to have enough liquor. It is embarrassing to run out. And consider carefully where your bars are placed. You want to avoid lineups and congestion. Are you being charged per drink, or can a flat rate be worked out? Do you need to obtain any special permits to have a bar or to extend the hours? Do you need to enclose the area where drinks can be served? Do you need to limit the type of drinks served—such as shooters or expensive brandies and wines—when the host is picking up the tab? Guests can quickly become intoxicated drinking shooters, particularly when contests start up, and your bar bill can quickly go through the roof. Rare brandies, ice wines and champagne are expensive and can have a major impact on your budget if everyone decides to sample them. Give precise instructions to the bartenders and waiters about how you want them to handle requests for such items. You may decide guests will be told that they can have champagnes or specialty items, but they have to pay for it themselves. Alternatively, you may decide that while it is not being promoted or offered openly, if a guest makes a specific request it is OK to fulfill it. If wine is included with the dinner, do you want the wine poured by the waiters or the bottles left on the table? Is the quantity unlimited, or is there a set number of bottles per table? How are requests for additional wine above the limit to be handled?

Include in your budget a provision for tipping the staff. Most facilities will calculate the gratuities based on a specific percentage and bill your master account. That percentage varies from venue to venue, so you need to ask in every case. In some areas they also apply a government tax on the amount being tipped. That may not seem like an important consideration, but these pennies can add up. If this applies, include it in your budget calculations.

Don't assume taxes on food and beverage are one and the same. If you are bringing any items into the facilities, find out what the "corkage" charges are. This charge applies if you are providing your own wine or liquor. For example, at fund-raisers a sponsor who is a winemaker may donate the wine for the event, and the facility will charge a corkage fee.

If you have an open bar but want to maintain some control, ask the beverage manager to let you know when you have reached the halfway point of your estimated budget so you can decide whether or not to slow service down.

With both food and bar service, make sure that teardown does not begin until staff has received clearance from you to do so. You may have to be flexible. With everything in full swing, guests may not want the party to end, and the client may decide to extend things. Find out about overtime charges—what would apply if you decided to extend the party? Make sure that all staff are aware in advance that this could be a possibility.

On an incentive program in Jamaica, the event planners were sitting in the dining room discussing the schedule and how important it is to be at hand during setup—you never know what can happen and when you will be needed to step in and make major decisions that could affect the success of your event. At that moment, kitchen staff came running to report a fire in the hotel's oven. The gala dinner was up in flames. The fire was quickly put out, but in the process the meat had been doused with fire extinguisher chemicals. Guests were about to arrive, and all the kitchen had prepared was chemically-soaked prime rib.

The kitchen staff wanted to just wash the chemicals off and serve the meat! Needless to say, this idea was vetoed, but the problem was that the hotel had no more prime rib. In the end, the solution was to borrow some from another hotel. The meat covered in chemicals was put aside but in plain sight so that it would not be used by accident or otherwise. That way, the result was not a planeload of passengers suffering from food poisoning or worse. Had event staff not been there at that precise moment, would they have been told what had gone on? What would have been the outcome if the chemically soaked meat was served? The event proceeded seamlessly, and the client was not even aware that there had been a problem.

Menu Planning

Take the time to do an initial budget before you begin to plan your menu. Start with all of the fixed costs—those that are not flexible—like room rental or bartender charges that could apply if you were taking over a facility exclusively. You can always have a custom menu created to fall within your budget guidelines and switch from a full bar to serving just wine and beer to bring costs in line. Knowing your fixed costs will help you determine what you can afford to spend on food and beverage and where you need to negotiate a better rate.

If the facility is receiving extensive revenue from food and beverage, there will generally be no charge for room rental. However, if you require extensive setup time for staging, lighting and decor, and the facility needs to close to handle your requests, you may be asked to compensate them for lost revenue in the form of room rental charges. These amounts can be negotiated, but you need to know what you are prepared to spend on food and beverage so that the facility can make a fair assessment based on what is coming in from your event versus what could be lost revenue.

A cardinal rule of menu planning is not to run out of food, but that sounds a lot simpler than it really is. Think about what will be put out and when. If you are setting out a lavish display of appetizers for guests to help themselves, you need to consider when the guests are arriving. Will there be anything left for latecomers if everything is put out at once? If you estimate four hors d'oeuvres per person and your guests come directly from work, perhaps having missed lunch, you may have a problem. Famished guests will not stop at four and you will quickly run out. The same applies to receptions where you may have two different groups attending. Group A could be attending a pre-reception event and Group B only the reception, which is scheduled to begin at a specific time. If Group A is delayed and Group B is at the reception first and all the food is put out at once, there may be only slim pickings left for Group A when they do show up. You could request that the food be brought out in staggered amounts, have someone from your event planning committee call to advise you when Group A will arrive so that you can have the tables replenished, and ensure that Group A is met with an attractive display ready and waiting for them.

You also need to give consideration to where the kitchen is and how items will make their way to your guests.

At one black-tie event with more than 1,000 guests, all the food and drink was coming from only one main area, and it never made it past the first wave of guests who had stationed themselves strategically to ambush the food and drink as it emerged from the kitchen. There were no separate food stations or satellite bars set up that would allow the waiters to approach the guests from another direction. Waiters attempted to move through the crowds carrying trays of wine and beer. It was very difficult for them to move in the congestion, and they had to take extreme care not to spill the content of their trays on the guests. Wine bars placed around the room would have helped to move guests from the one central area and lessened the congestion.

It was also impossible to find a place to lie down empty glasses and dishes. No side tables had been set up. Obviously, the venue had planned to have the staff circulate and clear away used glasses and dishes, but the congestion made this nearly impossible.

Hors d'oeuvres were being passed, but care had not been given to their selection. Items included those served on skewers, as well as shrimp with their tails on, and guests disposed of these discreetly in their cocktail napkins. Unfortunately, the staff was unable to circulate and clear the guests' garbage. The waiters were so busy trying to serve everyone that no one had time to clear the used dishes away. Designated staff to serve and others to clear would have helped to alleviate this.

In the end the waiters came out with bottles of wine in hand and began to try to maneuver around the crowds to top up the glasses of the guests who were fortunate enough to have them. To an observer it looked as though the venue had run out of glasses. It was nearly impossible to get a nonalcoholic beverage or a glass of water. You must give care and attention not only to the selection of the food and beverage but also to room layout, presentation, service and removal.

How will you handle early arrivals? Do you have a plan for what to do if you have a lineup at the door half an hour before you are scheduled to begin? If the client has told you to open the doors and serve everyone, are you able to do this? Do you have the bartenders, the waiters, the food and the music ready? Who has the authority to give the staff the official go-ahead? Make sure that all staff are on hand well before the event is scheduled to begin. This is particularly important, as staff may be hesitant to open just on the event planner's say-so.

As you begin to plan your menu take into consideration the season, the country, the local specialties and how adventuresome your guests are. Not everyone will be open to sampling rattlesnake, alligator or even buffalo meat. In Barbados and Florida, they often serve "dolphin," but they are quick to point out that it is not the "Flipper" variety—this is a fish, while the other is a mammal—as people begin to turn up their noses. In Morocco, a local delicacy is made from pigeon, which throws westerners, but the meal can also be made with chicken. Guests will appreciate knowing what they are eating, be it rabbit, goat or anything that may not be standard fare to them. Frog legs look a lot like chicken—and taste like it, too—but have a waiter discreetly ask if guests would like to try some frog legs. Some will be game and others not. But at least they were free to choose.

How will your guests react to live shrimp being cooked at the table in front of them (drunken shrimp cooked in beer)? Will they enjoy this local favorite or not? For events in other countries, a good way to experience local cuisine is to have a welcome buffet dinner that includes a sampling of local fare. Have staff explain to guests how each dish has been prepared or post a description by each serving tray. Always make sure that you offer a choice of entrees, a selection of salads and side dishes and an interesting array of desserts when you are including anything a little on the more "interesting" side.

How will your overall food presentation look? Does each dish complement one another visually and in the choice of selection? Is it vibrant and colorful? How will it look as it is presented? Is it tasty? Do the food choices work well together? Have you taken the time to ensure that the menu is balanced and that you have not designed one that is too heavy or not filling enough? If you are planning a heavy entree, you will want to offer a lighter selection of appetizers, salads and desserts. Foods that are too heavy, too hearty or too rich could leave your participants or guests feeling sleepy and lethargic. It is especially important at a meeting that the midday meal leave your participants ready to return to the meeting refreshed and full of energy, happy to continue on for the rest of the day. For this reason, it is probably not a good idea to include alcohol at lunch; instead offer a selection of beverages such as iced tea and lemonade, soft drinks, fruit juices and water. Keep the alcohol for the reception at the end of the day once the meeting has come to a close.

Breakfast

You have many options for breakfast at meetings, conferences, conventions or incentives. You may decide to arrange a breakfast buffet so that everyone can eat as a group and give them a chance to interact.

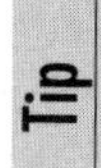

When you are doing a buffet, whether it is breakfast, lunch or dinner, try to have a two-sided layout, each set with the same items, so that you have two lines moving at once.

If possible, have more than one buffet station so that everyone is not standing in line at the same time. If you require portion control to save money and ensure food for all, have staff members serving. To limit the number in line, move the peripheral items, such as juice, cereal, fruit, desserts and coffee, to separate food stations. Always make sure that there are sufficient utensils for all. Watch out for areas that could cause congestion. Some resorts have toasters set up for guests to use, but the toasters have very limited capacity and are often bottlenecks. One solution would be to have baskets of toast brought to the tables instead. And whenever you are in a hot tropical climate, make sure that the food is kept at proper temperatures, is not sitting out too long and has a fan or some other device in place to keep insects and birds away.

Generally the hotel offers an array of buffet options at varying prices but read the fine print. What is the minimum charge to set up the buffet? Often the cost for the buffet in the hotel's food and beverage menu is based on a minimum of 50 guests, and there could be an additional surcharge if your numbers fall below that. Surcharges could also apply for a chef to prepare individual omelettes, pancakes and waffles or to carve a breakfast ham. For smaller numbers the venue may be able to create a buffet with fewer choices, or you may need to consider a sit-down breakfast where a set breakfast on a plate is brought to each guest. Wherever possible, try to avoid limiting options too severely and offer a menu that has variety and choice for breakfast, especially if lunch and dinner menus will be plated, which provides even less choice.

Remember that planning breakfast is not just about feeding your guests, but about your objective. Do you want to bring people together first thing in the morning, or do you want to give them some breathing room because they will be together the rest of the day?

If your meeting is for an extended period of time, you want to make sure that you offer some variety. If budget is a concern, and you need to stay within certain parameters, find out if you can work within one buffet budget range but offer different options each day. You will need to work with the catering staff on this. For instance, you may not be able to offer both fruit juices and slices if you are requesting they change the scrambled eggs to something that could be more labor intensive, such as omelettes or poached eggs. In order to offer a variety in the choice of eggs while remaining on budget, you may need to offer only bacon and sausage and forgo the ham.

You also have to take into consideration that people are becoming more health conscious. Make sure that, along with standard buffet fare of eggs, bacon, sausages and ham, you include yogurt, fresh fruit, juices, cereal, herbal teas and decaffeinated coffee. When given the choice, many people are opting for milk rather than cream in their coffee. Make both available to your guests and pay attention to future trends; guests have recently begun to request soy milk. And make sure that the milk and cream are fresh.

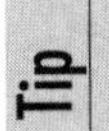

Wherever possible, have the milk and the cream in servers rather than in individual plastic containers. It is a much better presentation.

In some areas of the world you can also do fun interactive breakfast buffet events. In Arizona, you may want to consider a sunrise trail ride with a cookout in chuck wagons set up as buffet food stations. Guests choosing not to ride horseback can be transported by jeep. (Remember to cost in and arrange for porta-potties.)

Another breakfast option is to make arrangements for guests to dine at one of the hotel's restaurants, where they can choose anything off the menu and sign their bill to their guestroom. Most hotels offer a full buffet breakfast in their main restaurant, and the cost is often the same as a private buffet and sometimes less. If guests choose just juice, coffee and toast, that is all you will be charged for.

When planning meetings or events, never forget that there is a psychology behind everything you choose to do, and this psychology extends well beyond what you are serving your guests at a particular meal. Take something as simple as coffee. If your guests' internal time clocks are still set on a hectic city pace, and you want to ease the transition to the more laid-back local ways, you can help by immediately delivering a whole pot of coffee—not just a cup—to each guest table. That way guests can relax, serve themselves and adapt to a more leisurely pace. Otherwise, they could initially become unhappy with the speed of the service and that unhappiness could spill over into your meeting.

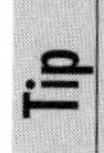

Know your client. For example, a nice touch at a breakfast for stockbrokers is to have newspapers such as the *Wall Street Journal* available.

You can make arrangements with the restaurant to have block seating for your group and have a staff member on hand to greet the guests to ensure that they are not left standing in line. If they all have to be out by a specific time, advise the restaurant of this in advance so they can plan accordingly. If guests have the option of ordering room service, again, let management know in advance so that they can have enough staff on hand. There are ways to ensure that room service staff are not overwhelmed by a flood of orders coming in at the same time. Many hotels have express breakfast cards that can be filled out in advance, and you may be able to design custom ones for your group.

To help them adjust to five-hour time differences, one group in Hawaii got fresh orange juice, thermoses of hot coffee and a basket of fresh-baked pastries delivered each morning with their newspaper to enjoy on their

(continued)

terrace. This gave them a leisurely beginning to their day before having breakfast in the main restaurant when the rest of Hawaii woke up.

When budgeting for clients allowing their guests to eat off the menu, assume that the cost is the same as the breakfast buffet. That is generally the most expensive item, and it builds a buffer into your costs. Some guests may have only juice, cereal and coffee. Remember to adjust meal orders and food guarantees on departure days. Depending on flight times, you may want to make arrangements for early departures to have just a continental breakfast before heading to the airport, especially if the flight will be serving breakfast on board.

At the end of your stay, before the individual room bills are printed and distributed to each guest, sit with accounting to make sure that all authorized charges, such as breakfast in the hotel's restaurant, have been pulled and do not show on the guest's room bill. The authorized charges should be posted to the master account—leaving guests with their incidental charges, such as the minibar or gift store purchases, which are not being picked up by the host company. The time spent doing this is minimal compared to trying to do it at checkout time, particularly since, as event planner, you will have your hands full with things such as guest luggage collection and transportation to the airport.

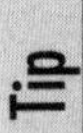

What is and is not included should be clearly outlined in the itinerary of events that each guest is given—make sure that it clearly states what charges, meals and activities they will personally be responsible for. Some companies have even been known to pick up the entire tab, but do not advertise the fact. That is a nice surprise at checkout.

One final option for those staying overnight in hotels is to compare the regular guestroom rates to those offered on the concierge floors. These floors are available worldwide at most five-star hotels and resorts and offer private check-in, upgraded amenities and special services, which can include continental breakfast, afternoon tea and pre-dinner appetizers. It is worth doing a cost comparison. For example, a group had taken over the entire concierge floor of a hotel in Los Angeles. They had all flown in from separate parts of the country, and this was the only time they were all together. The trip had been extremely busy, so they decided that what they most wanted to do was sit around somewhere other than in another restaurant and spend one evening together before heading home. Because they had the entire floor booked for themselves, special arrangements could be made. A pizza pajama party was quickly arranged. Everyone showed up in their hotel robes in the private lounge area, relaxed, ate pizza and had a great time together.

Coffee Breaks

Coffee breaks during conferences can be fun. Milk and cookies was a hit at one meeting, while an ice cream sundae bar turned up the excitement at another. Remember to keep the season in mind when you are planning. Find out when and where other meetings are holding their breaks so that you can schedule yours to avoid conflict.

Lunch

For luncheon meetings at a hotel or resort, you can have a served lunch, a buffet, an outdoor BBQ or a boxed lunch that is brought to the room or set up just outside. If breakfast has been buffet style, you might want a plated lunch so that guests can enjoy a different style of service.

Served or Buffet

With lunch, it is easier to choose a menu that will have something for everyone. If you are having a fish-based appetizer or soup, don't repeat fish as the main course for lunch, but instead go with an alternate like chicken or a light pasta dish. If time is a key factor, the table can be preset, with the salad or appetizer waiting. Have one person in the meeting room ready to alert luncheon staff when the meeting is close to breaking—the timing of the advance notice will vary depending on the number of guests being served—so that they can start to lay out the salads and fill the water glasses. The waiters will need to know how to handle requests for alcoholic beverages. Will such beverages be available and, if so, will they be charged to the master account or billed to the individual? You have to tell the waitstaff how to word their reply to guests.

Outdoor BBQ

If you are considering a BBQ or other outdoor function, make sure that you have a room reserved for backup in case of bad weather. It does not matter that it "never rains at this time of year." You will need to make the call on the day of the event, but at least if you have protected yourself with backup you do have an option available. Something else you need to be aware of for daytime outdoor events is shade. What protection is available and what needs to be brought in?

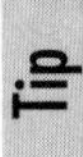

If your hotel has a permanent BBQ area that is close to the guestrooms, take a close look when you are doing your site inspection. Do those rooms fill up with smoke every time the BBQ is used? If so, you will want to exclude the rooms from your room block.

Boxed Lunch

Boxed lunches are often very popular at golf tournaments following a morning meeting because participants are anxious to tee off. Having the boxed lunches, along with golf balls and the appropriate logoed towels waiting in their preassigned golf carts, is a great way to get guests onto the golf course quickly. Their golf clubs can be transferred while they are in the meeting and set up in their carts, along with any rental clubs that may be required. Arrangements can be made to have a beverage cart assigned exclusively to the group and all beverages and snacks billed back to the master account. The minute their meeting breaks, guests are able to hop on waiting shuttles and head over directly to the golf course. Arrangements can also be made to have refreshments at the clubhouse at the end of their game billed to the master account. When all have arrived back at the clubhouse, return transfers can take them back to their hotel.

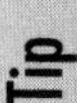

Whenever possible, try to use different rooms for different meals—using the same room for all meals every day of your guests' stay can get boring. With meeting rooms, the opposite is true. What usually works best is having a 24-hour hold on your meeting room so that you can leave everything as is for the next day. The rooms can be locked and secured.

Cocktails

Cocktail receptions can last anywhere from one hour to two and a half hours. Generally, though, a cocktail reception is scheduled to take place one hour before a dinner. If you are doing cocktails only, and your guests are on their own for dinner, the reception can be up to two and a half hours long, and the hors d'oeuvres served are usually more substantial.

You will need to base your room requirements on the type of food and beverage layout you plan. Will you have food stations set up, passed hors d'oeuvres or a combination of both? Will there be entertainment, scattered seating and tables? As a rule of thumb, have seating for about one-third of your guests, but if a high proportion are elderly you will probably want to increase that number.

As your guests begin to arrive, have an icebreaker ready. This can take the form of a specialty drink or entertainment, or even food such as oyster bars, sushi bars or California wrap stations that will provoke interest and comments. That way, the food becomes part of the entertainment. Have professionals on hand to explain the dishes and their preparation to your guests. Let guests have the opportunity to try something new, such as a local specialty. You want your guests to be drawn into the event, relaxed, mingling and entertained.

It's important that you take care when planning the music for a cocktail reception. You are looking for something low-key: it should be background music—something your guests can easily talk above. You don't want your guests to have to shout at one another. On the other hand, your entertainment should be heard.

For example, at a function for over 1,000 guests the entertainment was a trio, located in the center of the room. However, with the acoustics of the long and narrow room and the group's inadequate sound system, they might as well not have been there. No one could see them and no one could hear them—they were totally lost in the crowd. Most of the people away from the center of the room were not even aware that they were there. They actually packed up and left before the cocktail party was finished (which should never be done).

A more effective and dramatic welcome would have been a strolling violinist, saxophonist or classical guitarist to greet guests, or a white baby grand with the pianist in white tux and tails at the entrance where all guests could see and hear him as they passed. Staff could be on hand with silver trays of champagne and canapés to greet the guests as they arrived and let them know that the bars are open and that a lavish display of food awaits them inside. All guests would have a moment to enjoy the entertainment before moving farther into the room. If you are holding the cocktail reception outside and can time it to take in the sunset, you have added ambiance at no additional cost. Do it whenever and wherever you can.

Take the time to look at all the viable options when it comes to selecting where to hold your cocktail party and, in fact, any of your food and beverage functions. You can always hold your cocktail reception in a traditional room, but if you can instead do it on the terrace overlooking the ocean at sunset, it would be a shame not to utilize what is available to you. The function room can be your weather backup. Don't pass up a setting that is absolutely magnificent.

One resort has a wonderful private courtyard complete with an outdoor fireplace and a working fountain that is beautifully lit at night. Add to this a classical guitarist, some exquisite floral arrangements and twinkle lights in the greenery and you have a beautiful setting for very little cost. It is simple and elegant. There is no need to bring in additional decor.

If you are planning an evening outdoor setting, do your site visit at night. A location may look wonderful in daylight, but you need to see it at the same time that you plan to hold your event to be able to visualize how the area can be best utilized. Will it need extra lighting or heaters? Is there weather backup? If you don't have dollars to spend on decor, take a look at what is around for you to use to create an area of ambiance. Most hotels are more than accommodating in this area. Sometimes you can even borrow items from one of their restaurants that may be closed for the evening you are holding your event.

A Pacific Rim dinner was planned for the ballroom at one of the top hotels in Vancouver. The cocktail reception was in full swing. The drums were beating and the lion dance began to lead guests into the ballroom. Between each course, an array of children were set to perform, featuring local dances and gymnastics to tie in with the particular region of the Pacific Rim whose food was served as that course. It was a memorable evening. The show plates—the plates at each place setting as guests arrive that can be used as a decorative base—were from the hotel's gourmet restaurant. Valued at over $200 each, the plates set off the tables wonderfully. The restaurant was closed and the hotel graciously loaned them at no additional cost.

Another time, at a hotel in Florida, huge potted palms with uplighting—that lights the tree from the base—were moved into the cocktail area for only minimal labor costs. No one else was using the facility that night and the guests had it all to themselves. Moving the palms did not inconvenience any other guests by spoiling the look of the decor in the other sections, but the clusters of palm trees provided a warmer atmosphere.

In the Caribbean, cocktails are often done at poolside. What you need to find out in advance is whether the other hotel guests will have access to the pool area while your cocktail reception is going on. At what time would setup begin? To open the area up, you will have to move the furniture such as the lounge chairs. Will they be moved to a location out of site or simply stacked to the side in unsightly piles? This also applies when you are doing events at restaurant takeovers. You want to make sure that any furniture that has been removed is completely out of sight of guests.

Bathroom facilities are important at any event. If you are taking over one section of a restaurant exclusively for a cocktail reception, realize that the bathrooms for the whole restaurant might be in that area. How will this affect your setup? Will you have uninvited guests wandering through your cocktail reception searching for the washrooms? There is one restaurant that is on three levels with washrooms only on the first and third level. When using the top floor for an event, you can get management to direct guests dining on the second floor to use the facilities on the first floor and have staff stationed by the door to make sure that any regular restaurant guests are redirected back downstairs. You could also have signs put up.

One important factor to keep in mind when selecting the best site for your cocktail reception is the layout of the room. Do you have one large area where guests can gather, or is it an area that has multiple rooms and a lot of nooks and crannies? If you want your guests to mingle, you want to have them together in one area. If there are multiple rooms and the space is too large or too spread out, you will lose the energy of your party. Guests arriving will see only a few people and not all those spread out in the various alcoves.

Another consideration in holding receptions is the weather. In a location where guests are cooled by tropical breezes, it is fine to do cocktails and dinner outside. But if you are doing an event at a time of year when the weather is known to be hot, sticky and humid or with extremely intense heat—such as in a desert destination during the day (evenings cool down)—you may be wise to move your reception inside. This can even work in your favor.

For example, suppose guests are attending a convention. Suppliers are vying to have them attend their individual evening functions. The goal is to make the party interesting, have guests stay as long as possible and thus limit their availability to other suppliers. Two parties are going on: one outside and quite spread out; the other in a smaller location. The party in the smaller location is full of energy, atmosphere, great music, great food and air-conditioning. With temperatures well over 100 degrees Fahrenheit, guests who chose the event with the air-conditioning never made it to the other party. They were in no hurry to leave. Guests who had gone to the outdoor party first were quite appreciative—and very vocal when they arrived at the second party—of being inside in the cool air. They stayed, too. The party needed to be extended. Guests and hosts were having a fabulous time. Had both parties been outdoors, guests most likely would have showed up at both and then moved on to somewhere cooler.

At another event, the weather was the same—hot, sticky and humid. Guests were attending a convention and suppliers were inviting a very well-traveled and sophisticated crowd out for the evening. The goal once again was to interest them and keep them at the event. The first virtual reality Olympics at a brand-new entertainment complex was exactly the right fit. It was being held indoors and that translated to air-conditioned. The venue had just opened. It was exciting. It was fun. Guests came for cocktails. Rules were explained over drinks and hors d'oeuvres. Teams were sent out with their mission—fun. They were involved in the games for two hours and then met back to hand in their scorecards, relax and enjoy a tempting array of food and beverages. The winning team was announced and then guests were free to use the facility and enjoy all of the games. At midnight, guests were still hard at play. It was the perfect choice for this group, and the company achieved their objective. Because the room was large and it was open to the public, the event planner needed to address how to bring guests together as a group and to spend time with one another without getting lost in the crowds. The upstairs section could be taken over exclusively for groups. It was private but overlooked the activity on the floor below. You could feel the energy around you. By having guests come together for cocktails in a private area, sending them out in assigned teams, and bringing them back together at the end of the games to compare scores before letting them enjoy the balance of the evening at leisure, they had a presence even in the midst of a major complex. And having it inside on a hot, sticky night added to their enjoyment and was a definite plus.

With newly opened restaurants or venues, it is usually recommended that you wait six months before planning an event there to give them time to work the kinks out of the system. If you feel comfortable working with them because of your past experience—either because you have personally worked with new venues before, or because of the quality and caliber of their facility and staff—you could hold your event sooner, but be prepared to spend the time it will take from both you and the facility to work together to make it successful.

In addition to room layout and weather, food presentation plays an important part. Pay attention to eye appeal. It is one of the ingredients that adds immeasurably to the success of your event. For example, when you are having appetizers passed, the most visually effective method is to have only one type of food on each tray. This suggests a feeling of abundance and plenty. Instead of one lonely shrimp on a tray mixed in with many other selections, a tastefully presented tray featuring just shrimp stands out. Tray presentation is more pleasing to the eye with garnishes such as fresh herbs, flowers or other items that tie into your theme. Limiting the number of pieces per tray helps to achieve a more elegant presentation. Overall, you can offer an array of choices, but limit it to between 8 and 10 items—this is the selection of types of appetizers, not quantity per person—in total. Make sure when planning your menu that you take the time to balance your choices and include a meat, poultry, fish, dairy and vegetarian selection. Remember that not all vegetarians eat dairy, so ensure that you include some non-dairy vegetarian choices as well.

Make sure that the pieces served are bite-sized and do not require the use of a knife and fork. At one reception they served shrimp with their tails on, wrapped in noodles. These were passed around with just napkins. The noodles were greasy, slippery to the touch and dripping in the sauce they had been tossed in. Leaving the tails on the shrimp just left people looking for places to dispose of them. The whole thing was awkward and messy, certainly not the best choice to serve to guests in tuxedos and ball gowns. It was also very unappealing to see piles of discarded shrimp bits lying around waiting to be collected.

If you are having hors d'oeuvres passed with dipping sauces, serve the sauces on the side so that guests can make their own choices with regard to how much or how little they would like. For formal affairs, it is best to avoid them entirely.

In addition to the hors d'oeuvres, you can also set out items on display for your guests to help themselves to or have waiters on hand to assist them with their selections. Make sure that these items are replenished often and that each food station is set with appropriate utensils and napkins. Place the tables in different areas of the room to avoid congestion and long lineups.

You may want to set up food stations to feature specialty items or dessert and coffee if you are doing a cocktail reception that is featuring what is referred to as "heavy" hot and cold hors d'oeuvres. When the cocktail reception is taking the place of a dinner, the choices for the canapés will be a little heartier, the quantity per person is increased and coffee and dessert is served. With the desserts, as with the hors d'oeuvres, make them manageable, bite-sized and easy to cut with just a fork. You can make arrangements to have specially trained staff on hand to prepare gourmet coffees at the end of your cocktail reception as a special treat for your guests.

If dinner follows the cocktail reception, calculate on six to eight hors d'oeuvres per person but if you are not including dinner, the cocktail reception will run longer and the guests will fill up on hors d'oeuvres. Count on guests eating between 18 and 30 pieces per person, depending on how substantial the selections are (hence the name "heavy" hot and cold hors d'oeuvres).

Make sure that you give consideration to how guests will be disposing of empty glasses, plates and napkins. Do you have enough waiters to clear the debris efficiently? Have you provided scattered tables—high bar tables or smaller round ones—for guests to set their glasses on? Count on each person using at least three cocktail napkins, glasses and plates. For a stand-up cocktail reception, quality paper napkins are acceptable. Budget permitting, you could even have them logoed to enhance your theme. For example, in the Midwest at a Diamond and Denim theme party, the napkins were the color of blue denim and had "diamonds" glued to them. The cost was minimal but people noticed the extra touch.

At any stand-up reception or buffet, always try to utilize plates that have a slight lip on them. It helps to ensure that the food stays on the plate.

Dinner

There are many options for dinner. It can be a stand-up or sit-down buffet, a plated dinner, formal, themed, fun and/or casual. The choices are endless. When you are planning a dinner, the purpose is always more than just dinner. As with any event, each time you bring people together you need to look at how you can design your function to achieve your objectives. There is meaning behind the meeting.

Guests may be coming from across the continent, and one of your objectives is probably to have them mingle and interact with one another. With this in mind you may want to consider doing a buffet, either stand-up or sit-down, where guests are moving around freely. Seating is not structured. Rather than having one long buffet, one way to get people to meet each other would be to have a variety of interesting food stations with entertainment scattered around the room. It is always good to have something to break the ice when standing in line or simply enjoying the event. The objectives you set for a particular event will help to define its content.

Consider these two scenarios:

In Singapore, your guests are led poolside where they are greeted by staff in local costume with tropical beverages—perhaps even a Singapore Sling. The area is filled with the smell of exotic foods being prepared. Tropical flowers are everywhere, candles are flickering, local artisans are at work and entertainers perform at tableside. There is an abundance of things to see, do and sample. All the senses are awakened. You present featured entertainment and then a fireworks finale. Guests are relaxed and talking openly with one another.

In another scenario, you are in Morocco and for the evening you have taken over a series of fantasy tents. Great care and thought has gone into where guests will be seated and with which other guests. The company wants to make sure that certain guests get to spend quality time with one another and have ample opportunity to talk. Everyone is seated on pillows, leaning back and relaxing. Sheer fabric is draped everywhere, and it billows gently in the evening breeze. Here, the food is brought in on huge platters for guests to sample with their fingers. Entertainment moves from tent to tent and the medina—the old Arab quarter—comes to life in front of you. After dinner, guests move outside their tents to marvel at the horsemanship display, and for the finale the company's corporate logo is emblazoned against the black desert sky.

These are two very different events designed with two very different purposes in mind. One aims to have guests mingling with one another, and the other encourages specific guests to spend time together.

If the objective of your evening lends itself to a buffet dinner, there are several factors to consider when you start to plan your menu selections. Take into account the temperatures the food is best served at. What has lasting power on a buffet? You want to avoid ending up with food that has crusted over, changed color or dried out because of the length of time it is sitting out. Remember to think of food and health safety, as well. Pay careful attention to how long the food will be on display. Avoid dishes such as those with mayonnaise in them unless they are kept chilled. Make sure that your dinner foods do not mimic the hors d'oeuvres you have served. Look for variety in your menus. If you can project an image of lavish abundance, say, with a large display of fresh, lush strawberries dipped in chocolate, don't think just chocolate-dipped strawberries but rather strawberries dipped in a working chocolate fountain. This unusual conversation piece is inexpensive and will have more of an impact than an endless variety of traditional standard choices (and could actually end up costing less). Choose one standout item that guests will not soon forget. Remember, it does not have to be expensive to stand out.

When renting an item such as a chocolate fountain, remember to include the cost of trained personnel to run it.

If you have designated your buffet to be a stand-up event, make sure that the food can be eaten with just a fork and that your guests are not left wrestling with large pieces of meat, chasing slippery mussels around their plates or attempting to break through deep-fried batter or phyllo pastry that really requires the use of both a knife and a fork. At one black-tie affair, the stand-up buffet featured food that was so hearty—thick slices of prime rib, lamb chops, ribs, chicken, spinach baked in phyllo, deep-fried egg rolls, lasagna—that it was unmanageable. Guests unwrapping their napkins thought that their knife was simply missing and went back to get another set.

If you choose to serve a slice of beef at a stand-up buffet, make sure that it is thinly sliced and that bread is available so that guests can eat it like an open-faced sandwich.

Make sure that guests are not left waiting in line for clean plates or utensils. One way to ensure this is to have the hotel or facility pre-wrap extra setups (knife and fork or other cutlery wrapped in a napkin) and have staff ready to bring in more sets before they are required. Find out in advance the exact number of forks, knives, spoons, dishes, napkins and glassware that are available to you.

Consider both the size and the shape of the plates you will be using. As mentioned previously, for a stand-up buffet it is best to use plates that have a raised lip because they're better to contain the food on the plate. You will need to decide if you want to go to a full-size dinner plate or something smaller. Keep in mind that a smaller plate could mean multiple trips to the buffet and a fresh plate each time. Planning ahead will allow you to have sufficient quantities of utensils as well as staff on hand to clear away used ones. If you plan a sit-down buffet or plated dinner, make sure that the facility has extra napkins to replace those that are dropped or soiled. An oversize napkin is recommended for stand-up buffets—should guests find a seat other than at the scattered seating and tables, they can place it on their lap and it will provide better protection. Remember to have seating for at least one-third of the guests and more if your guests are older.

In Mexico, your group can dine on the fish they caught that afternoon when they were out deep-sea fishing. The cost is minute compared with the pleasure it brings. Schedule the deep-sea fishing tournament to take place the same night that you are doing a beach lobster bake and fish fry—it becomes the highlight of the evening—and should no one catch anything you can still have a wonderful dinner. You will have to negotiate in advance with the hotel to clean and prepare the fish and with the fishing boat charter, as generally they take home the catch of the day. They may each ask for compensation. Discuss details with the hotel and the charter. One more note about deep-sea fishing—guests will not come in if they have the big one on the line.

If you are doing a sit-down buffet you need to consider how to arrange access to the food. Do you have everyone line up at their leisure, or do you have designated tables take their turns and have the banquet captain and their staff inform guests when it is their turn? Whatever option you choose, consider having an appetizer or salad served at the table so that initially everyone has something to eat while they await their turn at the buffet. The number of buffet tables required will vary depending on room layout, menu selection and whether or not you will be having items like the appetizers and salad served at the table. Visualize the feel that you want in the room. Is the buffet set up to move people quickly in and out so they can get back to their meeting, or has it been designed to give your guests an assortment of local specialties?

Sit-down dinners can be handled two ways: open and preassigned seating. Open seating allows guests to select their own dinner companions and sit wherever they choose. With preassigned seating they are allotted a particular spot.

When you choose the preassigned route it is imperative that you have a seating plan and a simple, clear way of telling guests where they are seated. You can do this in a few ways. A seating chart can be posted, or table numbers can be included on the guest security passes or given out at registration.

Regardless of which method you select, make sure you have staff who are familiar with the room layout and, if applicable, the table numbers with the seating assignments to help direct guests to their seats. To reduce congestion and confusion, have signs made up and posted outside the ballroom telling guests which doors to use based on their table assignment.

Make sure the tables are clearly numbered, and think about how you will display the numbers. Does the facility have table numbers and holders? Not all do. If they do, ask to see a sample to make sure they are of good quality and not chipped or broken. How are they displayed? Do they have stands to set them in? Do you need to have tent cards made up? You can have your calligrapher number these stand-up cards, and they can be designed to match the theme decor. If you decide to have them professionally made to tie into the decor, make sure the cards will sit securely in the facility's holders. Test one to make sure that it will not slip out.

How do you want the overall table presentation to look? Do you want the table numbers removed once all guests have been seated? Make sure that they are clearly visible when the guests arrive and do not get lost among the centerpieces.

You will also need to decide whether or not guests are free to sit anywhere at their assigned table, or if they also have a preassigned seat. If the latter, you will need to have individual place cards made up and set at each guest's seat. When one of the objectives of the event is to bring key people together, guests are assigned strategically, not randomly. But be prepared to have guests switch place cards so that they can sit next to the person they want to be with. This happens even among senior company executives.

If you are doing a seating plan, you have to know when to stop fiddling with the revisions. Revision after revision will lead only to error and confusion. However, flexibility is key when planning events and that includes the ability to handle last-minute changes. Just be very aware of when those changes could affect the success of the event and work against it. Table location can be key at an event when you are honoring top suppliers or employees. You don't want to risk offending one group by placing them in a faraway corner at a table that had to be made up at the last minute because ongoing changes muddled the table assignment. Such gaffes cannot be tolerated and reflect badly on the entire organization.

When planning table assignments and layout, the number of people at each table—whether it seats 8 or 10—will have an impact on your overall budget. Obviously if you have 8 people at a table that could have 10, your guests will be more comfortable but you will need more tables, as well as table linens, overlays—the cloths that are layered over each table linen on an angle that often provide a splash of color or allow the color of the table linen to show through—centerpieces, pinspotting (lighting designed so that each individual table is lit), tent cards and waitstaff. Tables may have to be positioned closer together. Each of these will increase your budget, so remember to factor them in. It is always advisable—budget and room size permitting—to make sure that your guests are comfortable and not sitting on top of one another.

Seating Capacity and Tablecloth Sizes for Round Tables

Seating	**Table Size (Round Diameter)**	**Floor-Length Tablecloth (Rounds)**
10–12	72″	132″
8–10	60″	120″
6–8	54″	114″
4–6	48″	108″
4	36″	96″
Waiters		
Number Needed	Type of Event	No. of Guests/Waiters
1 Per Two Tables	Informal/Casual Dinner	Maximum 20 Guests
2 Per Table	Formal Dinner	Maximum 10 Guests

When you are in the initial planning stages of your event, try to visualize the room as a whole. What color are the walls, the carpet, the chairs, the linens, the overlays, the napkins, the glassware, the dishes, the cutlery? If you are doing a black-and-white theme dinner, you don't want a hotel to use their signature cobalt blue glasses. How does your menu selection tie in with all of the above? Visualize it. How can you pull in all the colors? The room colors could influence the colors in your centerpiece. Will the menu you have selected compliment the colors you are working with? Does it enhance the total picture presented visually?

Of course, budget permitting, you are never limited to working with the colors in a room. Rooms can be totally transformed with the proper specialty lighting, draping, chair covers—the covers that fit over standard banquet chairs and can totally transform them in appearance—and decor.

Some theme dinners have been known to feature food of one color, either in actual color tones, in name or both, and that tie in with special lighting and decor. A menu for a "Rhapsody in Blue" evening could feature martinis with a touch of blueberry, and perhaps grilled blue marlin as the entree. Now here's where the hotel's signature cobalt blue glassware would be an appropriate choice.

A gala dinner being planned to take place out of country had chair covers, linens and napkins all being flown to the location at great expense. Customs had to be cleared and local transportation arranged to get everything to the site. It was the first time chair covers had been used in this locale, and staff had to be shown how to put them on. It was important that the event reflect the client's corporate colors, and they were sparing no expense to do so. But someone had neglected to check the color of the dinnerware. It was assumed that it was white. It was white, but covered in blue flowers, which clashed loudly with the corporate colors. By reviewing the dishes in advance, they were able to find a suitable solution and borrow china from a neighboring hotel. The dishes should have been reviewed during the initial site inspection, and all-white dishes should have been stipulated in the functions sheets. A detail like checking the color of the dishes could be thought of as relatively unimportant, but consider the overall effect it would have had on this event.

Find out if there are any areas of protocol that need to be addressed. In some cultures it is appropriate that the VIP table have a more elaborate centerpiece; in others, the color of ink used to spell out someone's name on place cards could have a negative meaning, the number of flowers in a centerpiece can matter, and the color and type of flower can be very important as well. On your function sheet, take the time to find out and to explain to the venue, suppliers and your staff why specific things must be done as outlined and requested. For example, in Asian protocol, you need to do everything to ensure that nothing causes another to lose face, and this applies to everyone. Never do anything to cause anyone else to lose face. What may seem ordinary to you could be something

At one event, chair coverings were being introduced, and a walk-through was done with senior officials. As soon as they spotted them, they discreetly asked how they would "unwrap" the chairs to sit down. Of course, you do not have to open them, you simply sit down on them, but this was something new to them and they wanted to know in advance the proper protocol and procedure. Never take your own industry knowledge for granted as it could cause embarrassment to others as in the example of the chair covers.

It is important to honor beliefs and customs of others and to take them into account in any planning. A senior delegate was entrusted to take back home a gift that had been given to the president of his company, but it was lost or misplaced somewhere between the hotel and the airport. It was of utmost importance to the senior delegate that a replacement be found—he would lose face if it wasn't on the president's desk on Monday morning. This was not a matter to be taken lightly. There were urgent calls from the airport, many calls from the plane and many from the connecting airport, but the answer was that there could be no replacement available for another two weeks—the department that handled them was closed for until then. They were very sorry, but nothing could be done. When the general manager of the hotel heard about the situation, he informed his staff he had an exact replica of the very item in his office and offered it as a replacement. It was on the next plane and would be on the senior delegate's desk Monday morning. The senior official was greatly relieved. The hotel general manager knew how important finding a solution was.

new to them. Always take the time to explain anything new you might be introducing.

Always take one step more to understand customs and protocol. Roger E. Axtell has written several excellent books on international protocol, which are all entertaining and informative, including *Do's and Taboos Around the World* (Wiley, 1993).

If you are taking guests out to dinner in a restaurant as a group, you can do this as a group dinner or as a dine-around. The latter allows guests to choose between two or more restaurants on a given night, and the group divides into smaller numbers. This can be done for different reasons. For example, some may wish to try local cuisine, while others want to try a popular seafood restaurant. An added benefit is that one or more representatives from the host company are usually assigned to each restaurant and get to spend quality time with their guests. Dine-arounds can also be preassigned, the reason being once again to bring certain individuals together for a period of time.

If you take over a restaurant exclusively you can have your guests order off the menu if the numbers are limited, or for larger groups the restaurant will prepare a specially printed menu. Make sure that you work with the kitchen to prepare a menu that offers some choice. Two entrees are enough, but offer variety with the appetizers, salads, soups and dessert. If guests are ordering off the menu, go through it carefully to make sure that there are no hidden surprises. At one very upscale restaurant in Miami, a very extensive, very special selection of very old brandies starting at US$100 an ounce are available. Do you want your guests to order them? Brief the waiters in advance how to handle the situation if it comes up. This also applies to champagne and other expensive items. Know in advance what can and cannot be offered.

If you are looking at having your event catered, be sure to ask for recommendations from the facility—some have a very select list of who they will work with. Get references and talk to staff that were on duty when the caterers handled a function there. Find out what worked and what didn't. If the facility does not have caterers that they recommend, check with quality rental companies, florists and other top venues to see who caters their events. The same names often come up time and time again.

Make sure that you do a site inspection with the caterers. Are they comfortable with the layout, the capacity, the size of the stove and fridge? Will their cooking pans or serving dishes fit inside the existing spaces? Do you need to bring in any additional equipment? What are their electrical needs? Will you need to bring in a backup generator? Will they need a cooking or a food preparation tent? If so, it will probably involve permits. Do they have a liquor license, or will you need to provide one? Will you need to rent tables and chairs or other items for them? What are they providing, and what are you providing?

Make sure that you receive all quotes in writing and that these include details on the menu, quantity, price, all taxes and gratuities, delivery charges, how many staff will be on hand, how many hours they are contracted to work and a detailed account of what they are providing. What will the caterers' staff be responsible for? Are they assisting with food preparation, acting as waitstaff and busboys, passing food, replenishing items from the buffet tables, clearing the tables and taking care of all cleanup, including the dishes? Find out what time the caterers will be arriving and where the food will be prepared. Will it be at their premises with final preparations at the site, or will all cooking and food preparation be handled on-site? Are there any special arrangements you need to make on their behalf for parking and off-loading of equipment? Find out how the staff will be dressed. How experienced are they?

Wherever you are holding your event, be sure to inform the cleanup staff that when dishes are cleared, the plates are not to be scraped in front of the guests—that looks unprofessional.

Make sure that the banquet manager is familiar with the schedule of events. If there are to be speeches, do you want service to stop while the speeches are going on? Make sure that waitstaff has received clear instructions on how to proceed.

Cocktail Receptions

Cocktail receptions can include a full open bar, wine and beer only, or feature specialty drinks. With an open bar, you can be billed on actual consumption or on a negotiated flat rate. With the former, you are paying for every drink consumed. When you are paying a flat rate, it is based on a flat hourly rate multiplied by the number of guests attending. The facility may have a rate for one hour, three hours or more. Do you know the guests? What is their history? Do they like to party? Do they enjoy fine wines? The advantage of a flat rate is that you know what your bar bill will be in advance, whereas consumption can be hard to estimate. One rule of thumb often used to budget is two to three drinks per person per hour, but it will vary from group to group.

If you are paying a flat rate your bar will probably be limited to standard house brands unless you pay a premium. The brands offered will vary greatly depending on the venue and location. And while the pricey drinks may not be visible, guests may still ask for them, and your bartender needs your direction. Shooters will probably not be included in a flat rate. You need to verify that and make a decision as to how to handle requests. Will you be charged for opened bottles or just the number of drinks consumed? Have staff on hand to do an immediate sign off on the cocktail reception bill. If you are concerned with exceeding your proposed spending limit, ask staff to let you know when you have reached your halfway point. The decision is then whether you would prefer to have the service slowed down. Make sure that if there is the possibility of the host wanting the party to be extended, you have an adequate liquor supply and you are in no danger of running out. Always make sure the bar is stocked with more than you need. One fund-raiser has run out of both food and beverage so often that it has acquired a reputation for it. Think about the image that you are trying to project and how your actions might affect it.

Count on having at least one bar for every 40 to 50 guests, and ideally not more than 40 guests per bartender. Depending on the room layout, you could have a double bar set up—two bar stations placed side by side—or have several bars set up in various locations. Having multiple bar locations helps to alleviate congestion and long lineups. You can use the bars to draw your guests farther into the room by locating bars away from the registration and check-in area. Take into account the kitchen area and the doors where the waitstaff will be constantly going in and out, and make sure that the position of the bars will not hinder their service in any way.

Will the bartenders need help restocking the bar and preparing time-consuming specialty drinks like frozen daiquiris and margaritas? Make sure that your bartenders are professional and experienced. (Six months' experience is recommended.) What is the staff dress code? When will the bartenders be setting up, and what time will they be scheduled to start? What is their break schedule, and how will it be covered? Discuss with them in advance how to handle early arrivals and any other special areas of concern.

At one fashion fund-raising event, the bartenders were giving the models bottles of wine to take upstairs. Many bottles of wine. This could have jeopardized the quality of the show, but luckily it was stopped before all the good wine disappeared. Your client may want to extend an invitation to the models or entertainers—depending greatly on who they are and whether it is appropriate—to join the reception, or may send food and drinks backstage after the show. Discuss this with your client in advance and advise your bartenders and banquet manager accordingly. Remember to factor the additional demand into your food and beverage counts when you are calling in your guarantees—you do not want to underestimate the amount of food and drink you need to have on hand—and include the cost in your budget calculations.

When you are contracting entertainment be sure to read their "rider" carefully, because it not only outlines their terms and conditions, how many encores they will do, if any, if they require first-class air travel and accommodations and for how many, and so on, but also details specifically what food and beverage must be provided for them backstage. Riders can affect your budget, so know in advance what needs to be included—food and beverage will be just one of the items.

Make sure that the bar area is kept clear; floral arrangements and candles may look attractive, but they are not practical. Busy bartenders do not need to worry about maneuvering around the decor. Also it is best to keep open flame away from high-traffic areas where guests could accidentally walk into it. Find out the type of bar that is being used for your event and make sure that the area looks as polished and professional as possible—both in front (should you be setting up a banquet table instead of a standard bar station) and behind the bar setup. Always keep in mind what your guests will be seeing and what you can do to enhance it

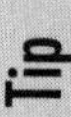

If you are having a specialty bar—such as a martini bar—set up and staffed by outside suppliers, make sure that you have everything that is needed: glassware, garnishes, beverages, spirits, shakers, napkins, tables and all related equipment, and have it all ready when staff arrives. As well, make sure that you discuss dress code, protocol, break schedule and tipping with them.

If you are bringing in specialty beverages with you, or are doing a fund-raising gala where some of the beverages/alcohol may be donated, find out the facility's policy in advance. As mentioned earlier, the venue may charge a fee per bottle corkage, and you need to include that in your budget calculation.

Liability

With respect to liability, find out the responsibility of your client, the facility and yourself. Determine what is needed in terms of permits and securing professional licensed bartenders in order to protect everyone including the quests. Venue owners and bartenders have been charged with man slaughter in the event of a death from not taking proper social host responsibility, e.g. serving someone who is already intoxicated, etc. What insurance (host liability) do you need to make sure that everyone is covered in case of an accident on the property or on the drive home?

What is the legal drinking age where the event is held? This can differ from country to country and area to area. Make sure that you are aware of local restrictions and age requirements for drinking. Will any minors be attending your event? How will you monitor this? If there is a concern about serving minors, a visible means of identification could be used, such as hand stamps, wristbands or different-color security passes. You can be held legally responsible for any underage individuals being served. Make sure to always include an assortment of nonalcoholic beverages, and if you are offering specialty drinks, make them available with and without alcohol so that your non-drinking guests are not excluded from the festivities.

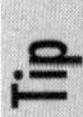

Be mindful of local laws and customs when doing out-of-country events. How would you deal with a participant of a program who has been arrested? It has happened. Take the time to figure out in advance what should be done. Sometimes the situation may be out of your control, and you need to know in advance how best to deal with it.

It is important to decide how to handle any guests who become a danger to themselves and to others. Find out how your client would like you to deal with such issues as a guest who has had too much to drink or who ends up in a brawl. It can be as simple as having two people—never send out just one person on his or her own—assigned to take the drunk back to the hotel room or home. This is where it is beneficial to have off-duty police hired as security; they have the experience to handle such situations effectively and efficiently. A security company may have certain restrictions with regard to how they would be able to handle such a situation, so discuss this with them in advance.

It is important to know the laws and customs not only at the location where you are holding your meeting but also for any off-property venues you may be using. The rules and regulations could be different; sometimes off-property venues can come under a different jurisdiction.

Make sure that quality ingredients are used at the bar. Freshly squeezed juices, lemons and limes, garnishes and spices all add to the appeal of the drink, the bar and the event in general. Use quality paper napkins—budget permitting, you can have these custom logoed—and avoid plastic glassware wherever possible. Make sure that in everything that you do the attention to detail and quality shows through.

Cocktail Reception:
Basic Bar for 50 Guests—Beer, Wine and Spirits

Beer	
Light/Dark/Imported	Five cases mixed selection (120 bottles)
Wine	**Cocktails Only**
Red Wines	Five 750 ml bottles (cocktail reception only)
White Wines	Eight 750 ml bottles (cocktail reception only)
Spirits	**One Bar Station***
Gin	Two 1140 ml
Rum (Light)	One 1140 ml
Scotch	Two 1140 ml
Tequila	One 1140 ml

(continued)

Vermouth (Dry)	One 750 ml
Vermouth (Sweet)	One 750 ml
Vodka	Two 1140 ml
Whiskey	One 1140 ml**

Liqueurs can be customized to include any specialty drinks you may want to serve. If champagne is to be offered calculate 12 bottles for 50 guests.

*Specialty Drinks/Blender Drinks/Champagne Not Included.

**Whiskey is usually bourbon in the United States and rye in Canada

1140 ml = 40 ounces = 26 × 1-1/2 ounce drinks

Ice	1-1/2 pounds of ice per person, 2-1/2 pounds of ice per person if you will be chilling wine and beer. Additional ice will be required for specialty blender drinks.

Glasses

Napkins/Coasters

Mixers (to be available at each bar station)

Clamato Juice—Especially for Canadian guests
Cranberry Juice—All-Natural Whenever Possible
Cola—Diet and Regular
Ginger Ale—Diet and Regular
Grapefruit Juice
Lemon Juice
Lemon-Lime Soft Drink (Sprite or 7UP)
Lime Juice
Orange Juice
Sparkling Water
Tomato Juice
Tonic Water

2 liter bottles = 67.6 fluid ounces = eight 8 ounce servings

Estimate a minimum of three drinks per person.

50 Guests × 3 Drinks = 150 Drinks × 8 Ounces = 1200 Fluid Ounces = Approx. 18 × 2 Liter Bottles

Garnishes (At Each Bar Station)

Angostura Bitters
Bar Sugar
Black Pepper (freshly ground)
Celery
Cinnamon (freshly ground)
Cinnamon Sticks
Cocktail Olives
Cocktail Onions
Grenadine Syrup
Jalapeño Peppers (pickled)
Lemon Slices
Lime Slices
Maraschino Cherries
Margarita Salt
Mint Sprigs (fresh)
Nutmeg (freshly ground)
Orange Slices
Tabasco Sauce
Worcestershire Sauce

Glassware (customize to beverage selections/available at each bar station)

Beer Glasses
Wineglasses
Cocktail Glasses

Note: You can customize glassware according to your event's particular needs. For instance, you may want red and white wineglasses, martini glasses or brandy snifters and champagne flutes. If you are planning on any glassware being used as serving dishes for desserts, order extra and keep these separate from the bar requirements. Calculate on using a minimum of three glasses and three cocktail napkins per person.

Bartending Equipment (available at each bar station)

Bar Spoons (long handled)
Blender

(continued)

Bottle Opener
Champagne Pliers
Citrus Reamer
Coasters
Cocktail Napkins
Corkscrews
Cutting Boards
Funnels
Garbage Cans and Liners (tastefully draped, covered, lined)
Garnish Bowls
Glass Pitchers
Glassware (minimum of three glasses per person. In a pinch, a water glass can be used for wine and partially filled.)
Hand Towels
Ice Buckets/Tubs (For Wine/Champagne)
Ice Scoops
Ice Tongs
Jiggers
Lemon and Lime Squeezers
Measuring Cups
Measuring Spoons
Mixing Glasses
Mixing Pitchers (large)
Nutmeg Graters
Paring Knives
Pepper Mills
Plastic to protect area behind the bar
Serving Trays
Shakers and Strainers
Sponges

When serving wine with dinner, decide how it will be poured. Will the opened bottles be left on the table for guests to help themselves or will the waitstaff be responsible for pouring the wine and topping up glasses? Have the waitstaff fill the wineglasses about a third to half full, never more—you want to leave room for the wine to breathe.

Again, as with the open bar, you must instruct staff to keep you informed on how the wine consumption is going, and monitor the rate at which it is poured. Staff can give you a count of how many bottles have been served, and you can decide how to adjust service based on that.

Know in advance how you will handle requests for additional bottles or beverages other than wine. Clients may decide to provide their guests with their individual requests and pick up the tab for it, or they may instruct the waitstaff to say that what is being provided is all that is available. How it is worded is key—it could reflect on your company image. Make sure that you give staff the exact wording you would prefer.

Make sure that you have more than enough wine on hand. You will not be charged for unopened bottles, and in most cases if you have purchased them they can be returned if the seal has not been broken and the label is intact. If you are doing an outdoor event and chilling the wine on ice, slip the wine into clear plastic bags so that the labels are not damaged.

In certain areas of the world, particularly warm, tropical locales such as the Caribbean, wine may not be as popular as tropical blended drinks, and some hotels carry only a limited number of bottles. The venue may not be able to meet additional demand and have to substitute another type of wine. This could be an issue in other parts of the world as well and in any restaurant where you have specifically ordered one type of wine.

When calculating the amount of wine per person, take into account the rest of the evening. After dinner, will the bars be reopened or will the waiters take drink orders? Will there be speeches and presentations? In the latter case, you may want to increase the amount of wine served and have guests remain seated instead of opening the bar and having the presentation disturbed by guests getting up and down.

Wine with Dinner Following a Cocktail Reception

Wine	Per 50 Guests
Wine (Red)	Eight 750 ml Bottles Based on 2 Glasses/Person
Wine (White)	Twelve 750 ml Bottles Based on 2 Glasses/Person

Wine with Dinner Only (No Pre-Dinner Cocktails)

Wine	Per 50 Guests
Red Wine	Ten 750 Bottles Based on 1/2 Bottle/Person
White Wine	Fifteen 750 ml Bottles Based on 1/2 Bottle/Person

Wine Servings

750 ml = six × four ounce servings

Special Note: These amounts are based on 60/40 white to red ratio, but will vary based on your menu choices and your guests' personal preference. Red wine consumption is on the increase and often goes as high as 60 percent. If you are planning on speeches or entertainment after dinner, and you are not reopening the bar, increase your consumption estimate to one bottle of wine per person.

An alternative to an open bar after dinner could be liqueurs and cigars, but keep in mind what it will do to the energy of the main room if some of the guests scurry off to the cigar room. If the guests do go and enjoy a cigar, you want them to return to the main area afterwards, especially if there will be entertainment following dinner. Bear in mind that a quality cigar will take some time to smoke, so you will lose part of your audience for up to an hour.

If you set up a smoking room, make sure that it does not take away from your overall objective. At one gala fund-raiser they had an extensive array of items for a silent auction, but the smoking room became the focal point of the event once dinner was over. Guests went to the smoking area and stayed because there was seating, a bar and monitors showing the entertainment that was going on in the next room. Guests were content just to sit and relax in the smoking room. Going back into the cocktail area to revisit the silent auction was the last thing they were prepared to do. Planners were pulling guests in three separate directions—silent auction area, dinner and entertainment, and smoking room.

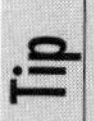

When planning to include smoking areas, consider how they can affect the energy level and overall atmosphere of your event.

If you are planning on beginning or ending your event with a champagne toast, be certain that the facility has proper champagne flutes—not saucers—available in sufficient numbers. It may be necessary to rent some. Corporate clients for special occasions have also been known to provide their own logoed champagne flutes, which the guests keep as a memento after the toast. Arrangements can be made to have them washed and packaged, but this will be

Champagne Toast	**Per 50 Guests (Allows for 2 Glasses Per Person)**
Champagne Toast	18 750 ml Bottles

750 ml = 6 × 4 Ounce Flute Glasses of Champagne
1500 ml = 12 × 4 Ounce Flute Glasses of Champagne
1 Case (12 Bottles) = 72 × 4 Ounce Flute Glasses of Champagne

Champagne Bottle Sizes

Magnum	=	2 Bottles
Jeroboam	=	4 Bottles
Rehoboam	=	6 Bottles
Methuselah	=	8 Bottles
Salmanazar	=	12 Bottles
Balthazar	=	16 Bottles
Nebuchadnezzar	=	20 Bottles

labor intensive and there could be additional charges to have this done. If you want to add a really festive air to the occasion, you may want to consider ordering champagne in oversize bottles, from magnums to Methuselahs. You will be ordering the same amount of champagne, but it provides a more elaborate and memorable show for your guests.

The party is over. The bar has been closed down. Once again, be sure to sign off on the bills for food and beverage and take a copy with you. At one event, the venue lost the entire record of charges and had to receive a copy from the event planning company. If there are any areas of dispute, you will be able to address them immediately. Always take the time to note specific items on your bill while they are fresh in your mind, such as the bottle of champagne that was ordered to celebrate someone's birthday. Three weeks after the event you may not remember why it was ordered and who gave their approval. Making clear notes will assist you with your reconciliation. If the facility is sending a final bill to you after the event, you will be able to compare it with your original copy and address any changes or adjustments that have been made.

Staffing

Let all staff—suppliers, volunteers, in-house staff—know how the event will unfold and what is expected of them (dress codes, protocol, behavior). They play a major part in the success of your event and need to be—and feel—a part of it. The staff needs to be motivated to want the event to succeed as much as you do. Treat everyone with respect and consideration, including such simple things as saying please and thank-you.

When and where will staff take their breaks and meals? Is there a secure area for them to leave clothes and valuables? What arrangements do you need to make and include in your budget?

Part of an event was a team-building exercise where a group had to cook dinner and set it out buffet style for themselves and the other 200 guests. This was done in a proper professional kitchen under the supervision of experts who do it every day. The group was divided into teams to prepare and cook certain items. Each was thoroughly briefed. Word came down that the meeting was breaking early and that the buffet had to be ready an hour ahead of schedule. That announcement galvanized the group, and they worked even faster. The team effort was a success. They managed to prepare the food on time and learned to appreciate and respect the hard work each contributes. The key ingredient in any successful event is the ability of everyone to come together as a team.

Information and communication is key when it comes to having an event without incident. The more the staff are aware of your needs, the better they will be able to meet them. When you do a pre-con it is important to meet with not only your key contact but also the others who will be working behind the scenes.

If you are doing an event at a hotel, the bell captain will need to know a number of things: What time are the guests arriving? Who is listed on the flight arrival manifest? Is it a local or an international flight? Has customs been cleared in the originating city, or does it have to be cleared upon arrival? This will affect the timing. Will guests be coming by taxi, limousine or motor coach? Each mode of transportation will have its own challenges. Will the hotel receive a call from the airport letting them know that the guests are on their way?

All of this information will help the bell captain and staff to be in a position to do their jobs to the best of their ability, handle the needs of your arrival and get your guests and their bags to their rooms as fast as possible. They also need to know if they will be delivering any room gifts and when. Do these gifts have to be in the guestrooms before the guests arrive or after? This will affect the number of staff available to handle the luggage and the room deliveries.

The rooms manager will need to know when the guests are arriving at the hotel, if they are to take credit card imprints, if there are any VIPs who will be signing all their expenses to the master account, if two room keys must be in each packet in addition to the minibar keys and express checkout forms, if there are any room upgrades or special room requirements such as handicapped rooms (rooms close to the elevator for persons with disabilities or for someone who has a heart condition and may need to limit their walking), and if anyone will require accessibility to a computer hook-up or fax machine. What is the protocol for VIPs' accommodations? This can be important to Asian clients, where the president is often located on the top floor with no staff or other VIPs on the same level. Will guests require two double beds or just one—may friends or siblings share a room? Will any guests need connecting or adjacent rooms? Will any guests want early check-ins or late checkouts? The location of the satellite check-in is yet another consideration among many.

Housekeeping needs to know arrival times as well, to have sufficient staff on hand to turn the rooms around quickly. They also need to know if you will be using any day rooms as group change rooms so that they can have extra towels and other bathroom amenities ready. They will need to make sure that a person is assigned to check on and freshen the room. The person who handles the minibars will need to be advised if there are any special requests, such as stocking it with only cola or fruit juice. This can be arranged, but he or she needs to have advance notice.

All these items are covered in the function sheets and the arrival and departure manifest lists you prepare and give to the hotel, but having a representative from each section at your pre-con gives you a chance to review everything with them to ensure the information has been passed down and hear any concerns they might have regarding your planned itinerary. On the day of arrival, make sure that you have enough staff to allow you to do a walk-through of as many rooms as possible, especially the VIP rooms and the rooms that have special requirements.

> *Twice now, in five-star properties, one in California and one in the Caribbean, I have walked into completely empty rooms. In California it was very obvious that the room had not been used or even cleaned in a long while. This was to be a VIP room with access for a computer and was supposedly the only one of its kind in the hotel at the time. An army arrived to put the room right—it was cleaned and sprayed, and furniture was raided from other rooms. It was ready (absolutely spotless) when the client arrived, but had we not checked she would have walked into a room that was empty of everything but cobwebs.*

The concept of attention to detail applies not only to meetings, conferences, conventions and incentives but also to fund-raising, weddings and any other special events. Success is in the details, someone once said, and they were absolutely right. Effective communication is the key. Sharing information is of utmost importance. Finding out what you don't know is crucial. The secret is to never ever assume anything.

Make sure that everyone is aware and knows exactly what is expected, how it is expected, when it is expected, where it is expected, and why it is expected so that you have a successful event that meets everyone's expectations and is without surprises and incident.

Charitable Donations

Many hotels now have policies and procedures in place that make it easy for organizations holding meetings at their hotels to donate any used or leftover display samples to a local charity after their event is complete. The clients save the time and money of shipping items back to their head offices, help those who are less fortunate and may be eligible for a tax deduction for the donation. In addition, although the purpose of the program is not public relations, quite often the organizations donating also receive good press for their efforts.

The same can be done with the abundance of food that is often left over after an event. Check with your venue and local food banks or shelters to see what can be donated. The charity will arrange for the pickup of items and can advise you of any special requirements. For example, they may be equipped to receive only the non-perishable items.

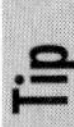

You can look to recycling in other areas as well. You can use the centerpieces as part of your event and reuse them afterwards. You can make them a part of your event by holding a draw, having one person at each table win them. If you are doing a meeting the next morning you can use them to enhance the buffet table.

9

Other Considerations

When the event planning world is vying to capture guests' attention and attendance and have their client's industry buzzing about their upcoming event, it is important that you devise a way in which to stand out from the crowd. Creative events that are strategically planned to ensure a return on the event, client objective, and the client's investment of time, money and energy, and meet and exceed guest expectation, require a mastery of event design and attention to detail in every event element—from guests' well-being and safety to making sure the guests, your client's company and your company are protected from liability should anything go wrong. There is a skill to producing events that deliver results and what you include and how you present them can make a world of difference to the event experience.

Entertainment

Great care must go into choosing your entertainment. Plan this element carefully. Know your audience. What kind of event are you holding? Is it social, artsy or corporate, or a mixture of all three? What is the age range? What may be appropriate for one group may be totally inappropriate for another. Make sure that strict guidelines are given to the MCs, comedians, musicians and performers. Use good judgment. For detailed information on business ethics, business etiquette and business entertaining refer to *Event Planning Ethics and Etiquette.*

Live entertainment enhances any event as a wonderful icebreaker. If you are doing an event out of country, find out what is special to the region and would be enjoyable to your guests. Here are some ideas of entertainment to begin or end your event: acrobats; arcade games; belly dancers; caricaturists; casinos (complete with slot machines, roulette, craps, baccarat, trained staff and showgirls); chili cook-offs; church choirs; cigar rollers; classical guitarists; dance bands; dance instructors; dessert chefs (waffles or crepes); disc jockeys; ethnic music and dancers; fiddlers; fire-eaters; folksingers; fortune tellers; handwriting analysts; harpists; Hawaiian dancers; ice cream specialty carts/stations; Indian sitar players; indoor fireworks or confetti bursts; interactive games; jukeboxes; line-dance instructors; magicians; marching bands; mariachi bands; mimes; miniature racetracks; one-man bands, opera performances; oyster shuckers; photo booths; pianists; pool sharks; popcorn maker machines; reggae, steel drums or calypso music; saxophonists; specialty bars; specialty coffeemakers; square-dance callers; string quartets; sushi makers; tea leaf readers; and virtual reality games. The list goes on—limited only by your imagination.

Look for what is fun, new and available in your area. You can have armadillo races in San Antonio. Finding Hawaiian dancers in Nashville to launch an incentive program can be difficult, but not impossible.

Do your homework when it comes to selecting your entertainment provider. Does the band have a reputation for being reliable? Will the talent show up? Check references. Get referrals. Make sure they are professional. Read contracts carefully, and check riders for any hidden provisions. If you want encores, ensure you've added that into your budget and the contract. Be specific.

Know your entertainment and know all of their act. Andre-Philippe Gagnon is a fabulous, world-renowned entertainer. He was scheduled to appear at an event whose planner had not seen his act. Doing a final check of the ballroom before dinner and the private performance the planner saw what looked to be the remains of the crew's lunch—fast-food wrappers, containers and beverage glasses were piled in a corner in disarray. Just as a staff member was about to throw out this "garbage," he was stopped. It was actually part of Gagnon's props!

A detailed schedule of events or show flow will need to be prepared, outlining all that will be happening onstage—the minute-by-minute action that will be taking place—taking into account the MC, the audio, the lighting and what is happening on-screen. More and more companies are turning to entertainment specialists to help them meet this challenge as their age base grows and there is more diversity and sophistication in their workforce.

Today, companies are looking to have their guests engaged from the moment they walk into their event and they are hiring professional MCs and hosts to keep their event's energy level up and consistent. New entertainment activities include numerologists, glass blowers, poetry doctors, beading, game shows and customized songs. Some of the latest "how to" entertainment event inclusions are salsa dancing, ballroom dancing, wood carvers and even interactive centerpieces where guests create and customize their own tabletop decor that they can take home with them.

Working with a professional entertainment management company can be a great investment. They are on top of what is new and fresh, and, most importantly, who can be counted on to deliver your entertainment in a professional manner.

Entertainment Q&A

Q&A

What time will the performance take place? Will rehearsal time be required?

In the contract, specify what time you want the performers ready and dressed to go on. Always plan to have the music or entertainment begin at least 15 minutes before guests are scheduled to arrive. That way, they won't be greeted with dead air. Emphasize to the

Q & A

performers how important it is that they are ready before your guests arrive. Are they performing elsewhere on the same day? Is there sufficient time left between engagements? Are they scheduled to be anywhere else after your engagement? Do they have a plane to catch? This can be the case sometimes with prominent entertainers and guest speakers.

When you are scheduling rehearsal time, take into consideration what else will be going on in the room. Will the audiovisual crew need to be running sound checks at the same time the band is scheduled to begin their rehearsal? Will rehearsals be taking place while cocktails are going on in the reception area? Will guests be able to hear them from there? Do you need to adjust the timing in any area?

Q & A

What time will the event end?

What are the chances that presentations and speeches could go on longer than planned? You may want to build in an extra hour as a buffer.

Q & A

Will you require the entertainers to extend their hours if the event is in full swing?

In different areas of the world you can arrange for the party to extend past 1 a.m., but you will need to obtain permission and a permit. You may want to have this option available to you should the host want the party to go on. Prepare the band for the possibility of playing longer than contracted. Find out the additional costs involved. Make sure that they know that they are not to start tearing down their equipment until they have been advised that it is OK to do so.

Q & A

What is their equipment like?

Is it tasteful, trashy or in disrepair? Does it fit the company image? Are there any areas of concern? Are there any objectionable pictures or words displayed? Don't be surprised by the caliber of the equipment on the day of the event.

Q&A

When will their equipment be arriving? How long will setup take?

Find out how the equipment will be arriving, and determine if you need to make any special parking arrangements for off-loading the truck. Will union crews and fees be involved? Will someone be available to set up immediately? Will the band, you or the venue supply the setup person? How long will it take to set up the instruments and do a sound check?

If your entertainment hasn't worked at the facility before, then schedule a site inspection with them. Are there any areas that could be a concern, such as stairs without an elevator, narrow passageways, pillars or hanging light fixtures to work around?

All the equipment must be ready before the decor and table setup begins. How will this fit into what else is taking place in the room. What is the order of sequence?

Q&A

Do they have any special requirements for off-loading and setting up of equipment?

Will they require the use of dollies? Will they need any assistance to off-load? If the hotel is unionized, that help could be mandatory and you must include those dollars in your budget as they will affect your bottom line. What equipment has to be rented and what costs are involved? Who is licensed to operate them? If you have complicated or extensive staging, lighting, audiovisual and entertainment move in, setup, rehearsals, event day and teardown, then union costs could be high, in some cases $100,000 and more. That is why it is essential that these items be fully researched and incorporated into your budget. Will the entertainment require the use of an elevator, and do you need to schedule a time? Do you know the dimensions and weights of what is being moved in? For example, if you are moving in a piano, will it fit in the freight elevator? Will you require a piano tuner? What if one of the pieces of entertainment for an ice fantasy theme party is a working,

Q&A

self-playing ice piano? What will you need to do to make sure that the piano is still intact at move in—as well as at showtime and during the show? Find out all the entertainers' equipment needs to make the move in as smooth as possible.

Q&A

Will you have anything onstage with the company logo on it?

Check with the agents and review your contracts. Some celebrities will not perform onstage with your product as it could suggest an endorsement. You may have to receive written permission or set up a separate staging area.

Q&A

Will the entertainers require a dressing room?

How many rooms will they need and how large? Are there any special requirements such as mirrors, special lighting, tables, chairs, hanging racks, storage space or refreshments? At one Oscar party, one of the entertainers was painted gold from the waist up, and the gold paint needed to be removed at the end of the event. This had to be planned for. Who would be responsible for doing it? And how?

If the entertainment includes animal acts—for example a jungle party theme—what do they and the facility need for the care and safety of the animals and the guests? Visually, it may be exciting to have a live baby elephant or tiger as part of the entertainment, but what food and water or other special requirements will this entail? How hot is the lighting? Will the animals be protected from the guests? Will the guests be protected from them? What is your plan of action should the baby tiger escape among your guests? And who is on cleanup detail?

Q&A

Do meals and refreshments for the entertainers need to be included in the budget? Will they be treated as guests, or will meals be set up in a separate room?

If they are having their meals or refreshments in their dressing room make sure that you arrange for tables and chairs to be set up for

Q & A

their comfort. Performers are often delayed, so select food that will keep well, and do not have the area cleared until you check to see if they have had the opportunity to eat.

At one gala fund-raiser, by the time the performers went to get their meal it had been cleared away. Because this happened in a convention center and not a hotel, replacement food was difficult to find. In the end, all that was available was leftover hors d'oeuvres. The entertainers give the event their best; it is a sign of respect and appreciation to give them your best in return. And that may not be an option but a condition clearly outlined in their contract rider. Assign a staff person to oversee entertainers' needs.

Q & A

If entertainers are being served a meal, is there a specific time that is best, and do they have any special needs or requests?

Some performers choose to eat after their performance and not before. Find out if there are any special requirements and make sure that someone is responsible for overseeing this area. When a celebrity performer at a gala fund-raiser had still not eaten at the end of the evening, it was discovered that he was a vegetarian and could not eat the meal that had been provided. The staff managed to put together a suitable meal once his needs were known, but this should have been known and addressed before the event. Entertainers' meals do not need to be the same as those served to the guests.

Q & A

Is the entertainment—bands, models or other performers—permitted to drink or to otherwise join the event at any time?

Make sure that you discuss dress code and conduct with all contracted entertainers. You will need to decide if drinking and smoking are permitted or not. Are the performers to be included as a part of the party? You may want them to be. If you are doing an event with name entertainers you may want them to join in and mingle with your guests after their performance. For instance, at a

Q & A

theater evening, you may want to invite some of the cast to your private post-theater event. If the affair is held in a location away from the theater, make arrangements to get them there and back. Find out what would be required in advance should they choose to accept the invitation. The performers will probably need time to change from their costume and makeup, so it is important to know how long you anticipate your post-theater party to go on.

Q & A

What is the band's break schedule?

Work out the band's break schedule in advance. Does it need to be adjusted to work with the schedule of events? Will there be continuous play with staggered breaks or taped music? If using taped music to fill in at the breaks, do you want it to be the band's own music, or can it be low-key background music?

Q & A

Are there any songs that the band should not play?

You will need to see the band's repertoire of songs so that you can select a specific song list. Schedule a time to review them. Remember, you are the client and they are the supplier. If they insist on playing songs that are not appropriate for your audience—words or lyrics—they are not the right band for your event. Do you want to work with prima donnas?

Tip

Audition your entertainment. Try to see a live performance, and note how they interact with the audience. Many performers have CDs available, but be absolutely certain—spell it out in your contract—that what you hear on the CD is who will actually be performing at your event. All the band members may not be the same, and the quality of the performance could change.

Q & A

Are they insured? Is their equipment insured?

Find out what insurance the entertainers have. They will need to have enough to cover damage to their equipment or to the facility. Do you need to arrange for additional coverage? Do they? What is outlined in the facility's terms and conditions?

Q & A

What additional entertainment-related costs need to be factored into the budget?

You will have to consider things such as music royalties and rights under ASCAP or BMI in the United States or SOCAN in Canada, electrical power, rehearsals, overtime, encores, meals, and terms and conditions included in your entertainers' contracts known as riders. Riders could include items such as air transportation, accommodation, meals, shipping of equipment, dressing rooms, equipment rentals, move in and setup costs, rehearsal fees and similar items. All of these items have a cost attached and must be included in your budget.

Are cartage or freight costs included in the quote you received? Is their equipment being shipped to you? What are their electrical power needs? Will they be tapping into the existing sound system, or will they be providing their own? Will you need backup generators? Is the power at the venue sufficient to meet all of your event needs? Consider not just the entertainers but everything that needs to use power. What else is going on in the room and in the facility?

What equipment do you need to provide for the entertainers? Will they require draped tables or chairs on the stage, say, for a disc jockey? Do you have sufficient electrical outlets and extension cords? Where are they set up in relation to the available outlets? What do you have to do to avoid having guests tripping over any plugs and wires? Always review the entertainers' and the facility's terms and conditions before you begin to prepare your budget so that you know in advance what has to be included.

Q & A

What are the dress requirements? Have the entertainers been informed?

How will they be dressed? Will they arrive dressed, or will they need to change once they get there? Do they require access to anything special, such as a private bathroom or shower (in case of extensive makeup or body paint)? Does their dressing room need to be secure? Can it be locked? Will they require storage space?

Q & A

What are the home phone and cell phone numbers of the entertainers or their managers and agents in case of an emergency?

Make sure that you obtain home numbers, cell phone numbers or pagers. If something unexpected happens on the day of the event, you need to be able to know who to reach, where to reach them and how best to do it. Keep in mind that entertainers generally perform in the evenings and may be difficult to reach first thing in the morning. (They could be sleeping.)

Q & A

How are requests to be handled?

Make sure this is reviewed with all involved. For example, if you are doing a low-key jazz reception designed specifically so that people will mingle and talk, and a request is made for something else (like hard rock), how do you want the DJ to handle this? For example, the DJ could say that the host has pre-selected the music and that all that is available to play is jazz, and then ask if there is a specific jazz artist they would like to hear. Different music will change the whole tone of the evening, and it will be difficult to get back the mood you want.

Photographers and Videographers

Event photographs and films of the event become a lasting memory to guests; a marketing opportunity for clients when used as an event follow-up or to publish in their industry magazine, on their website or in some cases even on YouTube in hopes of attracting new business, creating brand awareness and star industry performers to their company. A film can be turned into a motivational message for a corporation; and a portfolio of very select pictures, a testimony of an event planning company's creativity (with permission from the client to use the photographs to showcase their event talents). When you are hiring a photographer or videographer to capture an event, make sure that you have found out from both your company and the company hosting the event's legal departments as to what will be required to obtain guest permission to be captured on film and have their likeness posted on a website, printed in a magazine or displayed or distributed in any other way. You also need to negotiate ownership rights with the photographer and videographer and in the case of filming an event, if music is to be added to the final version you need to find out what must be done legally with regards to music royalties, etc.

It is of key importance that you:

» Know the best style of photographer to give you the results you are looking for—traditional photographer (posed shots) or a photojournalist-style photographer (capturing what is going on in the room)
» Think carefully about how many photographers you need (you may want one photographer stationed in a central spot for specific shots of celebrity guests, for instance, and another to cover the ongoing events in the room as they are happening)
» Consider hiring a professional videographer to video your event, either in addition to or in replacement of a photographer
» Know the reputation of the photographer and/or videographer you are hiring

What are your needs? You may miss a priceless photo opportunity if there are not enough photographers on hand, or they are not stationed in the right places. You don't want your photographers to be continually pulled in all directions, which can happen if you have a number of committee members all issuing different directives. For gala fund-raisers a fabulous photo can be of tremendous value and result in more media exposure. Imagine what would happen if a celebrity unexpectedly pops in for a quick hello, and you miss the chance for a wonderful endorsement of your cause because your photographer is tied up in another part of the event. The moment is gone and so is the celebrity.

While the media may bring their own photographers, it is still a good idea to have your own on hand. You will want specific pictures taken and can't expect the media photographers to be at your beck and call. The media's focus would probably be on any celebrities, and they may not include the sponsor in their shots of well-known stars. On the other hand, you want the sponsor's name to appear with that of the star especially if you hope to have this sponsor back again next year and to attract others. It is a good marketing move for them and for you. With your own photographer, you will be able to ensure that specific shots are taken and are sent out to the media.

As with all elements of event planning, expect the unexpected and think outside the box to find solutions to problems. At a top hotel in Puerto Rico, the evening was festive and everything was moving along very well for a group that was holding their private gala event at a fort attached to a hotel as opposed to on their cruise ship. The photographer had been doing a wonderful job until the presentation began. The moment was now at hand to take photos of key individuals receiving their awards, and his camera batteries went dead. No problem! He had been requested to have a backup battery and camera. Problem! Both the backup camera and battery gave out. As fate would have it, there was a dance club at the hotel, and it was Valentine's Day. The photographer who was on hand to take pictures of the happy couples quickly agreed to help out. He was very well compensated for snapping a few pictures of the presentation before he returned to his happy Valentine couples in the dance club. The original photographer adjusted his bill to compensate for not being able to complete his job.

If you are doing special events in a port of call, always budget for staff to fly in ahead of the ship to advance each event and to make sure that all is in readiness.

You can plan, you can prepare, and you can have Plan B (the backup cameras, batteries and assistant) at the ready, but you still have to be able to think on your feet and think fast to find the solution. Sometimes it's just down the hall on Valentine's Day. Another answer could have been to have the remaining official photos taken back on ship by the ship's photographer, while everyone was still dressed up. A near disaster could be turned into a triumph—a VIP moonlight champagne reception—as the ship set sail. What would have been missing, though, would be the beautiful themed decor in the background that the client felt was important to the client to capture.

Tip

Event planning companies should plan on hiring their own photographer to take pre-event photographs without client identification or guests in the shot so that they can use them in their own marketing endeavors to potential new clients, e.g., a close-up of tabletop decor, room transformation, food presentation, etc.

Photographer Q&A

Q&A

When do you want the photographer to arrive? How long do you want him or her to stay?

Will you require pre-event shots to be taken to show the room setup and decor? Will the photographers have to stay to take pictures of the final addresses or of the winners of door prizes? Do you want them to stay for a set time period or until the very end? What will best fulfill all of your needs?

Q&A

Will you want black-and-white prints, color or both?

Where will you be using your photos, and what will work best? Will they be submitted to the media, used in company newsletters or shown at staff meetings? Will you be hanging a copy on your company's hall of fame or sending them to each participant? Consider the areas where they can best be used and what will best fit your needs and your budget. You will also need to discuss with the photographer the cost of having the prints produced. Will you be able to purchase the negatives (some photographers will not sell them), and, if so, at what cost? Does the photographer retain copyright? Will the photographer need to be credited for all shots sent to the media? You will need to know this in advance.

The same will apply to the films your videographer is taking. And remember, for both candid and posed photographs and videos being shot, you need to know what legally has to be done to obtain guests' permission and signoff for their likeness to be used and posted, printed or shown anywhere. If you are bringing in celebrity entertainment, their riders may stipulate that they are not to be photographed or captured on film with the client's logo as it would show them to be endorsing a product they are not being paid to endorse or be a spokesperson for. You also need to find out from both companies' legal representatives how guests' cell and BlackBerry cameras and videos are to be handled, e.g., will they be permitted to bring cameras of any kind into the event. Today, event missteps and bad guest behavior are often captured on guests' cell cameras and videos and could be uploaded to YouTube in minutes with your guests' privacy being violated. The potential of lawsuits and how to protect the client's company, your company and the attending guests needs to be discussed in advance of the event.

What size and quantity of prints will you want?

On incentive programs, photographs are often taken and sent out later in custom frames or albums as a record of the event. If time permits, these can be prepared and left as a farewell pillow gift on the last night of the event. Purchase your frames and albums in advance so that you know the exact dimensions of your prints. It is easier to order pictures to fit the perfect frame than trying to find a frame that will fit the perfect picture.

Will you want photos shot vertically or horizontally? In a particular spot?

Does the venue have locations that are ideal for photographs? As you do the site inspection of the property, think about what area would visually lend itself to the photographs you want taken. At the Opryland Hotel in Nashville, they have a wonderful staircase, a beautiful atrium area and delightful fountains. In all three of these spots, vertical pictures would be preferable. Because of the

Q & A

height of each locale, you would lose much of the beauty of the background if you were to do a horizontal picture.

Look at each area as if you were looking through a camera lens. Is there anything hanging, like wires, that would interfere with the picture? Sure, the picture can be cropped, but that might throw off the balance of the picture, and cropping isn't cheap. If you need a professional eye to scout locations, get the photographer to advise you. You will have to pay for this, but it may be worth it in the long run. If the photographer has not worked in the location before, he or she may need to do a site inspection, particularly if you are doing specialty shots, to assess what lighting and equipment will be needed.

Q & A

How will the photographer and/or videographer be paid? If charging by the hour, what is the rate? Is there a minimum number of hours? Is there a flat rate? Does that rate include film, contact sheets, negatives, prints? What are the rates for black-and-white and for color film? How much are prints?

Make sure you receive a quote in writing and have all costs itemized. Some clients choose to simply pay for the photographer's time, film use and a contact sheet, preferring to have extra prints made at their own convenience.

Tip

Most professional photographers and videographers guard their creative rights. If your event is a celebrity event, it is unlikely that the photographers will release the film rights to you. They will work with you to send them to the media, but they will want their work credited.

Q & A

What is the turnaround time? How quickly will the photographer be able to provide you with contact sheets or prints?

At some events, photographs are taken at the beginning of the evening, developed immediately, put in custom frames and are

Q&A

ready for the guests to pick up on their way out. There are extra charges to do a rush job of this nature, and it can be a real stampede depending on the number of guests in attendance. At a dinner in Portugal, individual pictures of the group were taken during cocktails and by dessert a carton of matchbooks was delivered with the restaurant's logo and each member's personal picture on the front cover. You can come up with many different ideas, but the key is whether your idea is doable logistically and how quickly it can be turned around. It is a wonderful idea to present prizewinners with an album full of pictures at the end of an incentive program, but if something goes wrong with the developing, or there isn't enough time to mount all the photos, it could be an expensive and unproductive proposition. Mailing the photo albums to prizewinners after the event is better than nothing but loses the energy, spark and surprise of the original idea.

Q&A

Are there any additional charges to factor into your budget? These would include such things as couriers, meals, refreshments, costs to transport equipment and parking.

Will there be any additional charges if photographers have to take part in a site inspection of the facility? Have you made arrangements for them to be able to eat, either with the guests or in a separate area? Have you factored these costs into your budget? Will any charges apply for transporting equipment? Will you be charged gas and mileage? Find out in advance what costs could apply. For example, on an incentive program while the winners are meeting, it is possible to set up a glamour photo shoot with hair and makeup artists, clothing props and light refreshments to entertain the spouses. Each guest receives notification of their shoot time in advance. A professional photograph can be a wonderful treat and something they might not do for themselves. Costs for the suite, makeup artists, hairdressers, props and refreshments would all need to be included in your budget in addition to the

Q&A

photographer and film. The guests' spouses will probably be so pleased with the results that they will want copies for their families. How will you handle that request? Will it be the responsibility of the company to pick up the cost, or the responsibility of the guest and billed to their room? Find out in advance.

Q&A

Do photographers and/or videographers have any special requirements? Are they familiar with the venue they will be shooting in? Is there sufficient light, and are there any other areas of concern?

These photographers are experts in their field, or at least they should be—it's your job to find out. Some companies choose to bring their own photographers with them around the world, while others will work with locals. If you do, get referrals. Check with the hotels and florist shops to see whose name keeps coming up. Listen to their advice and suggestions. It is important that the photographers be familiar with the property and, if they haven't worked there before, available for a site inspection. They need to know the locales, what light they will be working in and the equipment they will need.

Q&A

Have you advised the photographers and/or videographers of dress code and protocol?

Be very specific about proper dress and conduct. How do you wish them to be dressed—subdued or flamboyant? You don't want your photographers' mode of dress to become the talk of the evening. Make sure that it is never revealing or loud. You want them to blend in, not stand out from the crowd. As well, discuss what you expect from them in the form of their conduct, from eating and drinking to the accepted way of speaking with guests.

Q&A

If this is a high-profile event, is the photographer and/or videographer you are considering familiar with key celebrities and society guests?

It is imperative to have a photographer who is familiar with who is who. They need to know instinctively who will be newsworthy and

Q & A

make a terrific picture. You need someone who can recognize a dignitary's car and who is well aware of proper protocol.

Q & A

Are you familiar with the photographer's and/or videographer's work? Have you seen samples and talked to references?

Looking at local newspapers and magazines, study the photo credits on the types of photographs you want. Look at the quality of their work—does it meet your needs? Study the composition, sharpness and color balance. This is a good starting point when selecting a photographer. Be sure to check references and dig around to find out if there are any unsatisfied customers not mentioned in the references. Keep an open mind, but try to get the complete picture.

Q & A

Do you have specific groupings of photos that you want taken? Who will be preparing the list, reviewing it with the photographer and assisting them during your event to help identify and bring together the people that you want photographed as a group?

If you have specific photo groupings that you want taken, make sure that the photographer has been provided with a list. Assign a staff member who is familiar with the invited guests to assist the photographer in obtaining the photos.

Q & A

Will you or the photographer be sending copies to the media? Have you included the cost for reprints and couriers in your budget?

Who will have the final say on which photographs are being released to the media? The media, of course, makes the final decision on what they print or show, but what needs to be established is who will sign off on the prints being released to them. You may want the photographer's advice on the best pictures, angles, colors, compositions and the like, but you must make it crystal clear that you have the final say. Find out in advance the

Q & A

media deadlines, and make sure that you meet them. Call the media to let them know when to expect the photographs, follow up to ensure that they have received them and find out when the photos will be appearing. Have you included in your budget all applicable costs for the reprints, envelopes, letters, couriers and additional time for the photographer? The same will apply to video footage. Another area to consider is whether you will be using the photographs or videos on the company website or posting photos on the event website so the media can download whatever they want. But—and this is a big but—before pictures are even taken at an event, remember to find out from the client's legal department, your company's legal department and the photographer's legal department or representative what legal requirements have to be met with regards to posting the pictures on the Internet and guest privacy issues; how they may be distributed, e.g., can someone else take the picture and use it on their website, etc.; and who owns the legal rights to the pictures.

Themes and Programs

Centerpieces

Centerpieces can range from very cheap and simple to very extravagant and elaborate. They can be a dramatic array of orchids or exotic tropical flowers bathed in candlelight or a single, perfect rose. Centerpieces can be beautiful. They can be imaginative. They can be interactive. They can be fun. They can encompass everything from fishbowls with real or blown-glass fish floating around, to a beach party theme in the middle of winter, to loot bags filled with childhood toys and candies from the past to tie into a theme (for a '50s, '60s, or '70s party).

You create a visually dramatic centerpiece by selecting just one color and/or one type of flower. Varying the height and the width of the arrangements provides added interest. If you choose to include an assortment of flowers, remember to take into consideration not only how they will look but also the overall effect of the combined fragrances—do they complement one another or are they overpowering together? Have you considered all customs and protocol and made sure that no flowers, colors or numbers—white, 13—in a centerpiece will be a breach of what is appropriate? Also, be aware that VIPs often demand more elaborate centerpieces.

Find out from the florist the best delivery time. How long will it take the flowers to be fully opened and at their absolute best? Should they be refrigerated to prevent them from opening prematurely? Are there any special care arrangements? Can the facility accommodate this? How long will the flowers last, and what is the florist's policy on substitutions? Make sure that they outline in the written contract what is being sent, the time, the delivery instructions and all costs for delivery and setup.

Suppose you are doing a theme dinner in the Caribbean and the only flowers that will tie in must be pure white. At that time of year there are no white flowers in bloom on the island, so you arrange to have them brought in from Miami. They arrive, but instead of the flowers you expect, you find they sent a substitution—daisies with bright yellow centers. There is no time to have others flown in, so what do you do? Do you use flowers that would take away from the total effect, or do you get creative? One of the colors in this theme dinner was gold. It was amazing how a little artfully applied gold spray paint salvaged this situation.

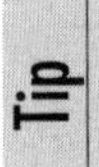

There is not always a large selection of materials such as gold spray paint on all Caribbean islands, so plan ahead, and, like the Boy Scouts, be prepared.

At an event in Mexico—flowers were being delivered for a Valentine's Day program—pink roses were to be tied with pink ribbon. The hotel claimed over and over that it had pink ribbon. It did, but it read, "It's a Girl." White ribbon was used. Check and double-check.

If you are doing a product launch in your home city, you can almost guarantee that the number of guests invited for dinner will increase, sometimes without notice. At one product launch, calls started to arrive at the hotel for instructions on where the dinner was to take place. This was a tad suspicious, since all invited guests were staying at the hotel. Senior VIPs had extended last-minute invitations to key suppliers to join them for dinner and the show but had not told anyone. Extra tables were hurriedly thrown together, but that may not always be possible. How quickly could your florist respond to a call for additional centerpieces? Would they have sufficient supplies on hand? Do you need to look at initially building in a buffer and ordering additional centerpieces that could be set out on display tables if they were not required? Check with your client to see if having additional last-minute guests could be a possibility and if they want to order additional centerpieces to cover this. Another reason it's important to know in advance if there will be additional guests is that the room capacity may not be able to handle more people and there may not be sufficient meals to go around. If the event is open-seating, there may be no way to tell who is an invited guest and who is an addition. Your client must keep you informed of any changes. And, as an event planner, it is your responsibility to keep your client informed of room capacity, fire regulations and the effect of having last-minute invited guests.

There are two things to remember when deciding on centerpieces: first, make sure guests can see each other over them, and second, expect guests to walk off with them.

Keep the centerpieces small enough so that guests can see each other across the table when seated. They can be low, raised high on clear pedestals or a mixture of both; they don't have to be one or the other. Have a sample made and test it out beforehand by actually sitting down at a table.

At an industry function for event planners in Chicago years ago, the guests walked in, sat down, and almost in unison, each table immediately moved the centerpiece; they could not see the person across from them. The centerpieces looked wonderful but defeated their purpose. They became a barrier and an obstacle, not a centerpiece that added to the event.

The second item to remember is to be prepared for your centerpieces to walk away at the end of the night. If they are rented, you could end up with a major unexpected cost added to your budget. And if someone has spent $5,000 to purchase a table at a charity event, the last thing you want to tell them is that they can't take the centerpiece. Prepare for it and plan for it in your budget. That way, you avoid unexpected surprises.

If you are considering flowers for meeting rooms, make them potted—that way they can be sent to a nursing home or hospital after the event. Little cards can be printed stating that they are being donated.

The client may want the flowers or centerpieces sent to their guestrooms or to those of the VIPs. In these cases, arrange for a bellman to deliver them. Don't have your clients carrying them around in their evening dress; have it done with finesse. On one two-stage incentive program, the client and guests were so enchanted with the floral arrangements that they had to be shipped from one hotel to the next.

Advise the facility in advance what you will be doing with the centerpieces. You don't want them to clear them away and discard them if you are planning to use them again the next morning or to send them on to a nursing home or hospital.

There are centerpieces that involve indoor pyro (fireworks that are designed for indoors), but they can be very dangerous and should be handled with extreme care. At one event where centerpieces with pyro were used at each table, they were set off by a charger that was located in the service passageway. Afterwards the charger was left unattended and caught fire, but fortunately was discovered by a waiter who just happened to be walking by.

Anything involving fire and fireworks requires extreme care. Know the risks and what insurance, permits and safety precautions you need. Whenever indoor pyro is used, make sure that you work with professionals who are specialists in this field. Ask them for suggestions that will dazzle your guests.

And ensure you know what the facility's policy is regarding pyro. Some venues will not even allow candles.

There are some other wonderful alternatives to centerpieces with indoor pyro that you can use instead. These might be a good idea, since pyro can startle guests if they are not expecting a fireworks display coming from their centerpiece, and because once guests have been seated and placed items on the tabletop you have no control over what can be leaning up against the pyro. An airburst of indoor pyro over the service doors as dessert is being wheeled out, specialty firework candles in a cake, or an indoor fireworks display with a custom logo as the grand finale are alternate suggestions to consider.

Other ideas for centerpieces can include water fountains and wet rock gardens. The important thing is to be creative.

Decor

The term decor includes all of the furnishings and decorations in the room, but just what elements you include can be a problem. Look around at your selected venue. What color is the carpeting? What color are the walls? What about the chairs? Look at the dishes, the silverware, the glassware. Do they all come together? What needs to be done to make it feel more special? Will it have an impact or be lost in a sea of hues?

Look carefully at the dollars you are spending on decor. Will you be better off spending them all on one area rather than spreading them around and not getting the same results? For example, are you better to use the venue's linens and spend more money on the floral arrangements or bring in something special? Picture black linens, oversize black polka-dot overlays, black chair covers, red glass plates, black-stem wineglasses, black napkins with red trim or black-and-white polka-dotted with red trim and a bouquet of fresh full red tulips. Alternatively, think about plain white linen, china, silver and crystal with a striking centerpiece.

What is the look, the feel, the mood you want to create? What do you remember most from the events you have attended? At one dinner event in Singapore, everything was very elegant and traditional until the end. Then, all at once, the floral centerpieces were removed and baskets filled with truffles descended from the ceiling to land precisely in the middle of each dinner table. People walked away talking about that for some time to come. The dinner, the dishes and the food were all excellent but it was the presentation of the truffles that was memorable.

Another part of decor is the print materials—custom menus, place cards, table number signs, programs and signage—that need to be included your budget. All of these could be tied together, part and parcel of the total picture. Know how long it will take to have everything prepared. There have been events where the programs arrived after the guests, and custom-designed T-shirts showed up literally hot off the press, still hot to the touch.

You may be surprised at the endless number of items that are available for rent—everything from hangers and coatracks to elegant serving pieces and silver candelabra. You can rent tables and chairs in any number of combinations, from formal elegance to casual and fun. You are not limited to the banquet chairs the facility offers and, even if you choose to use them, they can be covered for greater impact. Along with chairs, tables and chair covers, you can rent linens, overlays, napkins, high-top bar tables, banquet tables, registration tables, half-moon tables and serpentine tables.

Make sure that the tables you will be using are a solid unit in the size requested. Some facilities and rental companies put plywood over smaller tables, which, if not properly attached, can easily tip if leaned on.

Find out if the rental prices include setup, or if the company will just drop off the items. You need to know this in advance because setup could take some time and you may need to bring in additional help.

Schedule a time to meet with the rental company to see the quality of goods they offer. Look beyond their display area. Ask to see samples of what is in back. Spot-check items. You need to make sure that their linens are free of cigarette burns, stains and visible mends. It is important that the linens are delivered to you in pristine condition.

Table settings for rent run from designer selections to those more appropriate for a company BBQ. You can rent show plates, dinner plates, salad plates, dessert plates, side plates, flat plates, rimmed plates, soup bowls, consommé cups and saucers, regular cups and saucers and demitasse cups and saucers. Cutlery can range from gold plated and sterling silver to plastic. Each has an appropriate use. There are dozens of types of dinner knives, fish knives, butter knives, dinner forks, fish forks, salad and dessert forks, dessert spoons, soupspoons, teaspoons and demitasse spoons.

Glassware can be rented in everything from the finest crystal to everyday glass, both plain and colored, and you can rent glasses in every conceivable shape—highballs, old fashioneds, martini glasses, wine glasses in a variety of sizes, brandy snifters, liqueur glasses, champagne saucers, champagne flutes, sherry glasses, shooters, pilsner glasses, beer steins and water goblets. Glassware can be used for beverages, desserts and to hold individual floral displays at each place setting. Make sure that you have more than enough on hand.

You need to find out in advance how the rented items are being delivered, when they are being delivered, who will be unpacking them, who will be setting them out, who will be collecting them, who is responsible for cleaning them and who will be repacking them and sending them back. Know clearly what the rental agency will be doing, what the facility staff will contribute and what you will be responsible for. Make sure that it is clearly listed on your invoice and contract who is supplying what number of staff for the move in, setup and teardown. Make sure all special requests are noted and that the supplier confirms in writing (known as "signing back") all items, pricing and timing. Find out if they are licensed and insured, and who incurs what costs should any items be broken or damaged.

Fountains (actual working ones), water art (walls of water that can be lit, waterfalls and an array of other items) and fiber optics through which colors of light shine (the lights can be programmed to change color throughout the evening; walls and ceilings can be done this way) are all very dramatic enhancements that can be rented in a variety of sizes. What will be of extreme importance is how much time will be required for setup and if suppliers have any special requirements.

Along with rental companies, check with decor companies; prop houses that work with theater or movies; florists; antique shops; art galleries; specialty lighting and furniture stores; and even nurseries for new and interesting ideas. Be sure you discuss rental costs, delivery charges and insurance with each of them. Check the rental costs against the cost to buy. Sometimes it can be less expensive to purchase the item, but the question then is what do you do with it when the event is finished? You could ask the hotel or venue if they are interested in purchasing it from you, or once again you may want to have the item donated.

Special Effects

Special effects are well named—they are not called special for nothing, and they can have a spectacular effect at any event. Imagine walking into a ballroom that has been turned into a forest, with the scent of pine reaching into the lobby. Or perhaps into a room that has been transformed into an ice-skating rink, complete with falling "snow."

Special effects can affect all your senses—sight, sound, smell, taste and touch. You can fill a room with sound coming at you from all angles (surround sound) instead of just the stage area. You can fill a room with scent. You can light up the room with a laser show, fireworks or robotic lighting and bring in sweeps of colors. You can create high energy with fast-rolling light beams or have undertones of light crawl across the floor.

Smoke (dry ice) can be brought in to give more effect. Custom images or logos can be inserted on clear walls or floors. Events can be cybercast live. Take the opportunity to touch all of the senses and seek to stimulate all of them.

Check to make sure your special effects meet and exceed all safety regulations. Are there any safety regulations to be aware of? Are the materials being used flameproof? Find out what can go wrong, and what can be done to prevent it. Let your suppliers know what else is going on in the room. Consider the consequences of having candles burning on the tables during a confetti shower. That sounds like a recipe for disaster. The confetti is supposed to be flameproof, but is it? If not, you could end up with a little more excitement than you bargained for.

Special effects can be extremely complicated, so it is essential that you find out how much setup time is required and know all costs involved, including labor and power. Are there permits required? Again, you may need to budget for a fire watch to be on duty during the event. A fire marshal and the venue may have to approve all proposed plans. They will advise you of what needs to be done for your event to move ahead. They may require detailed floor plans, a schedule of events and a show flowchart.

Specialty Acts

Cirque-style performers creating magic overhead, fashion shows using holograms instead of models, contortionists turning themselves into a multitude of shapes, underwater ballets being conducted in an aquarium that is suspended overhead and dramatic dancing water displays set to music and lighting are the norm today, and it is important that you find out each and every requirement that needs to be provided. Technical and entertainment riders, which are terms and conditions you will be contractually agreeing to, need to be fully understood at planning time—not at contracting. Charges related to these policy clauses can be twice, three or more times the actual cost of the act once every cost is factored in.

For example, Cirque-style performers may require Marley floors installed, have all their costumes shipped and have care requirements (cleaning, pressing, repairing) that need to be costed in, and that can be just the tip of the iceberg. You may only have six performers but their technical rider may have a staff of 18 that needs to travel with them to ensure that rigging is safely installed and that all of their technical needs are met. If it is a union facility that you are setting up at, you may have to cost in for a union staff member to be assigned to each Cirque-style technical team member, and if a certain number of attendees is reached then you have supervisory staff costs to add in. It is imperative that you carefully research all technical and entertainment riders that may apply when you start to prepare your cost sheet. *The Business of Event Planning* includes other areas of cost consideration for the strategic planning and staging of successful events.

Parting Gifts

Parting gifts are always a nice way to mark the culmination of a special event. Make them meaningful. Make them a part of everyone's take-away memory. They don't have to be expensive, but they should be memorable.

> *A pre-theater party was held by the reflecting pool at the Westin Century Plaza in Los Angeles. Guests were then taken to see* Forever Plaid *and after the performance they were brought back to the hotel's incredible presidential suite , which has balconies that wrap around the entire floor. The view was spectacular. The cast of the play arrived and mingled with the guests, and when guests returned to their rooms they found, waiting on their pillows, a CD from* Forever Plaid *tied with a piece of plaid ribbon. It was simple and inexpensive but it captured the memory perfectly. It was very well done.*

On one incentive program, the welcome gift arrived as all the guests were heading back to the airport. The client had been advised of the deadline to get the gifts out on time, but had not sent them on schedule. Items can and will be held up at customs, and that needs to be factored into the logistics and timing. Find out well in advance what customs will require, what your broker will require and how much time is needed to get the item there well in advance of the guests' arrival. The hotel will store all shipped parcels in a secure area until you arrive.

Final Touches

You have chosen the site, you have selected the food and beverage and you have worked with the facility, staging, lighting and audiovisual people to make sure that the room layout and timing logistics will work. You must also take into account the decor and entertainment before you are ready to sign contracts. If you are doing an elaborate decor setup, you need to factor in move in, setup and teardown time. You need to know that all the pieces will fit together and how, because each is linked and can have an impact on one another. You can't have the tables moved into position and set up if the entertainment and decor need room to bring in their equipment. Planning ahead helps eliminate the need of doing things twice. You lose time, energy, money and sometimes even patience if proper thought and planning have not gone on beforehand.

First consider what atmosphere you are looking to create and how you go about doing that. Then work out the logistics behind it. What will you need to achieve it? Each event is different, but what you learn from one you can often apply to the next. Are you looking to achieve a warm, welcoming ambiance, or are you searching for something of a decidedly different nature?

> *A* Ghostbusters *theme event was held in the dungeon of a real castle. Candles flickered in the darkness, eerie sounds emanated from the background and an unexpected laser show greeted guests as they made their way through the narrow, damp tunnels. Guests then suddenly emerged in the old stables where a lively party atmosphere beckoned. The planners had wanted a dramatic entrance to their party, and they exceeded everyone's expectations.*

If you are doing a theme event as part of your meeting, you can set the party mood from the moment guests leave the meeting and get into their hotel rooms. Glow-in-the-dark hands can hold an invitation to the evening's events for a party that is taking place over Halloween. Inflated dolphins can be placed in the room—or even in a bathtub filled with water—with an invitation to an exclusive dinner set in an aquarium. Children's in-line skates can hold fun candy and an invitation to a day event that will include in-line skating lessons, and deliver one skate to each room as part of the invitation prop. (The next day, a skate exchange can be held at the hospitality desk and guests with young children, nieces, nephews and grandchildren can exchange sizes and find a match. The remaining skates can be donated to charity.)

You want guests to feel a sense of anticipation, a sense of celebration as they arrive. What will they see first when they arrive? Will it have visual impact? Will there be someone on hand to greet them and welcome them into the event? Does the room have the feeling of all details being attended to in advance of their arrival, or are people running around trying to pull together last-minute changes? At one restaurant opening, the owners kept changing the time and announcing it with a hand-written sign. Guests arriving at the appointed hour peered through the blinds, saw that nothing was ready and left. How is the room temperature—is it too hot or too cold? As more people arrive, this is something that needs to be monitored. How long does it take for the air-conditioning to kick in and cool down the room?

Is the food and drink readily at hand? Does it look and smell inviting? Is it nicely presented? Is there enough staff to properly service the event? One facility that was attempting to showcase its capabilities underestimated the number of cooking staff it would need for the number of guests invited. Inevitably they rushed things and tried to turn everything around too quickly. They served mussels that were undercooked and unopened. They attempted a too-intricate dish for a buffet. The lineups were long, and there were not enough other foods available. One yacht cruise being launched had set up a casino to show what could be done on board. There was taped music, but the guests were businesspeople coming together, without spouses, for the first time, and dancing was not appropriate. The yacht provided only enough casino chips to last each person about 10 minutes. The cruise was more than three hours long, and there was no other entertainment on board. This was only fun play, not for money or prizes, so there would have been no more added expense to have brought along sufficient tokens to allow for unlimited play by those guests who wanted to partake. To top things off, the yacht ran out of food. They had a television crew aboard and instead of an air of excitement and fun, they got fizzle.

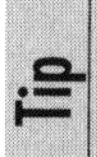

With private yacht charters, determine the plan of action should the boat run into difficulties. One yacht simply stopped mid-cruise, and it took hours to get it going again.

Take the time to visualize all aspects of your event. Put yourself in the room. What does it feel like? What does it look like? In your mind walk through the entire event from the moment guests arrive until they leave. What do you need to make it the absolute best? Go through contracts with a fine-tooth comb, making sure that all costs have been included in your budget. Read the terms and conditions—have they all been met?

Do you have all appropriate permits? Take the time to do a check. And if you can, it is always advisable to have someone else double-check your contracts and costings. A fresh pair of eyes may catch something that has been overlooked. If the proper research and development has gone into your costing and creative, the operations on the project will fall easily into place. If it hasn't, and you have already signed off on contracts, it can have a tremendous effect—financially and operationally—on your proposed project.

Staff, Supplier and Entertainment Work Permits

Another key area that needs to be addressed is required work permits for entertainment, suppliers and event planners themselves operating or taking part in an event out of country.

Exactly how the question "Are you traveling for business or pleasure?" is answered and how the reply is backed up is taking on new importance in the event planning industry for planners traveling outside their country to run a client's program. Cautionary tales are now circulating and the consequences run far deeper than just missing a flight—they can jeopardize both a planning company's events and their ability to successfully execute them, as well as limit an event planner's livelihood.

Imagine, as a freelance planner, trip director or vital on-site member of an event planning company's travel staff, being banned from entering a country for professional and personal travel—including connecting through it—and the long-term repercussions it could have on their event planning career and/or meeting planning company. That's what could happen if they were caught by customs and immigration not being truthful as to the real reason for their visit—by claiming pleasure instead of business. They would end up being denied entry if found to be deceptive—not just for that one trip but flagged forever. Or if they claimed business as their reason for traveling and cited running an event as a supervisor, but were deemed by the deciding powers that day to have required a valid work permit, treaty trader work visa, temporary business visitor documentation or other if-applicable certification that may be required to enter that country to do work on behalf of their client. Event planners being refused boarding or entry driving across the border can and is happening and the reasons vary.

In airports around the world, event planners can be found overseeing their participants' departure, making sure that their groups check in smoothly and that they encounter no problems with missed connections, seating, lost luggage or immigration issues. Making sure that their client's guests are well taken care of from start to finish is standard out-of-country event planning procedure. Once everyone is present and accounted for, the event planners traveling with their group then proceed to the departure lounge and get ready for their next stage of their journey, which will be assisting advance staff already in place with airport transfers upon arrival and then, without missing a beat, jump immediately into their on-site role requirements.

But that was not the case for one event planning company's staff at the airport to check in their group and then fly with them into the United States. The immigration authorities in charge that day did not allow them to board the aircraft and travel with their group because they did not have the proper work visas. Their passengers flew down to their destination unaccompanied, and the event planning staff already in place, advancing the program, had to move immediately into crisis management mode to deal with an immediate unexpected staffing shortage.

And planners do not only have to ensure that they have proper documentation for business travel to the country their event is taking place in, but that their suppliers who are coming down to lend their expertise or services to the event have all their affairs in order as well, so that on travel days there will be no unexpected surprises that could drastically hinder the successful execution of their event. Be aware that the legal requirements and documentation for each category—planners and suppliers—can be different.

Legal Requirements and Documentation

It is imperative that you do your homework to be 100 percent compliant with all the rules and regulations involved with working in another country. In all things legal, the responsibility is with each level of supplier and planner to ensure they are abreast of all the changing customs regulations as they apply to each country. For example, you may attend a conference, give a lecture or supervise an event without a work permit; but, actually installing and producing an entire event does not fall into the same category.

If you are working in another country on a regular basis, you may need to have visas and permits. If, however, your work in the country is very sporadic, you may be able to travel under a legal letter, with your key people as "supervisors," only to ensure the "look or the branding" is in line with client mandates, and hire a team of suppliers and installers in the location to carry out the vision. It is for that very reason many of the technical companies who often work in a specific country have opened offices there.

Not only does proper documentation need to be in place for those supervising events, but also material being brought into the country carries its own set of rules and regulations that must be met. For example, you may be able to temporarily import the products on a return basis into the country for a show (that is, all goods entering the country will return to the originating country), but the manifest documents must be detailed and the process is intensive. For instance, in one country, in the past you simply needed to list the country of origin of every product you were sending. Now, you must list the country and the manufacturing company for many products. That information may not always be available. For example, you may have difficulty if your decor company purchased anything by retail or through brokers overseas. Fabrics and feathers set off alarm bells, so your decor company might be required to have full documentation on all such items. (Officials wonder if the feathers are from an endangered species, are fire retardant and according to which nation's code, etc.) Some products are simply not welcome because of their country of origin and customs brokers will be able to provide you and your suppliers with a list of them.

Establishing a relationship with a great customs broker who keeps up with the ever-changing categories will save countless hours. To ensure a smooth international entry and exit, be sure you declare fully on the manifest everything both going and returning. Be sure to edit the document if things are "taken" from an event by attendees, as it won't match return documentation.

Planners need to make sure that their suppliers' staff are all able to travel freely as well. There are horror stories of a simple misdemeanor some 15 years earlier halting a person from entering another country because it is still lurking on an archived record. The employee may not even know a record still exists.

Be forthright and say what you are actually going to do, such as supervise a show, and have your signed contract with your client, the contracts with co-suppliers in the country, and details of the labor source to be used, and that will make the process go much smoother as all your documentation is in place. There really are no shortcuts.

The more time you have to plan all the paperwork, the better. Make sure key people in your organization are keeping passports up to date, and make sure you have a great database of associates in other cities to partner with.

Some planners do hire their decor company of choice in their home city so that they have the same level of comfort when they are executing internationally. Knowing they are in good hands, they can concentrate on the big picture while having all other aspects taken care of by those who regularly partner with them. But it is important to work with professionals who have done events internationally to avoid any issues. Working in unfamiliar territory is stressful enough. Be sure you are working with those who increase your sense of security and don't add to the stress.

Booking performers through a professional entertainment and talent management company, one that is experienced in out-of-country requirements for their talent, can be a time- and stress-saver for planners. The entertainment management company will ensure that everything that is required by their acts has been obtained in advance. This way, planners don't run the risk of no-show appearances if entertainment performers or speakers they have booked on their own have not followed through and obtained proper legal documentation for performing in the country they are traveling to. And entertainment and talent management companies can apprise planners of other out-of-country legal and travel rider considerations that come with costly fees that need to be accounted for in advance so that planners' clients are not fielding additional costs that should have been anticipated and incorporated into proposal budgets. Hitting a client with additional costs—which can go up the thousands for work permits—at final reconciliation only serves to diminish the event planning company's reputation. It is clearly important to work with professionals that can prepare planners and their clients in advance as to what to expect. Time needs to be factored in as well. Some work permits can take up to three months or more to process.

There can also be additional costs that may need to be included. One entertainment management company had to make arrangements with the local union in Mexico, which required a performance fee equivalent to what the Mexican band would have been paid if they had performed at the group function instead of the entertainment that was being brought in. An additional $3,000 had to be added to entertainment costs.

Local destination management companies experienced in dealing with customs and immigration can be an invaluable resource as well for planners and any suppliers and entertainment they may be bringing in.

Shipping as much meeting material as possible in advance with experts in this area can ease customs and immigration clearance for planners. It ensures that there will be no holdups clearing goods upon arrival, is one less concern for travel staff clearing customs and immigration, and preempts any delays from being interviewed by officials and having business goods traveling with them subjected to exam. Many planners travel today with just computer memory sticks and limit the program documents they carry with them.

Some major courier companies also offer printing services through which meeting planners can post large files of up to 60 MB and avoid the expense of shipping printed materials to the event venue. Using their hub-and-spoke system, a store located near the venue can print the documents, provide a wide variety of finishing services and deliver the completed order on-site. Rush jobs that are required during the event can also be sent to the store via e-mail or posted to their site for printing and delivery. Companies such as The UPS Store provide the full range of printing services including offset and wide-format (poster printing), and graphic design. Supplies needed at a conference, such as binders, notepads, pens, flip charts and packaging supplies can be obtained from The UPS Store using their online service. Orders placed online can be delivered on-site at the conference venue.

Companies like The UPS Store can also provide on-site packing and shipping services from the event venue. Delegates returning home from a conference often find themselves loaded with various materials, including treasures from local art galleries and gift shops, that can't easily be packed in their luggage or carry-on bags. Such companies would also be able to advise planners on what their participants would need to do to comply with customs and immigration regulations upon return.

Event Risk Assessment

Today, risk assessment plays a very important part in event design and it is not limited to just one area. Risk assessment and event liability can include everything from location and weather considerations to financial issues (from a client wanting their event planning company to finance their event or from financial repercussions from an event) and actual event inclusions, and each must be carefully appraised—with protective measures costed into your program—before moving forward to contracting.

Some main risk assessment areas to consider include those that would make it impossible for the event to be held, such as:

- » A decrease in attendance
- » Bad weather
- » Non-appearance of a major speaker
- » Company emergencies
- » Other events and their timing
- » Force majeure

Logistical risk assessment areas include:

- » Necessary permits
- » Access to up-to-date information on telephone, gas and hydro lines
- » Available washroom facilities
- » Available power hookups
- » Ground coverage
- » Noise regulations on music levels if private homes are nearby
- » Preparation of evacuation and emergency procedures (e.g., water taxis if on an island)
- » Renewal of union venue contracts
- » Being limited to in-house suppliers
- » Verified, up-to-date licenses and certificates , such as liquor licenses and insurance certificates (ask for copy of all relevant licenses and insurance certificates)
- » Local events or festivals taking place at the same time that could result in disrupted transportation, poorer service and substantially increased expenses for staffing and other labor

There are many ways to reduce or eliminate event risk to your client, your company, the participants and your suppliers, and they can range from finding logistical solutions to ensuring your contract is amended to protect everyone involved and taking out event insurance. Contract clauses that planners should look out for include attrition, cancellation and force majeure. Planners should negotiate to have any forfeited monies applied as deposits on future business booked to deliver within a reasonable period of time (to be specified in the contract) after the original event. One event planning company that didn't invest in event cancellation insurance had to cancel a large conference on a week's notice. Had insurance been in place, the $50,000 in cancellation charges their client was charged may have been recoverable.

Planners should always review the venue's security plans and ask for a "heart of the house" tour. Ask for their Emergency Procedures Manual or how they have handled a situation, whether a labor conflict (picketers) or a death or injury.

With regards to contracts, responsibilities and liabilities should be mutual—look for mutual indemnification; insurance evidenced by both parties and a reciprocal cancellation clause. Do include clauses requiring the vendors to provide timely notice regarding renovation, construction and change in ownership; flag or brand, and indicate the consequences should any of those occurrences happen. A non-competitor clause can also be added, but you do need to specify who would be considered a competitor.

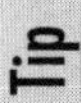

The Special Events Advisor: A Business and Legal Guide for Event Professionals (Wiley 2003) written by David Sorin, an attorney and consultant to companies in the special events industry, is a recommended read on the event planning business and legal issues. Sorin has been involved with many high-profile events, including the 1996 Olympic Games in Atlanta. He has been active in event industry organizations for many years, and has served as president of the International Special Events Society (table of contents: http://www.wiley.com/WileyCDA/WileyTitle/productCd-0471450103,descCd-tableOfContents.html).

Always have company lawyers review and approve contracts and find out when and where waivers will be required, such as in the case of event elements involving physical activity. Also find out if you can be added onto riders for insurance certificates in addition to taking out event cancellation insurance, which can cover cancellation charges for all expenses incurred to promote and produce the event. Require that your suppliers and venues provide you with evidence of their insurance, including supplier-specific insurance such as worker's compensation coverage, vehicle insurance or loss/damage of equipment insurance, etc.

Reducing exposure and lessening event risks for clients, guests and the event planning company and their staff and suppliers is extremely important in today's litigious society. It can be a costly step to overlook. and not just in financial terms—one florist was sued for thousands of dollars for substituting pastel-pink flowers for the contracted rust flowers—but guest safety as well, as in the case of a garden party event where a rotting willow tree fell and killed an attending guest and injured others, and when a deck collapsed from the weight of too many guests gathered on it for a photo shoot. Deaths and serious injuries have taken place during an event. The responsibility is on the event planning company to ensure that they have shown they have done everything possible to prevent injury, and that insurance coverage is there should anything go wrong. For example, an event planning company designing a team-building ski race event would need to take into account that safety nets would need to be installed on the runs as a protective measure; that the participants are being physically protected with quality equipment, safety headgear, etc.; that highly trained staff are supervising the event; that EMS has been included in case of any accidents; that waivers have been signed, permits are in place and insurance has been taken out; that a backup weather plan is prepared; and that all other event design logistical and legal requirements are in place. Each event element's risks must be carefully assessed and the event planning company's and their client's legal departments do need to become involved and sign off on an approved course of action. Event risk assessment needs to take place at the planning and pre-contracting stage so that informed decisions can be made, amendments to contracts can be made and all costs for insurances, permits and logistical solutions can be factored into proposed budgets. Event risk assessment is a vital part of successful event execution and budget management, and a skill that is required in today's event planning industry.

Conclusion

It's a Wrap!

The last guest has departed. Your event has concluded. At the end of the day, remember that only you and the people involved in the planning and operations will know if it all came about exactly as planned. Your event may have had some unexpected twists and turns, but isn't that what life is all about? If you have managed to meet the challenges calmly, serenely and with a smile, no one will really know what actually took place backstage. Keep in your mind the image of a swan gracefully gliding on water, while underneath, its feet are paddling furiously. And during the event, try to take time to savor it, if only for a moment, before moving on to the next item in your function sheets. Remember to make note of any observations directly on your function sheets. They will refresh your memory when you have your wrap-up review.

If you can, plan to do nothing the next day but pamper yourself. There is always an emotional impact the day after an event. You have put your heart and soul into it, worked day and night to bring it about and now it's over. Sometimes it can be a year in the planning and other times three weeks, but, either way, you are probably exhausted. It's a time to reflect and bask in the success of a well-orchestrated event.

Take the time to review your event with all those involved, but don't schedule it for the very next day. Give everyone time to review their notes, gather their thoughts and get some rest, but do hold the review while the event is still fresh in everyone's mind.

When you do the event evaluation, make it clear that you are not looking at areas of blame but rather areas of learning and growth. What worked? What would you do differently next time? To this day, there is not one event from which I haven't learned something that I can bring to the next one. Were your objectives met? If not, what could be done differently to bring about different results? Did you come in on budget? Did you spend more in one area than anticipated? What were the reasons? Were they valid? What was the feedback?

Record all relevant thoughts and observations. They will be valuable to you as you prepare your executive event review summary for your client and your in-house post-event history—the copy for your files that will go with the stored material once your event and final reconciliation have come to a close—and again later when you begin to plan your next event for the same client or use the same venue, suppliers and event learning for someone new.

A post-event history—both the executive event review summary and the event planning in-house post-event history—contains valuable information that can be used as a blueprint that will provide a solid foundation on which to build future events. When a company decides to hold an event, one of the very first questions their event planning company or venue, such as a hotel or convention center if they are handling the event in-house, will be asking is the history of the events they have held. This information aids them in many ways. First off, they will be able to tell from the caliber of the properties your events have been held at whether or not the property they are considering would be the right fit or if they may be better served by a different property.

There is an art to designing events that will successfully build on one another, and a detailed post-conference history can help companies avoid taking any backwards steps. For example, if a company has traditionally only held events in five-, six- and seven-star hotels and resorts and then dramatically downgrades to a four-star property for their next event, the choice of hotel or event inclusions could send out a message to your employees, suppliers and industry that your company might be experiencing hard times. And there can also be pitfalls if you go in the opposite direction.

If your company has been successfully building on their past events and then takes a leap to a much higher level, they need to be fairly certain that they will not have to go backwards the following year because of budget constraints or fail to achieve their company objectives because the property and program are not the right fit for their attendees. A new company president decided to choose a location and a luxury resort property for an incentive program that fulfilled his personal desires. In the past, their company had staged incentive programs that met sales targets but selected all-inclusive properties and cruises for three- and four-day getaways. They were the perfect match for their employees, who wanted to enjoy a stay that presented no personal financial concerns and not have to stress when someone was asked to pick up the next round of drinks. Because they were staying at properties where everything was included, they could totally relax and joke about being the one to take care of the drinks. In order to stay within budget and afford the seven-night stay the new company president wanted meals and drinks and other all-inclusive features dropped from their program. Winners at that year's incentive struggled as they found they personally could not afford to pay for their meals at leisure at this resort. Also the property was so far away from shopping areas that it was not affordable to jump in a taxi to town for an inexpensive meal, so they resorted to filling up their beach bags with rolls, muffins, fruit, etc. from the breakfast buffet in order to tide them over to dinner. They did not come away feeling like winners on this trip. They incurred many additional expenses they had not run into before, and when the next year's program was launched there was no motivation to achieve sales goals because many preferred to simply win the lesser prizes than to qualify for a trip that they could not personally afford to take. Once the company president studied the past event history and measured the sales results against his initial program and the following year's, he was able to assess the situation and go back to what was working, with a company objective in mind to elevate their events but to do it in a way that the company could still pick up the majority of the costs for their incentive winners. Their next program tapped into what held value to their employees and was an overwhelming success. Instead of an exotic location and luxury hotel for a seven-night program halfway across the world, they opted to do a family incentive to Disney with a shorter stay but all meals and activities provided for the winners and their families. Had the company president taken the time to review the wealth of information that lay in his company's post-event executive event review summaries, and had their event planning company used them as a teaching guide as to what worked best and had a proven history of delivering company and event objectives results, the company would not have lost the momentum they had been building on. They would not have been in a situation of having to make up time and recoup lost sales for the previous two events that they had designed around a personal whim instead of on a successful company event history that was readily apparent from the detailed information found in the post-event history.

By now, it probably goes without saying that not taking the time to write an effective post-conference history can be very costly in terms of money, energy and time.

Effective post-event history summaries should include:

» Company and event strategic objectives and how the event was strategically designed and planned to meet these objectives
» The company and event return on investment

It is important, as you move forward through planning, operations and on-site execution, to track pertinent information that you will need to include in a post-event history and not depend on memory after your event has run. One way to do this successfully is to have the account executive and planning, operations and lead on-site staff keep an event journal listing key elements in point form, including revised costings, any issues, additions, and major scope changes. Visual reminders can be very good as well. The Polaroid Digital Instant Mobile Photo Printer could be a very useful event planning tool for capturing and recording visual elements reminders in journals. This printer fits easily into a pocket and allows you to print pictures instantly from a cell phone with a Bluetooth connection or from a digital camera with a USB cable. The printer does not require any ink as it uses a special brand of paper, and it prints out a 2 × 3-inch photo that has an adhesive backing. The backing turns it into a sticker that can then be placed in the journal as a reminder, e.g., if you happen to note an area of concern regarding move in on a site inspection, a quick picture taken, printed and in your journal with logistical notes would be very useful for operations and serve as a concern consideration to be noted in a post-event history for future events held at that location.

Remember to get meal numbers and guestroom pickup (how many rooms were actually assigned and used) data daily from the Conference Services Manager and keep it on file for preparation of the report, and include the actual number guaranteed, number served and number paid for.

A post-event summary for an event planning company or supplier to use in-house for future reference and an executive summary that will be presented to their client will contain different information. For example, an event planning company will be compiling a report that will help them when working on future business with their client, give them insight on a property, supplier, product, etc., for future events with different clients using the same facility or some of the same event elements, and provide notes on how to improve for next time. This is a confidential in-house report but is kept on file for all future programs. It is important for internal records to keep samples of materials used as well as contracts, critical paths, final meeting specifications, challenges and changes. It is also important to include observations taken as the event was unfolding and record the turnout, feedback from delegates and the little information they see and hear that could be of value to future event design and event execution applications.

A client's post-conference report should be prepared as an executive summary. Remember, they will be preparing their own internal post-conference report as well, with confidential information that the event planning company will not be privy to. Your report will act as a supplement to theirs. It is important to keep the report clear, concise and easy to either duplicate or share with the client's stakeholders. It is essential to ask the client what their stakeholders will want to see in the post-conference report to ensure that the data and documentation is captured from the beginning. Ensure that there is backup for all financial information. Include the outcome of company and event objectives and highlights of the program. Keep the communication simple and include the contracted amount and final billing in a comparison chart; visual accents; and event program survey results.

You will want to hold an in-house post-conference review in order to make sure that you have captured all essential elements for your company's event history as well as your client's. It is important to remember that the intent of the meeting is to learn and grow from each event, not to cast judgment. The focus needs to be on what worked, what did not work and actions to move forward. This meeting should include the full internal planning and operations team and on-site team. Keep the review very structured and focused on the topic, not on any emotion surrounding the event, and if possible limit the meeting to one hour in length.

Client post-event presentations are usually done in person but for small meetings it may be acceptable to just submit the executive summary for review. It is important to know the client's expectations up front to ensure that the final delivery of the report meets their requirements. The final executive event summary report presentation can also be used as a presentation or opportunity to close future business and/or develop the relationship. The report should be presented at the same time as the financials are closed off. Remember that this is a business document and should be written and presented as if the CEO and CFO will see it.

A post-event summary is an important event planning tool both for the client and for the event planning company. It gives you the framework from which to build your next program and teaches you what needs to be done to maximize the company's event investment and meet and exceed attendee expectations. If the event produced outstanding results, the post-conference summary can also pave the way for increased budgets and expanded event programs. It is a valuable part of the event process that needs to begin at the planning stages. And it should never be missed.

Within a post-event summary, include:

» Layout all of their proposed event objectives, prioritized while keeping in mind past, present and future objectives and critiqued as to how they will help you meet specific objectives
» Date of travel
» Actual number of participants
» Guest profile/demographics
» Gateway cities (if air travel was involved)
» Total airfare spent
» Total number of participants that required air transportation
» Average air cost per person
» Guestroom breakdown, e.g., how many suites, how many single/king guestrooms, how many double guestrooms (shared two-bed accommodation) and room rates

» Total accommodation costs
» Meeting room spending and meeting room charges
» Audiovisual spending
» Total food spending
» Total beverage spending
» Total group activities spending
» Total entertainment spending
» Total spending (including expense reports related to the event)
» Total cost per person
» Company objectives going in
» Company objectives met
» Executive history success summary

Corporations are now discovering massive overspending on events due to each department handling their own arrangements as opposed to having it placed under one department's control. When they compiled all the numbers, one company found out that they were spending one billion dollars annually on events—twice what they thought they were spending—and they are not alone. What was showing up were areas where costs could have been contained. For example, one department would cancel their meeting and be hit with cancellation charges that could have been applied to another department that was looking at having an event at the same hotel at a future date. Companies are now taking steps to get control over what is being spent and how it is being spent. One way to capture total event costs that some companies are no longer turning to is meeting charge credit card programs that are set up to capture all event costs, as well as on-site meeting expenses.

In an effort to bring down costs, some corporations are having their procurement department—not sales and marketing—solicit quotes from event planning companies and suppliers.

Your executive event review summary can become a powerful marketing tool when event planners and a corporate company's sales and marketing teams are faced with an emerging trend of having a corporation's procurement department do the event buying. Procurement—not sales and marketing—are determining who is awarded the business and once the proposed event has gone to contract only then does the procurement department turn the event over to sales and marketing to be managed and live with the results. If the event planning can show that they are consistently coming in, on or under budget and meeting and exceeding company, event and guest objectives, then a company making the move to having the procurement department make a decision based on dollars and cents, not dollars and sense with the dollars strategically spent on working to achieve company goals, could be sidestepped. Procurement may work on securing the best price for couriers, buying office equipment, etc., but for event planning, pricing alone is not the way to ensure that the results the company is looking for can be achieved. To learn what event planning companies can do when faced with preparing a quote for a procurement department, please refer to *The Executive's Guide to Corporate Events and Business Entertaining*.

Developing long-term relationships with your clients is imperative. It can be an expensive venture to solicit new clients. An event planning company can conceivably spend up to $15,000 on a proposal when you factor in the hours spent researching, developing, preparing and presenting it with no guarantees of securing the business. You always want to be in the position of being the incumbent, with other companies vying to secure the business.

Working in partnership with your client as a vital part of their sales and marketing team is how you want them to perceive your value—not as a service industry where you can be easily replaced. The role you play and how you present yourself and your company will matter from beginning to end—and the executive event summary review process is a stepping stone to their next event and company referrals. One company president was so pleased with the results of his event that he made sure to introduce his event planning company heads to key decision-makers from other companies attending his event. That is the goal you are working towards—repeat and referral business—and establishing long-term business relationships as opposed to soliciting new business by cold calls and being one of many competing for the same piece of business. For ways on how to set you and your company apart from your competition, please refer to *Marketing Your Event Planning Business*.

Applause! Applause!

Remember to schedule time to say thank-you. The best time is in the days immediately following your event, when everything is still very fresh in your mind. Be as specific as you can be. If there were people who went above and beyond to make sure that your event was successful, let them know how much you appreciate their efforts personally and mention them by name in your letter to your main contact.

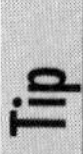

Take care with the wording of your letters and how much confidential information is in them. They may be seen by others and could be used as reference letters to other potential clients, so do not name your client but talk specifically about the event and their involvement in making it a success.

At all costs, avoid form thank-you letters. It destroys the whole message if two or more people discover they have received identical letters. Put the same thought and care into your letters that you want them to put into your event. You never know when you may find yourself working together on another project.

Use your function sheets as a tool to remind you who needs to be thanked. Collect business cards as you go along so you can refer to them for the correct spelling of names, titles and addresses. And, once again, remember to include in your budget an estimated amount for cards, letterhead, envelopes, postage, couriers and any thank-you gifts you may be sending. Put some thought into the thank-you gift you send. Ideally, it will be a reminder of the event. If you had a featured singer, you could have a CD personalized and signed for them. If in conversation you learn what their interests are, perhaps by what they display in their offices, take the time to use that knowledge to make their thank-you gift special. The gift doesn't have to be expensive, but it must be thoughtful and most importantly fit into their company gift policy—you do not want to be perceived as trying to buy their future business. You may even want to come up with a signature gift. I have always loved to give miniature inukshuks, which are the traditional stone structures built as directional markers by the Inuit, leading the way for others. They are symbolic of our responsibility to each other and our dependence on one another. They are the perfect symbol for event planners. When you do an event you are dependent on one another, and each of us is responsible for leading the way for the others who follow behind.

Your Next Event

The skills learned to plan successful meetings, conferences, conventions or incentives transfer over to other special events. What you learn from one event can help you with your next one. While it may not be exactly the same scenario, what you learned and experienced may trigger an interesting twist you can bring to your next event.

You now have an invaluable record of suppliers, phone numbers and key information. Take the time to record all of these numbers and contact names, organize your files and transfer all the information to one central place. Leave no messy files, no bits and pieces of paper floating around. As you take apart your files, secure them with an elastic and place each section in a separate unsealed envelope that is clearly labeled. Then place them in order—bound together again—in a larger container such as a box or envelope that has been clearly labeled with key information. You will find that you will go back to this information and refer to it for a variety of reasons as you begin to plan your next event. Having the majority of the event planning stages organized and easily available makes it so much more effortless when you need to find something that is critical to the success of your next event. What was the name of that balloon company? They were wonderful. You want to include them in your next event, but you just can't remember their exact name. Store all your related material together—cost breakdowns, payment schedules, critical path and function sheets with a backup copy of your computer disk as well as sample invitations, promotional items, etc.

Start fresh with each new event. Set up new files. There will be a new set of logistics to consider and work your way through. Start at the beginning and begin to fill in the detail.

Appendix A

Sample Cost Sheets

Gala Fund-Raiser

A cost sheet is a detailed breakdown of the costs related to your specific event. It is used to provide an overview of items that you will need to include to produce a successful event. It shows you clearly what each item will cost and helps you determine whether or not it is an expense that you wish to include. Once you've had an opportunity to review the total estimated costs as listed you may decide that the money being spent on centerpieces would be better applied to one lavish memorable "wow" item like a chocolate fountain. Itemizing your costs allows you to see all the elements that must be included in each area and laying them out "storyboard fashion" allows you to do a visual walk-through ensuring that you do not miss a step. For example, if invitations are being included in the costing, items you would need to consider and account for under invitations would include: the quality, the size (has a bearing on postage), the printing, the special touches, the quantity required, etc. Envelopes for the invitations would also need to be considered. You would need to detail all the elements and costs that could apply to them: the quality, the quantity (have you costed in sufficient envelopes to cover any addressing errors or damage) or the printing (return address), how they are being addressed—by hand, printed labels, or will the addresses be printed directly on the envelopes. All of the items mentioned above have a cost attached to them—be it the actual cost of the item or the cost of labor. All these cost items must be accounted for in order for your projected budget to be based on realistic costs. No one wants to be presented with a $100,000 costing error after contracting—it can and has happened. By taking the time to lay each item out and factoring in all possible costs that could be incurred you can avoid costly errors. Walking through your event step by step on your Cost Sheet with the same detail and thought given to each item, no matter how seemingly insignificant, will help you to fine-tune your budget and reduce/eliminate mistakes.

The Cost Sheet is the foundation on which your event is built and it is a multi-purpose tool. You can use it as the base for your Critical Path because many of the elements that need to be handled are outlined in both. The same applies for your Payment Schedule—your Cost Sheet can be copied and reformatted to work out your Payment Schedule, reducing the time spent re-inputting the same information. As your event progresses and items are continually updated and subtracted and final costs are input—what was once your original Cost Sheet becomes your Final Reconciliation—and you will be going into your event knowing exactly where you stand.

The following sample Cost Sheet for a gala fund-raiser includes three columns at the top. This is just one example of how a Cost Sheet can be laid out (a second example is provided in Appendix B). Here the headings displayed are LOT COST, P.P., and # of PAX.

The LOT COST is the total cost of the line item. This can be based on either a flat rate cost, i.e., room rental charge; the total cost, i.e., the cost of table linens based on x number of tables multiplied by the per table linen cost; or a cost that has been calculated on a cost per item multiplied by the number of guests attending.

P.P. refers to the Per Person cost. This is calculated by dividing the LOT COST by the # of PAX (the number of guests attending). A formula can be worked out in either Excel, or any other accounting system.

This formula can be used to calculate the Per Person cost which is based on the LOT COST divided by the # of PAX. The LOT COST when based on a per item cost such as dinner and multiplied by the number of guests attending may also be calculated using the same formula.

Having formulas in place allows you to quickly see the impact on your budget should you increase your guest list, for example, from 72 guests to 100. But when you are changing the number of guests remember to pay attention to line items where the cost has not been based on a flat rate or a rate based on a per item cost multiplied by the number of guests. In the case of rented table linens—if you were doing tables of eight you would have multiplied the cost of the rented linens by nine tables—changing the number of guests to 100 would increase the number of table linens required to 12 (providing 2 of the tables of 8 then became tables that could accommodate 10), you would need to ensure that you have gone in and made the change.

SAMPLE GALA FUND-RAISER–TRIBUTE	**LOT COST**	**P.P.**	**# OF PAX**
Estimated Sponsorship Dollars Required *Special Note: Items have been laid out in "menu format" so that they can be added and subtracted to meet your budget guidelines. A detailed payment schedule will also be provided.*			
Pre-Event			
Invitations (Estimated based on 4,000)			
Detail			
Envelopes (Based on 4,000)			
Detail			
Order Forms (Based on 4,000)			
Detail			
Mailing			
Addressing/Labels			
Mailing – Estimated			
Couriers – Estimated			
Ticket Sales			
Ticket Coordination			
Ticket Processing			
Liquor Licence			
Special Occasion Permit.			

SAMPLE GALA FUND-RAISER–TRIBUTE	LOT COST	P.P.	# OF PAX
Special Event Insurance Host Liquor Liabilities/Property of Others. Estimated.			
Charitable Event Licence/Permit			
Room Rental Room Rental Access from 5:00 a.m. onward			
Based on the proposed number of guests there is no room rental charge. If numbers drop below 700 guests the following rates will apply: $2,000.00 Room Rental 500–700 Guests $3,000.00 Room Rental 300–500 Guests			
Audiovisual/Staging			
One Way Transmission			
Satellite Requirements Detail Inclusions			
Visuals Detail Inclusions			
Image Magnification Detail Inclusions			
Composite Switching Kit Detail Inclusions			
Audio Detail Inclusions			
Lighting Detail Inclusions			
Miscellaneous Detail Inclusions			
Setup (6 Hours) Detail Labour			
Operate Detail Labour			
Strike Detail Labour			
Technical Phone Line and Audio Conference Line Detail			
On-Location Technical Support, Video, Lighting, Audio Support Detail			
Filmed for Television/Film Editing Costs Detail			

SAMPLE GALA FUND-RAISER–TRIBUTE	LOT COST	P.P.	# OF PAX
Delivery and Transportation Detail			
Charges for Use of Freight Elevator Detail			
Costs for Two-Way Transmission Detail			
Staging Detail			
Film Clips Editing of Film Clips – Estimated Film Clips – Transfer to Toronto Estimated *Special Note: Additional costs involved to secure rights to show film clips.* Script Writing – Introductions, Speeches, Show Flow, Visual Aids (Slides/PowerPoint) Estimated Power & Power Distribution Charges Estimated Award for Presentation *Special Note: All labor is estimated, actual hours to be invoiced. Prices subject to change based on final staging, lighting, audiovisual requirements.*			
Parking Valet Parking. 6:00 p.m. Start Parking Costs			
Crowd Control Pay Duty Officers. Estimated.			
Reception Estimate based on 2 drinks per person			
Entertainment Detail SOCAN (Paid to the Hotel – Music Royalty/Rights)			
Silent Auction Signage, Bid Sheets, Item Numbering, Pens, etc. Estimated			
Signage for the Four Doors for Table Assignments, i.e., Door One Tables 1-200, etc. Signage, Floor Plan, Table Assignment Floor Plans for Hostesses to Distribute. Estimated.			
Place Cards Place Card Settings. Estimated. Based on 700			
Table Numbers Table Numbers Cards. Estimated.			

SAMPLE GALA FUND-RAISER–TRIBUTE	LOT COST	P.P.	# OF PAX
Menu			
Menu			
Colour output 2 sides, laminated to cover stock			
Decor – Table Linens			
Based on 70 tables of 10. Maximum room capacity 700 for a sit-down dinner. Ticket sales cannot exceed 700 guests.			
Decor – Table Napkins			
Based on 700 guests 2 napkins per guest			
Decor – Chair Covers			
Based on 700			
Centerpieces			
Centerpiece. Based on 70 tables of 10			
Dinner			
Menu Detail			
Food. Estimated. Based on 700			
Tax			
Gratuities			
Beverages			
Wine. Estimated. Based on 700			
Tax			
Gratuities			
Photographer (2)			
7 Hours			
Tax			
Color Contact Sheets (Estimated 20 Rolls × 36 Print Exposures)			
Tax			
Delivery of Contact Sheets for Media Distribution			
Tax			
Return Delivery of Contact Sheets for Processing			
Tax			
Estimated Color Reprints to Media			
Tax			
Delivery of Color Reprints to Media			
Tax			
Media			
Meals for Media			
Advertising			
Full-Page Ad			
Camera-Ready Artwork. Estimated			

SAMPLE GALA FUND-RAISER–TRIBUTE	LOT COST	P.P.	# OF PAX
Press Kit Detail Inclusions and Organization **Take-Away Gift** Custom Memento. Estimated. **Custom T-Shirts for Volunteers (for ID Purposes)** Estimated **Communication Costs** Couriers, Site Inspection Costs/Parking, Function Sheets, etc. Final Reconciliation to be based on actual costs incurred **Program Directors** On-site Program Directors/Setup/Rehearsals and Day of Event Final Reconciliation to be based on actual costs incurred Walkie-talkies. Estimated.			
Estimated Subtotal in Local Currency			
Management Fee			
Estimated Total in Local Currency			

Appendix A

Sample Cost Sheets

Meeting

In the sample Cost Sheet for a Meeting you will see the addition of a grid. When an event encompasses more than one day it is helpful before costing to lay all your requirements out on a grid. This grid has a dual purpose—it can be used to help you visualize and capture all inclusions for your Cost Sheet and it can be used to send to the hotel or venue as an outline of the function space you will require.

CLIENT NAME:
TRAVEL DATE:

DESTINATION: JAMAICA
BASED ON:

PROGRAM OUTLINE	DAY ONE Saturday	DAY TWO Sunday	DAY THREE Monday	DAY FOUR Tuesday	DAY FIVE Wednesday	DAY SIX Thursday	DAY SEVEN Friday	DAY EIGHT Saturday
BREAKFAST		Breakfast at leisure	Breakfast Meeting 8 a.m. – 10 a.m.	Breakfast at leisure	Breakfast Meeting 8 a.m. – 10 a.m.	Breakfast Meeting 8 a.m.– 10 a.m.	Breakfast Meeting 8 a.m. – 10 a.m.	Breakfast at leisure
MORNING ACTIVITIES		Private Sail Dunn's River by Catamaran Pickup at the pier	Activity Allowance Choices could include: Deep-Sea Fishing Horseback Riding Scuba Diving Helicopter Ride (1.2 hr)	Morning Meeting	At your leisure	Activity Allowance Choice could include: Deep-Sea Fishing Horseback Riding Scuba Diving Helicopter Ride (1/2 hr)	At your leisure	Return Transfers will commence
LUNCH		Included at Your Leisure	Included at Your Leisure	Included at Your Leisure	Included at Your Leisure	Included at Your Leisure	Included at Your Leisure	
AFTERNOON ACTIVITIES	Private Transfer Hotel Refreshments Motor coach	The Spa Golfing Watersports The Choices are endless ... and included.	Choices continued Blue Mountain Bike Tour Shopping Shuttle Golf Tournament	Late Beach Olympics	At your leisure	Choices continued Blue Mountain Bike Tour Shopping Shuttle Golf Tournament	At your leisure	
COCKTAIL RECEPTION	Welcome Reception 7 p.m. – 8 p.m.				Private Sunset Sail Cocktail Reception		Farewell Reception 7 p.m. – 8 p.m. Military Band	
EVENING ACTIVITIES	Caribbean Buffet 8 p.m. – 11 p.m. Mento Band	Included at your leisure	Private Dinner in the Spectacular Green Grotto Caves 7 p.m. – 9 p.m. Folkloric Show Steel Band 9:00 pm – 11:00 pm	Lobster Bake & Fish Fry on the Beach 7 p.m. – 9 p.m. Reggae Band	Included at your leisure	Included at your leisure	Farewell Dinner 8 p.m. – 9:30 p.m. Cabaret Singer with Backup Band 9:30 p.m. – 11 p.m.	

* The hotel is an all-inclusive resort—all meals and beverages have been included.
Unless group functions, guests are free to enjoy their meals at their leisure at any of the hotel's four restaurants.

SAMPLE COSTING: CONFERENCE/MEETING JAMAICA **ESTIMATED LAND COSTING IN US DOLLARS**	**LOT COST $US**	**COST P.P. $US**	**# PAX**
Jamaica—All-Inclusive Resort			
Sports * Recreational Features			
Detail all activities available to guests at the hotel			
where there is no additonal cost, ie:		Included	
Tennis		Included	
Basketball		Included	
Golfing		Included	
Squash		Included	
etc.		Included	
		Included	
		Included	
		Included	
		Included	
		Included	
Watersports Features			
Detail all activities available to guests at the hotel			
where there is no additonal cost, i.e.:		Included	
Waterskiing		Included	
Banana Boat		Included	
JetSkis		Included	
Paddleboats		Included	
etc.		Included	
Scuba Diving		Additional	
Spa Services			
Full body massage ***		Included	
Neck and back massage ***		Included	
Reflexology ***		Included	
Dry sauna		Included	
Wet sauna		Included	
Whirlpool		Included	
(Appointments necessary for all services and treatments)			
*** One complimentary per person per stay. Repeats available at a modest surcharge. Choice of 25-minute full-body massage, 25-minute neck and back massage or 25 minutes with the reflexologist.			
Optional Activities and/or Services **<u>Subject To Surcharges</u>**			
Skin Care Treatments/Facials/Waxing/Styling Salon		Additional	

SAMPLE COSTING: CONFERENCE/MEETING JAMAICA **ESTIMATED LAND COSTING IN US DOLLARS**	**LOT COST $US**	**COST P.P. $US**	**# PAX**
Other Resort Facilities			
Nightclub		Included	
Piano Bar		Included	
Carbaret		Included	
Nightly dancing and entertainment		Included	
Large-screen TV in Game Room		Included	
Library with books and newspaper		Included	
Video Library		Included	
Currency Exchange		Included	
Gift Shop		Included	
Dining * Lounges * Refreshments			
Six restaurants on property		Included	
Selection of international wines at all resort restaurants		Included	
Accommodation			
Seven nights accommondation			
Hotel Taxes		Included	
Porterage at the hotel		Included	
Maid Gratuities		Included	
Day One: Saturday			
Arrival Transfers			
One way transfer by air-conditioned motor coach based on group arrivals		Included	
Airport porterage at $2.00 US per person, based on two pieces of luggage per person			
Beer and soft drinks on board motor coach			
Special Note: *The hotel is a scenic one and one half-hour transfer from Montego Bay Airport*			
Arrival at the Hotel			
Welcome rum punch upon arrival		Included	
Welcome Cocktail Reception and Dinner			
Native Bamboo Stalls will be set up on the lawn to display the tempting array of local food. Pepper Lights and Candlelight provide added ambiance.			
Cocktail Reception			
One hour open bar		Included	
Standard Bar to include Volka, Gin, Rum, Rye		Included	
Whiskey, Bourbon, Scotch, Cuevo White, Triple		Included	
Sec, Sweet Vermouth, Napoleon Brandy		Included	
House Wines Red and White		Included	
Red Stripe Beer		Included	

SAMPLE COSTING: CONFERENCE/MEETING JAMAICA ESTIMATED LAND COSTING IN US DOLLARS	LOT COST $US	COST P.P. $US	# PAX
Hot and Cold Hors d'Oeuvres			
Assorted Canapes		Included	
Private Welcome Dinner			
Caribbean Buffet			
Salads			
Buffet Platters			
Basket			
Entree			
Desserts			
Surcharge for private dinner.			
Beverages			
Standard Bar to include Volka, Gin, Rum, Rye		Included	
Whiskey, Bourbon, Scotch, Cuevo White, Triple		Included	
Sec, Sweet Vermouth, Napoleon Brandy		Included	
House Wines Red and White		Included	
Red Stripe Beer		Included	
Entertainment			
Mento Band			
Day Two: Sunday			
Breakfast at Your Leisure			
Morning Activity			
Private Sail. Dunn's River by Catamaran			
Pickup at the hotel pier			
Beer and soft drinks on board Catamaran			
Tipping of guides at Dunn's River Fall			
Special Note: Embarkation and Disembarkation is done in the water.			
Lunch and Dinner at Your Leisure		Included	
Day Three: Monday			
Breakfast Meeting			
Breakfast served in meeting room		Included	
Activity Allowance			
Deep-Sea Fishing *			
Horseback Riding			
Shopping Shuttle			
Scuba Diving			
* *Special Note: Should any of your guests catch a fish we can make arrangements to have the fish prepared and served at tomorrow night's Lobster Bake and Fish Fry.*			

SAMPLE COSTING: CONFERENCE/MEETING JAMAICA **ESTIMATED LAND COSTING IN US DOLLARS**	**LOT COST $US**	**COST P.P. $US**	**# PAX**
Lunch		Included	
At your leisure			
Private Dinner in the Spectacular Runaway Caves			
Green Grotto Caves – Round-trip transfers			
Hotel-catered 5-Course Meal			
Folkloric Show			
Steel Band			
Day Four: Tuesday			
Breakfast			
At your leisure		Included	
Morning Meeting			
Coffee, Tea and assorted cold drinks and ice water		Included	
Lunch			
At your leisure		Included	
Afternoon Activity			
Beach Olympics			
Beer and Soft Drinks during Beach Olympics			
Fun Prizes			
Lobster Bake and Fish Fry on the Beach			
Lobster Bake and Fish Fry			
Salads			
Buffet Platters			
Basket			
Entree			
Desserts			
Lobster Bake and Fish Fry Surcharge			
Reggae Band			
Day Five: Wednesday			
Breakfast Meeting			
Breakfast served in meeting room		Included	
Day at Leisure to Enjoy the Hotel's Facilities			
Special Note: A golf tournament could be an optional enhancement to your program, but it will require more money for refreshments, prizes, etc. Non-golfers could look at putting on a private shopping shuttle or additional spa treatments being made available to them.			

SAMPLE COSTING: CONFERENCE/MEETING JAMAICA ESTIMATED LAND COSTING IN US DOLLARS	LOT COST $US	COST P.P. $US	# PAX
Lunch			
At your leisure		Included	
Sunset Sail			
Sunset Cruise (2 Boats)			
Cocktail Reception			
Dinner			
At your leisure		Included	
Day Six: Thursday			
Breakfast Meeting			
Breakfast served in meeting room		Included	
Activity Allowance			
Deep-sea Fishing			
Horseback Riding			
Shopping Shuttle			
Scuba Diving			
River Rafting up the Martha Brae			
Lunch			
At your leisure		Included	
Dinner			
At your leisure		Included	
Day Seven: Friday			
Breakfast Meeting			
Breakfast served in meeting room		Included	
Lunch			
At your leisure		Included	
Cocktail Reception			
One-hour open bar			
Entertainment for Cocktail Reception			
Miltary Band (1hr)			
Hot and Cold Hors d'Oeuvres			
Assorted Canapés			
Hot			
Private Farewell Dinner			
Menu			
Entertainment			
Cabaret Singer with Backup Band			

SAMPLE COSTING: CONFERENCE/MEETING JAMAICA ESTIMATED LAND COSTING IN US DOLLARS	LOT COST $US	COST P.P. $US	# PAX
Day Eight: Saturday			
Breakfast			
At your leisure			
Return Transfers			
Delivery of departure notices			
One-way transfer by air-conditioned motor coach based on group departure			
Airport porterage at $2.00 US per person based on two pieces of luggage per person			
Beer and soft drinks on board motor coach.			
Airport Departure Tax (Current rate – subject to change)			
Room Gift Allowance			
Estimated Costing			
Optional Suggestions for Room Gifts			
Beach Wraps with Logo			
Beach Bags			
Golf Shirts			
Ray Chen's Jamaican Book			
Jamaican Plantation Hamper (Blue Mountain Coffee, Jamaican Cigars, Liquors)			
Jamaican Pastry Platter			
Sunrise Deluxe (Coffee, 2 Coffee Cups, Tia Maria, Preserves in a basket)			
Promotional			
Three rigid bag tags per person with your company logo based on two colors			
PST			
GST			
One soft vinyl ticket wallet per couple. Logoed based on two colors.			
PST			
GST			
One itinerary booklet per couple. Estimated costing			
PST			
GST			
Customized airport/hospitality desk signs			
Estimated costing			
PST			
GST			

SAMPLE COSTING: CONFERENCE/MEETING JAMAICA ESTIMATED LAND COSTING IN US DOLLARS	LOT COST $US	COST P.P. $US	# PAX
Screen Charges included in above costing. Estimated costing. Camera-ready art to be provided. Final Reconcilation will be based on actual costs incurred. **Site Inspection** Based on one (1) company executive and (1) J.A. Productions executive Estimated costing. Final Reconcilation will be based on actual costs incurred **Program Directors** Two Program Directors to co-ordinate all on-site aspects of your program. Estimated costing. Final Reconcilation will be based on actual costs incurred **Communication** Communication costs. Estimated (Long-Distance, Faxes, Couriers, Walkie-talkies)			
Subtotal Land in US Funds			
Management Fee			
Estimated Per Person Land Total in US Funds			

Appendix A

Sample Cost Sheets

Incentive Program

In the sample Cost Sheet for an Incentive Program you will see an example of where the costing shows both local (destination) currency and the currency the program will be contracted in. It is helpful to be familiar with local currency and to include it in your Cost Sheet. You will have a copy of your Cost Sheet with you on-site and you can use it to compare costs for any bills that may be presented to you for sign off in local currency.

As seen in the sample Cost Sheets for a Meeting, a grid is included here to help you visualize all your requirements.

CLIENT NAME:
TRAVEL DATE:

DESTINATION: BANGKOK–6 NIGHT PROGRAMME
BASED ON:

PROGRAM OUTLINE	DAY ONE Friday	DAY TWO Saturday	DAY THREE Sunday	DAY FOUR Monday	DAY FIVE Tuesday	DAY SIX Wednesday	DAY SEVEN Thursday	DAY EIGHT Friday	DAY NINE Saturday
BREAKFAST				Full American Breakfast	Full American Breakfast	Full American Breakfast	Full American Breakfast	Full American Breakfast	Full American Breakfast
MORNING ACTIVITIES	Depart Toronto	En route Crossing International Datelines	Arrive Hong Kong 6:45 a.m. Depart Hong Kong 9:25 a.m. Arrive Bangkok 11:25 a.m.	Half-day Bangkok Klongs and Grand Palace Tour	Activity Allowance Choice of: City&Temple Tour Rice&Barge Cruise Shopping Safari	Full-Day Tour Chiangmai Elephant Camp in jungle	At Leisure	At Leisure	Depart Bangkok
LUNCH				Buffet Lunch at Tiara Supper Club	On Own	Buffet Lunch Mae Su Valley	On Own	On Own	
AFTERNOON ACTIVITIES			Private Transfer to Hotel Light Refreshments in Guestroom	At Leisure	At Leisure	Handicraft Village Return Flight to Bangkok	At Leisure	At Leisure	Arrive Hong Kong 2 p.m.Depart Hong Kong 3:30 p.m. Arrive Toronto 5:45 p.m.
COCKTAIL RECEPTION								Rose Garden Farewell Reception and Dinner	
EVENING ACTIVITIES			At Leisure to relax, settle in and adjust to the time change	On Own	Thai Dinner & Classical Dances	On Own	Cash Allowance (or possible Dine Around)	BBQ Dinner Music Boat Along River Firework Display 30-Minute Show Loy Krathong Festival	

SAMPLE COSTING: INCENTIVE PROGRAM BANGKOK ESTIMATED LAND COSTING IN US DOLLARS (THAI BAHT TO US$ $1.00)	LOT COST THAI BHAT	LOT COST $US	COST P.P. $US	# PAX
Accommodation Six nights' accommondation at the Royal Orchid Hotel – Bangkok				
Day One: Arrival Transfers One-way transfer by air-conditioned motor coach based on group arrivals. Welcome Flower Garland by girls in Thai costume				
Private Check-In A private check-in will be provided for your guests Welcome drink upon arrival				
Welcome Refreshments in the Room Light refreshments including finger sandwiches, fresh tropical juices, mineral water will be waiting in each guest room. (Estimated costing) Guests will be arriving in Bangkok late evening if arriving by Northwest or Korean Airways. Cathay Pacific would arrive in at 11:25 a.m. We recommend a light beginning to your program to allow your guests to adjust to the time difference.				
Suggested Room Gift Ramayana mask with stand and box One set per room Enclosure provided by client Delivery of room gift (Estimated)				
Day Two:				
Full American Breakfast at the Hotel At your leisure				
Half-Day Bangkok Klongs & Grand Palace Tour Buffet Lunch Buffet Lunch Local Beer/Soft Drinks based on (2) per person				

SAMPLE COSTING: INCENTIVE PROGRAM BANGKOK ESTIMATED LAND COSTING IN US DOLLARS (THAI BAHT TO US$ $1.00)	LOT COST THAI BHAT	LOT COST $US	COST P.P. $US	# PAX
Dinner at Leisure				
Suggested Room Gift Thai Silk Shirt for the Men/Thai Silk Sarong for the Women — silk can be customized at an additional cost with company logo). Enclosure inviting them to wear this to dinner tomorrow night delivery of room gift. (Estimated)				
Day Three:				
Full American Breakfast at the Hotel At your leisure				
Activity Allowance Guests can pre-select their optional tour: City and Temple Tour Afternoon Rice and Barge Cruise Half-Day Shopping Safari Shopping tour will include visits to stores offering Thai Lapidary (Gemstones), Thai Silk or Casual Wear/Imitation Goods.				
Special Note: For costing purposes only I have based your costing on the highest possible option to present you with an idea of total budget costs should all guests choose this option. Final reconcilation will reflect costs based on actual tours selected. Until registration forms are received we will not know the guest's preference. It is better to cost on the highest-price tour and make sure that we still fall within budget guidelines than to average them out and possibly end up exceeding budget projections should all guests decide to take the most expensive tour.				
Evening Thai Dinner & Classical Dances Round-trip transfers to/from hotel. Thai Dinner including cocktails and wine with dinner				

SAMPLE COSTING: INCENTIVE PROGRAM BANGKOK ESTIMATED LAND COSTING IN US DOLLARS (THAI BAHT TO US$ $1.00)	LOT COST THAI BHAT	LOT COST $US	COST P.P. $US	# PAX
Suggested Room Gift Silk Photo Frame size 3″ × 5″. One per couple Enclosure Delivery of room gift (Estimated)				
Day Four:				
Full American Breakfast at the Hotel At your leisure				
Tour of Chiangmai Duration: 12 hours (6 a.m. – 6 p.m.) 6 a.m. Transfer to Bangkok Domestic Airport 7:30 a.m. Depart Bangkok for Chaingmai 8:30 a.m. Arrive Chaingmai Transfer to Elephant Camp 10 a.m. See elephants at work in teak forest 10:40 a.m. Depart for Mae Su Valley for lunch. Garden setting – lush green lawns and garden brilliant with colors of cassias, dahlias, daisies and poinsettia. Your guests will enjoy lunch overlooking Mae Sa Valley. 11:30 a.m. Buffet Lunch 12:45 p.m. Visit to the Handicraft Centre and gain insight into the making of teakwood furniture, Thai silk, silverware and Thai umbrellas 3:30 p.m. Transfer to Chiangmai Airport 4:45 p.m. Return flight to Bangkok 5:45 p.m. Arrive Bangkok 6 p.m. Arrive Hotel				

SAMPLE COSTING: INCENTIVE PROGRAM BANGKOK ESTIMATED LAND COSTING IN US DOLLARS (THAI BAHT TO US$ $1.00)	LOT COST THAI BHAT	LOT COST $US	COST P.P. $US	# PAX
Dinner at Leisure				
Suggested Room Gift				
Thai Cookbook				
Enclosure				
Delivery of room gift (Estimated)				
Day Five:				
Full American Breakfast at the Hotel				
At your leisure				
At Leisure for Personal Activities or Shopping				
Lunch on Own				
Cash Allowance for Dinner				
Suggested Room Gift				
Brass Elephant Paperweight with base and plaque. One per couple.				
Custom Invitation to Farewell Dinner (Estimated)				
Delivery of room gift (Estimated)				
Departure Notices				
Delivery of departure notices				
Day Six:				
Full American Breakfast at the Hotel				
At your leisure				
At Leisure for Personal Activities or Shopping				
Evening: Rose Garden				
Included in the evening:				
Round-trip Transfers				
Fresh Flowers in Company Logo				
Garland Welcome and Cold Towels				
Welcome Fruit Punch				
Elephant welcome with custom banners				
Elephants for VIP couple				
Elephant Show and Rides				
Fruit & Vegetable Carving, Garland-Making Demonstration				
One-hour open bar with hot and cold hors d'oeuvres				
30 Minutes in Handicraft Village				
Klong Sabatchai procession to riverside lawn for dinner barbecue and stalls				

SAMPLE COSTING: INCENTIVE PROGRAM BANGKOK ESTIMATED LAND COSTING IN US DOLLARS (THAI BAHT TO US$ $1.00)	LOT COST THAI BHAT	LOT COST $US	COST P.P. $US	# PAX
Barbecue Buffet Dinner and Food Stall				
Music boat along the river				
30-minute show (3 dances, sword, short/ long pole fighting, wedding ceremony)				
Loy Krathong Festival				
Fireworks and Logo, Farewell Message				
Rose Garden Dinner as outlined above				
One-half bottle of wine per person				
Police Escort (Estimated)				
Suggested Room Gift				
Thai Raw Silk Robe (solid color).				
One per person. Logoed or with guest's initials at additional cost				
Enclosure				
Delivery of room gift (Estimated)				
Day Seven:				
Full American Breakfast at the Hotel (At your leisure)				
Departure				
Departure Transfer from the hotel to the airport will be by River Jet Cruise. The River Jet Cruise is non-exclusive.* The River Jet Cruise can be bought out on an exclusive basis but based on 300. Alternate option would be to transfer by motor coach.The River Jet Cruise offers one final look at the city before flight. The minimum check-in time at Don Muang Airport is two hours prior to flight departure time. The Program Directors will assist with check-in and pre-departure formalities. All checked luggage will be transferred to the airport by separate van with a baggage master.				
** There will be other passengers on board who are not with the group. To have the transfer exclusive to the group we would need to purchase 300 seats.*				
International Airport Departure Tax (Current rate – subject to change)				

SAMPLE COSTING: INCENTIVE PROGRAM BANGKOK ESTIMATED LAND COSTING IN US DOLLARS (THAI BAHT TO US$ $1.00)	LOT COST THAI BHAT	LOT COST $US	COST P.P. $US	# PAX
Promotional/Communication Three rigid bag tags per person with your company logo based on two colors Taxes One soft vinyl ticket wallet per couple Logoed based on two colors Taxes One itinerary booklet per couple Estimated costing Taxes Customized airport signs. Estimated costing Taxes Screen Charges Included in the above pricing. Camera-Ready Artwork to be supplied. Final Reconcilation will be based on actual costs incurred. **Site Inspection** Based on one (1) Company Executive and (1) J.A. Productions Executive Estimated costing. Final Reconcilation will be based on actual costs incurred. **Program Directors** Two Program Directors plus Sales Executive to co-ordinate all on-site aspects of your program. Estimated costing. Final Reconcilation will be based on actual costs incurred. **Communication Costs** Communication costs. Estimated (Long-Distance, Faxes, Couriers, Walkie-talkies)				
Subtotal Land in US Funds				
Management Fee				
Estimated Per Person Land Total in US Funds				

Appendix B

Sample Payment Schedules

Corporate Event Costing

The first form in Appendix B is another example of a sample Cost Sheet. Here the event is a Wine Appreciation Evening. Remember that your Cost Sheet is the basis from which you generate your Payment Schedule. Here the client wanted to know exactly what they were spending in Food and Beverage, Decor and Entertainment, Miscellaneous Costs (such as Doormen, Security) and Onsite Staffing Costs, Promotion and Communications. This is just a variation on the original Cost Sheet. You are still dealing with LOT COST—just under different headings—P.P. cost and # of PAX.

In this particular example you will also see a GST column which is a specific tax that must be listed on invoicing in Canada. The GST would be included as a line item cost but a formula line can be included to list the GST under a separate column as well for a quick calculation of total GST costs only for invoicing purposes.

Once the costing has been finalized and the preparation of the contract is to begin you will need to work out a Payment Schedule based on your inclusions.

The Cost Sheet can be saved and copied under a new name. Depending on when your event is scheduled to take place and the payment requirements of your suppliers you may have several different payment dates to adhere to. Work with the various suppliers to bring the due dates of payments into line—you will usually find them more than accommodating—and make sure that they will work within your company/client's specific cheque runs as well.

SAMPLE COSTING: WINE APPRECIATION EVENING (ALTERNATE COST BREAKDOWN STYLE)

ESTIMATED LAND COSTING	LOT COST FOOD & BEVERAGE	LOT COST DECOR & ENTER.	LOT COST MISC	LOT COST STAFF/CO PROMO.	COST P.P. $	# PAX	GST
Exclusive Restaurant Takeover							
Date 6:00 p.m. – 7:00 p.m. Ice Wine Reception 7:00 p.m. – 10:00 p.m. Gourmet Dinner/Wines 10:00 p.m. – Dessert/ Coffee/Liqueurs/Cigars							
Parking Parking nearby. Guests to pay their own.							
Coat Check Tipping							
Doorman Estimated cost							
DJ Estimated cost							
Reception 6:00 p.m. – 7:00 p.m.							
Beverages Reception * Ice Wine Sampling Based on 2 per person – Estimated. Service Charge Staff Taxes Taxes							
Winemaster *							
*** Well Known Winemaster/Chef** Speaker's Fee – Estimated pending final confirmation Taxes							

ESTIMATED LAND COSTING	LOT COST FOOD & BEVERAGE	LOT COST DECOR & ENTER.	LOT COST MISC	LOT COST STAFF/CO PROMO.	COST P.P. $	# PAX	GST
Marriage Between Food and Wine							
Menu/Wine Coordination							
Taxes							
Winemaster's Dinner							
Eight Course Gourmet Dinner – Estimated							
Service Charge Staff							
Taxes							
Taxes							
To include:							
Fresh Foie Gras of Duck							
Live Lobster							
Oysters							
Servuga Caviar (Russian or Royal Iranian)							
Prime US Beef							
Various Organic Raised Game							
Fresh Seafood							
Wine with Dinner							
Appropriate Wines to accompany each course							
Service Charge Staff							
Taxes							
Taxes							
To Include:							
Opus One							
Cabernet Sauvignon – Unfiltered Napa							
Pinot Noir – Unfiltered Napa							
Chardonnay – Sauvignon Blanc (or Fume Blanc)							
A Dessert Wine							
Plus two others							
Place Cards							
Place Cards							
Taxes							
Taxes							
Dinner Menus							
Dinner Menus							
Taxes							
Taxes							

ESTIMATED LAND COSTING	LOT COST FOOD & BEVERAGE	LOT COST DECOR & ENTER.	LOT COST MISC	LOT COST STAFF/CO PROMO.	COST P.P. $	# PAX	GST
Table Cards Table Cards Taxes Taxes							
Entertainment (Soft Background Jazz) Trio (Piano/Vocals, Bass, Saxophone or Guitar) Taxes							
Yamaha Digital Grand Piano Cartage $250.00 Taxes							
The Yamaha GT2, a digital grand piano is very small and quite elegant – would be fitting for the evening/ambiance.							
Sound System/Technician and Cartage							
Meals for the Musicians – Estimated Service Charge Staff Taxes Taxes							
Souvenir CD – Estimated Taxes							
Music Royalities							
Special Note: I will have them autographed with actual guest's name							
Coffee/Liqueurs Based on 1 per person. Service Charge Staff Taxes Taxes							
Selection of world's finest handmade cigars. Cigars – Estimated ($20.00 – $50.00 each) Based on 1 per person. Service Charge Staff Taxes Taxes							

ESTIMATED LAND COSTING	LOT COST FOOD & BEVERAGE	LOT COST DECOR & ENTER.	LOT COST MISC	LOT COST STAFF/CO PROMO.	COST P.P. $	# PAX	GST
Cigar Hostess (3) Gratuities Lighters and Clippers Custom Logoed Banding **Roundtrip Transfers To/ From Hotel** Awaiting final decision re limos/motor coach **Communication** Communications Costs. Faxes, Couriers, Function Sheets, Cell Phone Misc. Tipping etc. Estimated. **Staffing** Onsite Program Management							
Estimated Subtotal (In Local Currency)							
Estimated Subtotal (Columns 1-4)							
Management Fee							
Estimated Total (In Local Currency)							

Appendix B

Sample Payment Schedules

Payment Breakdown

As seen in the following sample Payment Schedule for the Wine Appreciation Evening, payments are laid out as Payment A, B, C, etc., and assigned specific dates to each. Rather than re-input all the detailed description of the line items use what the you/your client is already familiar with—the Cost Sheet—and simply change the headings to reflect the payment dates. A supplier may want 50% of costs upon contracting/depositing, 40 % at a specified time prior to the event taking place, and 10% post event. It will vary with each supplier and the terms of their individual contracts. You will need to go in and adjust the formulas but you will be able to cross reference your Payment Schedule total costs with your Cost Sheet easily because you will not be working with two entirely different layouts.

It is important to look at not only the required payments and due dates from suppliers but also their cancellation policies as well. In order for event planning companies to fully protect themselves and their suppliers in uncertain economic times—when businesses are financially stretched and many have gone bankrupt without warning—event planners may want to factor cancellation penalties into their payment schedule requirements. For example, a hotel may only require an initial payment deposit of $3,000 for an event but should that same event cancel after signing tens of thousands of dollars may be the amount required in cancellation fees and if the event planning company has only collected $3,000 from their corporate client they could encounter difficulty collecting it. This pro-active protective thinking applies to all suppliers and to a percentage of the event planning management fee and hard costs as well. You always want to be in the position of having all required monies on hand to cover all cancellation charges whenever possible. And financing your client's event should never be a payment option.

SAMPLE PAYMENT SCHEDULE BREAKDOWN: WINE APPRECIATION EVENING

The cost sheet can be saved under a different name and changed to payment schedule format. Then it can be re-named and used for your reconciliation.

The sample payment schedule below will follow the same breakdown covered in the previous section.

To download the form in full, please visit www.wiley.com/go/event-planning

ESTIMATED LAND COSTING	DEPOSIT PAYMENT A	DUE DATE PAYMENT B	POST EVENT
Exclusive Restaurant Takeover Date 6:00 p.m.– 7:00 p.m. Ice Wine Reception 7:00 p.m.– 10:00 p.m. Gourmet Dinner/Wines 10:00 p.m. – Dessert/Coffee/Liqueurs/ Cigars			
Parking Parking nearby. Guests to pay their own.			
Coat Check Tipping			
Doorman Estimated cost			
DJ Estimated cost			
Reception 6:00 p.m.– 7:00 p.m.			

ESTIMATED LAND COSTING	DEPOSIT PAYMENT A	DUE DATE PAYMENT B	POST EVENT
Beverages Reception *** Ice Wine Sampling** Based on 2 per person – Estimated. Service Charge Staff Taxes Taxes			
Winemaster * **Well-Known Winemaster/Chef** Speaker's Fee – Estimated pending final confirmation Taxes			

Appendix C

Sample Function Sheets

Contact Sheets

Function Sheets become your onsite "bible" and need to contain as much detail as possible. They must include your instructions to your suppliers, staffing assignments, and the negotiated costs (as your suppliers will not be receiving a copy of your Cost Sheet, only the costs that are relevant to them). If there are any pricing discrepancies it is better to know in advance when they're reviewing your Function Sheets, rather than at the close of the event. They should be clearly laid out and in order of sequence of events.

The Function Sheets are sent to all suppliers. They are what the onsite staff work from. They ensure that everyone is working from literally "the same page." A hotel, for example, may have there own variation for their internal staff—they will review your Function Sheets, note any changes, and send you their version for your sign off and review—but both of you will have cross-referenced each others eliminating any potential problems/conflicts.

A key component of a Function Sheet is a Contact Sheet. It needs to be filled out in great detail, and as seen in the following example, should contain all of the information you need to have for each contact. On the following page is a list of all the different contacts you may need to compile this information for.

Possible Contacts

Limousines (List all drivers)
Media (List all)
Orange Cones
Photographer
Police (Security—List all)
Print Production
Road Permits
Ropes and Stanchions
Skytrackers
Speaker Support
Special Effects
Speech Writer
Street Permits
Staging/Lighting/Audio-Visual (List all key staff members)
Transportation (Motor coach)
Walkie-Talkies
All Other Applicable Suppliers

You should have every possible number to reach a supplier after hours—from cell phone numbers to pagers to after hour business lines. When you have an emergency and need to reach your supplier you need to ensure that you have a means to do so. This means the motor coach driver, the limousine driver, and everyone on up. Your Contact Sheets also become your checklist for sending out thank you letters after the day/event is over.

Appendix C

Sample Function Sheets

Meeting

In the following Function Sheet for a Meeting you will notice that instructions have been repeated for each day they occur. This laying out of items in storyboard fashion and in sequence avoids you having to continually search through your function sheet for information.

As each element is completed, relevant notes can be made on the page. You will not need to go back and refer to them again until it is time to do the reconciliation. Such items as staffing will change day to day and laid out this way makes it easy to see where these changes occur and how to deal with them.

THE EVENT	*Client Appreciation Sales Conference being held in London.*
THE GUESTS	*All male. They are all each others competitors. They are all from Montreal.*
THE ELEMENTS	*Inter-active events that evoke feel of play.* *Sales Conference*
THE VENUES	*Hockey Hall of Fame Exclusive for the guests.* *Reception and use of the full facility.* *Dinner at Wayne Gretzky's* *The Shot (Railway Station Restaurant with Pool Tables)* *Pool expert to teach guests trick shots*

SCHEDULE OF EVENTS: OVERVIEW

MONDAY

	Judy to pick up walkie-talkies and proceed to Sheraton to advance check-in and room gift distribution.
11:00 a.m.	Liane and Judy to meet at the Sheraton.
11:30 a.m.	Carol to advance Montreal airport.
12:00 p.m.	Guests to arrive at Montreal airport for group check-in
1:00 p.m.	Air Canada 413 is scheduled to depart Montreal.
1:00 p.m.	Liane to arrive at the airport to monitor flight arrival Toronto Airport. Meet with DMC and oversee motor coach transfer/ spotting. Room Gift Delivery – Welcome (Large Pretzels & Beer) Room Gift Delivery – Hockey Puck Custom Design Room Delivery – Invitation to this evening's event. Room Gifts to tie in with "Hockey Night in Canada" Reception and Dinner. Departure Notices and Baggage Pull Arrangements
2:08 p.m.	Air Canada Flight 413 scheduled to arrive. Liane and Carol to transfer with the motor coach to the hotel. Mr. *** will be arriving by train independently — he is unable to fly due to a medical condition.
3:00 p.m.	Estimated arrival at the hotel. Check in 21st floor. Carol to reconfirm arrangements for baggage pull the next morning and distribution of departure notices. Liane and Carol to do quick site inspection of Hockey Hall of Fame drop-off point and Wayne Gretzky's Restaurant.
5:00 p.m.	Judy and Liane to advance Hockey Hall of Fame.
5:30 p.m.	Motor coach to spot. Carol to oversee and transfer guests. Liane to meet motor coach and escort guests to the Hockey Hall of Fame.
5:50 p.m.	Motor coach to depart for Hockey Hall of Fame
6:00 p.m.	Motor coach arrival Hockey Hall of Fame
7:30 p.m.	Judy to advance Wayne Gretzky's. Carol to oversee motor coach arrival for transfer to Wayne Gretzky's.
9:00 p.m.	Carol and Liane to transfer with guests to the restaurant. Guests to make their own way back to hotel.

SCHEDULE OF EVENTS: OVERVIEW

TUESDAY

	Carol to oversee luggage pull
	Carol to oversee motor coach and hotel checkout
	Judy to advance and oversee breakfast.
8:00 a.m.	Private group breakfast
9:00 a.m.	Depart for London to attend conference.
	Guests to be dropped off at conference. Lunch is included.
	Carol and Driver to advance hotel and drop off luggage.
	Departure notice and baggage pull
	Carol and Driver to visit The Shot Restaurant and Pool Hall.
	Return to conference.
5:00 p.m.	Transfer guests to the hotel.
5:45 p.m.	Estimated arrival at hotel.
6:30 p.m.	Transfer to The Shot. Motor coach to remain with group.
9:30 p.m.	Return to the hotel. May want one early shuttle as well.
	Hotel porters will deliver bags to the guest rooms.
	Note to Liane/Carol: Please call the hospitality desk prior to leaving the airport to advise you are on your way.

WEDNESDAY

	Carol to oversee Luggage Pull
	Carol to oversee Motor coach and hotel checkout
	Carol to advance and oversee breakfast.
9:00 a.m.	Breakfast
10:00 a.m.	Depart for conference.
10:30 a.m.	Estimated arrival time conference.
	Carol to reconfirm flights.
12:30 p.m.	Lunch included at conference.
1:30 p.m.	Depart for factory (host's company factory)
2:00 p.m.	Tour of factory
3:30 p.m.	Depart for airport
	Check in at London airport.
	Toronto guests to remain onboard and transfer to the city.
5:40 p.m.	Air Canada 1218 is scheduled to depart London to Toronto.
6:18 p.m.	Air Canada 1218 arrives in Toronto.
7:00 p.m.	Air Canada 194 departs for Montreal.
	Carol returns with group.
8:05 p.m.	Air Canada 194 arrives in Montreal.
	Train passenger overnights at hotel and departs in the morning.

FRIDAY

J.A. Productions	Judy to reconfirm all arrangements for Monday for pick up walkie-talkies, headsets and batteries.
	(Both walkie-talkies and batteries to be fully charged)

Company
Address
Contact:
Tel:
Fax:
Email:
Cell:

MONDAY

J.A. Productions — Judy to pick up walkie talkies, headsets and batteries.
J.A. Productions: 3
1. Judy
2. Carol
3. Liane
Walkie-talkies to have earphones, belt and channel selector on top.

FRIDAY
HOTEL PRE-CON

10:00 a.m. — Location:
Set Up: Boardroom/Hollow Square
To attend: Sales
Club Room Check-In Manager
Catering Manager
Banquet Manager
Bell Captain
Please ensure that a list outlining all extension numbers, names and titles of all department heads has been prepared and is available for this meeting. J.A. Productions will require three copies.

11:00 a.m. — Approximate end of pre-con.

HOCKEY HALL OF FAME/MOVENPICK CATERING PRE-CON

1:00 p.m. — Pre-Con with Hockey Hall of Fame/Movenpick Catering
Location:
Hockey Hall of Fame
To Attend:
Hockey Hall of Fame: Contact Name
Movenpick Catering: Contact Name

WAYNE GRETZKY'S PRE-CON

3:00 p.m. — Wayne Gretzky's
Location: Wayne Gretzky's
To Attend:
Wayne Gretzky's: Contact Name

MONDAY
ADVANCE MONTREAL AIRPORT

Carol to arrive in Montreal August 13 (evening)

Hotel accommodation has been blocked at:
Montreal Dorval Airport Hilton
12505 Cote de Liesse Road
Montreal, Quebec
H9P 1B7
Tel: (514) 631-2411
Fax: (514) 631-0192
Reservation: 1664167
$127.62 inclusive of taxes ($112 base weekend rate)
Room has been guaranteed.
No guests will be staying overnight at the hotel.

11:30 a.m. Arrival at the airport. Seat selection has been arranged for the group. Group check-in has been arranged.
Contact Name:

12:00 p.m. Guests have been advised to check-in one hour prior to departure. They will be looking for Carol. Please display company sign.

1:00 p.m. Air Canada 413 is scheduled to depart for Toronto.

2:08 p.m. Arrival in Toronto. Liane will meet Carol at the gate. Look for the company sign.
Quebec departure taxes are pre-paid.

MONDAY
TORONTO AIRPORT ARRIVAL/TRANSFER TO HOTEL

1:00 p.m. Air Canada 413 is scheduled to depart for Toronto.

2:08 p.m. Arrival in Toronto.
Liane will meet the flight.
DMC will meet Liane at the Air Canada arrival area (section C).
Included in transfer cost:
One-way transfer by air-conditioned motor coach based on group arrival.
Airport Meet and Greet Staffing
Porterage at the Airport
Special Request: French Speaking Staff where possible. Same driver throughout program.
Liane to transfer with the group back to the hotel. Richmond Street entrance will be the motor coach drop-off point.
Hotel porters will deliver bags to the guest rooms.
Note to Liane/Carol: Please call the hospitality desk prior to leaving the airport to advise you are on your way.

MONDAY

HOSPITALITY DESK HOTEL/PRIVATE REGISTRATION CLUB FLOOR

Daily Requirements: One house phone/no long distance access, one skirted table (6 x 3), three chairs, two flip charts/easel, markers, (two colours), one waste basket, one table lamp (only if not in a well-lit area)

10:00 a.m. Registration set-up to be ready. Desk to remain in place for 24 hours.

MONDAY

HOTEL CHECK IN PROCEDURES

Hotel check-in is 3:00 p.m. but early check-in has been requested. The majority of the participants will be arriving as a group. Early arrivals may be the Toronto head office staff who will be overnighting at the hotel. Other guests will be arriving on Air Canada 413, which is scheduled to arrive at 2:08 p.m. Guests will be arriving by motor coach as a group.

Motor coach Drop-off point and hotel porterage to be arranged: Richmond Street entrance.

One guest will be arriving by train and three by car.

Parking to master for overnight Toronto guests has been arranged. They will be leaving their car at the hotel while they are in London travelling with the group.

A private, satellite check-in desk is to be set up beside hospitality desk on the 20th Floor. This is to be ready by 11:00 a.m. Check-in to be manned by staff exclusively for group. **French-speaking staff requested. All guests are from Quebec.**

Please ensure adequate staff scheduling has been provided for the private registration desk, the bell desk and the lounge.

All check-ins are to be pre-registered and rooms to be preassigned.

No room rates are to appear on individual folios.

Express check-out forms to be included in each key packet along with room key, mini bar key and hotel information.

Separate key packets to be prepared for each guest. Two keys per packet.

Key packets to be ready and waiting in alphabetical order prior to guests' arrival at the satellite check-in desk.

Upgrades or changes of room are not permitted unless authorized by J.A.\Productions.

Four copies (both alpha and numeric) of rooming list will be required.

Scheduled welcome room gift deliveries to be in each guest room at least one hour before guest arrives.

MASTER ACCOUNT

Client # 1

All to master (room, taxes, all meals and incidentals signed to the room) including valet parking *

Client # 2
All to master (room, taxes, all meals and incidentals signed to the room).

* Their cars will remain at the hotel while the group is in London. They will be returning late Wednesday evening to pick up their cars. All parking charges to go on the master account.

Judy Allen Productions

1. All to master including valet parking
2. All to master

Balance of Guests
All guest room charges and taxes are to go to the master account, but participants are to give a credit card imprint to cover incidentals such as room charges for meals in restaurants, room service, laundry, health club and mini-bar. Unless specified the client will not be responsible for participants incidental accounts.

AUTHORIZED SIGNATURES FOR THE MASTER ACCOUNT

Client

1. Name and Title
2. Name and Title

Judy Allen Productions

1. Judy
2. Carol

ACCOUNTING

Judy Allen to meet with hotel's accounting department on August 14th (approximately 10:30 p.m.) to review all individual room charges (guest folios). This must be done prior to the folios being delivered to any guest rooms.

All bills to be posted to the master account must be signed off by an authorized member of J.A. Production staff. Judy Allen will meet with accounting Tuesday, August 15 once guests have departed for London. Please have two copies of all bills and folios available.

ROOM BLOCK

Please see attached rooming list.

City Hall view and all guests to be located on the same floor have been requested.

Guest room rate $000.00 Commissionable at 10%.

Special Note: Every room must have two beds. A bed and a pull out couch is not acceptable.

SHERATON CLUB ROOM EXCLUSIVE SERVICES AND AMENITIES

These include:

» Complimentary local calls
» Dataports in room
» Separate concierge service on 20th floor
» Private lounge serving complimentary:
  Continental Breakfast (6:30 a.m. – 10:30 a.m.)
  Afternoon Tea & Cookies (3:00 p.m. – 6:00 p.m.)
  Evening Hors D' Oeuvres (5:00 p.m. – 7:00 p.m.)

» Guest rooms with bathrobes, valet stand, skirt hangers, specialty lotions, mineral waters and extra bathroom amenities
» Complimentary access to the Adelaide Club, featuring squash, aerobics and weight equipment.

FUNCTION SPACE
Conference Room D&E

Breakfast August 15	Sit Down	Double-Sided Buffet 7:00 a.m. – 9:00 a.m.

MONDAY
ROOM DELIVERIES
ROOM GIFT – WELCOME

Giant Pretzels with condiments (mustard) –two per person.
Iced Beer – two per person.
Both items to be provided by Sheraton.

<u>Bill To Master Account</u>

Pretzel and Condiment	$0.00 +++
Iced Beer	$0.00 +++
Delivery Charge	$0.00 + 0 % taxes

MONDAY
VIP ROOM GIFT DELIVERY:

Judy Allen will bring gifts with her. To be delivered to:
1. Name
2. Name

MONDAY
TRAIN TRANSFER

Mr. *** is unable to fly due to an inner ear problem.
He will be arriving by train. He will be met by limo driver at the station and transferred to the hotel. Client has advised him that he is being met.
Train 57 departs Montreal 10:00 a.m. and arrives Toronto 3:30 p.m.
Limo driver to call hospitatlity desk upon departure from the train station to advise Liane that he has met the guest and they are on their way to the hotel. Liane to meet guest at the front door with porter and transfer him to check-in.
Limo driver's name:
Cell number:
License number:
Description of limo:

MONDAY
HOTEL ARRIVAL

Arrival Schedule:
Air Canada 413 departs Montreal 1:00 p.m.
Air Canada 413 arrives Toronto 2:08 p.m.
Guests will be met at the airport and transferred to the hotel by motor coach as a group. Luggage will be transferred with the group.

2:30 p.m. Hotel staff (French-speaking requested) to be in place at the satellite check-in.

Hotel staff members to take credit card imprints when guests arrive with the exception of those whose expenses are going on the master account.

1. Name
2. Name

Participants will be arriving at the Richmond Street entrance.

Upon arrival at the hotel, luggage is to be taken from the participants and delivered directly to their rooms. Their guest rooms are all located on the Club Floor.

Hotel porterage is included in their stay.

Please ensure that valet parking has been advised that parking for:

1. Name
2. Name

be charged to the master account and that their cars will be at the hotel until late evening on the 16th. All parking charges up to and including the 16th are to be put on the master account.

All guest rooms are blocked into the hotel's Club Level accommodation. Guests should proceed directly to the 20th floor via the express elevator for private check-in. A French-speaking guest services agent has been requested.

Bill to Master Account

Room:	$000.00
Taxes:	00%
Porterage:	$0.00 + 0% taxes roundtrip
Valet Parking:	$00.00

MONDAY
LUGGAGE PULL/DEPARTURE NOTICES

Departure notices will be given to the bellmen for delivery this evening while the guests are out for dinner.

Bags are to be left inside the room. Pick-up will be at 7:30 a.m. on the 15th. Motor coach to depart at 9:00 a.m..

ROOM GIFT

Hockey puck (customized) to be delivered to each guest.

Letter/card to accompany gift.

Hockey Pucks will be delivered to the hotel by noon.

To be placed in each guest room once guests have departed for their evening's event. Scheduled departure time from the hotel 6:00 p.m.

Bill To Master Account

Delivery Charge $0.00 + 0% taxes

MONDAY
TRANSFERS FROM HOTEL TO HOCKEY HALL OF FAME

5:35 p.m.	Motor coach to spot.
5:50 p.m.	Departure from the hotel (Richmond Street entrance) to the Hockey Hall of Fame. Carol to travel with group. Liane will meet motor coach at the 181 Bay Street entrance to the Hockey Hall of Fame.

TRANSFERS FROM HOCKEY HALL OF FAME TO WAYNE GRETZKY'S

8:45 p.m. Motor coach to spot.

9:00 p.m. Departure from 181 Bay Street entrance to Wayne Gretzky's:
99 Blue Jay Way
Toronto, Ontario
M5V 9G9
Guests will make their own way back to the hotel. Motor coach is required to be on standby to extend pending weather conditions for return transfer to the hotel. Carol will advise driver before disembarking.

MONDAY

HOCKEY HALL OF FAME RECEPTION

Insurance faxed August 10 for their files.

4:30 p.m. Judy and Liane to advance.

6:00 p.m. Welcome Reception Esso Theatre located in the Hockey Hall of Fame.
Wine and beer to be passed on trays. Hot and Cold Canapes.
Mixed Drinks will be brought upon request (served to the guests).
Facility exclusive to the group.
Attach Menu – Description of Inclusions.
Clip-on microphone has been ordered.
Briefing on what they will be seeing, doing and experiencing
Special Note: Some of the guests do not speak English and French-speaking staff requested. Carol, Liane and Marguerite will be on hand to assist with translation. Details about the departure for Wayne Gretzky's to be given at this time. Also guests to be advised that the store will remain open from 6:00 p.m. – 7:30 p.m.. Purchases at their own expense. Maps of the facility will be given out.
6:30 p.m. Wall goes up.
Guests will be given a quick walk through of the facility. Would like them divided into two groups. Carol to accompany one group to assist with translation. Liane to accompany the second group. Marguerite to help where required.
Be sure to mention how they can have their personal hockey team photos in the Hockey Hall of Fame should they be interested in doing so.
Group to be at leisure to enjoy facility. It is their's exclusively.
Central food and bar station will be set up with a Satellite bar with light snacks Hall.
Please ensure both areas are covered on the walk through.

9:00 p.m. Guests to depart to Wayne Gretzky's.

MONDAY

WAYNE GRETZKY'S

7:30 p.m. Judy to advance

9:00 p.m. Guests scheduled to arrive via motor coach
Guests will be arriving from the Hockey Hall of Fame. They are taking over the facility for a private reception. They will be there from 6:00 p.m. – 9:00 p.m.
VIP Line Pass — Tables to be waiting for the group. Group to be seated immediately. No standing in line.

Private section to be reserved for the group. Smoking Section.
Number of guests:
Tables not to be positioned too tightly to allow waiters to manoeuvre between chairs and guests can easily get in and out.
Menu to be specially printed for the group. Notice to be placed on the bottom of the menu that two drinks per person will be compliments of client and that additional drinks will be at their own expense. For example, a group of four could split a bottle of wine but if they wanted more, they would have to pay for it themselves. Carol will be available should the waiter have any questions on how things should be addressed.
Need separate area for J.A. Production staff to be out of sight from the guests but close enough that we can check on them from time to time. If the Studio (adjacent private room) is not in use could a small table be set up there?
Requested waiters assigned to the group be exclusive to the group.
Choice of one of the following two appetizers:
Caesar Salad
Soup of the Day
Bread
Cheesy Garlic Flatbread
Choice of one of the following entrees:
Half Chicken with Fennel, Chilies, Oregano, Cinnamon
BBQ Back Ribs
Atlantic Salmon Grilled with Black Bean Sauce
Linguini with Shrimp, Clams, Mussels, Squid, Garlic, Tomato, Green Onions in Traditional Clam Sauce
Choice of one of the following desserts:
Chocolate "Evolution"
Homemade Apple Cake with Whisky Sauce
Hot Fresh Fruit "Calzone"
Ice Cream or Fruit Ice
Beverages
Coffee or Tea

TUESDAY
PRIVATE GROUP BREAKFAST

7:00 a.m. Judy to advance breakfast
Conference Room D & E
Rounds of 10 but set for eight.
Double-sided buffet

7:45 a.m. All to be ready to go in case of early arrivals

8:00 a.m. Breakfast
Buffet Set Up not Plated
Chilled Apple and Freshly Squeezed Orange Juice
Scrambled Eggs
Choice of Bacon or Sausage Links
Roasted Potatoes
Croissants and Muffins

Fruit Preserves and Butter
Coffee, Assorted Teas, Decaffeinated Coffee.
Ensure tear down does not start while guests are still in the room.
Special Note: Menu to be served buffet style at no additional cost.

Bill to Master Account
Buffet Breakfast $00.00 +++ per person.

TUESDAY
TRANSFER TO CONFERENCE

7:30 a.m. Luggage transfer will begin. Porterage has been prepaid.
8:15 a.m. All luggage to be down and in a secure area.
8:45 a.m. Motor coach to arrive at the Richmond entrance. Luggage to be loaded.
9:00 a.m. Motor coach to depart for conference.
Smoking in not permitted on motor coach. Carol to advise.
The driver will be French-speaking. Same driver as airport transfers will stay with you for duration of the trip.
Map to conference has been given to driver. Please review with driver. The number to call show you run into any difficulty is 1-800-000-0000.
10:30 a.m. Estimated time of arrival at conference.
Lunch provided.
Carol and driver to continue to London to drop-off the luggage.
Carol please give client the phone number of the motor coach.
Parking has been requested at the hotel for the motor coach and a room has been arranged for the driver. Room and tax will go the master account. Hotel will ask for credit card for incidentals.
Carol and driver to proceed to The Shot to advance.
Carol to give driver money to purchase cooler, beverages, ice, glasses garbage bags etc. for drive from conference to hotel. Have him provide receipts for everything.
Driver to stock cooler with soft drinks, juices mineral water, ice, cups and garbage bags. Drinks to be offered only on drive from conference to London.
Carol and driver to return to conference to wait for guests. Advise client when you have returned in case they would like an earlier departure. Cell number: Hotel is approximately 45 minutes from the conference.
Parking at conference. There is ample parking and a spot has been reserved for you # 123. There is no charge for parking.
5:00 p.m. Guests scheduled to depart conference for London.
Beverages to be served onboard.
5:45 p.m. Estimated arrival time in London.
Note to Carol: Call hotel to let them know you are en route so that they can ensure all is in place.

To be billed to client
Additional cost for beverages – .

TUESDAY
ADVANCE HOTEL
HOSPITALITY DESK/PRIVATE REGISTRATION
DELTA LONDON ARMOURIES

Daily Requirements: one House Phone/No Long Distance Access, one skirted table (6 x 3), three chairs, two flip charts/easel, markers (two colours), one waste basket, one table lamp (only if not in a well lit area), 11:00 a.m. registration desk to be set up and to remain in place for 24 hours.

Bill To Master Account

Flip Charts
House Phone
Balance of items provided by the hotel at no charge.

TUESDAY
HOTEL CHECK IN PROCEDURES DELTA LONDON ARMOURIES HOTEL

Hotel Check-In is 3:00 p.m. The participants will be arriving as a group.

Guests will be arriving by motor coach. Carol will drop them off at 10:30 a.m. at conference and will proceed to the hotel with their luggage. Carol will also meet with the front desk manager to review procedure for private check-in. Carol will return to conference to pick up the group and return with them to the hotel.

» Motor coach drop off point will be in front of the hotel.
» Overnight parking for motor coach has been requested.

Overnight parking charges to be billed to the master account for motor coach.

A private, satellite check-in desk is to be set up beside hospitality desk. This is to be ready by 4:00 p.m. Check-in to be manned by staff exclusively for client. **French-speaking staff requested. Guests are all from Quebec.**

Please ensure adequate staff scheduling has been provided for the private registration desk and the bell desk.

All check-ins are to be pre-registered and rooms to be preassigned.

No room rates are to appear on individual guest bills.

Express check-out forms to be included in each key packet.

Separate key packets are to be prepared for each guest, two keys per packet.

Key packets to be ready and waiting in alphabetical order prior to guests' arrival at the satellite check-in desk.

Upgrades or room changes are not permitted unless authorized by J.A. Productions.

Four copies (both alpha and numeric) of clients rooming list will be required.

Scheduled welcome room gift deliveries to be in each guest room at least one hour prior to guest arrival.

MASTER ACCOUNT

Client

1. Name All to Master
2. Name All to Master

Judy Allen Productions
1. Carol All to Master

Balance of Guests
All guest room and taxes are to go to the master account. Participants are to give a credit card imprint to cover incidentals. Unless specified client will not be responsible for participants incidental accounts.

AUTHORIZED SIGNATURES FOR THE MASTER ACCOUNT

Client
1. Name
2. Name

Judy Allen Productions
1. Carol

ACCOUNTING
Carol to meet with hotel's accounting department on August 15th (approximately 10:30 p.m.) to review all individual room bills. This must be done prior to the folios being delivered to any guest rooms.

All bills to be posted to the master account must be signed off by J.A. Production staff. Carol will meet with accounting Wednesday, August 16 before guest departure (10:00 a.m.). Please have two copies of all bills and folios available.

ROOM BLOCK
Please see attached list.

FUNCTION SPACE
Gunnery Ballroom Breakfast August 16 Sit down Double-sided buffet 7:00 a.m. – 10:00 a.m.

TUESDAY
HOTEL ARRIVAL **ARRIVAL SCHEDULE:**
Guests will be transferred to the hotel by motor coach as a group.
Luggage will have been delivered to the hotel earlier in the day while guests were attending conference. All luggage to be waiting for guests in their rooms.
Estimated arrival time 5:45 p.m. Carol will contact the hotel when they are en route from the show so that staff will be ready.

5:15 p.m. Hotel staff (French-speaking requested) to be in place at the satellite check-in.
Hotel staff members to take credit card imprints when guests arrive with the exception of those where all is to the master account.
Participants will be arriving at the Dundas Street entrance.
Hotel porterage is included in their stay.
Note to hotel: Some guests will have an understanding of English but I have been advised that there may be some who speak no English at all.

Bill to Master Account

Porterage $0.00 + 0% taxes roundtrip
Parking Motor coach. Reserved Parking

TUESDAY
ROOM GIFT

Welcome gift to be delivered to each guest room. Carol to receive from client prior to advancing the hotel along with a letter from the company to accompany gift. Gift to be waiting in each guest room.

Bill to Master Account

Delivery $0.00 + 0% taxes roundtrip

TUESDAY
LUGGAGE PULL/DEPARTURE NOTICES

Departure notices will be given to the bellmen for delivery this evening while the guests are out for dinner.
Bags to be left inside the room. Pick-up will be at 8:30 a.m. on the 16th. Motor coach to depart at 10:00 a.m. Bell staff to advise if they will require more time for luggage pickup.

TUESDAY
TRANSFER/RECEPTION AND DINNER AT THE SHOT

6:30 p.m. Depart Hotel for The Shot Restaurant
(The restaurant is no more than a five minute drive from the hotel)
Enter parking lot. There is a charge for parking. Carol to pay.
The back section of the restaurant and pool tables have been reserved exclusively for the group.
The pool tables as you enter the restaurant will be for the restaurant's other guests.
Guests seated in raised section of dining room. Please ensure that there is sufficient space between tables and seating.
Client would like to have all guests in pool area to see beginning of demonstration first. Drinks and snacks in will be served in this area. Guests will probably be hungry as they will only have had a light lunch at the show.
Need separate area for J.A. Production staff to sit out of sight from the guests but close enough so that we can check on them from time to time. Could a small table be set up for Carol in the patio?
Requested waiters assigned to the group be exclusive to the group.
Pool expert will perform from 6:30 p.m. to 7:15 p.m. and he will stay and interact with the guests. Meals and beverages are included.

7:30 p.m. Dinner to be served. Two beverages in addition to the beverages (2) served during the reception to be compliments of client Additional beverages to be at guests own expense.

9:00 p.m. Shuttle to begin.

9:30 p.m. Last transfer complete.

WEDNESDAY
HOSPITALITY DESK HOTEL OUTSIDE GUNNERY BALLROOM (PRIVATE BREAKFAST)

Daily requirements: one house phone/no long distance access, one skirted table (6′ x 3′), three chairs, two flip charts/easels, markers (two colours), one waste paper basket, one table lamp (only if not in a well lit area) 6:00 a.m. the registration desk set up and to remain until 10:00 a.m.

Bill To Master Account

Flip Charts
House Phone
Balance of items provided at no charge from the hotel.

WEDNESDAY
PRIVATE GROUP BREAKFAST GUNNERY BALLROOM

8:00 a.m. Carol to advance breakfast
Gunnery Ballroom to the right of main dining room.
Round tables of ten but set for 8.
Double-sided buffet
8:30 a.m. All to be ready to go in case of early arrivals.
9:00 a.m. Breakfast
Buffet
Orange Juice, Grapefruit Juice, Apple Juice, Cranberry Juice
Scrambled Eggs with Chives
Strip Bacon, Peameal Ham, Breakfast Sausage
Home-Fried Potatoes
Grilled Tomato
Fresh-Baked Danish Pastries, Bran and Fruit Muffins, Butter Croissants
Mini Bagels with Cream Cheese
Fruit Preserves and Sweet Butter
Coffee, Assorted Teas, Decaffeinated Coffee.
Ensure tear down does not start while guests are still in the room.

Bill to Master Account

Buffet $00.00 +++ per person.

WEDNESDAY
TRANSFER TO CONFERENCE/FACTORY/AIRPORT/TORONTO

8:30 a.m. Luggage transfer will begin. Porterage has been prepaid.
9:15 a.m. All luggage to be down and in a secure area.
9:45 a.m. Motor coach to spot. Luggage to be loaded.
10:00 a.m. Motor coach to depart for conference. See attached.
10:30 a.m. Estimated time of arrival at conference.
Motor coach Parking pre-reserved.
12:30 p.m. Lunch included at the conference.
1:30 p.m. Depart for factory.
1-519-000-0000
2:00 p.m. Arrival factory
3:00 p.m. Depart for airport. Recommend at least one hour for transfer due to traffic. Carol to reconfirm.
4:00 p.m. Arrival at airport. Carol to handle porterage at airport.
Those departing on the flight to disembark.
Air Canada 1218 departs London 5:40 p.m.
Air Canada 1218 arrives Toronto 6:18 p.m.

Air Canada 194 departs Toronto 7:00 p.m.
Air Canada 194 arrives Montreal 10:05 p.m.
Carol departs with group.
3 head office staff plus 1 guest to continue to Toronto
1 client staff member to be dropped off at Yorkdale Shopping Centre.
Motor coach drops off remaining guests at the Sheraton.

WEDNESDAY
OVERNIGHT HOTEL ACCOMMODATION FOR TRAIN PASSENGER

Overnight accommodation has been blocked for Mr. *** for the night of the 16th. Club Room. Bill to master account.
Liane to meet motor coach at hotel and assist Mr. *** with check-in and head office with valet parking — making sure all costs are charged to the master account.

THURSDAY
TRANSFER FROM THE HOTEL TO THE TRAIN STATION

A driver will meet for Mr. *** in the hotel lobby. He will have company sign.
Note: Liane please ensure that you advise him to be at the front doors at 9:00 a.m. for transfer to the station. Continental buffet included with his stay on club floor.
Driver's Number:
Train 56 departs Toronto 10:00 a.m. arrives Montreal 2:41 p.m.

Index

A

accessibility, wheelchairs, 82, 155, 175–176, 202, 207

add-on fees, 94–95, 96

airports, 136–137

air travel, 136–140

alcohol, 286, 291, 305–306

arrivals, 149–150, 166–170, 201, 327–330

associations, listed, 404–407

attrition dates, 49

audiovisual, 208, 212, 213, 214, 216, 217, 220–221

Axtell, Roger E., 281

B

babysitters, 242

balloons, 183

banners, 197–198

bar, 253, 284–290

barge charters, 134

"barn to barn" charges, 135, 146

bartenders, 253, 283, 284–286

bathrooms, 101, 105, 113–114, 122, 123, 126, 268, 296, 307

batteries, 199, 200, 310

BBQ, 263, 264

bell captain, 295–296

beverage, 248, 251–254

BlackBerries, 199

block seating, 261

blueprints, 194, 213

BMI, 307

boat charters, 134

"book," 54

boxed lunch, 263, 264

breakfast, 259–263

budget, 219–222, 255–256, 307, 321–322
buffet, 259, 263, 274–276
bus, 145–147
business days, 74
The Business of Event Planning, 3, 17, 247, 326

C

cake-cutting fee, 224
calligrapher, 235, 276
cameras, 181–182, 310, 312
cancellation dates, 49
car, as indoor display, 189, 205
carpeting (venue), 203–205
caterers, 98–99, 125, 251–255
Cattle Baron Ball, 251
CD invitations, 233, 244–246
cell phone activation fee, 95
cell phones, 181–182, 199–200, 201
centerpieces, 247, 317–321
CEO Challenges, 24–25, 28
chairs, 195, 196–197
champagne toast, 293–294
charitable donations, 297–298
charting (critical path), 74–79
checklist
  arrivals, 201
  contact sheets as, 56
  critical path, 73
  event design principles, 45
  guest list, 233
  invitations, 237–239
  move in requirements, 126–127
  setup, 128–131
  teardown, 131–132
  transportation, 164–165
  venue and event supplier, 222–223
children, 242–244
choosing a date, 58–72
cigars, 207, 250, 292
Cirque du Soleil, 36
Cirque-style performers, 37, 188, 209, 325–326
cleaning, room, 217
client executive summary, 345
client objectives, 7–9, 24–33
client post-event report, 345–347
coat check, 178–179, 180
cocktails, 265–272, 283–294
coffee, 261
coffee break, menus, 263
communications requirements, registration, 199–201
company event objectives, 229
concierge floors, 262–263
conferences, timing, 62–63, 65
contacts, listed, 387
contact sheets, 56–58, 313–314, 386–388
continental breakfast, 262
contractor general information literature, 223–224

contracts, 108–110, 109, 224, 333
convention centers, 93–98
conventions, timing, 62–63, 65
Cool Yule, 227
corkage fee, 285
Corona, 251
corporate events, 35–36, 65–66, 226–229, 376–380
costs, 22–24, 192, 200, 222, 324
cost sheets, 41–44, 50, 90, 353
councils, listed, 404–407
couriers, 237, 314–315, 335
credits, photos and videos, 313
crew meals, 219–220, 222
critical path, 47–51, 50–51, 73, 353
customs, 279–281, 327
customs brokers, 333
cutlery, 119, 120, 275, 323

D

dance floor, 204–205
Dancing Water, 186–187
date, choosing, 58–72
day rooms, 296
"dead" file, 78
decor (venue), 321–324
departure (transfer), 149–150
dessert and coffee station, 53–54
Diamond & Denim, 248, 250–251, 272
dine-around, 281
dinner, 272–283
"dirty" rooms, 184
disappearing centerpieces, 319, 320
Disney, 83
Disney World, 173
domino effect, 48, 78
Don Strange Catering, 249
doormen, 176–177
Do's and Taboos Around the World, 281
draping and skirting, 195–196
dress code, 284, 305–306, 307, 315
drinks per person, cocktail reception, 283
D.R.I.V.E., 46
drunk guests, 286–287
DVD invitations, 233, 244–246

E

early check-in, 169
easels, signage, 197
education, as objective, 29–30
Eid Festival—Hari Raya Puasa, 61
electrical requirements, 191
Emergency Procedures Manual (venue), 337
empty rooms, 297
end-of-year celebrations, 226–229
energy, 9, 16–17, 28–29, 82
engagement (objective), 28
enhancements (transfer), 150
enlightenment (objective), 26–28

entertainment, 29–30, 207, 209, 284–285, 299–308, 325–326
entrance attendant, 177
envelopes, 235, 236, 246
Equine Experience, 27, 28
event budget, 3, 5–7, 41–45, 90–93, 135
Event Planning Ethics and Etiquette, 6, 300
event vision questionnaire, 17–20
e-vites, 233, 244–246
executive event review summary, 341
The Executive's Guide to Corporate Events and Business Entertaining, 2–3, 46, 60, 230, 348
express breakfast cards, 261
extension cords, 198–199

F

fanfare, 182–192
Father's Day, 61
Festive Frolic, 228–229
fiber optics, rentals, 324
film rights, photos and videos, 313
final walk-through, 56
fire, regulations, exits, 205–206, 212
fireworks, 320–321
fit, 82–83
Five Steps to Overcoming Fear and Doubt, 27
flights, winter, 88
flip charts, 197
floods, 59, 87
flooring, 203–205
floor plan, 212–213
floral arrangements, 250, 320
fondue, 227–228
food
  allergies, 243, 252
  banks, 298
  choosing types, 252
  guarantee, 252–253
  presentation, 270–271
  as staging tool, 248
  stations, 247–248
  tax, 254
force majeure, 59–60, 336, 337
Forever Plaid, 326
forfeit monies, 337
form letters, 349
fountains, rentals, 324
freight elevators, 189
function sheets, 52–58, 386–403
fund-raiser, 63, 65–66, 193, 352–358
future events, 350–351

G

Gagnon, Andre-Philippe, 300–301
gala openings, 107–126

General Catering Information booklet, 224
glasses, empty, 256–257, 272
Glass Orchestra, 227
glassware, 252, 323
Glenlivet, 248
global warming, 59, 87
gobos, 167, 204, 209–210
green events, 21–22
group photographs, 316
GST, 376
guest arrival, 167, 169–182, 189–190, 201
guests
  cameras, 312
  charges and itinerary (tip), 262
  demographics, 226–229
  interaction, 230
  list, 230–234
  list checklist, 233
  numbers, 231–232
  pass security, 193–194
  profile, 232–234
  safety, 72, 338
  ticket pick-up, 193–194
  unexpected, 253

H

handicaps, 18, 82, 155, 175–176, 202, 207, 296
hangers (coat check), 179
Hannah Montana, 36
"heart of the house" tour, 337
helium balloons, 183
Holiday Fun Do, 227–228
Holiday Magic, 228
holiday parties, 226–229
holidays, 60, 67–68
homeless people, 176–177
horses, 27, 28
hotels, 63–64, 93–98
house brands, 283
housekeeping, 296
"how-to" entertainment, 301
Hurricane Katrina, 60, 72, 136
hurricanes, 59, 87

I

icebreakers, 248, 249, 265, 273, 300
"impossibility" (insurance), 59–60
incentive programs, 40–41, 65, 368–375
indoor pyro centerpieces, 320
infectious diseases, 87
in-house post-conference review, 345
initial planning, 33–38
intelligent lighting fixtures (gobos), 210
international considerations, 330–335
International Special Events Society, 337

invitations, 233–239, 244–245
It's Not About the Horse, 27

J

Jack Daniels, 249
Jack Frost, 227
Jingle Bell Rock, 226–227, 229

K

kidnappings, 136

L

land transfers, 140–141
last-minute guests, 318–319
late RSVPs, 252–253
layout, 194–195, 212
Le Flame, 187
Le Scandinave Spa Blue Mountain, 29
liability, alcohol, 286
lighting, 209–210, 218, 221–222
limousines, 141–144
liquor, 253, 283–284
live video coverage, 212
Llano, 249
local laws, customs (tip), 286
logo, 22, 173-174, 204, 304, 312
Lone Star, 249
long weekends, 69
losing face, 279–280
Lot Cost, 353–354
Luggage Forward, 139
luggage shipping, 138–139
lunch, 263–265

M

mail delivery schedules, 236–237
mail house, 235–236
mailing, 50–51
major events (transfers), 151
Marketing Your Event Planning Business, 349
Marley floors, 326
maximum guest attendance, 232
meal rooms, 265
media, 160, 240–242, 316–317
meditation, 26, 27
meeting charge credit card programs, 347
meetings, 62–63, 65, 359–367, 389–403
Memorial Day, 63
menus
- breakfast, 259–263
- and choice, 259–260
- cocktails, 265–272, 283–294
- coffee break, 263
- custom, 255
- dinner, 272–283
- lunch, 263–265
- planning, 255–258
- printing, 234–235

milk and cream servers, 260

minimum rental charges,
transport, 135
Miraval Life in Balance, 27
Mistletoe Magic, 228
M&Ms, 247
modems, registration, 200
Mother's Day, 61
motor coaches, 145–147
move in requirements, checklist,
126–127
Mövenpick Marché, 83
Moving Toward Balance, 26
murder, 136
Murphy's Law, 1, 7
"must-haves," 10–11
mutual indemnification, 337

N

name tags, children, 244
napkins, 272, 275, 287
"need dates," 63–64
new restaurants, 270
new venues, 107–126
9/11, 72, 136
noise, 192, 211–212
non-competitor clause, 337
nonprofit organizations, 35
no-shows, and catering, 252–253
number of guests (PAX), 353–354
number of vehicles (transfer),
150–151
Nutcracker Sweet, 228–229

O

office holiday parties, 226–228
open seating, 276
Oprah Winfrey Show, 26
Opryland Hotel, 312
orientation, photographs, 312
Original Runner Co., 174
Oscars, 72
outlets, registration, 200
"overage," 253
oversized envelopes, 236
overspending, 347

P

parking, 133, 143, 145, 147–148,
314–315
parking lots, 151–157, 163
parking (transfer), 151–160,
162–164
parting gifts, 326–327
party, event requirements,
231–232
PAX (number of guests), 353–354
pay phones, 199
peanut allergies, 252
penalties, 49
People, 26
people per table, 209
Pepsi, 249
permissions, 309, 312
permits, 158–159, 185, 191–192,
206–207, 212

per person cost (P.P.), 353–354
personal space requirements
chart, 210
personnel changes, 54
Pez, 229
photographers, 308–317
photo shoot list, and event, 240
pillars, 212
pin-spotting, 185, 222, 277–278
place cards, 234–235
plates, 252, 256–257, 272, 275
Polaroid Digital Instant Mobile
Photo Printer, 344
popcorn, 100, 101
postage rates, 236–237
postcard invitations, 234
post-event history, 341–348
postponing, 38
P.P. (per person cost), 353–354
pre-assigned seating, 276
pre-con, 1, 49, 56, 109, 295
pre-event photographs, 311
preferred suppliers, 56
preliminary budget, 6–7
preliminary cost estimates, 22–24
preliminary visual walk-through,
39–40
prepaid parking, 154
press, 240, 242
"prevailing" rate (unions), 188
printing, 234–235, 335
prints, photographs, 311–313
private
air charter, 134, 139
check-in, 168–169, 193
gala dinner, 66–67
venues, 98–99
procurement department, 348
progressive dinners, 134
proms, 59, 67
propane flame walkway, 187–188
prop houses, 324
public transport, 160–161

R

Radko, Christopher, 227
rear-screen projection, 208
reciprocal cancellation clause,
337
records, for future events, 350–351
recycling, 298
rehearsal time, 217, 301–302
religion, 61, 68
requirements grid, 90–91
responsibilities
contracts, 337–338
rentals, 323–324
restaurants, 83–85, 98–99, 125
restrictions, arrival, 192
risk assessment, 59–60, 87, 108,
335–339
risks, event elements, 338–339
room gifts, 295–296
rooms manager, 296

room (venue)
  decor, 321–324
  requirements, 203–225
route choices (transfer), 149
RSVP, websites, 246
rush-hour traffic, 64, 151

S

safety, 192, 205–206, 325
samples, 316, 345
SARS, 72, 87, 136
schedule of events, 47
school breaks, 69
seafood allergies, 252
security, 72, 180, 236
self-drive, 147–148
seniors, 81–82
service charges, 96
set breakfast, 259
setup
  checklist, 128–131
  time, special effects, 185–186
setups (cutlery), 275
7UP, 249
shelters, 298
Shiner Bock, 249
shooters, 283
show flow, 301
shuttles, 133, 157, 164
Sierra Tucson Treatment Facility, 27
sight lines, 212, 214, 319
signage, registration, 197
signature gift, 350
sign holders, easels, 197
"signing back" (rentals), 323–324
sign language, 216
Singapore Airlines, 139–140
sit-down buffet, 276
sit-down dinner, 276–278
site inspection, 102–103, 121–122, 158–160, 184–185
site selection, 81–90
Slice soda, 249
smoking areas, 292–293
snowstorms, 59
Sorin, David, 337
sound booths, 208
Southern Comfort, 249
space, 34
space requirements, 80
special effects, 184–188, 191, 206, 215, 324–325
special events, 65–66, 71
The Special Events Advisor, 337
special requests, 252, 253
specialty acts, 325–326
specialty bar, 285
sports, 70–71
spring break, 61
staff, 135, 164, 178, 179, 254, 296–297
stage, 195, 217–218
staging, 208, 210, 214–216, 217–219

stand-up buffet, 274–275
starting point (transfer), 150
Starwood's Luxury Collection, 139
static lekos (gobos), 210
storms, 59
street permits, 148
street vendors, 159–160
style (event), 3, 15–16
sunsets, 86
supplies, centerpieces, 318
Swarovski crystal, 227
synagogue services, 68

T

tables, 174, 195–196, 224, 279–280, 322, 323
Taste of Texas, 248–250
"tasting" station, 248
taxes, 96, 254
taxi stands, and parking, 160
team building, 28–29
teardown checklist, 131–132
teaser cards, 234
Tecata, 251
technical riders, 325–326
telephones, registration, 199–200, 201
teleprompter, 217
tent cards, 276–277, 278
10 (the movie), 126
tents, 55, 101–107
Texas Black-Tie and Boots Ball, 251
Texas theme parties, 248–251
Thanksgiving, 63
thank-you gifts, letters, 349–350
theaters, as event location, 99–101
theme parties, children, 243
third-class mail, 237
tickets, mailing, 236
Time, 26
time buffers, 77
Time Management for Event Planners, 36, 37, 61
time of year, 62
time requirements, initial planning, 37–38
timing, entertainment, 302
timing, invitations, 233
tip
  bathrooms, 105
  BBQ, 264
  beef at buffet, 274
  blueprints, 194
  breakfast newspapers, 261
  breakfast planning, 260
  buffet, 259
  cell phone activation fee, 95
  chocolate fountain, 274
  church services, 68
  contracts, 109
  cost for staging, lighting, audiovisual, 222
  "dirty" rooms, 184
  event websites, 246

guest charges and itinerary, 262
hors d'oeuvres, 271
Las Vegas, 184
legal issues, 337
live video coverage, 212
local laws, customs, 286
long weekends, 69
maximum guest attendance, 232
meal rooms, 265
meeting room flowers, 320
milk and cream servers, 260
"need dates," 63–64
new restaurants, 270
parking lot as venue, 163
plates, 272, 275
pre-event photographs, 311
preferred suppliers, 56
recycling, 298
restaurant with catering, 125
risk assessment, 59–60
risk-assessment insurance, 108
RSVP websites, 246
school prom, 59
smoking areas, 293
specialty bar, 285
stage, 195
street permits, 148
supplies, centerpieces, 318
synagogue services, 68
table runners, 174
tables, 322
thank-you letters, 349
third-class mail, 237
time of year, 62
union staff, 97–98
volunteers, 57
websites, 246
yacht charters, 329
toasters, 259
tornadoes, 59
total event costs, 347
traffic, 64, 150–151, 161–162
transferable invitation, 230
transfer as event, 135
transfer options, 149
translation booths, 208
transportation, 148–164, 164–165
tsunami, 60, 72, 136
turnaround time, photos and videos, 313–314

U

umbrellas, 172, 173, 179
unions, 96, 97–98, 100, 213–214
UPS Store, 335
USA Today, 26

V

vacancy rates, hotels, 63–64
valet parking, 162–163
vegetarian selections, 252

venue and event supplier checklist, 222–223
venue requirements, 202–223
videographers, 308–317
violent outbreaks, 136
VIPs, 138, 157–158, 297
visualization, 8–24, 38–41
volunteers, 57–58, 178

W

waivers, contracts, 338
walkie-talkies, 199–200, 201
walkways, 174
Wall Street Journal, 261
war, 72, 136
weather, 86–89
Webb, Wyatt, 27
Web check-in, 137
Web conferences, 72
websites, events and RSVP, 246
weddings, 59, 67
weekend traffic, 64
What To Do When You Don't Know What To Do, 27
wheelchair access, 155, 175–176, 202, 207, 218
when and where (transport), 148–149
W Hotels, 139
window drapes, 212
wine, 253–254, 290–291, 292
work permits, 330–335
World Series, 70
the "wow" element, 187
wrap-up review, 340–341
wrist ID, children, 244

Y

yacht charters, 329
Yee, Rodney, 26, 27
yoga, 26, 27
Yoga: The Poetry of the Body, 26
YouTube, 308

Z

zoning, arrival, 192